MAHAN ON SEA POWER

Captain Alfred T. Mahan in 1894. Sketch made at Gravesend aboard the U.S.S. *Chicago* while on European cruise, 1893–1895, from the *American Monthly Review of Reviews*, July, 1894.

MAHAN ON SEA POWER

BY WILLIAM E. LIVEZEY

University of Oklahoma Press
Norman

ISBN 0–8061–1569–6

MEMORIAE
PARENTIUM MEORUM
CHARLES LIVEZEY
ELIZABETH LIVEZEY

PREFACE TO REVISED EDITION

IN THE FIRST EDITION of this book, my attempt to give "an appraisal of Mahan's ideas, a correlation of them with the climate of opinion in which they took shape, and an estimate of their influence upon the course of events," was generally well received. Interest in Mahan, judged at least from the scholarly writing he evokes, continues to be strong.

The new insights derived from these scholars, the opportunity for further evaluation of the impact of certain technological and political changes, and the perspective gained from the passage of time form the basis of a new chapter, "Mahan Revisited." It is my belief that these comments will contribute to a better understanding of Mahan and his influence in both his own time and in ours. Some ideas have been clarified, others expanded, some new ones introduced, and some old ones modified. The original text remains unchanged with the exception of the correction of typographical errors, a minor stylistic change throughout, and some modification of chapter 14 to correct misleading or erroneous statements. This not only avoids the criticism of my attempting to profit from hindsight but permits the reader to know what my views were at that time.

There is no longer any dissent as to the primacy of Mahan's concern emphasized in the first edition. Scholars are not suggesting, as one did in the 1930's, that the United States from 1885 to 1914 was "distant and shadowy" for Mahan, or that "most of his more important essays were written for English magazines and were never republished in his own country." Rather, all agree with my thesis, and nowhere is it more succinctly stated than by the able historian of the British navy, Professor Arthur J. Marder, when he writes that Mahan's "main purpose was to wake up his countrymen to the supreme importance of sea power."

Moreover, there has been general support for my contention that Mahan's role as expounder and promoter of the large policy and the outward view should not be overemphasized, and that we would do well to accept his own evaluation that he had "to some extent helped turn thought." Indeed, as will be later developed, the pendulum may be swinging a little far in the opposite direction, at least from my viewpoint, as some scholars portray Mahan as one who came late on the scene, or as one who recorded events after the fact, rather than as the influential publicist-propagandist that I believe he was.

It has not been possible to integrate these several new contributions into the new final chapter without sketching a little background from time to time and consequently repeating some information previously given. I hope this has been kept to a minimum and will not unduly distract the reader.

The number of illustrations has been increased and legends added where appropriate, even to those which appeared in the first edition. Acknowledgment is gratefully made to the Navy Department for furnishing several photographs and to the University of Oklahoma through its research funds-for the acquisition of other illustrations. Permission to use the photograph of Admiral S. G. Gorshkov was kindly granted by the Information Department of the Embassy of the Union of Soviet Socialist Republics.

William E. Livezey

Norman, Oklahoma
January 1, 1978

PREFACE TO FIRST EDITION

ALFRED THAYER MAHAN has been associated frequently with the European naval and imperial rivalry of the later nineteenth and early twentieth centuries, and rightly so. European statesmen were in need of a rational justification of their acts and Mahan was the author of the gospel from which their texts most often were drawn. To view him from this aspect alone does justice neither to his own innermost conviction and purpose nor to his wider influence upon his contemporary world. Mahan's chief concern was the indoctrination of his fellow countrymen with the importance and significance of sea power.

The present study does not ignore the foreign repercussions of the doctrine of sea power; an evaluation of Mahan's influence upon the programs and policies of Great Britain and Germany and, to a lesser extent, upon Japan and France is made. Mahan's primary concern, however, receives the major attention. Few Americans were more anxious for the United States to assume a commanding position among the powers of the world; few Americans saw as clearly the implications, responsibilities, and obligations inherent in the assumption of such a position; few Americans contributed so significantly and so ably to the formation of private and public opinion on matters of naval and foreign policy in the years that the United States became such a power. This approach has demanded an analysis of Mahan's major interests for the United States, a consideration of the manner and method by which these interests were transferred to others, and an investigation of the degree to which these interests were translated into action. Naturally an extensive use of Mahan's own published writings has been made. Furthermore, to ascertain the reception accorded his letters to the press, his numerous magazine articles, and his many books, and to determine the extent of their use by presidents, cabinet members, congressmen, editors, and other publicists and statesmen has required an examination of presidential messages, pertinent Senate and House documents, reports, and committee hearings, Congressional debates, and contemporary periodical literature. The search for thought and influence via the friendly letter has called for an investigation of the private papers of Theodore Roosevelt, Henry Cabot Lodge, Sr., Samuel A. Ashe, Stephen B. Luce, John D. Long, John Hay, William McKinley, and Mahan. The archives of the Navy and State Departments have been utilized.

Though a chronological narrative of the life of Mahan appeared a few years ago, there remains a definite need for an appraisal of Mahan's ideas, a correlation of them with the climate of opinion in which they took shape, and an estimate of their influence upon the course of events. The present study seeks to meet this need. My own views appear occasionally in the course of the presentation and are clearly indicated in the final chapter, yet my objective has been to offer an analytical, critical, evaluative, and, so far as possible, impartial treatment of one of the most important figures of recent times.

I wish to take this opportunity to thank again the following persons: Dr. Thomas P. Martin of the Manuscripts Division of the Library of Congress, who showed friendly interest and assisted in making available the Roosevelt, McKinley, and Mahan papers on deposit in that division; Mr. Lyle E. Mahan, who gave permission to quote from the letters of his father; Mrs. C. C. Williams and Henry Cabot

Lodge, Jr., who granted the right to use certain correspondence of Henry Cabot Lodge, Sr.; Mr. A. B. Forbes of the Massachusetts Historical Society, who made the Lodge papers accessible and accorded the right to examine the Long papers; Captain D. W. Knox, chief of the Office of Naval Records and Library, who gave opportunity to use the Luce papers and pertinent records under his care; Professor Tyler Dennett, who permitted the selection of certain letters from the Hay papers; the Curator of the Flowers Collection at Duke University, who placed at my disposal the Mahan-Ashe correspondence; Professors Lawrence F. Hill and Homer C. Hockett of Ohio State University, who have long desired that this study be pursued and its results published; Dr. Royden J. Dangerfield of the University of Oklahoma, who, while in war service at Washington, D. C., read the manuscript and offered helpful criticisms; and Martha Taylor Livezey, who throughout the months of research and composition has given invaluable assistance and unfailing encouragement. A grant from the Faculty Research Committee of the University of Oklahoma provided funds for the preparation of maps and the acquisition of additional illustrations.

I wish also to acknowledge my indebtedness to the following publishers, who kindly gave permission to quote from the copyrighted material indicated: Charles Scribner's Sons, from Henry Cabot Lodge, *Selections from the Correspondence of Theodore Roosevelt and Henry Cabot Lodge,* and from Anna Roosevelt Cowles, *Letters from Theodore Roosevelt to Anna Roosevelt Cowles, 1870–1918;* D. Appleton-Century Company, from Andrew D. White, *Autobiography;* John Murray, from C. C. Taylor, *Life of Admiral Mahan;* Little, Brown and Company and Atlantic Monthly Press, from L. S. Mayo, *America of Yesterday as Reflected in the Diary of John D. Long;* The Johns Hopkins Press, from

Julius W. Pratt, *Expansionists of 1898,* and C. C. Tansill, *The Purchase of the Danish West Indies;* Princeton University Press, from Harold and Margaret Sprout, *The Rise of American Naval Power;* Harper and Brothers, from A. T. Mahan, *Armaments and Arbitration* and *From Sail to Steam.* Special thanks are extended to Little, Brown and Company for permission to quote freely from the many books of Mahan's which they published, especially the following: *The Influence of Sea Power upon History, 1660–1783; Lessons of the War with Spain and Other Articles; The Interest of America in Sea Power, Present and Future; Some Neglected Aspects of War; The Problem of Asia; Retrospect and Prospect; The Interest of America in International Conditions; Naval Administration and Warfare; Sea Power in Its Relation to the War of 1812,* and *Naval Strategy.*

WILLIAM E. LIVEZEY

Norman, Oklahoma
January 7, 1947

CONTENTS

ILLUSTRATIONS

MAPS

MAHAN ON SEA POWER

I

THE MAN

IT WAS a foreboding first of December in 1914. The armies of embattled Europe were engaged in a life-and-death struggle. The first battles of the Marne and Ypres had been fought, and though all was not quiet on the Western front, there was a relatively stabilized war zone. In the East, enormous armies swept backward and forward over wide regions; the battle of Tannenburg had been partially neutralized by that of Lemberg. In the Far East, Kiaochow had fallen, and the various Pacific island possessions of the German Empire had been taken by Japanese or British forces. The Grand Fleet, the most powerful concentration of naval force the world had ever seen, was mobilized at Scapa Flow in the windy Orkneys. It was hoped that this fleet, by its command of the sea, might serve in the hour of crisis a role comparable to that of "those far distant, storm-beaten ships" which had stood so valiantly and successfully a century earlier between Napoleon and "the dominion of the world." Still a week in the future was the naval engagement between lesser contingents of the British and German navies off the Falkland Islands. Here the courageous Admiral von Spee and all save one of his vessels perished in the icy waters of the South Atlantic, only a few hundred miles from where the pocket battleship named in his memory was scuttled by her crew in another December of another world war a quarter of a century later.

One great power, the United States, stood bewildered as these events of 1914 transpired. Americans in general possessed little comprehension of the forces that had impelled the world toward this major tragedy. Only a limited few appreciated the nature and significance of the balance-of-power system and its lack of stability; nor were many Americans truly cognizant of the orgy of militarism, imperialism, and nationalism in which the Old World had been indulging. This was not the case, however, for one retired rear admiral of the United States Navy, who for years not only had feared and forecast this holocaust but by his activities had partially armed the foes ideologically and physically for the terrible contest. Born on September 27, 1840, at West Point, New York, on this foreboding December 1, 1914, in Washington, D. C., Rear Admiral Alfred Thayer Mahan died, a citizen of the world.

Though this internationally known American had achieved a distinction and renown accorded few, in his reminiscences written late in life we learn that he seriously questioned the wisdom in his choice of a naval career. Here he gave his father's opinion and his own later judgment concerning this decision: "He told me he thought me less fit for a military than a civil profession, having watched me carefully. I think myself now that he was right; for though I have no cause to complain of unsuccess, I believe I should have done better elsewhere."[1] This verdict of father and son is borne out to the extent that Mahan's fame today rests not upon his working for the navy from within the navy as a ship or fleet commander but upon his reputation as an outstanding naval historian, philosopher, strategist, publicist, and propagandist. It is highly problematical whether he would have followed the course which led to such eminence had he chosen a civil profession; it is certain he would not have possessed the first-hand experience of the service which proved such an invaluable background for his study of naval history and international affairs.

[1] Mahan, *From Sail to Steam*, xiv.

4

Alfred Thayer Mahan's naval career is unusual in that it was not until mid-life that the events occurred which gave him the opportunity to develop his hidden talents with resultant world-wide renown. There was comparatively little in his early life that suggested an extraordinary or brilliant future. His paternal grandparents, who were Irish Catholic, came to the United States early in 1800 and shortly settled in Norfolk, Virginia.[2] Dennis Hart Mahan, born two years later, was a lad in his early teens during the War of 1812. It scarcely need be said that in this Mahan home no love was wasted on the English. Dennis Hart entered West Point in 1820 and was graduated four years later, head of his class. He was commissioned second lieutenant in the United States Army with assignment to the Corps of Engineers. Much of his time during the next few years was spent in Europe in the study, both in the classroom and on inspection tours, of field and permanent fortifications and allied military topics. In 1830 he returned to West Point to become acting professor of engineering. There he renewed his acquaintance with the Academy's most able superintendent, Colonel Sylvanus Thayer, subsequently called the "Father of West Point." The confidence of Thayer in his appointment of the young army engineer was fully justified, for Professor Mahan shortly published several treatises on field fortifications and civil engineering which gained recognition in the United States as authoritative and standard works.

Dennis Hart Mahan was made dean of the faculty at the Academy in 1838. In the following year he married Mary Helena Okill of English-Hugenot ancestry. Though she was thirteen years his junior, it was disposition rather than age that gave her vivacity in such marked contrast to the taciturnity of her mate. On September 27, 1840, a son was born who was christened Alfred Thayer, in honor of the superior

2 For further biographical data see Captain W. D. Puleston, *The Life and Work of Captain Alfred Thayer Mahan.*

5

officer and close friend. The son was as much an Anglophile as his father was a Gallophile, for Dennis Hart gloried in the deeds of the French and the great Napoleon in much the same manner as Alfred Thayer near-deified the exploits of the English and the immortal Nelson. Writing nearly two-thirds of a century later of his one-half Irish, one-quarter English, and one-quarter French-American ancestry, he stated: "As far as I understand my personality, I think I see in the result the predominance which the English strain has usually asserted for itself over others."[3]

Alfred Thayer Mahan's early boyhood was spent at West Point. At twelve years of age he was sent to St. James, a boys' school closely associated with the Protestant Episcopal church, near Hagerstown, Maryland. The father was desirous that his son grow up a Southerner, a factor which partially determined the choice of St. James; yet dissatisfied with the lad's progress at the Maryland school, he transferred him to Columbia College for the next two years. In 1856, at sixteen years of age, rather against his father's wishes, Alfred Thayer entered the navy as acting midshipman. Because of his advanced preparation, he skipped the first year, becoming one of the " '55 Date." He was graduated three years later, ranking second in a class of twenty. Among his mates, though not of his class, were Dewey, Schley, and Sampson. Samuel A'Court Ashe, who later achieved distinction as a North Carolina historian, was his classmate. Ashe dropped out of school, for he was too severely afflicted with sickness on the practice cruises to continue in the service. However, the friendship established at Annapolis lasted throughout life; though in later years their letters were infrequent, Mahan and Ashe were correspondents until the former's death.[4]

3 Mahan, *From Sail to Steam*, xiii.

4 The Mahan to Ashe letters (about one hundred) have been saved and are deposited in the Library of Duke University. Those from October, 1858,

Steam sloop on which Lieutenant Mahan was Executive Officer during Civil War. *Official U.S. Navy photograph*

The story of Mahan as a line officer is comparatively un-
eventful. He rose from the rank of midshipman to that of
lieutenant, to lieutenant commander by 1865, to commander by 1872, to captain in 1885, and with that rank he retired
in 1896 after forty years of service. A decade later he was
promoted to rear admiral on the retired list.

His first naval service after graduation from Annapolis
was on the frigate *Congress* at the Brazil station. During the
Civil War he served in various blockading flotillas or squadrons, principally off Charleston coast and Sabine Pass. This
tedious duty was broken by a cruise to Europe on which
Mahan was first lieutenant with Stephen B. Luce in command. This chance association with Luce, as will be seen,
played its role in Mahan's later activities.

Following the war a three-year cruise on the steam sloop
Iroquois to the Asiatic station via Cape of Good Hope was
"the dream of years" to Mahan. He saw Japan in the days
of its medievalism; Osaka and Kobe had just been opened
to the outside world. Detached in 1869, Mahan returned via
Suez, Rome, and Paris. Forty years later he recalled the
ubiquity of the English soldier. Wrote he:

An impression which accumulates upon the attentive travel-
ler following the main roads of maritime commerce is the continual outcropping of the British soldier. It is not that there is
so much of him, but that he is so manywhere:[5] in our single voyage, at places so far apart as Cape Town, Aden, Bombay, Singapore, Hong Kong.[6]

to July, 1859 (about thirty), have been edited by Rosa Pendleton Chiles and
published as the Duke University Library Bulletin, No. 4 (July, 1931). The
remaining letters, the more interesting and valuable for this study, are still
in manuscript form.

[5] Mahan held it legitimate to coin new words "if they be congruous to
standard etymology"—hence "manywhere" if "anywhere," "nowhere," "some-
where," "everywhere" were acceptable; similarly he defended "eventless,"
"thitherto," and "ex-centric."

[6] Mahan, *From Sail to Steam,* 222.

Subsequent to this Asiatic adventure, Mahan served in various places at sundry tasks: on the Receiving Ship at New York, at the Navy Yards in Boston and New York, at the Naval Academy at Annapolis, and as commander of the U. S. S. *Wasp* at Rio de la Plata and of the U. S. S. *Wachusetts* of the South Pacific Squadron. In 1872, prior to much of the service noted above, he was married to Miss Ellen Lyle Evans of Philadelphia; to this union were born two daughters, Ellen (1873) and Helen (1877), and one son, Lyle (1881).

The routine of intermittent land and shore duty was not calculated to call forth much originality or give opportunity for distinction. Yet Mahan had the scholar's bent; though not given to "protracted mental labor" (to use his words), he read widely in current affairs and military literature, including the foreign service journals. It was during the Asiatic cruise that he began the systematic perusal of history which was to be a lifelong habit, a habit he frequently urged on his fellow officers. His first published work, an essay on "Naval Education for Officers and Men" won the third prize in a competition of the United States Naval Institute in 1878. In addition to a schooling in the professional subjects, he advocated not only a knowledge of French, Spanish, and international law, but also a wide reading in English and foreign literatures. Mahan personally carried out a considerable portion of this program and profited greatly thereby. For example, Napier's *Peninsula War* brought him into "a new world of thought" and made him keenly aware "of the military sequences of cause and effect." This study very definitely influenced his approach in his first book, *The Gulf and Inland Waters*. Published in 1883 as the concluding volume in the series on the navy in the Civil War, it is a competent account but in no way foreshadows his sea-power studies.

From a larger point of view, Mahan's career began with

the founding in 1884 of the Naval War College for advanced study in naval matters and international law. The college had a very unpretentious beginning. For several years an almshouse situated at Coaster's Harbor in Naragansett Bay served as the only building facility. Commodore Luce, then president of the college, under whom Mahan had served on his European cruise during the sixties, asked Mahan to join the teaching staff to direct the work in strategy and tactics and also to instruct in naval history. The middle-aged captain eagerly accepted the invitation as lecturer, and in 1886 succeeded Luce as president of the college. He remained in that capacity for three years and after a brief lapse of time again served as its head. Though written nearly a quarter of a century later, Mahan's own account of this vitally important turning point in his life well summarizes its significance. He wrote:

With little constitutional initiative, and having grown up in the atmosphere of the simple cruiser, of commerce destroying, defensive warfare and indifferent to battleships; an anti-imperialist, who for that reason looked upon Mr. Blaine as a dangerous man; at forty-five I was drifting on the lines of simple respectability as aimlessly as one well could—my environment had been too much for me; my present call changed it.[7]

It was in answer to this call of Luce's that Mahan evolved the concept of sea power and its influence on empire. The first set of lectures, commencing with the old Dutch Navy and carrying the story down to the close of the American Revolution, proved unusually popular with the officers in attendance. His "clearness of statement and a certain elegance of diction" interested, even "charmed" the men. His "faculty for generalization and his readiness in drawing conclusions from the lessons of history" greatly appealed to President Luce.[8]

7 *Ibid.*, 274.
8 Luce to Barnes, August 5, 1889, Luce Papers.

11

As early as September, 1887, Mahan had hinted to Ashe that his lectures might materialize in a critical military history of naval events popularly told. Various attempts were made to secure a publisher for them. Publication, it was urged by Luce, would relieve Mahan of the care of a large amount of manuscript material and permit a continuation of the study, which would result, it was hoped, in the development of the science of *modern* naval warfare. It was also believed that their publication would "assist the college," which had hitherto been "obliged to fight its way for bare existence."[9] Eventually (evidently with a guarantee of $2,500) Little, Brown and Company was persuaded to undertake the venture,[10] and in May, 1890, these lectures only slightly revised appeared under the title of *The Influence of Sea Power upon History, 1660–1783*.

The War College shortly fell under departmental displeasure and was transferred to the care of the commander of the Torpedo Station located near by. Mahan was shifted to special duty in the Bureau of Navigation as a member of a commission to choose a site for a navy yard at Puget Sound. This assignment was soon completed, and as there were no college sessions in 1890 and 1891, Mahan had virtually no care other than writing. For two years "the college slumbered and I worked," he wrote.[11]

Prior to the Puget Sound trip, some preliminary general reading and a modicum of writing had been done on the next phase of the sea-power studies; and despite time out for a short *Life of Farragut* (1892), it seemed as if the succeeding chapters in the story would soon be ready for the printer. However, a "formidable enemy" came upon the scene with a change in the Bureau of Navigation, under the

9 Luce to Barnes, August 5, 1889; Meigs to Luce, October 27, 1888: Luce Papers.

10 Mahan to Luce, October 7 [1889?], Luce Papers.

11 Mahan, *From Sail to Steam*, 303.

direction of which the college lay subsequent to its merger with the Torpedo Station. The new chief thought Mahan's assistance to the college less necessary than his going to sea. To one of Mahan's advocates for an allowance of time, this bureau chief categorically replied, "It is not the business of a naval officer to write books."[12] But the Secretary of the Navy, Benjamin F. Tracy, came to the rescue and Mahan was given respite. The manuscript was completed, used once in lecture form in the first session of the college (which had now gained a new building and separate existence), and then published late in 1892 in two volumes as *The Influence of Sea Power upon the French Revolution and Empire, 1793–1812.*

Mahan was now even more reluctant to put to sea, as authorship, promising "a fuller and more successful old age," had definitely "greater attractions" than the pursuit of his profession. He recognized that he had had no sea service as captain and that indisputably his turn for such service had come, yet he sought special consideration. He rested his plea upon the fact that his retirement after forty years of service would fall within the term of the administration granting his request, and that certainly his contribution in the continuance of his sea-power studies would be of greater value than a couple of years at sea, so shortly followed by his final retirement.[13]

Roosevelt and Lodge, already disciples of Mahan, sought to lend their influence to the endeavor. Roosevelt asked Mahan to send him all the data available, pro and con, upon his request. Luce, Lodge, Harry Davis, and Roosevelt held a "council of war" to determine plans and lay strategy.[14] Lodge wrote the Secretary of Navy:

12 *Ibid.,* 311.
13 Mahan to the Chief of the Bureau of Navigation, March 18, 1893, Navy Department, Bureau of Naval Personnel, General File, No. 26806.
14 Mahan to Roosevelt, March 1, 1893; Roosevelt to Mahan, May 1, 1893: Mahan Papers.

I dislike to trouble you any further in the matter. . . . At the same time, discretion is left to the Secretary who can make exceptions if he thinks it for the best interests of the service. . . . It seems to me very clear that this is one of the exceptional cases. Captain Mahan is doing a work which reflects the greatest credit on the American Navy and America's literature, work which no one else can do. . . . I enclose an extract from the London *Times* . . . which will show you that the opinion of the merit of his work from competent and disinterested judges does not differ from mine.[15]

The pleading was in vain. Mahan thought Secretary Tracy would have granted the request;[16] but the new Secretary of the Navy under the Cleveland administration, Hilary A. Herbert, had not yet become, as he was later, a Mahan convert.

Defeated, but not downcast, Lodge, Luce, and Roosevelt now endeavored to have the sea-power author given command of the *Miantonomah*, a vessel which would not take him "so far away as to compel him to sever all connection with his work and with his libraries of reference."[17] Even this indirect maneuver fell short of achievement, and Mahan was ordered to the *Chicago*, which was sent to Europe as flagship of that station. In his truly inimitable style, Roosevelt bemoaned, "Oh, what idiots we have to deal with!"[18] Mahan was resentful at the time, resentful toward both the department and his youthful folly. He wrote Ashe:

I am enduring, not living; and have the painful consciousness that I am expending much labor in doing what I have indifferently, while debarred from doing what I have shown particular capacity for. It is not a pleasant feeling—especially when accompanied with the knowledge that the headstrong folly of

15 Lodge to the Secretary of the Navy, April 18, 1893, Lodge Papers; see also Mahan to Roosevelt, March 26, 1893, Roosevelt Papers.
16 Mahan to Ashe, November 24, 1893, Flowers Collection.
17 Lodge to the Secretary of the Navy, April 29, 1893, Lodge Papers.
18 Roosevelt to Mahan, May 1, 1893, Mahan Papers.

my youth started me in a profession which, to say the least, was not the one for which I have the best endowments. . . . I have become exceedingly interested in professional literary work, and have now a fair promise of success in it.[19]

This resentfulness later turned into thankfulness; in retrospect he stated: "The request was probably inadmissible. . . . at any rate, it was not granted, luckily for me."[20]

This change of sentiment was due to a combination of unforeseen circumstances. The trip proved of value in several respects. It offered a chance for experience with one of the ships of the new fleet; it presented opportunity for the collection of first-hand information for a life of Nelson, the groundwork of which had been laid in his preparation of *The Influence of Sea Power upon the French Revolution and Empire, 1793–1812;* best of all, it gave occasion for recognition and acclaim in England with repercussions in the United States extremely favorable to Mahan. The attention paid Mahan during this European cruise did much to convince his skeptical brother officers and his indifferent fellow citizens that the sea-power studies were works of first order. Receptions by the Queen, the Admiralty, the exclusive Royal Navy Club, and others of the higher nobility, as well as honorary degrees from Oxford (D.C.L.) and Cambridge (LL.D.) were among the honors accorded the author in England. Mahan's reaction, judged from contemporary correspondence, was neatly summed up by him in his reminiscences: "This brought my name forward in a way that could not but be flattering, and affected favorably the sale of the books."[21] American recognition was soon forthcoming. Harvard, Yale, Columbia (later Dartmouth and McGill) granted him honorary degrees; and in 1902 he was elected president of the American Historical Association.

19 Mahan to Ashe, November 24, 1893, Flowers Collection.
20 Mahan, *From Sail to Steam*, 313.
21 *Ibid.*

In characteristic fashion Hay is reported to have said that he was "so glad Mahan had been publicly recognized, as Theodore [Roosevelt] would now no longer feel obliged to make them all go to Annapolis to hear his lectures."[22]

Is not the irony of fate made manifest in this call of Mahan to the sea, a call which proved in its wider ramifications of well-nigh incalculable value? On the one hand, Mahan, Lodge, and Roosevelt arduously sought escape for the author from his sea duty, and failing in that, begged for a near-by station; while on the other hand, Ramsay, Herbert, and probably others, unwilling to grant exceptions or in any way lessen the rigor of circumstances, gave Mahan the needed boost on his way to fame.

When the orders to sea appeared irrevocable, Mahan immediately dropped research on the next and final study in the sea-power series, the War of 1812, and turned his attention to a life of Nelson. His study of the Anglo-French duel at the close of the eighteenth and the opening of the nineteenth century convinced him that no existing biography of this great naval leader "filled the bill." In light of this fact and aware that his own name was "closely associated" with "the very great interest in naval matters," Mahan may not have been greatly influenced by his publisher's prediction that a life by him on Nelson would be "a pecuniary success."[23] Because of unavoidable delays, it was not until the fall of 1896 that Mahan sent to the publishers the manuscript for his two-volume study of Nelson. It appeared early the following year and immediately took a high place among the several biographies of England's great naval hero. Two comparatively minor errors, one relative to Nelson's activities at Naples in 1799 and the other concerned

22 Anna Roosevelt Cowles, *Letters from Theodore Roosevelt to Anna Roosevelt Cowles, 1870–1918*, 145.

23 Mahan to Ashe, November 24, 1893; November 7, 1896: Flowers Collection.

with Mahan's appraisal of Lady Nelson, were corrected in a second edition (1899).

In the writing of biography, Mahan followed a guiding principle closely akin to the part which sea power played in his treatment of history. He defined this leading idea as one in which he sought "to realize personality by living with the man, in as close familiarity as was consistent with the fact of his being dead."[24] He thought that a biography which presented a man's thoughts and acts, yet did not over and above them fashion his personality to the reader, was a failure. In none of his biographical writing did he come more nearly achieving this goal of the portrayal of personality, the portrait of the man as he was, than in *The Life of Nelson.* In his reminiscences he wrote, "Amid approval sufficient to gratify me, I found most satisfaction in that of a friend who said he felt as if he had been living with my hero; and of another who told me that after his day's work, which I knew to be laborious, he had refreshed his evenings with *Nelson.*"[25]

Allusion has been made to Mahan's growing restlessness and discontent with the naval profession as a career. Its routine was irksome to him; the problem of discipline was burdensome; its duties prevented him from giving undivided attention to his heart's desire, a literary profession. Prior to 1896 Mahan had written, in addition to the two sea-power studies, the *Life of Farragut,* the nearly completed manuscript on Nelson, a few significant articles for *Atlantic Monthly, Quarterly Review, Forum, North American Review, Century Magazine,* and *Harper's Monthly.* The opening of a magazine field and the reception accorded his two major books at home and abroad, especially in England, and the firm belief that the United States would become more and more maritime minded convinced Mahan that he had a fair chance of successful livelihood in the literary world. He recognized that

24 Mahan, *From Sail to Steam,* 318.
25 *Ibid.,* 322.

like all other moves there is a risk of failure, but I think the chances are good. The pay of literature is not great—except in fiction—not at all proportionate, in my case, to the labor I put into it; but upon the whole I like it, and at present there seems a sufficiently fair prospect of demand.[26]

The tenseness of Anglo-American relations occasioned by disagreement about the applicability of the Monroe Doctrine in the boundary dispute between Venezuela and British Guiana briefly delayed Mahan's application for retirement from the active list; he told Ashe he did not wish to retire "while possible trouble from an overt source remained."[27] Once that difficulty was cleared up, he sought and received release from active service.

The opportunity for uninterrupted research and writing failed to materialize wholly. The Spanish-American War brought orders for his return from Italy (where he had gone for a short vacation with his family) to serve as a member of the Naval War Board along with Admiral Sicard and Captain Crowinshield. Shortly after his release from this duty, service as a member of the American delegation at the First Hague Conference was another temporarily disruptive factor in the life of the full-time author. Service on the Naval War Board gave Mahan an opportunity to utilize and test his strategical principles; participation in the Hague Conference broadened and deepened his knowledge of world politics; both duties publicized the author, increased his audience, and furnished him ammunition for magazine articles which were republished in *Lessons of the War with Spain and Other Articles* (1899).

Following his retirement, Mahan became less and less the historian and more and more the publicist. This was rather a matter of degree than of kind and was probably due more to his basic desire to influence public opinion than

26 Mahan to Ashe, January 3, 1897, Flowers Collection.
27 *Ibid.*

to any sense of relief from restrictions felt while an active naval officer. In this period the only study of a thoroughly historical character was his *Sea Power in Its Relation to the War of 1812*. It was not until 1902 that Mahan again took up this story, which he had been forced to drop by his sea duty in 1893, and then "rather under compulsion" of completing the series as first designed "than from any inclination to the theme." The task occupied three years, with research in Washington, Ottawa, and London. As history, Mahan considered it the most thorough work he did; yet he thought it lacked interest, primarily because it was "impossible to infuse charm" where from the facts of the case it did not exist. It reminded Mahan strongly of the Chinese portrait-painter who remonstrated with a discontented patron, " 'How can pretty face make, when pretty face no have got?' "[28]

The lure of magazine writing had captured Mahan. Having achieved his niche in the hall of fame, possessing a following and wielding an influence naturally quite pleasing to the ego, he might have rested upon his laurels. But no, with an adulatory audience and a timely thesis, with a tinge of mysticism, a touch of dogmatism, and an air of omniscience, in schoolmaster fashion and in language with a strong moral undercurrent, often even Biblical, the ardent and sincere advocate could not forego to pontificate. Pecuniary considerations could not be ignored, for Mahan was not financially independent. With articles bringing in some cases as much as five hundred dollars and with right of subsequent publication in book form reserved, a right almost always capitalized,[29] Mahan assiduously applied himself to the role of an international observer and world commentator. After 1896 over one hundred articles—not to mention

[28] Mahan, *From Sail to Steam*, 317.

[29] In fact, slightly over two-thirds of Mahan's 120 magazine articles were reprinted and served largely or entirely to form over one-half of his 21 major works.

letters to the press—were published and added to the near dozen previously written. These articles were popular in treatment, general in interest, and usually propagandistic in purpose. The wisdom of American expansion, the desirability of the participation by the United States in world affairs, current fallacies in naval subjects, the beneficence of force as a factor in international relations, conditions determining naval expansion and preparation, and similar subjects were discussed.

The world thus became his province and a consideration of the external policy of nations and their mutual international relations his task—a task not self-assigned, he stated, but assumed at the request of editors. He examined the extant conditions and attempted to evaluate "their probable and proper effect upon future events and present action." His approach was essentially military, with these conditions viewed as forces, contending and perhaps even conflicting, which had to be considered and handled as a government would dispose of its fleets and armies. This was not an advocacy of war, he held, but merely the "recognition that the providential movement of the world proceeds through the pressure of circumstances; and that adverse circumstances can be controlled only by organization of means, in which armed physical power is one dominant factor."[30]

After retirement, in addition to his activities during the Spanish-American War and at the Hague Conference, Mahan frequently was called upon to perform limited public service. In 1903 he was ordered to appear before a Congressional committee which was making a study of the American merchant marine; in 1909 Roosevelt appointed him on a commission to investigate the reorganization of the Navy Department; in the same year the President named him chairman of a joint commission charged with the consideration of national defense. Moreover, from 1898 through

30 Mahan, *From Sail to Steam*, 323–24.

1912 Mahan was often associated with the War College as summer lecturer on naval history and strategy. In 1912, at seventy-two years of age, he was undecided whether to apply himself "casually to passing topics of interest, letter writing for the press, etc." or to devote himself to "some long work of more permanent character."[31]

As it resulted, he chose both avenues of employment. He continued to contribute articles to magazines and letters to the newspapers until this activity was largely restricted by orders from the Navy Department shortly after the outbreak of the war in Europe. With a grant-in-aid from the Carnegie Endowment, Mahan essayed to write a history of American expansion and its bearing upon and relation to the problem of sea power. In the fall of 1914 he left his home at Quogue, Long Island, and went to Washington, where he could be near the necessary sources. This study was cut short by his rather sudden death on the first of December, with only a few introductory pages written.

His death was probably hastened by too great preoccupation with the diplomatic and military events of the struggle, the approach of which he had clearly foreseen. In 1898 Mahan saw no folly in the German imitation of British policy which had gained for Britain her empire. Whether the British and the German peoples proved equal to their ambitions time alone could tell, but the sea-power analyst of power politics held that it was "a noble aim in their rulers to seek to extend their influence; to establish their positions, and to knit them together in such a wise that as races they may play a mighty part in the world's history."[32] Yet four

31 Mahan to Ashe, June 17, 1912, Flowers Collection.

32 Mahan, "Current Fallacies upon Naval Subjects," *Harper's Monthly*, June, 1898, reprinted in *Lessons of the War with Spain and Other Articles*, 293–94. Privately to his British friend, J. R. Thursfield, he had stated in a letter of December 1, 1897, that Germany represented for the United States and Great Britain "a probable element of trouble in the future." Mahan Papers.

years later in the English *National Review,* Mahan called British public attention to the fact that German industrial and commercial growth, with its overseas ambitions and naval rivalry, was threatening England. In almost blunt language, he wrote: "The danger appears to exist; and if so the watchmen of the British press should cry aloud and spare not until all classes of their community realize it [this threat] in its fundamental significance."[33] In justice to this Anglophile it should be said that theoretically he conceded that Germany's maritime and commercial ambitions gave "no cause of offense" and that her creation of a large navy was the exercise of an "indisputable right"; he merely insisted that "watchfulness" and "counteraction" were required.[34]

In light of this background it is not surprising that, when hostilities started, Mahan gave the British further counsel. The climax came on August 3, 1914, when he advised England to strike at once, for otherwise the Central Powers would overcome France and Russia and then turn on Great Britain; Italy, he maintained, should forsake Germany and Austria.[35] In a country with a heterogeneous population and with a chief executive who was shortly to urge his fellow-Americans to be "neutral in fact as well as in name," perhaps it would have been surprising if no protests had been made and no restraining action taken. At any rate, telegrams and letters came to the President and to the Secretary of the Navy inquiring whether such advocacy of "war measures upon Great Britain against Germany" coming

33 Mahan, "The Persian Gulf and International Relations," *National Review,* September, 1902, reprinted in *Retrospect and Prospect,* 246.

34 Mahan, *The Interest of America in Sea Power, Present and Future,* 81–82; 166–67. See also letters to the London *Daily Mail:* "Britain and the German Navy," July 6, 1910; "Britain and the World's Peace," October 31, 1910; "Declares British Navy Weak," January 4, 1914. For British reaction, see "Excubitor" (pen name), "Admiral Mahan's Warning," *Fortnightly Review,* Vol. LXXXVIII (August, 1910), 224–34.

35 Statement to the press, August 3, 1914, prior to Britain's declaration of war.

from a "prominent and influential officer of the United States is not in spirit at least a violation of true neutrality," and whether naval regulations would not permit disciplining Mahan for the advocacy of "such a treacherous attack by Italy upon her allies."[36] Initiated by President Wilson, a Special Order was issued by the Navy Department, August 6, 1914, which prohibited officers of the Navy and Army of the United States, active or retired, from publicly commenting upon the military or political situation in Europe. The historian-commentator was besieged by requests from both sides of the water for an analysis and interpretation of the conflict from a naval point of view; he sought special exemption from the restrictive order, but in vain.[37]

Intimate contemporaries of Mahan were acquainted with certain aspects of his life and personality of which no mention as yet has been made. The intensity of his spiritual beliefs, his profound knowledge of the Scriptures, his charity, his ardent support of foreign missionary work, his habitual attendance at church, his certainty of God's guidance, his sense of duty and scrupulous honesty, his mild unassuming manner, his quiet conversation—here was a composite which drew from the Protestant Episcopal bishop in New York this tribute at the time of Mahan's death: "I share with all the world the admiration for his eminent service to his chosen profession and yet, beyond and above all that, I admired him for the beauty and charm of his Christian character." A similar appreciation was manifested in a memorial tablet erected by friends and fellow worshippers of his church at Quogue, Long Island: "Great among the na-

<hr>

36 Brumder to the President, August 6, 1914, Navy Department, Bureau of Naval Personnel, General File, No. 2473–63; Schilling to the Secretary of the Navy, August 4, 1914, *ibid.*

37 Mahan to Daniels, August 15, 1914, Navy Department, Bureau of Naval Personnel, General File, No. 2473–64; Daniels to Mahan, *ibid.*

tions as an expounder of Sea Power; greater in the Kingdom of God as an example of a Christian man."[38]

Though it may be held by some persons that the doctrines of sea power and empire are incompatible with if not antithetical to Christianity, such views were never held by Alfred Thayer Mahan.

[38] Bishop Greer to Mrs. Mahan, cited by C. C. Taylor, *Life of Admiral Mahan*, 271; At Church of Atonement, Quogue, Long Island, *ibid.*

II

THE HISTORIAN

VIEWED IN RETROSPECT, Mahan's West Point environment, his training at Annapolis, the blockade duty during the Civil War, the long cruises to Europe, Asia, and South America offering opportunity for leisure, reading, and observation, his professional knowledge gained in the handling of both sail- and steam-propelled vessels had prepared him, unconsciously to be sure, for his work as lecturer and writer on naval strategy and history. The origin, nature, and implications of Mahan's sea-power doctrine will be discussed in the following chapter; it is here proposed to inquire into his general concept of history, its purpose, its method of treatment, and allied topics.

Mahan's view of the world and mankind might be called "Jewish-Christian," with history as a kind of divine drama in which God's will or overruling purpose was revealed by personalities and events. In fact, in one instance history was defined as "the plan of Providence . . . in its fulfillment."[1] He believed the United States had a divinely commissioned responsibility in China. "The part offered to us is great," he wrote, "the urgency is immediate, and the preparation made for us, rather than by us, in the unwilling acquisition of the Philippines, is so obvious as to embolden even the

[1] Mahan, "Subordination in Historical Treatment," presidential address at the American Historical Association Meeting, December 26, 1902, reprinted in *Naval Administration and Warfare*, 267–68.

least presumptuous to see in it the hand of Providence."[2]
On another occasion in a similar vein he spoke of the Philippines as a "task" to which God had "led" us, and added that "if the careful effort at each successive step to do aright does not assure that the guidance in the course of events has been Providential, there is no test by which such guidance can be known."[3] Perhaps a still more striking illustration of his concept of history is that in which he suggested the hand of God behind the maritime greatness of Britain. Said he:

When one recalls that it [Jamaica] passed into the hands of Great Britain, in the days of Cromwell, by accidental conquest, the expedition having been intended primarily against Santa Domingo; . . . that by all probabilities, it should have been reconquered and retained by Spain in the war of the American Revolution; and when, again, it is recalled that a like accident and a like subsequent uncertainty attended the conquest and retention of the decisive Mediterranean positions of Gibraltar and Malta, one marvels whether incidents so widely separated in time and place, all tending toward one end—the maritime predominance of Great Britain—can be accidents, or are simply the exhibition of a Personal Will, acting through all time, with purpose deliberate and consecutive, to ends not yet discerned.[4]

In these lines may be seen the devout, orthodox Christian, the Anglophile with a touch of reverent mysticism.

The new history with its emphasis upon social and cultural elements was beyond Mahan's purview. His particular interest was the significance of the control of the sea, commercial and military, in the formation and development of

---

[2] Mahan, "Effect of Asiatic Conditions upon World Politics," *North American Review*, November, 1900, reprinted in *The Problem of Asia*, 175.

[3] Mahan, "The Philippines and the Future," *The Independent*, Vol. LII (March 22, 1900), 698.

[4] Mahan, "Strategic Features of the Gulf of Mexico and the Caribbean Sea," *Harper's Monthly*, October, 1897, reprinted in *The Interest of America in Sea Power, Present and Future*, 307–308.

national policies. Military and political history were inextricably linked, yet Mahan necessarily stressed the former. This type of history might be the simple chronicle, a mere annal devoid of explanation and interpretation; or it might be a general running narrative with an attempt at coherence and consistency; or the treatment might be more intellectual and philosophical with the war as a whole kept constantly in mind and each event properly allocated and interpreted.[5] The latter type was Mahan's ideal, and from a historiographical point of view he may be regarded as the founder of a new school of historical study.[6]

In an appraisement of this statement, one should bear in mind that Mahan was not the first diligent student of naval history. John K. Laughton, professor at the Royal Naval College, in some respects the spiritual father of Mahan, was the most notable of the few pioneers and the first to base his studies on a thoroughly scientific method.[7] Professor Laughton's most important researches were embodied in contributions to the British professional journals, the Navy Records Society, and the *Dictionary of National Biography*. Rear Admiral P. H. Colomb's *Naval Warfare: Its Ruling Principles and Practices Historically Treated* (1891) was appearing serially when Mahan's *magnum opus* was published. One reviewer characterized Colomb's work as "little learned and perfectly unreadable,"[8] and the English officer stated in his preface that he was "delighted" to see that "on

5 Mahan, "The History of Our Navy, from Its Origin to the Present Day, 1775–1897," *American Historical Review*, Vol. III (July, 1897), 747–51. This is a book review of John R. Spark's study of the navy with the same title.

6 G. P. Gooch, *History and Historians in the Nineteenth Century*, 423; Theodore Roosevelt, "The Influence of Sea Power upon the French Revolution and Empire," *Political Science Quarterly*, Vol. IX (March, 1894), 171–73.

7 H. H., "Naval History: Mahan and his Successors," *The Military Historian and Economist*, Vol. III (January, 1918), 7–10; see also H. M. Stephens, "Some Living American Historians," *World's Work*, Vol. IV (July, 1902), 2316–27, especially 2322–23.

8 "Sea Power: Its Past and Present," *Fortnightly Review*, Vol. LIV (December, 1893), 855.

the other side of the Atlantic, an abler pen and a deeper thinker" had been at work on thoughts something like his own.

Mahan acknowledged indebtedness to both these men, some of whose essays had appeared in the *Journal of the Royal United Service Institution;*[9] he soon repaid any obligation due them, for his studies were a major factor in the revival of interest in naval history in Great Britain. Moreover, the accelerated naval building program and the activities of the Navy League, also forces in that revival, were closely correlated with Mahanism. The Navy Records Society took a new lease on life, printing rare or unpublished works on naval subjects. A further and more careful investigation of the close relationship existing between the history of the British Empire and that of the Royal Navy was made. In a bibliographical article, Professor W. F. Craven has evaluated the important contributions of the naval historians as "second only to the economists in determining the modern interpretation of colonial policy," and Mahan was accorded first place as their "Seeley."[10] Indeed, not only was he the "Seeley" among this school of new writers but these men—Laughton, Oppenheim, Hannay, and Corbett, to mention the more prominent of his contemporaries—pursued their historical investigations and were "enabled to make them public largely through the stimulus of Mahan's writing."[11] All in all, Mahan's facts were so freshly and powerfully presented against the background of naval history in its wider bearings and in such a popular nonprofessional style that both from manner of treatment and resulting creation of interest, he may rightly be called the father of modern naval historiography.

9 Mahan, *From Sail to Steam*, 279–80.
10 W. F. Craven, "Historical Study of the British Empire," *Journal of Modern History*, Vol. VI (March, 1934), 40–69, especially 60–61.
11 Stephens, *loc. cit.*, 2322–23. See also Auguste Moireau, "La Maîtresse de la Mer," *Revue des deux Mondes*, Vol. XI (October, 1902), 688.

Mahan frequently expressed his belief that history should be considered primarily as a utilitarian, even didactic, study. History contained "lessons" which "well digested" were "most valuable for future guidance." "The value of history to us," he wrote, "is as a record of human experience; but experience must be understood."[12] Thus the function of history was not merely the accumulation of facts but their presentation "in such wise that the wayfaring man, whom we now call 'the man in the street' shall not err therein."[13] The historian therefore became a collector, assimilator, interpreter, instructor, and moralist.

This problem of the purpose of history early claimed Mahan's attention. While still engaged in study prior to writing his lectures for *The Influence of Sea Power upon History, 1660–1783*, he confided to Luce:

Of course the question thrusts itself forward; under all the changed conditions of naval warfare of what use is knowledge of these bygone days? Here I am, frankly, a little at sea how to point my moral. I have stuff enough to work up several popular lectures, but how to turn this into instructive matter for the future?[14]

When these lectures emerged in book form, Mahan did not seek to conceal a very definitely didactic objective; he was no longer at sea about how to point his moral. He clearly stated that the "practical object" of his sea-power study was to "draw from the past lessons . . . applicable" to his own country and service.[15] He sent a complimentary copy of this volume to Henry Cabot Lodge, then a member of the Naval Affairs Committee of the House of Representatives; and in

---

12 Mahan, *The Problem of Asia, vi;* Mahan, "Lessons of the War with Spain," in *McClure's Magazine,* December, 1898, reprinted in *Lessons of the War with Spain and Other Articles,* 26.

13 Mahan, "Subordination in Historical Treatment," reprinted in *Naval Administration and Warfare,* 258; 351–52.

14 Mahan to Luce, January 22, 1886, Luce Papers.

15 Mahan, *The Influence of Sea Power upon History, 1660–1783,* 83–84.

an accompanying letter he stated that he had endeavored "to make the experience of the past influence the opinions and shape the policy of the future." Mahan alluded to his own change of view on the matter of the value of the past for the present despite altered conditions and apologized for an explanation of this sort to a man of Lodge's intelligence and breadth of reading. It is appropriate as well as significant to note that Mahan stated he was sending the copy because of Lodge's interest in history and naval matters and also because of his membership on the Naval Affairs Committee.[16]

This purpose of drawing lessons from the past was equally avowed and more fully developed in some of his magazine articles. Relative to his essays on the conduct of the Spanish-American War, he wrote, "A principal object of these papers . . . is to form a correct public opinion." He thought the importance of a popular understanding was twofold:

It promotes interest and induces intelligent pressure upon the representatives of the people, to provide during peace the organization of force demanded by the conditions of the nation; and it also tends to avert unintelligent pressure which, when war exists, is apt to assume the form of unreasoning and unreasonable panic. . . . It is, of course, vain to expect that a great majority of men should attain even an elementary knowledge of what constitutes the strength or weakness of a military situation; but it does not seem extravagant to hope that individuals . . . may be numerous enough, so distributed throughout the country, as to constitute rallying points for the establishment of a sound public opinion.[17]

Mahan had a high regard for the role played by public opinion. He judged:

16 Mahan to Lodge, May 19, 1890, Lodge Papers.
17 Mahan, "Lessons of the War with Spain," McClure's Magazine, February, 1899, reprinted in Lessons of the War with Spain and Other Articles, 110; ibid., v–vi.

Questions connected with war—when resort to war is justifiable, preparation for war, the conduct of war—are questions of national moment, in which each voter—nay, each talker—has an influence for intelligent and adequate action, by the formation of sound public opinion; and public opinion in operation, constitutes national policy. . . . [And] our leaders, when a call for action comes, cannot outstrip by very much the recognized wishes of the people.[18]

Mahan was not blind to at least some of the difficulties which confront the student who would seek to point the way to the future through a study of the past. He recognized that contemporary conditions were so altered from those preceding them that, when the attempt was made to utilize the teachings of the past, "application becomes a matter of no slight difficulty, requiring judgment and conjecture rather than imparting certainty." Hence this "instruction from the past must be supplemented by a particularized study of the indications of the future." Assuredness of conclusion could not be guaranteed by this process; nevertheless, "we can still be confident that under all surface conditions, present or past, there must lie permanent facts, and factors, the detection and specification of which ascertains at least the existence and character of certain determinative features and the relations subsisting between them."[19]

This conscious motive of making history didactic naturally influenced Mahan in his treatment of historical data. His plea throughout was for the general reader. He believed that the historian was inclined to burden his narrative with a mass of detail which the general reader had the time neither to read understandingly nor to work out therefrom for himself the leading features, the determinative lines. He by no means disparaged thoroughness or accuracy of

18 *Ibid.*, 10; "Effect of Asiatic Conditions upon World Policies," *North American Review*, November, 1900, reprinted in *The Problem of Asia*, 157.
19 *Ibid., vii.*

knowledge critically arrived at through the mastery of sources and intimate acquaintance with facts; yet the accumulation of facts at once in entirety and in accuracy was not the real function of history. "The significance of the whole . . . must not wait too long upon unlimited scrutiny . . . fine dust of the balance rarely turns the scale," and mere "observation heaped upon observation remains useless to men at large."

In different words and in Biblical phraseology he maintained that elaborate research was "encumbered with over much serving" and was forgetful of the "one thing needful."[20] He believed:

The matter is one of utility. . . . for the onward movement of the whole body of mankind—which we call the public—is dependent upon each man's thorough, consummate knowledge of his own business, supplemented by an adequate understanding of the occupations and needs of his neighbors. . . . Adequate understanding can be had if the determining features of the particular subject are exposed clear of the complication of details which cling to them, and even in part constitute them; the knowledge of which is obligatory upon the specialist, but to the outsider impedes acquirement.[21]

In reality it was Mahan's concept of the purpose of history that caused him to stress the significance of the whole and to urge its portrayal to the public in such a manner that it might be grasped and utilized. In the final analysis this resolved itself into the problem of presentation. Mahan gave particular attention to this subject in his presidential address, "Subordination in Historical Treatment," given before the American Historical Association in 1902.

Able presentation did not consist of the enumeration of every fact and in the omission of none; for however ex-

20 Mahan, "Subordination in Historical Treatment," reprinted in *Naval Administration and Warfare*, 249–52; 259–61.
21 *Ibid., vii.*

haustive and laboriously acquired, facts were only the "bricks and mortar" of the historian—"fundamental, indispensable, and most highly respectable, but in their raw state" they were the "unutilized possession of the one or at most the few." To be of use, these data had to be studied analytically, their broad leading features detected, their mutual relations recognized, and their respective importance assigned. With analysis, insight, imagination, and a gift of expression, facts were to be turned by the historian into a work of art, a "picture comprehensible by the mass of men." Emphasis, so essential to comprehension, could be achieved less by color than by the proper disposition of details with due subordination to the central idea. Unity of the whole thus became the primary requirement, but

unity is not the exclusion of all save one. The very composition of the word—unity—implies multiplicity; but a multiplicity in which all the many that enter into it are subordinated to the one dominant thought or purpose.[22]

Each incident of history, whether it was the tactics of a battle, the strategy of a campaign, or the policy of a war, possessed intrinsic unity. Each accordingly had to be treated as a work of art in which the details were kept subordinate, but as succeedingly larger views were taken, these incidents, though intrinsic in themselves, in turn assumed subordinate positions. Mahan possessed to an unusual degree this ability to subordinate details and present a telling and impressive view of the whole. The none-too-friendly *Nation*, in an editorial at the time of his death, paid tribute to this characteristic by saying that he had "the insight and grasp to wrest the core of truth out of the period of which he wrote."[23]

His literary activities were remunerative. A few articles

22 *Ibid.*, 253–55; 262.
23 *The Nation*, Vol. XCIX (December 10, 1914), 680–81.

for the English *National Review* brought $500 each, with right for republication in book form. American magazines paid much less, though some articles returned as much as $150 each.[24]

Mahan's literary habits were not unusual. He used the notebook rather than the loose-leaf system for note-taking. His wife typed his manuscripts for the printer. He spent the morning hours at his desk writing what he could; whether the result was ten words or ten hundred, he sought to regard it with equanimity. The afternoons and evenings were given over to reading, exercise, and association with his family.

It was Mahan's practice to put down his thoughts in the first words in which they occurred and later to elaborate and polish them. He was guided by Dr. Johnson's maxim: "Do not exact from yourself at one effort of excogitation, propriety of thought and elegance of expression. Invent first and then embellish."[25] He strove for lucidity and accuracy, though these were not always compatible. In fact his besetting anxiety for accuracy led to diffuseness and complexity, and his writings are frequently marked by laborious fullness of statement and burdened with qualifications. In many instances they make difficult reading, and as time progressed he became more and more abstract and metaphysical, partly because of the nature of his thesis and partly because of his own nature and his style. Mahan was conscious of this tendency to diffuseness and he defended it as natural. He wrote:

It is to this anxiety for full and accurate development of statements and ideas that I chiefly attribute a diffuseness with which my writing has been reproached; I have no doubt justly. I have not, however, tried to check the evil at the root. I am built that way, and think that way; all around a subject as far as I can see it. I am uneasy if a presentment err by defect, by

24 Various letters from publishers, Mahan Papers.
25 Mahan, *From Sail to Steam*, 286.

Captain Alfred Thayer Mahan, U.S.N. (1840–1914). "The profundity of his views and the lucidity of his reasoning attracted the attention of the statesmen of all nations; and more than any American scholar of his day, he has affected the course of world politics."—From resolution adopted by the American Historical Association, December, 1914. *Library of Congress.*

Admiral Luce and the original Naval War College. Stephen B. Luce (1827–1917) played a crucial role in the creation of the new Navy and was primarily responsible for the establishment of the Naval War College at Newport, R. I., in 1884. *Library of Congress; Official U.S. Navy photograph*

excess, or by obscurity apparent to myself. I must get the whole in, and for due emphasis am very probably redundant. I am not willing to attempt seriously modifying my natural style, the reflection of myself, lest while digging up the tares of prolixity, I root up also the wheat of precision."[26]

Style, Mahan thought, had two sides. Primarily, it was the expression of a man's personality, and from this point of view it was "susceptible of training, of development or of pruning; but to attempt to pattern it on that of another person" was a mistake. Secondarily, there was to style an artificial element which was confined more to the technique of sentence structure, and this to an even greater extent was capable of improvement.[27]

Critics generally have agreed that Mahan had a power of expression above the average, yet the majority would add that his skill in this respect was inferior to that of most historians of equal prominence.[28] Most readers find Mahan difficult, and few would be as generous, or perhaps as discerning, as the reviewer who wrote at Mahan's decease:

His style was, indeed, well fitted to the task he set himself. It was clear though not picturesque, was of cumulative weight. To get the real impact of his argument you had to have a patience and a comprehension something like his own in marshalling facts and compelling them to yield their true meaning. His conception was original and powerful, but it took time and iteration to work it out.[29]

Mahan took himself, his task, and his writing seriously, and the degree of success attained bears warrant of this endeavor. It is quite certain, however, that his permanent rank as a historian will be somewhat less than was his contemporary fame. This is due in part to his preoccupation

26 *Ibid.*, 288–89.
27 *Ibid.*, 287.
28 Gooch, *op. cit.*, 422.
29 *The Nation*, Vol. XCIX (December 10, 1914), 680–81.

with the sea and consequent neglect of other items. The contributions of the Prussians, the British Army contingent, and the English-subsidized German mercenaries in the Seven Years War were dispensed with in a sentence; the significance of the Industrial Revolution in undergirding England during the Napoleonic struggle was not appreciated; and despite his considerable researches, the agricultural imperialism of the War Hawks as a provocative factor leading to the War of 1812 totally escaped his view. Nor does the present generation generally accept Mahan's concept of history; "his naive and sometimes contradictory moral judgments and his confident interpretations of the will of Providence" mar his greatness for those of a more sophisticated and critical age.[30] Add to these points the realization that much of Mahan's contemporary fame actually rested upon his activities as publicist-propagandist, and it seems safe to conclude that strictly as a historian his status is less enviable than at the time of his death. His achievements in biography have probably stood the test of time more successfully than his sea-power series, for they do not rest upon so restricted a basis.

Mahan himself recognized he could lay no claim to breadth and depth of historical research. His study of history began late in life and rather incidentally. He never deluded himself with the belief that he had become a historian "after the high modern pattern,"[31] and at times one may almost read between the lines his prayer of thankfulness. Laborious monographic research he saw as necessary, though he stressed its limitations; more difficult, more essential, and more pleasing was the role of him who attempted to lay hold of and present the significance of the whole. With a bent for

30 Julius W. Pratt, "Alfred Thayer Mahan," in William T. Hutchinson (ed.), *The Marcus W. Jernegan Essays in American Historiography*, 225–26.
31 Mahan, "Subordination in Historical Treatment," reprinted in *Naval Administration and Warfare*, 247–48; Mahan, *From Sail to Steam*, 278.

insight, a grasp of meaning, and an artful subordination of detail, Mahan shares with Frederick Jackson Turner the honor, among American historians, of being the creator of a new philosophy of history. To an analysis of that philosophy attention will now be given.

III

THE DOCTRINE OF SEA POWER AND THE PRINCIPLES OF NAVAL STRATEGY

THE CALL TO DUTY at the War College set Mahan on the trail which guided him to his philosophy of sea power and directed him to his analysis of naval strategy. Indeed, this service placed Mahan on the road which led directly to unexpected fame.

In certain respects Mahan was not a systematic thinker or writer; except in rare instances, he mixed together, wherever they happened to come in his chronological narrative, discussions of his philosophical concept of sea power, his strategic views on capital ships and allied thought, and his tactical analyses. This chapter indicates the processes by which Mahan arrived at his views in the related fields of sea power and naval strategy and briefly analyzes their content. In the following chapter the reception accorded these views and their influence upon foreign powers will be sketched.

Commodore Stephen B. Luce—detached from the command of the North Atlantic Fleet to assume the presidential duties of the newly created college, where for a few brief weeks the naval officers were to study the higher art of their profession—asked Mahan whether he would care to direct the work in strategy and tactics and instruct in naval history. Mahan replied enthusiastically; although he was fearful that he lacked the special knowledge required, he was confident that he possessed the capacity and perhaps the inherited aptitude for the position.[1]

This call from Luce came in 1884 while Mahan was on

1 Mahan, *From Sail to Steam*, 273.

duty off the coast of South America, but because of disturbances in some of the Central American states and a lapse of departmental interest in the college in the new Cleveland administration, nearly a year passed before the vessel returned to San Francisco and Mahan was detached. At the time Mahan welcomed neither the scene of delay nor the delay itself. From Panama he wrote to Luce in May, 1885: "If you can, do get me ordered home. I have applied by this very mail; on my own account simply, without reference to the future."[2] Certain restrictions entailed by this forced delay were offset by definite benefits. Though he told Ashe that "to excogitate a system . . . on wholly *a priori* grounds would be comparatively simple and . . . wholly useless,"[3] Mahan's subsequent lectures undoubtedly showed increased originality, for few pertinent books were available, while time for reflection was abundant. In his autobiography he evaluated this enforced procedure in these words: "Spinning cobwebs out of one's unassisted brain, without any previous absorption from external sources, was doubtless a somewhat crude process; yet it had advantages."[4]

Contemporary correspondence with Luce and Ashe confirms the account given in his reminiscences of the genesis of the sea-power doctrine. He described his experience in this manner:

While my problem was still wrestling with my brain there dawned upon me one of those concrete perceptions which turned inward darkness into light, gave substance to shadow. . . . He who seeks finds, if he does not lose heart; and to me, continuously seeking, came from within the suggestion that control of the sea was a historic factor which had never been systematically appreciated and expounded. Once formulated

2 May 16 [1885?], Luce Papers.
3 Mahan to Ashe, February 2, 1886, Flowers Collection.
4 Mahan, *From Sail to Steam*, 274.

consciously, this thought became the nucleus of all my writing twenty years then to come.[5]

This general view was given special direction by his reading on the ship and in the English Club's library at Lima. Mommsen's *History of Rome,* especially the Hannibalic episode, played an important part in the development of the idea.

It suddenly struck me, whether by some chance phrase of the author I do not know, how different things might have been could Hannibal have invaded Italy by sea, as the Romans often had Africa, instead of by the long land route; or could he, after arrival, have been in free communications with Carthage by water. This clew, once laid hold, I followed in the particular instance. It and the general theory already conceived threw on each other reciprocal illustration; and between the two my plan was formed by the time I reached home, in September, 1885.[6]

It was Mahan's ambition to investigate coincidentally the general and naval history from the middle of the seventeenth century to the close of the Napoleonic wars; he proposed to demonstrate the influence of the events of the one upon the other and to call attention particularly to the role played by the control of the sea, or the absence thereof, upon the course of history. He realized that time was not available for, and believed that necessity did not require, original research for a program of this sort. He thought:

The subject lay so much on the surface that my handling of it could scarcely suffer materially from possible future discovery. What such and such an unknown man had said or done on some backstairs, or written to some unknown correspondent,

5 *Ibid.,* 276–77.

6 *Ibid.,* 276 ff. See also Mahan to Luce, May 16 [1885?], and January 22, 1886, Luce Papers; Mahan to Ashe, January 13, 1886, and February 2, 1886, Flowers Collection. Mahan further developed Hannibal's dependence on the sea in *The Influence of Sea Power upon History, 1660–1783,* 13–21.

if it came to light, was not likely to affect the received story of the external course of military and political events.[7]

Mahan's first study covered the period from 1660 to 1783. The initial date was chosen largely because the years following Westphalia marked the emergence of European nations in their modern positions struggling for existence and preponderance; the end was dictated by "necessity to stop and take breath."[8] The increasing tendency in the subsequent four volumes of the sea-power series to rely less upon secondary authorities and more upon original research leads one to the conclusion that it was partially, if not largely, a matter of time which forced Mahan to rest so exclusively upon the available published materials in preparing his first book.

Three authors—Lapeyrouse-Bonfils, Jomini, and Martin—sufficiently influenced his line of development to merit comment.[9] In his study of naval history, the first book upon which Mahan chanced (the word is exact) was Lieutenant Lapeyrouse-Bonfils' story of the French Navy. Its chief value was "the quiet, philosophical way of summing up causes and effects in general history, as connected with maritime affairs," which "corresponded closely" with Mahan's own purpose. While this treatment was with the Frenchman only casual, it opened to the American "new prospects."[10]

Mahan's indebtedness to Jomini was considerable, especially in the realm of strategy. By him he was led to a critical study of naval campaigns; with naval conditions constantly in mind, Mahan read and by analogy sought to develop a systematic study of naval war. Jomini's dictum that "the organized forces of the enemy are ever the chief objective"

[7] Mahan, *From Sail to Steam*, 284.

[8] Mahan to Luce, January 22, 1886, Luce Papers; Mahan, *From Sail to Steam*, 281.

[9] For other authors used, see Mahan, *From Sail to Steam*, 279–80; Mahan to Luce, April 24, 1886, Luce Papers.

[10] Mahan, *From Sail to Steam*, 278.

sank deep into Mahan. From the military strategist he also imbibed a fixed disbelief in the commonly accepted maxim that the general and the statesman occupy unrelated fields; from his striking phrase, "the sterile glory of fighting battles merely to win them," the sea-power philosopher deduced the succinct, pregnant sentence, "War is not fighting but business."[11] In 1907 Admiral Luce wrote Mahan that he had said at the opening of the Naval War College, "We must find one who will do for naval science what Jomini did for military science," and that after the sea-power lectures he had added, "He is here; his name is Mahan."[12]

Mahan's close interest in the interdependence of commercial and maritime policies was awakened by a study of Colbert's manipulation of trade as given by Henri Martin in his *History of France*. This book served as "an introductory primer to this element of sea power. . . . New light was shed upon, and new emphasis given to the commonplace assertion of the relations between commerce and a navy; civil and military sea power."[13]

Arriving at home in September, 1885, Mahan spent the winter in study and research, and it was not until near May that he began to write.[14] By September, 1886, he had the whole, except the concluding chapter, on paper in lecture form These lectures, slightly revised and enlarged, were published in 1890 as *The Influence of Sea Power upon History, 1660–1783*. The first eighty-nine pages in this book are of a philosophical nature and contain, in more or less developed form, Mahan's concept of sea power and, to a lesser degree, his views on naval strategy.

11 Mahan to Luce, January 22, 1886, Luce Papers; Mahan, *From Sail to Steam*, 278, 282–83.
12 Luce to Mahan, July 15, 1907, Luce Papers.
13 Mahan, *From Sail to Steam*, 281–82.
14 In *From Sail to Steam*, 285, Mahan wrote that it was the end of May; an examination of Mahan-Luce correspondence shows that on May 1 he had sent some eighty pages for Luce's scrutiny. Mahan to Luce, May 1, 1886, Luce Papers.

He expressed the need for a substantiation of the sea-power doctrine in these words:

It is easy to say in a general way that the use and control of the sea is and has been a great factor in the history of the world; it is more troublesome to seek out and show its exact bearing at a particular juncture. Yet, unless this is done, the acknowledgment of general importance remains vague and unsubstantial; not resting, as it should, upon a collection of specific instances in which the precise effect has been made clear, by an analysis of the conditions at the given moments.[15]

Consequently, in this and subsequent volumes in the series, as well as in other books and articles, the concept of sea power was bolstered by supporting evidence drawn from the pages of history; it was given life and blood by a detailed treatment of the naval wars from Louis XIV to the fall of Napoleon, which period marked the gradual mastery of the seas by England; it was reinforced by accounts of the contemporary battles of Yalu, Santiago, Manila, and Tsushima; it was elaborated and developed in his voluminous magazine writing on contemporary international politics.

Sea power was by no means synonymous with naval power; in the hands of this analyst it included not only the military strength afloat that ruled the sea or any part of it by force of arms, but equally "the peaceful commerce and shipping from which alone a military fleet naturally and healthfully springs, and on which it securely rests."[16] Naval history became more than a mere chronicle of events; in the hands of this philosopher it became an analysis of the meaning and significance of events with a deduction of their governing principles. The record of man's past no longer ignored the role and importance of the sea; in the hands of this historian nearly the whole of history was an epic of the sea.

[15] Mahan, *The Influence of Sea Power upon History, 1660–1783*, iii.
[16] *Ibid.*, 28.

The sea was a great highway, a wide common over which men might pass in all directions with travel and traffic easier, safer, and cheaper than by land. Domestic trade was only a part of the business of a country bordering upon the sea; exchange of produce with foreign powers was an essential corollary. This necessitated a carrying medium, and every nation naturally wished this shipping business to be handled by its own citizens. Vessels sailing to and from needed secure home ports, safe points for trading, refuge, and defense, as well as potential protection en route. This interrelation Mahan summarized in the following sentence:

> In these three things—production, with the necessity of exchanging products, shipping, whereby the exchange is carried on, and colonies, which facilitate and enlarge the operations of shipping and tend to protect it by multiplying points of safety—is to be found the key to much of the history, as well as of the policy of nations bordering upon the sea.[17]

A broad general consideration of the sea, with its uses to mankind and the effects which its control or lack of control had had upon the peaceful developments and the military strength of nations, led to a discussion of the elements or sources of sea power. Mahan enumerated the following as the principal conditions which had affected sea power: (1) geographical position; (2) physical conformation and, as connected therewith, natural production and climate; (3) extent of territory; (4) number of population; (5) character of the people; and (6) character of the government, including the national institutions. There was considerable scope within this framework for comments of a broad and general nature. Comments of this kind, however, were always supported by specific examples drawn primarily from Spain, France, Holland, England, and the United States. The primacy of Mahan's concern to draw lessons applicable

17 *Ibid.*, 25–28.

to the United States appeared throughout the discussion; though a detailed examination of these references relative to the contemporary American situation will be found in subsequent chapters, allusion to them will be made here to give greater definiteness to his generalizations on the component factors of sea power.

Geographical position was of prime importance.[18] First of all, a nation might be so located as to be neither forced to defend nor induced to seek extension of its territory via land with specific military and financial results, e. g., England as compared with France or Holland. Or again, position upon two large bodies of water tended to disperse rather than concentrate naval force, e. g., France or the United States in contrast to England. Finally, a central position, with ports near major trade routes and a good base for hostile operation against probable enemies, was of great strategic advantage. England's position, which gave her control of the Channel and North Sea trade routes, was vastly superior to that of the United States, which possessed no ports near the great centers of trade.

The seaboard of a country was one of its frontiers and the deeper and more numerous the harbors, especially if they were outlets of navigable streams, the greater was the tendency for intercourse with the outside world.[19] The importance of actual separation of a nation's territory by water was significant, e. g., Great Britain and Ireland, Spain and Spanish Netherlands. Natural endowments of soil, climate, and the like might draw or force a nation to the sea. England and Holland, little endowed by nature, took to the sea; while France, blessed with "delightfulness and richness of the land," did not. The United States, similarly blessed, had also ignored those pursuits which promote a healthy sea power, and until the day should come when shipping again

18 *Ibid.*, 29–35.
19 This second element is discussed in *ibid.*, 35–42.

paid, "those who follow the limitations which lack of sea power placed upon the career of France may mourn that their own country is being led, by a like redundancy of home wealth, into the same neglect of that great instrument."

The extent of territory was the last of the conditions, pertaining to the country itself as distinguished from its people, which affected the development of sea power.[20] It was not the area but the proportion of the country's population to the length of its coast line and to the character of its harbors that was of prime importance.

When consideration was given to the number of inhabitants, the more martial aspect naturally was uppermost.[21] It was not the total population but the percentage which followed the sea, as shipbuilders or seafarers, that constituted a strong element of sea power. The staying power of a commercial and maritime England in contrast to an agricultural France was proved time and again during their long colonial wars; the deficiency of the United States in this respect was "patent to all the world" and could be remedied only through foundation of a large commerce under her own flag.

History affirmed "almost without exception" that aptitude for commercial pursuits had been a distinguishing feature of nations great upon the sea,[22] e. g., the shopkeeping Dutch and English, the gold-thirsty Spanish and Portuguese, and the thrifty, hoarding French. The natural bent of a people toward trade, involving not only the production of something to sell but also the belief that commerce was an honorable as well as a lucrative calling, was "the national characteristic most important in the development of sea power." National genius likewise manifested itself in the

20 *Ibid.*, 42–44.

21 *Ibid.*, 44–49.

22 For a discussion of this fifth element, the character of the people, see *ibid.*, 50–58.

capacity to plant "healthy colonies"—colonies that sprang from the felt wants and natural impulses of a whole people. The "healthy colony" rested upon more than placid satisfaction with gain alone; it contained the principle of growth accompanied by political ambitions, e. g., the English in contrast to the Dutch. The character of the colonist rather than the policy of the home government, Mahan thought, was the basic principle upon which the growth of the colony depended. The good colonist settled down and identified himself with his new land, and even though he might maintain recollections of his former home, he had no restless eagerness to return. In this respect, the English settler was viewed as superior to the French. The wise colonist immediately and instinctively sought to develop, in the broadest sense of the word, the resources of the new country. Here the dissimilarity between the English and the Spanish was noted. Mahan believed that in this most important single element of sea power, the character of the people, Americans ranked unusually high.

From a study of several specific instances drawn from the history of England, France, and Holland, the philosopher of sea power concluded that the influence of government upon the sea career of its people worked in two distinct but closely related ways.[23] In times of peace governmental policy could either favor or oppose the natural growth; or that wanting, seek artificially to stimulate or throttle industries and activities which contributed to the development of strong commercial power. The Colbertian policy of building sea power through attention to production, shipping, colonies, and markets, which "withered away like Jonah's gourd when government favor was withdrawn," served as the shining example of the influence of government upon both the growth and the decay of sea power. In the specific preparation for war, the attitude of the gov-

[23] *Ibid.*, 58–83.

ernment was manifest in the attention or lack of attention given to the creation, equipment, and sound maintenance of a naval force which included not only "a fleet but reserves and bases for operations." Mahan deplored the absence of a sound American policy for the encouragement of its sea strength. The United States was woefully weak in the matter of foreign establishments of either a colonial or a military nature. He pointed out the evil effects of the false economy of the Dutch in their general commercial policy and urged that their lesson should serve as a constant warning to the United States.

Critics of Mahan have often ignored these general characteristics or conditions which he laid down as affecting the development of sea power. Mr. Godkin, for example, in disparaging the bellicosity of Mahan manifest in *The Interest of America in Sea Power, Present and Future* (1897), asserted that it was not ships and artillery "but the character of the people themselves and the government which owned the fleet" that made England supreme. Could Godkin have forgotten, or possibly never have read, these pages in Mahan's *magnum opus* in which he dealt with the nature of the government and the character of the people?[24]

Having disposed in this general way of the six basic features affecting sea power, Mahan paused for a moment before starting his detailed analysis of naval wars of a century and a quarter, to which the rest of the volume was devoted, to state succinctly the inclusive role which the navy should play in a nation's life. Naval strategy, he thought, had "for its end to found, support, and increase, as well in peace as in war, the sea power of a country." For the accomplishment of this objective his examination of history showed that a decisive command of the sea was of prime importance. He declared:

24 *The Nation*, Vol. LXVII (September 15, 1898), 198–99.

It is not the taking of individual ships or convoys, be they few or many, that strikes down the money power of a nation; it is the possession of that overbearing power on the sea which drives the enemy's flag from it, or allows it to appear only as a fugitive; and which by controlling the great common, closes the highways by which commerce moves to and from the enemy's shores. This overbearing power can only be exercised by great navies.[25]

These navies, it might be added, had to operate according to certain general laws of strategy which had been fully established as a result of long years of naval combat. Ships of the line, not overly large but numerous, well manned, with crew thoroughly trained, if adequately provided for with outlying bases, history had shown most efficacious.

From a military standpoint naval forces existed for offensive purposes; that is, the best defense was offense, with the fight carried to a definite issue. This necessitated the concentration of the fleet at decisive points, and under no circumstances was the fleet to be divided or dispersed. The final destruction or total mastery of the enemy fleet was the primary consideration; privateering was definitely secondary. Such command of the sea not only permitted the maintenance of one's own lines of communication while throttling enemy trade, but, if necessary, provided the means for the close supervision of neutral commerce.[26] With each of these items in mind—the ruinous consequences of inadequacy of preparation, the futility of privateering, the overwhelming importance of concentration of the fleet, and the validity of blockade—Mahan drew lessons for America.

Little that was new from a strictly factual point of view can be found in the general and philosophical manner in which Mahan interpreted the control of the sea as the major determinant in the destiny of nations. The idea of sea

25 Mahan, *The Influence of Sea Power upon History, 1660-1783*, 82, 138.
26 *Ibid.*, 8-9, 82-88.

power, if not the term itself, is as old as history, and a knowledge of its underlying importance was appreciated by Thucydides, Xerxes, and Themistocles; indeed, "as soon as it was found possible to use the seas as means of transport or communication the idea of sea power was born."[27] Mahan never laid claim to the right of discovery or even originality, though he was unaware, at the time, of predecessors such as Bacon and Raleigh, who had epitomized his theme in a few words. He did concede himself—and none can deny him the honor, though some might think it of dubious merit—a definite role in popularizing and making effective the doctrine of sea power.[28]

If any claim to originality be made for Mahan by his critics, it must rest upon his treatment or presentation of material. He clarified, formulated, substantiated, and expounded a doctrine history-old. In his hands sea power received a broad basis; the military and the naval, the political and the commercial, were as sword and sheath in his interpretation. Sea-borne commerce made a nation great; security for this was essential. Command of the sea which would assure the possessor of the potential strength to win was a prerequisite. This command of the sea guaranteed, in war or peace, the continuance of maritime commerce with its exchange of finished produce for supplies and raw materials; a close relation between foreign trade and the navy was thus affirmed. The effectiveness of the navy, however, was dependent upon bases and distant stations. Territories, though acquired with this in view, might prove valuable from point of raw materials or markets; in this respect, strategic needs and economic ambitions neatly bolstered each

27 J. M. Kenworthy, "Navy," *Encyclopedia of Social Sciences*, XI; see also P. A. Silburn, *Evolution of Sea Power*, 1; Bradley A. Fiske, "Naval Power," United States Naval Institute *Proceedings*, Vol. XXXVII (1911), 1684 ff.; J. M. Schammell, "Thucydides and Sea Power," United States Naval Institute *Proceedings*, Vol. XLVII (1921), 701–704.

28 Mahan, *From Sail to Steam*, 276, 325.

other. In a somewhat similar manner, merchant marine and navy were interdependent, for as the navy rested upon the marine in war, so did the marine rely upon the navy in peace. The sequence of industry, markets, marine, navy, and bases was firmly established with their interdependence forcibly brought home. In practice, sea power and mercantilistic imperialism became virtually synonymous. National life, national trade, national prosperity, and the command of the sea were most closely related. Wrote Mahan:

> The due use and control of the sea is but one link in the chain of exchange by which wealth accumulates; but it is the central link, which lays under contribution other nations for the benefit of the one holding it, and which history seems to assert, most surely of all gathers itself riches.[29]

Here in the doctrine of sea power as evolved by Mahan was a philosophy of history which neatly linked patriotism, politics, and economics; a philosophy of empire which was seemingly confirmed, moreover, by a study of the past. Fortunately or unfortunately, its formulation came in an era ready and waiting for such an exposition. The thesis by which Mahan hoped to convert his country to "go down to the sea in ships" was readily adaptable for use by other nations more eager than his own to heed this call of the sea, more anxious to accept the challenge of empire.

In the deduction of his strategic principles Mahan drew upon the lessons of history; in the enunciation of his strategic principles Mahan gave his country and the world a set of clearly defined rules. The exposition of these principles came at a critical time when it seemed to many that technology had made obsolete the ancient order. The new order had seen the stately ships of the line with towering masts, billowing sails, and wooden hulls supplanted by the steam-driven monsters of sleek, gray steel; and smooth-bore,

---

[29] Mahan, *The Influence of Sea Power upon History, 1660–1783,* 225–26.

muzzle-load guns replaced by built-up breech-loading rifles which could destroy an enemy vessel hidden from sight beyond the horizon. Amidst the confusion of thought and action resulting from these technical changes, Mahan asserted with firm but quiet insistence that the major strategical lessons of the past were valid still.

IV

GENERAL RECEPTION AND FOREIGN UTILIZATION

The *Influence of Sea Power upon History, 1660–1783*, released from the press in May, 1890, was immediately and warmly received in both the United States and Great Britain, although the acclaim was louder and more insistent in the latter. Translations were soon made into German, Japanese, French, Italian, Russian, and Spanish. With certain qualifications in the degree of praise and extent of translation, similar receptions were given *The Influence of Sea Power upon the French Revolution and Empire, 1793–1812* (2 volumes, 1892), *Sea Power in Its Relations to the War of 1812* (2 volumes, 1905), and *The Life of Nelson: the Embodiment of the Sea Power of Great Britain* (2 volumes, 1897).[1] The magazine articles, periodically compiled for book publication, as well as letters to the press—both of which were usually more contentious in subject matter and less historical in treatment—aroused definite dissension at various times in nearly all quarters.

So far as the sea-power series was concerned, a new de-

[1] *The Influence of Sea Power upon History, 1660–1783* went through fifteen editions in eight years and has to date appeared in forty-one editions, with a sale of nearly 29,000 copies. It is still in print. *The Influence of Sea Power upon the French Revolution and Empire, 1793–1812* had ten editions in six years, and in seventeen editions slightly less than 12,000 copies were sold before it went out of print in 1943. Almost 24,000 copies of *The Life of Nelson* in two- and one-volume editions have been sold. A new one-volume edition appeared in 1943. *Sea Power in Its Relation to the War of 1812* had a sale of a little less than 6,000 copies before it went out of print in 1935. (These figures were made available through the courtesy of Little, Brown and Company.)

parture was sensed and a veritable addition to naval history acknowledged.[2] Mahan's adept handling of the tangled thread of causation and his historically substantiated evidence of the controlling influence of naval operations over land campaigns appealed to Colonel George Sydenham Clarke, one of the ablest writers on military and naval matters in the British Army. Whitelaw Reid's New York *Tribune* considered the first book "sober, restrained, exact, and logical," with "critical commentary valuable and penetrating" and the vindication of the functions and uses of sea power "thorough."[3]

Theodore Roosevelt, then civil service commissioner, characterized the first study as "distinctively the best, the most important and also by far the most interesting book on naval history." In a personal note he told Mahan:

> During the last two days, I have spent half my time, busy as I am, in reading your book. That I found it interesting is shown by the fact that having taken it up, I have gone straight through and finished it. . . . It is a *very* good book—admirable; and I am greatly in error if it does not become a naval classic.[4]

At the time of Mahan's death he paid the book and its author this generous tribute:

> The book could have been written only by a man steeped

2 Charles Francis Adams, "A Plea for Military History," in *Lee at Appomattox and Other Papers,* 346; see also in addition to reviews subsequently cited, the following: "Nauticus" (W. Laird Clowes), "Sea Power: Its Past and Its Future," *Fortnightly Review,* Vol. LIV (December, 1893), 849–68; *American Historical Review,* Vol. IV (July, 1899), 719–21; Gaillard Hunt, "Sea Power in Its Relation to the War of 1812," *American Historical Review,* Vol. XI (July, 1906), 924–26.

3 G. S. Clarke (later Lord Sydenham), "Captain Mahan's Counsels to the United States," *Nineteenth Century,* Vol. XLIII (February, 1898), 293.

New York *Tribune,* May 18, 1890; for some other newspaper reaction see, Boston *Evening Transcript,* May 14, 1890; Portland *Oregonian,* June 2, 1890.

4 "The Influence of Sea Power upon History," *Atlantic Monthly,* Vol. LXVI (October, 1890), 563; Roosevelt to Mahan, May 12, 1890, Mahan Papers.

through and through in the peculiar knowledge and wisdom of the great naval expert who was also by instinct and training a statesman. . . . Admiral Mahan was the only great naval expert who also possessed in international matters the mind of a statesman of the first class. His interest was in the large side of his subject; he was more concerned with the strategy than tactics of both naval war and statesmanship.[5]

Fellow officers were "delighted" and "proud" of him. They congratulated him for having written an "admirable book" filled with "astonishing and convincing truths," and they thanked him for having aided them in crystallizing what before was "rather nebulous" in their minds regarding "the proper way to carry on war."[6]

No inconsiderable number of foreign commentators saw the Mahanian moral, the author's desire to arouse the United States to a realization of her needs on the sea. English critics wrote:

Though Captain Mahan is dominated by the philosophical spirit, and deals with his subject in a thoroughly scientific manner, a warmer motive than a love of science has led him to undertake the investigation. . . . The results of the inquiry are used didactically and for the benefit of the author's fellow citizens.[7]

He has, of course, the circumstances of his own country definitely in view; and it is allowable to suppose that in publishing these lectures he had hoped to rekindle in the hearts of his fellow-countrymen some desire to contest the supremacy of the sea.[8]

Nor did American reviewers fail to take note of the les-

5 "A Great Public Servant," The Outlook, Vol. CIX (January 13, 1915), 85–86.

6 C. F. Goodrich to Mahan, May 14, 1892; W. S. Schley, September 11, 1891; A. S. Barker, September 30, [1892?]: Mahan Papers.

7 Blackwood's Edinburgh Magazine, Vol. CXLVIII (October, 1890), 577.

8 J. K. Laughton, "Captain Mahan on Maritime Power," Edinburgh Review, Vol. CLXXII (October, 1890), 453.

sons which Mahan sought to impart. The folly of false economy, the stupidity of nonpreparedness, the impossibility of preparation on the spur of the moment, the unmanliness of submitting to wanton aggression, the too great reliance upon past records, the futility of privateering as more than a secondary factor—these "errors" of the past frequently caught their attention.[9] Some commentators sensed his larger concern and appreciated the concept of sea power as the basis of empire; they saw the interrelation of industry, · commerce, colonies, marine, and navy. The New York *Tribune* caught the vision, urged that here were "matters of grave importance" to the United States, and issued a stirring call for action. It is evident as one observes the language used by the editor of *Harper's* to characterize Mahan's philosophy that the sea-power author had not written in vain. The editorial showed not only an understanding of the doctrine but gave it its blessing and an additional circulation.

The lesson of this long story to the United States is not far to seek but it is deeper than appears on the surface. It is not only that without sea power a nation must take a low rank in this competing world, but that lacking this it lacks one vital element of internal prosperity. It is that it cannot properly develop itself if it permits itself to be hemmed in and shut from the markets and exchanges of the world.[10]

In 1890 one voice was raised against this sermonizing by Mahan. "In his constant tendency to point a moral for

[9] Theodore Roosevelt, "The Influence of Sea Power upon History," *Atlantic Monthly*, Vol. LXVI (October, 1890), 563–67; Roosevelt, "The Influence of Sea Power upon the French Revolution," *Atlantic Monthly*, Vol. LXXI (April, 1893), 556–59; Roosevelt, "The Influence of Sea Power upon History, 1660–1783" and "The Influence of Sea Power upon the French Revolution and Empire," *Political Science Quarterly*, Vol. IX (March, 1894). 171–73; *The Nation*, Vol. LXXXII (January 11, 1906), 39–41; Anna Heloise Abel, "Sea Power and the War of 1812," *The Dial*, Vol. XL (January 16, 1906), 45–47.

[10] New York *Tribune*, May 18, 1890, and January 22, 1893; *Harper's Monthly*, Vol. LXXXVII (November, 1893), 962–63.

our fresh water Congressmen, and to preach the gospel of American commerce, and a new navy, he mars to a considerable degree the force of his thesis."[11] Even this critic, however, granted Mahan great credit for having found "a subject comparatively so fresh" and for having exploited "the main idea so ably" and predicted that his achievement would exert "a strong influence" upon subsequent writers.

Not a few reviewers immediately sensed the probability of repercussions beyond the borders of the United States. They saw that though Mahan's moral might be intended for Americans, the thesis of sea power, as the author had presented it, could not be restricted. They recognized that here was a philosophy of power politics deduced from a study of the diplomacy, commerce, and wars of the seventeenth and eighteenth centuries which called for careful consideration by the molders and framers of contemporary state policy. While an English commentator in 1893 adjudged the initial sea-power studies as volumes "without rival" and found lessons "equally valuable to the historian, the statesman, the naval strategist, and the tactician," an American editor informed his readers that these were the "most striking and suggestive volumes that have appeared in many years touching the development and strength of national power."[12] "In the highest and best sense," wrote J. K. Laughton of the Royal Navy College, Mahan's first book was "a treatise on the philosophy of history, of history teaching by examples." The significance of facts now shone forth, "projected like an electric beam on the clouds of heaven, so as to compel the notice of all who come within its comprehensive survey." His second book, thought Professor Laughton, was addressed more to the general reader,

11 *Literary World*, Vol. XXI (July 5, 1890), 217–18.
12 A. H. Johnson, "Mahan on Sea Power," *English Historical Review*, Vol. VIII (October, 1893), 788; *Harper's Monthly*, Vol. LXXXVII (November, 1893), 962–63.

and in many respects was even more significant. Though it claimed the attention of naval men, it was more important to "the statesman, the administrator, the shipowner, the merchant, and the tradesman."[13]

As has already been indicated, Mahan's philosophy of world politics was compounded of two distinct but related theories: One was the thesis that national greatness rested upon mercantilistic imperialism; the other was the principle of the primacy of concentration of naval forces, in its applied form the doctrine of battle-fleet supremacy. Mahan's books had world-wide effects in the fields of expansion, naval armament, and naval strategy. Among foreign powers, his influence was most immediate and direct in England, Germany, and Japan.

The special import of Mahan's writings for the English was well brought out by their press. The English had done great deeds of which they were not unaware, but Mahan's analysis brought them an added understanding of the significance of these deeds. In evaluating *The Influence of Sea Power upon History, 1660–1783*, Captain C. B. S. Bridge, reviewer for *Blackwood's Magazine,* thought that "notwithstanding the more general scope indicated by its title, the book may almost be said to be a scientific inquiry into the causes which have made England great"; and though naval officers and students might find "instruction on nearly every page," he believed that the average British reader could and should learn from it how his "country acquired her present position amongst the nations, and how that position may be maintained."[14] Professor Laughton gave two reviews of thirty-four pages each in the *Edinburgh Review* of Mahan's first studies. He considered the books a "splendid

[13] "Captain Mahan on Maritime Power," *Edinburgh Review,* Vol. CLXXVII (April, 1893) , 484–85.

[14] *Blackwood's Edinburgh Magazine,* Vol. CXLVII (October, 1890), 576–84.

apothesis of English courage and English endurance, of English skill and English power."[15]

At this time the English were peculiarly in need of Mahan's analysis of the value, purpose, and function of a navy. The revolutionizing changes in propulsion, ordnance, armor, and the ever increasing differentiation of types of crafts had brought definite uncertainty about the most essential vessel or vessels and had created marked confusion concerning basic strategy not only in Great Britain but on the Continent. The resulting building programs represented a hodgepodge of coastal defense, commerce destruction, and battle-fleet supremacy. Partly from tradition and partly from new circumstances, the French had become intrigued with commerce destruction. They reasoned that the introduction of the steam ironclad and the torpedo craft and the altered position of a highly industrialized Britain primarily dependent upon foreign food and raw materials gave prospect of victory to a French Navy of fast cruisers and torpedo boats. They argued that the heyday of the battleship fleet had passed and that for the cost of one clumsy Goliath a nation could build sixty agile Davids. The *Jeune École*, led by Admiral Theophile Aube, not only greatly influenced French naval development until the end of the century but had ardent advocates in other European countries. At the height of the torpedo-boat craze several Continental navies abandoned their battleship programs; and though the British Admiralty was never won over to the extent of complete neglect of the ships of the line, its members did feel obliged at one time to apologize to Parliament for finishing such ships already under construction.[16] Ma-

15 "Captain Mahan on Maritime Power," *Edinburgh Review*, Vol. CLXXII (October, 1890), 420–53; "Captain Mahan on Maritime Power," *Edinburgh Review*, Vol. CLXXVII (April, 1893), 484–518.

16 Theodore Ropp, "Continental Doctrines of Sea Power" in E. M. Earle (ed.), *Makers of Modern Strategy*, 447. See also Margaret Sprout, "Mahan: Evangelist of Sea Power," in *ibid.*

han's doctrine of battle-fleet supremacy helped to turn the tide and to save the day in Britain.

Moreover, since the Crimean War, interest in the navy had lagged in Great Britain. The rapidity of decisions won by land forces in the German wars of unification and the limitation of recent naval operations to coastal forays had seriously undermined faith in the navy. Large sums were spent on the army and upon coastal fortification, while appropriations for the navy suffered; in fact, it was not until 1895–96 that the expenditure for the navy came once more to equal those of the army. The great resurgence in French naval activity coupled with the large naval appropriations by Russia in the late eighties provoked the British to pass the historic two-power Naval Defense Act of 1889. The Franco-Russian Alliance of 1894 and the increasing tension in world affairs in South Africa, Egypt, the Far East, and elsewhere gave no surcease to British fears.

Amid such circumstances it can readily be seen that Mahan's doctrine of sea power and his exposition of naval strategy were a godsend to the British. His interrelation of geographical factors, national character, commerce, colonial expansion, and navy as the forces which made for greatness on the sea and therefore for national greatness appealed to manufacturer, merchant, trader, and empire builder. His clarification of the fundamental principles of warfare and the affirmation of their continued efficacy, with the consequent insistence upon the battleship and its operation in fleet formation as the ultimate determinant in naval engagements, received the heartfelt blessings of statesman, navalist, and strategist. Mahan's stirring story of Britain's duels with Holland, Spain, and France in the seventeenth and eighteenth centuries challenged the indifference toward and rekindled a faith in the navy; his historical survey of Britain's rise to pre-eminence brought vitally needed support to the hesitant naval building program and strengthened materially the reviving maritime and colonial ambitions; his careful analysis of underlying principles of naval warfare brought order from the chaos and confusion created by the advances of naval architecture and technology, and indelibly left its stamp upon strategical principles employed.

Indeed, it is safe to conclude that the most important factor stimulating the English to a revival of interest in their navy was the appearance of Mahan's truly remarkable sea-power volumes in 1890 and 1892. British naval officers from the Admiral of the Fleet down wrote Mahan about his first great book. One officer acknowledged the pressing need for such a study; another predicted that it would "have great effect in bringing home to our statesmen and legislators the vast importance of sea power to England"; another wished that he had the power to place a copy in every home in Britain and the colonies; while another, writing less than a year following publication, stated that the book already had "had great effect in getting people to understand what they never understood before."[17] The publication of Mahan's following study brought other letters from English officers. One declared himself a Mahan "disciple" and as a member of Parliament proposed to work for a "big navy."[18]

The British government supplied Mahan's sea-power volumes for the libraries of the training ships. Gladstone, the arch opponent of armaments, called the second opus "the book of the age."[19] One British officer declared that no volume on naval or military subjects had attracted one-tenth the notice given this study.[20] Mahan was also a frequent contributor to the *Journal of the Royal United Service Institu-*

17 Admiral G. T. Phipps Hornby to Mahan, June 18, 1890; Captain Gerard H. V. Noel to Mahan, December 23, 1890; Captain Charles Beresford to Mahan, January 12, 1891; Admiral P. H. Colomb to Mahan, April 26, 1891: Mahan Papers.
18 Thomas Gibson Bowles to Mahan, January 14, 1893, *ibid.*
19 Arthur J. Marder, *The Anatomy of British Sea Power*, 47.
20 Captain F. N. Maude, "The Influence of Sea Power," *National Review*, Vol. XXIII (March, 1894), 110–17.

tion and to the *National Review*.[21] His views were disseminated through many magazine articles, reprints, and countless press quotations; and in press space devoted to Americans, Mahan rated close to Carnegie and Roosevelt.[22] By 1893 one writer stated that the sea-power "discovery" had been so widely discussed that its nature was now familiar to most Englishmen. Fifteen years later the *Standard* wrote, "It is no exaggeration to say that the publication of a new book by Captain Mahan is an event of international consequence."[23]

Many of the professional papers and discussions at the Royal United Service Institution forthrightly acknowledged indebtedness to this "very able American."[24] The navalists who believed that an adequate sea arm was an absolute bar

21 In the *Journal of the Royal United States Service Institution* see "Two Maritime Expeditions," October, 1893; "Blockade in Relation to Naval Strategy," November, 1895; "The Personality of Nelson," October, 1905; "Reflections, Historic and Others, Suggested by the Battle of the Sea of Japan," November, 1906. In the *National Review* see "The Influence of the South African War upon the Prestige of the British Empire," December, 1901; "The Military Rule of Obedience," March, 1902; "Motives to Imperial Federation," May, 1902; "Conditions Governing the Disposition of Navies," July, 1902; "The Persian Gulf and International Relations," September, 1902; "The Monroe Doctrine," February, 1903; "Principles of Naval Administration," June, 1903; "Principles Involved in the War with Japan and Russia," September, 1904; "The Strength of Nelson," November, 1905; "Retrospect upon the War Between Japan and Russia," May, 1906; "The Hague Conference of 1907 and the Question of Immunity for Belligerent Merchant Shipping," June, 1907; "The Hague Conference and the Practical Aspect of War," July, 1907.

22 See various letters from Leopold James Maxse, editor of the British *National Review* to Mahan, especially November 29, 1901, and May 29, 1902, Mahan Papers; also R. H. Heindel, *The American Impact on Great Britain*, 117, 133 n.

23 "Nauticus" (W. Laird Clowes), "Sea Power, Its Past and Future," *Fortnightly Review*, Vol. LIV (December, 1893), 849–68; The *Standard*, December 21, 1908.

24 In debate period see comments of Colonel Featherstonhaugh in *Journal of the Royal United Service Institution*, Vol. XLI (February, 1897), 191; also in *ibid.* translated article by Baron von Lüttwitz, Captain of the German Grand General Staff, "German Naval Policy and Strategy," 315–30; also professor J. K. Laughton to Mahan, March 11, 1893, Mahan Papers.

to invasion took as their slogan the immortal words of their American historian-analyst relative to the role of the British fleet in the days of Napoleon: "Those far distant, storm-beaten ships, upon which the Grand Army never looked, stood between it and the dominion of the world." Parliamentary debaters expounded the sea-power doctrine and buttressed their arguments with the words, "as Captain Mahan puts it."[25] Advocates for the maintenance of the historic British policy on the rights of maritime capture quoted Mahan upon the untoward effects on British naval power by the abandonment of such a policy.[26]

Lord Wolseley, writing in 1897 to his friend Sir Frederick Maurice, stated: "Mahan's books have done the country, and the Navy for that matter too, a world of good. It is a sad reflection that it has taken a Yankee to wake up this generation to the meaning and importance of sea power."[27] However, writing near the same time, Colonel George Sydenham Clarke expressed the view: "Speaking as an outsider, Captain Mahan wielded a force which could not have been extended by any British writer. . . . The importance of the service thus opportunely rendered by the brilliant American writer can hardly be overrated." Subsequently, in his autobiography, Lord Sydenham stated that Mahan's first book "powerfully reinforced our [naval] propaganda at this period. For the first time we had a philosophy of sea power built upon history from the days of the Punic Wars."[28] Admiral Sir Reginald Bacon, likewise in retro-

25 Sir Charles Dilke in Hansard, *Parliamentary Debates*, Series IV, Vol. XLVII, 68–70, cited by W. L. Langer, *The Diplomacy of Imperialism*, II, 425–26.

26 See secret memorandum prepared by G. S. Clarke, under the direction of the Prime Minister, for the Committee of Imperial Defense, May, 1906, in Campbell Bannermann MSS, cited in Heindel, *op. cit.*, 115.

27 Sir F. Maurice and Sir G. Arthur, *Life of Lord Wolseley*, 285. See also John Leyland, "Recent Naval Literature," in *Brassey's Naval Annual, 1897*, 210; also Lord Fisher, *Records*, 135.

28 G. S. Clarke, *loc. sit.*, 297; Sydenham of Combe, *My Working Life*, 144.

spect, could recall nothing during his years in the navy so significant as Mahan's sea-power studies.[29] The able English naval historian, Sir Julian Corbett, the nearest to a Mahan the British have produced, characterized Mahan's famous book "a political pamphlet in the higher sense," and added, "it has few equals in the sudden and far-reaching effect it produced on political thought and action."[30]

Allowing for exaggeration, some conception of how the English hung upon his word may be gained from the reaction of the New York *Tribune's* English correspondent writing in 1904: "The English people look upon him as a foreigner who understands the source of their power and influence in the world and . . . every word falling from his lips is listened to with eagerness as the judgment of an oracle."[31] No expression of British appreciation is stronger testimony of their high regard for Mahan than the near-royal reception given him in 1894 when he was dined by the Queen, by the Prime Minister, and the First Lord of the Admiralty, awarded honorary degrees by Cambridge and Oxford, and entertained as guest of honor by the Royal Navy Club—the first foreigner accorded this distinction.

Mahan made no secret of his admiration for British naval achievements or of his affection for many British institutions. He even went further, as has been noted, and from 1902 to the British declaration of war in 1914 called attention to the growing German menace, urging all good Britishers to rally to the historic call of their country. As the naval correspondent of the *English Morning Post* wrote at the time of Mahan's death, he was not only the first to formulate elaborately and comprehensively the philosophy of British sea power, but "from time to time, as occasions of

29 Reginald Bacon, *A Naval Scrap-Book*, 264–65.

30 Sir Julian Corbett, "The Revival of Naval History," *Contemporary Review*, Vol. CX (December, 1916), 735.

31 New York *Tribune*, July 22, 1904.

difficulty arose, he published an essay or an article which indicated the right course for Great Britain to follow."[32] It might be added that all Britishers did not always welcome his every suggestion.[33]

A discerning reviewer in *Blackwood's Magazine* of October, 1890, rightly predicted that once the causes and processes by which English greatness had been achieved were thought to have been divined and interpreted, there would be an immediate desire among the powers to imitate.[34] When Germany, with new leadership and under pressure of her growing industries and teeming population, was ready to forsake the Bismarckian ideal of a purely Continental empire for dreams of extra-European expansion, she found Mahan's books available for use. William II, even prior to his ascension in 1888, had manifested an unusual interest in things maritime. Infatuated by the might of the British Navy and intoxicated by the wealth of the British colonies, he ardently longed for the Reich to equal the British achievements. The telegram which the Kaiser sent Poultney Bigelow in May, 1894, is indicative of the reception accorded Mahan's views on the correlation of domestic production, foreign trade, merchant marine, colonies, and naval power by certain elements of the German state. Wrote the Kaiser: "I am just now not reading but devouring Captain Mahan's book [the first], and am trying to learn it by heart. It is a first class work and classical in all points. It is on board all my ships and constantly quoted by my Captains and officers."[35] The absence of any great naval tradition may partially account for the widespread appeal of Mahan's stra-

32 New York *Times,* December 2, 1914.

33 "Excubitor" (pen name) , "Admiral Mahan's Warning," *Fortnightly Review,* Vol. XCIV (August, 1910), 224–34.

34 *Blackwood's Edinburgh Magazine,* Vol. CXLVII (October, 1890), 576. For similar views see Charles A'Court Repington, *Vestigia,* 277, and General Sir George Aston, *Memories of a Marine,* 96.

35 Taylor, *Life of Admiral Mahan,* 131–32.

tegical concepts to the German naval command; at any rate, the German Admiralty wholeheartedly accepted Mahan's thesis that "the natural destiny of the navy was the strategical offensive."[36]

The German Colonial Society and the Pan-German League threw their support behind overseas acquisitions and enlarged naval appropriations. There can be no doubt but that German trade interests and increased dependence on overseas food supplies definitely contributed to German naval and colonial policies. The growth of German industry and trade in the years following her unification were remarkable, and the effects abroad no less significant than at home. Merchant tonnage increased about 150 per cent between the years 1873 and 1895, and the value of her maritime trade increased over 200 per cent in the same period. By 1897 in foreign trade Germany was second in the world, yet in naval power she was outclassed by four European powers, including Italy.[37]

The desire for colonial expansion likewise definitely motivated German policy. The close connection of Mahan with this development is seen in an article on German naval policy and strategy by Baron von Lüttwitz. This article drew heavily upon the American expansionist and strategist; it evoked much British interest and in translation was published in the *Journal of the Royal United Service Institution*. The German Army officer contended:

In the last century we were too late to partake of the general partition. But a second partition is forthcoming. We need only consider the fall of the Ottoman Empire, the isolation of China —that new India of the Far East, the unstable condition of many South American States, to see what rich opportunities await us. In order not to miss them this time we require a fleet.

36 Hans Hallman, *Der Weg zum Deutschen Schlachtflottenbau*, 128; Alfred Vagts, *Deutchland und die Vereinigten Staaten in der Weltpolitik*, Vol. II, 1420–21.
37 Langer, *op. cit.*, II, 429.

We must be so strong at sea that no nation which feels itself safe from our military power may dare to overlook us in partition negotiations, and there is no time to be lost.[38]

Mahan's insistence upon bases as an essential element in sea power greatly impressed the German Admiralty. Tirpitz and his aides employed Mahan's articles on "The Isthmus and Sea Power" and "The Strategic Features of the Gulf of Mexico and the Caribbean Sea," reprinted in *The Interest of the United States in Sea Power, Present and Future* (1897), in an attempt to convince the Foreign Office of the justification of German acquisition in these regions. Tirpitz accepted Mahan's views that sea power was concentrated in the Caribbean Sea as in but few places and believed that Germany needed territorial holdings in the region to have her share in it. To support further his case, Tirpitz attached to his memorandum the map of the Gulf and the Caribbean area taken from Mahan's book. Despite repeated pleas from the Admiralty, the Foreign Office took a negative attitude toward the acquisition of St. Thomas, Galapagos, and Curaçao.[39]

It was not until Alfred von Tirpitz became minister of marine in June, 1897, that the modern German Navy began to take clear form. In matériel, administration, and strategy Tirpitz was the formative and directive genius of the Imperial Navy from 1897 to World War I. Tirpitz brought to this new appointment a fund of knowledge gained from a long, active, and distinguished career in maritime matters. He had given much thought to strategy and tactics and had arrived at conclusions similar to those of Mahan. As early as 1891 he had stated "that the decision for our Navy must be sought in open battle." He never wavered from the conviction that cruiser warfare was of limited importance to Germany; he held firmly to the belief

[38] Lüttwitz, *loc. cit.,* 328; see also 330.
[39] Vagts, *op. cit.,* II, 1418–20; 1492–94; 1504.

that a considerable battle fleet in the North Sea was the primary objective of German naval policy. He never hoped to equal the *whole* British fleet; he did hope to make the German fleet so powerful that the British *home* fleet would not be willing to risk an engagement. Tirpitz was motivated by "the almost panicky fear that the rising Anglo-German economic rivalry would increasingly dominate the relations between the two nations and lead the British to crush German competition by brute force unless he could succeed at the last minute in building up a fleet sufficient to deter them from that course."[40]

Tirpitz' "doctrine of risk" was predicated upon the belief that the English would never be able to arrange their far-flung interests so as to concentrate all their squadrons in the North Sea, that the existence of a battle fleet near the nerve center of the Empire would immeasurably enhance Germany's power upon the Continent and her alliance-value, that the combination of the best army and a good navy with their resultant influence in power politics would cause Great Britain to make concessions to Germany rather than run the risk of imperiling her position in the world. As long as England was beset by the major threats of Russia and France in Asia, Africa, and the Mediterranean, the political value of Tirpitz' risk fleet strong enough to hold the balance of power between the Dual and Triple Alliances had some validity. Once England emerged from her "Splendid Isolation," this form of diplomatic blackmail not only lost its efficacy but tremendously embittered Anglo-German relations and contributed greatly to the eventual holocaust.[41]

40 Herbert Rosinski, "Mahan and the Present War," in Rear Admiral H. G. Thursfield (ed.), *Brassey's Naval Annual, 1941,* 200.

41 Alfred von Tirpitz, *My Memoirs,* I, 79, 84, 120–21. See also Tirpitz' draft of speech to the Reichstag, March, 1896, printed in Hans Hallmann, *Krügerdepesche und Flottenfrage,* 79 ff.; and memorandum appended to German Navy Bill of 1900 cited in Archibald Hurd and Henry Castle, *German Sea Power,* 348; and Theodore Ropp, *loc. cit.,* 451.

Wilhelm II (1859–1941). Emperor of Germany and King of Prussia, 1888–1918, he sought to make Germany a major naval, commercial, and colonial power. *Library of Congress*

Admiral Alfred von Tirpitz (1849–1930). Secretary of State of Naval Affairs, 1897–1916, he played a vital role in the creation and disposition of the German Imperial Navy. *United Press International photograph.*

The basic tenets of Tirpitz' philosophy of German naval policy were formulated and expressed before he took office as minister of marine. He knew what he wanted and cautiously yet positively moved for its achievement. His first problem was to persuade the Kaiser of the wisdom of his views; though William II in 1894 had been learning by heart Mahan's initial study and though he had received the sea-power author on his yacht at Cowes the following year, he was still disposed in 1897 to a cruiser rather than a battleship navy. Strangely enough, however, the Emperor made but slight objection and once converted became a most bitter critic of the "cruiser heresy."

Having cleared this initial hurdle, Tirpitz now engaged in a systematic campaign to win over not only the Reichstag but the German people.[42] He sought to popularize naval power and make the Germans sea-minded. Though there is an apparent air of artificiality about the propagandistic campaign of Tirpitz, it is true, as British critics have admitted, that German naval might was incommensurate with her economic and political developments.[43]

Tirpitz shrewdly analyzed the forces which could be employed for the advancement of his program. He capitalized upon the psychological atmosphere of a newly created state which was even then giving indications of wanting her "place in the sun." He sought to give direction to a people awakening to an interest in colonies and foreign commerce. He drew support from the munition makers (Krupps) and from large trading interests (Woermann of Hamburg). He secured the assistance of newspaper men, economists (Weber and Schmoller), and historians (Shäfer and Delbrück). Ernst Levy von Halle of the University of Berlin wrote *Die*

---

[42] Tirpitz, *op. cit.*, I, 121, 142–47; Eckart Kehr, *Schlactflottenbau und Parteipolitik, 1894–1901*, 93–110; Vagts, *op. cit.*, II, 1452–53; Langer, *op. cit.*, II, 436.

[43] Hurd and Castle, *op. cit.*, 118.

Seemacht in der deutschen Geschichte in which he applied
Mahan's doctrines to the events of German history. In the
introductory pages he paid tribute to "the epoch-making
work" of the American naval officer.[44] Admiral Tirpitz personally arranged for the translation of the second of Mahan's books; in order to get the two volumes to the public
before the new naval appropriations bill came before the
Reichstag, they were issued in sections, beginning in November, 1897.[45] Mahan's studies were designed to be sort
of a naval bible, and the complete sea-power series was supplied at government expense to all warships, public institutions, libraries, and schools.

Directly and indirectly the teachings of Mahan had profound and far-reaching influence upon the German state.
Though most of Tirpitz' views were undoubtedly derived
from his own vast first-hand experience, direct observation,
and study, yet from the American author he received encouragement, justification, and guidance. Even more important was the utilization of Mahan by Tirpitz and his
friends in selling the naval program to the German state.
Inasmuch as Mahan definitely influenced both Britain and
Germany in the fields of expansion and naval armament,
there attaches to him some of the responsibility for foster-
ing the imperial rivalry and the naval race which were two
of the causes of World War I. A commentator in the London
Nation at the time of Mahan's death made the following
provocative observation:

> The strategist who evolved the theory of sea power was
> much more than a historian. He helped to make history, much
> as Treitschke did. . . . One may doubt, indeed, whether Bern-
> hardi and all his school had as much effect in deciding Ger-
> mans to build a great navy as this American historian. . . . His
> books were quoted as classics by Count Reventlow and other

44 Pages 6–7.
45 Kehr, *op. cit.*, 45, 51 n.

leaders of the "Flottenverein." . . . The real motive which explains the rise of the modern German Navy is the lesson derived from Mahan, that sea power is essential to world empire. That at bottom is the reason why our attempts at discussion invariably failed. We were rather apt, on our side, to disguise the real facts, when we used to argue as though the sole functions of our Navy were to defend our shores. The Germans knew better; Mahan and history were their teachers.[46]

Nevertheless, it was a distorted Mahanism which the German state pursued. Mahan clearly distinguished between sea power and battle-fleet strength; the German Admiralty did not. Mahan warned that no nation could be both a great land power and a great sea power; Bismarck and William I were in essential agreement, but William II and Tirpitz believed otherwise. Mahan repeatedly pointed out the whip hand which a superior strategic position gave Great Britain vis-à-vis Germany; Admiral Tirpitz sought to offset this fatally inferior position in which geography had placed his nation by his famous doctrine of risk.

Despite Tirpitz' very definite errors of judgment in psychology, diplomacy, and strategy, his prestige was so great and the veneration in which he was held so marked that only in recent years has the wisdom of his policies been openly assailed by his fellow countrymen. The Nazi emphasis upon commerce destruction waged by submarines, airplanes, and surface raiders stands in sharp contrast to the Mahan-Tirpitz capital-ship theory. Indeed it is essentially similar to views held by the French *Jeune École* which Mahan had sought to combat.[47]

[46] London *Nation*, cited in Norman Angell, *The World's Highway*, 160–61.

[47] Herbert Rosinski, *loc. cit.*, 192 ff.; Vagts, *op. cit.*, II, 1524. For a most able analysis of the German postwar naval theory see Herbert Rosinski, "German Theories of Sea Warfare" in Rear Admiral H. G. Thursfield (ed.), *Brassey's Naval Annual, 1940*, 88–101. A discussion of Mahan's relation to the geopolitical views of Mackinder and Haushoefer will be found in the last chapter.

The sea-power doctrine reached Japan in her formative years when she was emerging as a world power. Mahan in his autobiography published in 1907 stated that, so far as he knew, more of his works had been translated into Japanese than into any other language.[48] He stated also that he had had much pleasant correspondence with many Japanese officers and that no people had shown closer or more interested attention and none more fruitfully so. The Japanese naval officer who translated *The Interest of America in Sea Power, Present and Future* wrote Mahan: "I trust that the great principles herein set forth by your forcible pen may even through this humble translation, awaken our nation and, as in Moses' time, be the pillar of fire leading our nation in the century to come."[49]

In Japan, too, the government placed translations of Mahan's more important books in all schools, and the naval and military colleges adopted *The Influence of Sea Power upon History, 1660–1783* as a textbook.[50] Thus did Japan prepare for Tsushima and lay the foundations of her so-called "Co-prosperity Sphere."

Within a few years after the appearance of Mahan's masterpiece, the great American author's name was known in every major admiralty and foreign office, and the influence of his views on colonial, maritime, and naval affairs was felt throughout the world. How is one to account for this immediate and world-wide acclaim? In the first place, Mahan had succeeded in presenting a somewhat novel interpretation of national power resting upon a broad foundation. He pre-

48 Mahan, *From Sail to Steam*, 303; E. A. Falk, *Togo and the Rise of Japanese Sea Power*, 379ff.; Admiral Viscount Nagayo Ogasawara, *Life of Admiral Togo;* C. S. Alden and R. Earle, *Makers of Naval Tradition*, 244; H. Morse Stephens, "Some Living American Historians," *World's Work*, Vol. IV (July, 1902), 2322–23.

49 M. Minakami to Mahan, July 15, 1899, Mahan Papers.

50 The Oriental Association to Mahan, April 1, 1897, *ibid.;* see also references in n. 48 above.

sented it, moreover, in a straightforward manner, with a strong didactic quality which gave it a definite appeal to the practical man. In simple, lucid manner, with eloquence and weight, the naval theme was the warp upon which the weft of national greatness was woven; with consummate skill, political, economic, and general military history were intertwined to form a pattern calculated to inspire and direct his fellow countrymen in their creation of national greatness. In that endeavor Mahan had unwittingly, or wittingly, revealed the modern world to itself and furnished it with perhaps the most systematic formulation of its guiding philosophy of action, power politics.

His formula for sea power called for developing domestic production, foreign trade, shipping interests, colonies, and a navy. His philosophy of sea power strengthened the economic and political forces already stimulating naval developments; this acceleration in navalism fostered and supported the new imperialism, which immediately called for still further naval construction. In Mahan's impact upon his contemporary world as in his analysis of the constituent elements of power on the sea, navalism and imperialism were inextricably linked; each was in turn cause and effect in the endless chain of national growth, national prosperity, and national destiny.

Timeliness contributed much to the acceptance and utilization of Mahan's strategical views. His concepts of strategy appeared at a critical juncture in naval development, when the impact of technological changes and political rivalries was calling for a clarification and even reorientation of naval programs and policies. Quite obviously, from one point of view, his concept of the command of the sea via concentration of force was not original; it had been derived historically, with some rationalization thrown in,[51]

[51] See Fred T. Jane, "Naval Warfare: Present and Future," *Forum*, Vol. XXIV (October, 1897), 240–41; and Jane, *Heresies of Sea Power*.

from an analysis of the success and failure of principles employed by the great powers in the naval wars of the seventeenth, eighteenth, and nineteenth centuries. Yet however successful the British had been in the utilization of sound principles, they had acted more or less blindly; it was Mahan's distinct contribution to organize ably into a logical system and present forcefully these strategic principles.

Admiral Raoul Castex of the French War College, in his *Les Théories Stratégiques,* holds that in the field of strategic theory Mahan was "truly creative." He adds:

> where only a vacuum had existed, his doctrine, based on historical analysis, established a solid structure of principles and ideas. . . . From 1892 on everyone quoted him and those who debated the subject endeavored to show their views were in agreement with his. . . . The true value of Mahan's theories lay in their innovating character. His works would doubtless have been less noticed in other periods.[52]

At the time of Mahan's death, the Paris *Figaro* in its analysis of his influence considered his genius had lain not so much in his new and highly original concept of history, remarkable as that was, as in the reduction of the principles of naval strategy to formulas workable by any great power. Continued this journal:

> Germany for instance, followed his teaching by strengthening her fleet until it involved risks, if challenged, to the supremacy of any power whatever. Japan took her cue from Mahan by making her squadrons effective against any feasible combination against her in the waters of the East. France abandoned her theory of tactical defensive afloat and made her fleet supreme in the Mediterranean waters. Great Britain altered her high-sea policy by adopting the plan of concentration in home waters.[53]

[52] *Les Théories Stratégiques,* I, 39 ff.
[53] Cited in *Current Opinion,* Vol. LVIII (February, 1915), 103–104.

An English appraisal at the close of World War I likewise asserted the impact of his views upon English and French policy in the prewar years. There was "little doubt," wrote this critic, that Mahan's advocacy of the principle of naval concentration "influenced in no small degree" the consummation of the Anglo-French agreement which provided for the allocation of the respective fleets in the North Sea and the Mediterranean.[54] In an evaluative discussion of "Lessons from Mahan for Today" an American commentator stated in 1919 that "in matters of naval strategy," Mahan was "the international court of last resort."[55]

Timeliness contributed also to the acceptance and utilization of Mahan's expansionist philosophy. This historically substantiated doctrine of power neatly synchronized with the new colonialism which was itself largely a product of the new industrialism. A resurgence of imperialism was in the making, and the last decades of the nineteenth century were years of transition that witnessed new departures in international affairs. Bismarck had been busy consolidating the empire established in 1871 and only reluctantly had followed merchant adventurers in their colonial enterprises, but *der Neue Kurs,* developing shortly after the ascension of William II, exhibited colonial expansion and world power as the ambitions of both sovereign and nation. The German Admiralty, separate from the War Office, was created in 1889; during the following year Helgoland was secured, African holdings confirmed and enlarged, and the Kiel Canal nearly completed. England, with France and Russia still her rivals and each embarked upon an enlarged naval program, was finally induced to pass the Naval Defense Act of 1889, which provided for an increase of seventy ships during the next four years and laid down the principle

54 Taylor, *op. cit.,* 138.
55 "Lessons from Mahan for Today," *Sea Power,* Vol. VII (September, 1919), 125.

of a British Navy equal to any two other countries. The United States was just making appropriations in 1890 for her initial battleships and Italy was laying the foundations of her navy. The nineties saw increased rivalry among the nations in commercial and colonial aggrandizement, marked by the downfall of the Spanish overseas empire, by the further partitioning of Africa, by the creation of spheres in China, by the emergence of Japan as a nation with which to reckon, by the appearance of the United States as a world power, and by the increase of importance attached to the control of the sea. As circumstances of the time gave to Seeley's philosophical study the actuality of a political pamphlet, so did Mahan's books serve as a gospel for the nations taking part in this expansion.

With writings weighty, well reasoned, provocative of thought and discussion, and timely in the extreme, "the ears of statesmen and publicists were opened, and a new note began to sound in world politics."[56] As early as 1902 a French critic stated: "After his first book and especially from 1895 on, Mahan supplied the sound basis for all thought on naval and maritime affairs."[57] Over a decade later a fellow-American scholar wrote: "Few historians have so greatly influenced men of affairs; indeed his first great book . . . may fairly be said to have achieved a greater influence upon the public mind of Europe and America than any other book of our generation."[58] At its annual meeting in 1914, occurring shortly after Mahan's death, the American Histori-

56 Julian Corbett, loc. cit., 735. See also C. O. P[aullin], "A. T. Mahan," *Mississippi Valley Historical Review*, Vol. I (March, 1915), 613–14; H. H., "Naval History: Mahan and His Successors," *Military Historian and Economist*, Vol. III (January, 1918), 7–19.

57 Auguste Moireau, "La Maîtresse de la Mer," *Revue des deux Mondes*, Vol. XI (October, 1902), 681–708.

58 C. O. Paullin, "The Major Operations of the Navies in the War of American Independence," *American Historical Review*, Vol. XIX (April, 1914), 689; also *American Historical Review*, Vol. XX (January, 1915), 445–46.

cal Association adopted a resolution drawn up by Carl Russell Fish, Guy Stanton Ford, and Charles W. Ramsdell in recognition of the services of its former president. With succinctness and accuracy it stated:

By the publication . . . of a series of studies of naval histories, he revolutionized the views of that subject held not only in this country, but in the world. Secure in an unsurpassed knowledge of this difficult and intricate field, he extended his vision to the bases upon which naval power rests, and to the relations of naval power to colonies, commerce, and national safety. The profundity of his views and the lucidity of his reasoning attracted the attention of statesmen of all nations; and more than any American scholar of his day, he has affected the course of world politics.[59]

In evaluating the influence of Mahan's works upon foreign powers, one must exercise discretion lest one fall into the fallacy of having sequence prove cause and effect. In light of the signs of the time—the increasing contraction of the world, the growing population, the entry of new peoples into the comity of nations, the expanding of industries with their demands for markets, raw materials, and capital outlets—one must acknowledge that the winds were already blowing in the direction of maritime expansion and new naval rivalries before Mahan's philosophical thesis was enunciated. Though these great developments probably would have taken place in due season for reasons of national policy aside from any Mahanian exposition or substantiation, it must be admitted that the convincing arguments for the renewed imperial and naval rivalry were often, if not chiefly, derived, directly or indirectly, from Mahan's analysis of the influence of sea power upon history; indeed "it is seldom . . . perhaps unique, in the history of the world,

[59] Navy Department, Bureau of Naval Personnel, General Files, No. 2473—75.

that historical writings have done so much to influence the policy of nations as have the writings of Captain Mahan."[60]

In the closing years of the nineteenth century and the opening years of the twentieth, navalists, merchants, capitalists, and statesmen were sorely in need of all available pretexts and rationalized supports for their neo-mercantilistic program of renewed expansion and increased armaments. It is Mahan's distinction—whether enviable or unenviable is irrelevant at the moment—to have been the chief author of the gospel from which their texts were chosen; he became their high priest and prophet, and his writings the justification of their acts. In these same years navalists, strategists, and statesmen were sorely perplexed and greatly confused concerning the soundest naval strategy. Mahan sifted the transitory and ephemeral from the permanent and fundamental; he dispelled the confusion and cleared away the perplexity. It is again Mahan's distinction—whether wisely or accurately followed is another point—to have formulated the basic strategic principles tacitly or openly espoused by the major naval powers on the eve of World War I; except for a feeble voice raised here and there in protest, his ideas were accepted as precepts of universal application and utility. At the time of his death Mahan reigned supreme in the field of naval strategy—he had no rival.

[60] Stephens, *loc. cit.*, 2322-23.

V

IMPLICATIONS OF THE SEA-POWER DOCTRINE FOR THE UNITED STATES

TO VIEW MAHAN on the European stage alone does justice neither to his own innermost conviction and purpose nor to his wider influence upon his contemporary world. His primary concern was the indoctrination of his fellow countrymen with the importance and significance of sea power for the United States. Though the policies of foreign governments were definitely altered by his teaching and though merchants, shipbuilders, big navy men, armament makers, high naval personnel, expansionists, statesmen, and publicists of foreign nations utilized his thesis for their own ends, Mahan was first and always a United States naval officer seeking to arouse his own country from its lethargy and indifference and calling it to assert itself, to take its place among the powers, and to gain for itself a fair share in the good things of life. To say that Mahan "thought and felt like an Englishman," that "his spiritual home was England," may serve a useful purpose; but to say that the United States (1885–1914) was "distant and shadowy" and that "most of his more important essays were written for English magazines and were never republished in his own country," even if intended to apply to the period after his retirement, greatly distorts the facts and calls for correction.[1]

Mahan's peculiar interpretation of history quickly led him to believe that "no nation, certainly no great nation,

[1] Louis Hacker, "The Incendiary Mahan: A Biography," *Scribner's*, Vol. XCV (April, 1934), 265, 312.

should henceforth maintain the policy of isolation." Imperialism, the "very suspicion" of which had been so "hateful" to him when the call came for service at the War College, now received his benediction.[2] Once his own outlook was broadened, once convinced of the vital truth of his sea-power doctrine for his own country, Mahan labored long and arduously to enlighten others. His conversion was followed by a proselytism marked with moral earnestness of purpose, mystical certainty of mission, evangelical fervor and unrelenting effort in prosecution, yet tempered withal by a fair appreciation of the difficulties to be encountered and the obstacles to be overcome.

In his very first lectures which dealt with the vital, natural, and human elements or conditions affecting sea power, from which were deduced certain relationships between prosperity at home, overseas trade and shipping, naval power, and colonial bases, Mahan continuously bore in mind the contemporary American situation. So frequently was the picture of his own country brought to the fore that one would have been safe in concluding, even if Mahan had not definitely stated it himself, that the whole analysis was merely an introductory historical background on which to sketch the real portrait.[3] He sought to evaluate the actual and potential advantages and disadvantages which the United States enjoyed in sea power; seldom were the conditions of the United States lost sight of or opportunities to moralize ignored. Indeed, one of Mahan's fellow officers wrote him:

I have just finished reading your book and cannot refrain from writing to congratulate you upon its value and success. . . . I was at first disposed to doubt the advisability of pointing the moral by referring to our conditions, our uncertain and

2 Mahan, *From Sail to Steam*, 324; Mahan to Ashe, July 26, 1884, Flowers Collection. Cf. Mahan, *Retrospect and Prospect*, 17–18; and Mahan, *From Sail to Steam*, 274.

3 Mahan, *The Influence of Sea Power upon History, 1660–1783*, 83–84.

erroneous policies, and want of strength, but finally concluded that, in and out of season, it is advisable and even a solemn professional and patriotic duty to call attention to the lamentable state of affairs and the ostrich-like conduct of those who legislate for us.[4]

It is now time to turn to a definite consideration of Mahan's reactions to the task he set himself in his *magnum opus* of examining "just how far the conditions of the United States involve serious danger, and call for action on the part of the nation in order to build again her sea power." Government action since the Civil War, faithfully reflecting the bent of the dominating, though Mahan hoped not the truly representative, elements of the country, had been concerned with production and internal development. Consequently peaceful shipping with its protecting navy and colonies, the remaining links in sea power, had suffered.[5]

The extent, delightfulness, and richness of the land had turned America's interests to internal development; and Mahan saw duplicated, in the blessings of Nature, those factors which had done much to turn France from a sea career. It was patent to the world that the United States did not have a seafaring group adequate to her needs or proportionate to her coast line and population, but a group such as this, Mahan thought, could be developed through a national merchant shipping and its related industries. The problem of the creation of a merchant marine, in the absence of strong interests convinced of its necessity, was one which called for governmental action and the solution of which, whether by subsidy or free trade, really rested with the economist rather than with the military officer.[6]

Mahan was convinced that if legislative hindrances were

4 Charles H. Stockton to Mahan, June 30, 1890, cited by Taylor, *Life of Admiral Mahan*, 161–62.

5 Mahan, *The Influence of Sea Power upon History, 1660–1783*, 83–84.

6 *Ibid.*, 39, 49, 88.

removed and more remunerative fields filled up, the appearance of sea power would not long be delayed. In national character—that most important of all conditions affecting the development of sea power—the Americans ranked high; "the instinct for commerce, bold enterprise in the pursuit of trade, and a keen scent for the trails that lead to it, all exist."[7]

Colonies attached to the mother country afford "the surest means of supporting sea power abroad," yet Mahan held no hope for his country in this respect. "Such colonies the United States has not and is not likely to have," for even if they were restricted to merely naval stations, the sentiment of the country was indifferent if not hostile to them. Yet without foreign establishments, either colonial or military, our warships would be

like land birds, unable to fly far from their own shores. To provide resting places for them, where they can coal and repair, would be one of the first duties of a government proposing to itself the development of the power of the nation at sea.[8]

Mahan believed that his country urgently needed a strong naval arm. The defense of seaports from capture, the prevention of an effective blockade, and the assurance that "the trade and commerce of the country should remain, as far as possible, unaffected by an external war," demanded a force afloat capable of taking the offensive as the surest path to certain defense. History had warned that a navy without national shipping as a basis was an artificial creation and sooner or later was bound to wither; but even granted the United States would develop a great national shipping—of which Mahan was none too hopeful—he was still skeptical, in light of her distance from other powers, whether a sufficient navy would follow.[9]

7 *Ibid.*, 57–58.
8 *Ibid.*, 83.
9 *Ibid.*, 84–88.

Save for Alaska, the United States had no possession inaccessible by land; and the weakest frontier, the Pacific, was far removed from the most dangerous of possible enemies. With internal resources boundless in comparison to present needs, Mahan said that we could live by ourselves and off ourselves in "our little corner." But, he continued:

Should that little corner be invaded by a new commercial route through the Isthmus, the United States in her turn may have the rude awakening of those who have abandoned their share in the common birthright of all people, the sea.[10]

Once this Central American canal was successfully built, the Caribbean would become one of the great highways of trade and would bring in its wake the interests of all the great commercial powers. Aloofness from international complications could then no longer be tolerated; preponderance of the United States in this geographical area would have to be secured and would involve, among other things, the acquisition of Caribbean bases and the creation of a navy capable of guaranteeing freedom of communications with the mainland.[11]

The primacy of Mahan's concern for his own country thus clearly seen in *The Influence of Sea Power Upon History, 1660–1783*, is likewise found in the other volumes of his sea-power series and especially in his numerous magazine articles. Mr. Horace E. Scudder, editor of the *Atlantic Monthly*, was greatly impressed by the general tone of the views which Mahan had advanced in his first sea-power book and particularly by the comment relative to "our little corner" and the exposed condition of the Pacific coast in the event of the construction of an Isthmian canal. He suggested to Mahan that he further develop his views in these respects. The result was Mahan's first important magazine article,

10 *Ibid.*, 42.
11 *Ibid.*, 33–35.

which Mr. Scudder entitled "The United States Looking Outward,"—appropriately called, thought Mahan, who subsequently wrote, "We were looking, but we had not got beyond that point where a baby vaguely follows with its eyes something which has caught its attention but not entered its understanding."[12]

Because of the nature of the various magazine articles and the manner of publication, they reached a wider audience in America than his more scholarly endeavors. Of the subjects dealt with, some were definitely professional, as the size, composition, and disposition of fleets, naval events in contemporary wars, and the like. Others were of broader scope and of more general interest, dealing with the whole gamut of international problems which claimed the attention of his country—the Monroe Doctrine, the acquisition and the fortification of the Canal Zone, the expansion into the Pacific, the annexation of Hawaii, the relation of the United States to her new dependencies, the Open Door, the World Cruise, naval expansion, the moral aspects of war, the scope and limitations of arbitration, and the possibility and desirability of peace.

Abundant opportunity was thus afforded for Mahan to develop, to enlarge, to expound further, and to justify his concept of the role which the United States should pursue. The habitual concentration upon internal affairs and the pursuit of a commercial policy wholly defensive in outlook provoked reprimand. He was distressed with the provincialism of America; she lived in her "own little corner," the Jack Horner of nations, indifferent alike to her own best interests and to the duties and responsibilities incumbent upon a great power. Though home markets might be preserved for home industries by protecting tariffs, yet the pol-

12 Mahan, "Retrospect and Prospect," *World's Work,* February, 1902, reprinted in *Retrospect and Prospect,* 12, 22; also Horace Scudder–Mahan correspondence, October 10, October 11, October 13, 1890, Mahan Papers.

icy was of doubtful validity in the development of those essential markets beyond the sea. Once the opportunities for gain abroad were understood and once the relation of foreign markets to her own immense powers of production was appreciated, the United States, he hoped, would alter her restrictive trade policies. He thought that Blaine and his reciprocity policy presaged a brighter future in this respect. Reciprocity was the logical corollary of expansion with resultant increase in power and scope to act.[13] "Joyfully," so Mahan asserted later, had he quoted Blaine in saying, " 'It is not an ambitious destiny for so great a country as ours to manufacture only what we can consume or produce only what we can eat.' " Mahan interpreted the tariff as an indication of undue concern with internal resources, production, and development. It was "American inventiveness and energy," triumphing over the "enervating influence of protection," and not a change in policy, that saved the day.[14]

In surveying the conditions of 1890, Mahan considered the restlessness in the world as significant if not ominous. The internal state of Europe affected us only indirectly, if at all. European states, however, were more than Continental rivals; they cherished also "aspiration for commercial extension, for colonies and for influence in distant regions which may bring and, even under our present contracted policy, have brought them into collision with ourselves." The unsettled political conditions prevalent in Haiti, Central America, and in the Pacific islands, especially Hawaii, when combined with great military or commercial impor-

13 Mahan, "The United States Looking Outward," *Atlantic Monthly*, December, 1890, reprinted in *The Interest of America in Sea Power, Present and Future,* 5; Mahan, "A Twentieth-Century Outlook," *Harper's*, September, 1897, reprinted in *The Interest of America in Sea Power, Present and Future,* 237 ff.

14 Mahan, "Retrospect and Prospect," *World's Work*, February, 1902, reprinted in *Retrospect and Prospect,* 20–22.

tance, contained dangerous germs of international strife. The Samoan and Bering Sea controversies and the aggressiveness of Germany in the Pacific, in Africa, and in South America were also noted.[15] It was necessary that the United States take cognizance of this restlessness and aggressiveness; it was time for her to awaken and look outward. Mahan would have agreed with Lowell that "new occasions teach new duties and time makes the ancient good uncouth." It was essential for national policy to be forward looking and for statesmen to keep abreast of the times. Conditions at the close of the century were fundamentally altered from those existing at the beginning:

it is not only that we are larger, stronger, have, as it were, reached our majority, and are able to go out into the world. That alone would be a difference of degree, not of kind. The great difference between the past and the present is that we then, as regards close contact with the power of the chief nations of the world, were really in a state of political isolation which no longer exists.[16]

The lapse of a century had altered international conditions; the face of the world had changed, economically and politically. Wrote the expansionist advocate:

Whether they will or no, Americans must now begin to look outward. The growing production of the country demands it. An increasing volume of public sentiment demands it. The position of the United States, between the two Old Worlds and the two great oceans, makes the same claim, which will soon be strengthened by the creation of the new link joining the Atlantic and the Pacific. The tendency will be maintained and

---

[15] Mahan, "The United States Looking Outward," *Atlantic Monthly*, December, 1890, reprinted in *The Interest of America in Sea Power, Present and Future*, 7–8, 15; see also Mahan, "The Future in Relation to American Naval Power," *Harper's Monthly*, October, 1895, reprinted in *ibid.*, 163.

[16] Mahan, "The Future in Relation to American Naval Power," *Harper's Monthly*, October, 1895, reprinted in *ibid.*, 146; see also 142–43.

increased by the growth of the European colonies in the Pacific, by the advancing civilization of Japan and by the rapid peopling of our Pacific States.[17]

There were calls other than the commercial, strategical, and political. Self-preservation demanded growth; a healthy nation had to look outward just as a healthy church had to have its mission posts, if stagnation and decay were to be avoided. But beyond and above all selfish interests was the welfare of Euro-American culture which was at stake. The Pacific was destined to be the scene not only of a thriving commerce but also of a gigantic struggle of races, civilizations, and religions. With her frontage on the Pacific, the United States stood guard over the preservation of Western Christian civilization. For that task the United States must not be found wanting; for that struggle she must indeed be well prepared.[18]

Just what would this "looking outward" and this taking "a twentieth-century outlook" involve? Primarily it would demand a fundamental change in the mental attitude of Americans toward maritime affairs. It would mean a shift from the complete occupation with internal problems; it would mean the construction of a modern navy and adequate coast defenses; it would mean the acquisition of outlying bases with special attention to the Isthmus, the Caribbean, and the Pacific; it would mean a revival of interest in American shipping—in brief, it would necessitate a recognition of the new and changed conditions of the day along with the realization of the rights, the duties, and the responsibilities of the United States as a world power.

As Mahan cast his glance outward, he found no reason to believe that the world had passed into a period of assured

17 Mahan, "The United States Looking Outward," *Atlantic Monthly*, December, 1890, reprinted in *ibid.*, 21–22.

18 Mahan, "A Twentieth-Century Outlook," *Harper's Monthly*, September, 1897, reprinted in *ibid.*, 264 ff.

peace. Neither sanctions nor international law nor justice of a cause would bring fair settlement if strong political necessity were opposed by comparative weakness. In such a world one would have to be ready to meet force with force; in the case of the United States Mahan maintained "every danger of a military character" could be met by naval preparedness. Yet it was a "sober, just, and reasonable cause of deep national concern" that the nation neither had nor cared to have its sea frontiers defended nor a navy of sufficient power to weigh seriously as a diplomatic or military factor.[19] This was no light matter; issues of vital moment were at stake and the present generation as trustee for its successors must not be faithless to its charge. Mahan was fearful of the fruits of improvidence and expressed himself in these words:

> Failure to improve opportunity, where just occasion arises, may entail upon posterity problems and difficulties which, if overcome at all—it may then be too late—will be so at the cost of blood and tears that timely foresight might have spared.[20]

This "looking outward," this keeping abreast of the times, required not only organized force which would weigh seriously as a diplomatic or military factor but also acquisition of such outlying positions as would confer mastery of essential water routes. The United States had reached her natural frontiers:

> arrested on the south by the rights of a race wholly alien to us, and on the north by a body of states of like traditions to our own, whose freedom to choose their own affiliations we respect, we have come to the sea. In our infancy we bordered upon the Atlantic only, our youth carried our boundary to the Gulf of

[19] Mahan, "The United States Looking Outward," *Atlantic Monthly*, December, 1890, reprinted in *ibid.*, 9, 14–15; Mahan, "Preparedness for Naval War," *Harper's Monthly*, March, 1897, reprinted in *ibid.*, 214.

[20] Mahan, "A Twentieth-Century Outlook," *Harper's Monthly*, September, 1897, reprinted in *ibid.*, 261–62.

Mexico; today maturity sees us upon the Pacific. Have we no right or no call to progress in any direction? Are there for us beyond the sea horizon none of those essential interests, of those evident dangers, which impose a policy and confer rights?[21]

"This is the question," continued Mahan, writing in 1893, "that long has been looming upon the brow of a future now rapidly passing into the present."

To this question, for Mahan, there was but one answer. The signs of the time bade us no longer be "bound and swathed in the traditions of our own eighteenth century."[22] The lessons of history, the fruits as it were of his sea-power studies, were called upon to bear witness:

Not all at once did England become the great sea power which she is, but step by step, as opportunity offered she has moved on to the world-wide pre-eminence now held by English speech, and by institutions sprung from English germs.[23]

Indeed, when England was confronted with the problem of expansion, Mahan thought:

It then could have been said to her, as it is now said to us, "Why go beyond your own borders? Within them you have what suffices your needs and those of your population. There are manifold abuses within to be corrected, manifold miseries to be relieved. Let the outside world take care of itself. Defend yourself, if attacked; being, however, always careful to postpone preparation to the extreme limit of imprudence. 'Sphere of Influence,' 'part in the world,' 'national prestige,'—there are no such things: or if there be, they are not worth fighting for."[24]

21 Mahan, "Hawaii and Our Future Sea Power," *Forum*, March, 1893, reprinted in *ibid.*, 35–36.

22 Mahan, "A Twentieth-Century Outlook," *Harper's Monthly*, September, 1897, reprinted in *ibid.*, 225 ff.

23 Mahan, "Hawaii and Our Future Sea Power," *Forum*, March, 1893, reprinted in *ibid.*, 50.

24 Mahan, "The Isthmus and Sea Power," *Atlantic Monthly*, September, 1893, reprinted in *ibid.*, 74–75.

Mahan's message for his fellow-Americans was: Read history carefully; appraise international questions intelligently; acquire true historical perspective; appreciate the quite obvious linking of national trade, national prosperity, and national greatness with an adequate control of the sea; learn to realize that as world conditions alter, so must also national policies; play a man's role and play it worthily; cultivate friendly relations with Great Britain; be not misled by false messiahs who speak of a perfect world; fear not the use of righteous force firmly and opportunely employed; be prepared to defend Christian civilization against the onslaughts of Eastern Asia; recognize, as trustees of future generations, that sins of omission may be more disastrous than sins of commission; be fully aware that not only national interest but the welfare of the world is advanced by expansion beneficently pursued.

This Mahanian message was translated into a definite program of action. It may be summarized as dominance in the Caribbean, equality and co-operation in the Pacific, and interested abstention from the strictly Continental rivalries of the European powers. The fulfillment of this program demanded the acquisition of strategic bases and the construction of a modern navy, supplemented by adequate coast defenses and a prosperous national shipping. Actual accomplishment, however, Mahan well knew would rest upon whether the arbiter, public opinion, cast a favorable or unfavorable decision. He expressed himself directly concerning the problems in hand, by writing for such magazines as *Atlantic Monthly, Forum, Harper's New Monthly Magazine, North American Review, McClure's Magazine, Independent, World's Work, Leslie's Weekly, Scribner's Magazine, Engineering Magazine, Collier's Weekly, Scientific American,* and *Century Magazine.*

In the following chapters attention will be concentrated upon the major interests of Mahan for the United States—

dominance in the Caribbean, co-operation in the Pacific, naval preparedness, naval strategy, and the morality or justification of expansion and of war. The reception given to his many books and to his numerous magazine articles, their use by congressmen, statesmen, and other expansionist publicists, and friendships with outstanding leaders of the day —all these will be called upon to testify. The difficulty of determining with a high degree of exactitude the influence which an individual exerts upon his contemporaries is recognized; nevertheless, a sketch, more or less distinct, with the general role portrayed, should be practicable, desirable, and valuable. If in the development of the story undue emphasis at times rests on Mahan, it is not Carlylean hero worship; Mahan is rather to be viewed as a child of his age, an age of budding imperialism. It was an imperialism, so far as America was concerned, which in the beginning was not primarily so much the fruit of capitalism and contemporary economic pressures as a recrudescence of the century-old, nation-old urge to expand—an urge most succinctly expressed in the wider meaning of the phrase "manifest destiny," a destiny which embodied inevitability in its nature, beneficence in its purpose, high duty in its execution, and the approval of the Divine in its fulfillment. Destiny, duty, and religion were intertwined; in his special emphasis upon strategy and sea power, Mahan did not ignore the driving power of these factors; he marshaled them in grand array to aid him in his attack upon American provincialism.

He was not ignorant of the forces in opposition, whether they were the economic preoccupation of the country with its own internal problems of exploitation, the political manifestations of indifference, the outright opposition to development of maritime power, or the deification of the past by worship of the policy of isolation pursued in Washington's day.

On the other hand, Mahan was not unaware of the forces

which were with him. He began his first major magazine article with the significantly prophetic sentence, "Indications are not wanting of an approaching change in the thoughts and policy of Americans as to their relation with the world outside their own borders."[25] Relative to this statement, the "prophet" acknowledged a dozen years later: "the presage has been fulfilled far beyond any consciousness then possible to the writer. . . . In writing on these themes in those days one felt that, while the chain of reasoning was eminently logical, yet there was a lack of solid foundation; that though argumentation were sound, premise was perhaps mistaken; and that when indulging in such forecasts one was in the fantastic sphere familiarized to us by Mr. Edward Bellamy and others."[26]

Mahan recognized that he was only one among many who was seeking to define and formulate the progress of national awakening. No evidence, however, has been found to indicate to what extent he was familiar with the activities of specific fellow intellectuals, such as John Fiske, Josiah Strong, and John W. Burgess. In the decade in which the United States embarked upon a program of overseas expansion, these men contributed views highly favorable to an aggressive policy. Mr. Fiske, in his essay on "Manifest Destiny" in *Harper's* in 1885, Reverend Strong in a chapter in his small volume published in the same year, entitled *Our Country: Its Possible Future and Its Present Crisis,* Professor Burgess in his *Political Science and Comparative Constitutional Law,* printed in the year of Mahan's first study, all asserted the superiority of the Anglo-Saxon race, though Burgess used the more inclusive term of Teutonic. They advocated and predicted the virtual dominance of the world by members of this God-favored and God-chosen

25 Mahan, "The United States Looking Outward," *Atlantic Monthly,* December, 1890, reprinted in *ibid.,* 3.

26 Mahan, *Retrospect and Prospect, vi,* 14.

group.[27] In the Roosevelt-Mahan correspondence there is a note from the former to Mahan stating that he had given the Reverend Josiah Strong a letter of introduction to him.[28]

At times the sea-power advocate indicated that he thought of himself as a chronicler solicited by the editorial watchers to report the progress of national awakening, a dictograph, as it were, to record from "time to time the stages of the antecedent process of preparation." At other times he came nearer reality when he humbly granted that he had "to some extent helped to turn thought." At all times, however, he definitely limited the role played by himself or others. "No man or group of men," he wrote, "can pretend to have guided and governed our people in the adoption of a new policy, the acceptance of which has been rather instinctive—I would prefer to say inspired—than reasoned."[29]

A much more accurate appraisal of Mahan's influence is obtained from a less partisan source, Mr. Frederick Greenwood of *Blackwood's Edinburgh Magazine*. To this English "Looker-On," immediately prior to the Spanish-American War, it seemed that the whole outlook of the United States —and of the world—had been recast by Mahan's writings. He thought Mahan's first study "an admirable book, but the most incendiary of modern times." He called attention to

the rising spirit in American affairs, which, with its fleets building, and its enthusiasms kindling, and its hidden spark in the heart of the most orthodox citizen, is preparing as much of a change as we saw in Japan the other day, and perhaps as sud-

[27] For further detail concerning the activities of these men in the development of the intellectual climate of period, see Julius Pratt, *Expansionists of 1898*, 3 ff.

[28] Roosevelt to Mahan, August 2, 1900, Roosevelt Papers.

[29] Mahan, "Retrospect and Prospect," *World's Work*, February, 1902, reprinted in *Retrospect and Prospect*, 24; Mahan, *From Sail to Steam*, 325; Mahan, "Retrospect and Prospect," *World's Work*, February, 1902, reprinted in *Retrospect and Prospect*, 16.

den. Even at this early time accidents are conceivable which would definitely alter the relations of the United States with the rest of the world in the small space of a week. . . . Mahan's teaching was as oil to the flame of colonial expansion everywhere leaping into life. Everywhere a new sprung ambition to go forth and possess and enjoy read its sanction in the philosophy of history ennobled by the glory of conquest. . . . I doubt whether this effect of Mahan's teaching has gone deeper anywhere than in the United States.[30]

With this cursory sketch of the more general implications of the sea-power doctrine as related to the United States, the further and specific development of Mahan's major interests should be simpler and more intelligible.

[30] *Blackwood's Edinburgh Magazine*, Vol. CLXIII (April, 1898), 563–65. "Looker-On" was the pen name of Mr. Frederick Greenwood.

VI

THE CARIBBEAN—DEVELOPMENT

REDOMINANCE OF THE UNITED STATES in the Caribbean was Mahan's cardinal interest. He was one of many who believed that an Isthmian canal under American control was essential to the welfare of the United States; he was one of few who stressed as an absolute concomitant of a policy such as this the acquisition of the approaches on either side of the canal and the creation of a navy capable of holding its own against any likely opponent. In light of the English fleet and English holdings in the Caribbean, Mahan also urged friendly relations with the former mother country.

In '885, prior to his own conversion to the "large policy" for the United States, he wrote his friend Ashe that he thought a "fleet of swift cruisers to prey on the enemy's commerce" the surest deterrent to foreign molestation. However, this view rested upon the supposition that America had no interests beyond her own borders. He continued:

If we are going in for an Isthmian policy we must have nothing short of a numerous and thoroughly first-class ironclad navy —equal to either England or France. To this I would add throw over the Irish vote (if you dare) and pursue a policy not of formal alliance but of close sympathy, based on common ideas of justice, law, freedom, and honesty, with England. . . . England is like every nation selfish but in the main honest— and the best hope of the world is in the union of the branches of that race to which she and we belong.[1]

[1] Mahan to Ashe. March 11, 1885, Flowers Collection. Cf. Mahan to Ashe. March 12, 1880.

99

After a few months' study of history Mahan openly avowed allegiance to the heretofore dubious Isthmian policy. It was in the Central American Isthmus that he saw quickening "the motive, if any there be," which would give to the United States a navy. A successful canal would change the Caribbean from a terminus and place of local traffic into one of the chief highways of the world with resulting international complications; "our little corner" would be invaded and a rude awakening would be our lot for having abandoned our share "in the common birthright, the sea." The geographical position of the United States, if supplemented by "proper military preparation," would give her paramount influence in this region. This military preparation was defined at the time in the most general terms; it would necessitate the protection of ingress and egress of the Mississippi, the possession of secondary bases of operation, and the assurance of continued communications between such outposts and home bases.[2]

In certain respects, there was nothing startlingly new or original about this outlook. Mahan was by no means the first to stress the significance of the West Indies. The naval and commercial importance of this region had been perceived immediately upon the disintegration of Spanish power in America resulting from the Napoleonic upheaval in Europe. The greatest prize of the Spanish possessions was Cuba, "the transatlantic Turkey," tottering to its fall yet sustained by the jealousies of the powers so desirous of gaining the spoils. In the early nineteenth century the United States sought the maintenance of the *status quo* of the island by opposition to the acquisition or the establishment of a protectorate over it by either Great Britain or France. In the decades of manifest destiny a bolder and more aggressive policy was pursued and attempts were frequent either

[2] Mahan, *The Influence of Sea Power upon History, 1660–1783*, 33–35, 42, 88.

to purchase the island or forcibly to bring it within our sphere by filibustering expeditions. Various motives existed. In these years, in certain quarters, the desire for the extension of slave territory was ever existent. The increased area on the Gulf as a result of the annexation of Texas brought additional significance to the Caribbean. The definitely defined and vastly increased territorial holdings on the Pacific following the Oregon and Mexican settlements, confounded by the discovery of gold in California, created the urgent problem of communication. At the moment, an interoceanic transit route seemed the only practicable solution and the strategic importance of Cuba in the control of such an enterprise was appreciated. Permeating all and furnishing additional driving power was the fast-growing conviction of the mission and the destiny of the country.

The abolition of slavery and the construction of transcontinental railroads permitting direct overland communication with the Pacific states removed the two primary factors motivating the expansion sentiment of the turbulent fifties. Seward, in untrammeled control of the conduct of foreign affairs, sought to carry forward the expansion program interrupted by the Civil War. The annual report of the Navy Department for 1865 stressed the necessity for more adequate protection of the fast-developing commerce of the country and pointed out especially the need for naval stations, calling attention to the new and different demands of the steam vessel. "A prudent regard for our future interests and welfare would seem to dictate the expediency of securing some eligible location for the purpose indicated [coaling and supply stations]."[3] Looking toward an increase of American influence in the Caribbean, Secretary Seward carried on negotiations with Denmark, Spain, Sweden, Nicaragua, and the Republic of Santo Domingo, but with no marked success. The American people were engrossed

3 39 Cong., 1 sess., *Executive Doc. 1, xv.*

with internal affairs; amidst the din and turmoil of a nation in the throes of political, economic, and financial reconstruction and exploitation, the call of destiny, duty, and defense fell on deaf ears.

So far as an Isthmian canal was concerned, United States official policy at first urged free and equal navigation by all nations. Even by mid-century the principle of neutralization under international guarantee was definitely incorporated in the Clayton-Bulwer Treaty with Great Britain. Never without its opponents in the United States, this treaty gradually became more and more objectionable as the power, prestige, prosperity, population, and self-confidence of the younger country grew. The tendency on the part of the United States government to turn from the policy of internationalism in the control of a transisthmian canal toward an American canal controlled by Americans was definitely discernible in the negotiated but unratified canal treaties with Colombia in 1869–70. The De Lesseps concession in 1878 filled American people with jealousy and alarm and directly influenced the introduction in both houses of Congress of resolutions which declared that control over any Isthmian canal must rest with the United States. President Hayes in his message of March 8, 1880, openly affirmed, "The policy of this country is a canal under American control." The ingenious arguments put forward by Blaine and Frelinghuysen in the vain attempt to prove the invalidity of the Clayton-Bulwer Treaty, the successful negotiations with Nicaragua for a canal entirely under American auspices, the withdrawal of this treaty from the Senate after Cleveland's first inauguration, and the 1887 concession to and the subsequent activity of the Maritime Canal Company were further indications of the growing importance being attached to the canal question in the eighties.

Mahan was cognizant of this growing interest in Isthmian projects; he knew that a canal under American control was attracting more and more attention.[4] He wanted enthusiasm tempered by reality; he desired that facts, not fancy, be kept uppermost. He had no time for wishful thinking. He was not unaware of the call of duty and the appeal of destiny, but it was to the problem of defense and to the field of strategy that he gave his special attention. Here he contributed telling thrusts at American self-contented provincialism; here he led the way in the formulation and carrying into effect of a strategic policy which had been gradually growing for many years in the minds of American statesmen and naval leaders. Though Mahan was the leader of this policy, he was, as Professor Inman says, "enthusiastically seconded by a group of enthusiastic nationalists, which included two brilliant young statesmen who were afterward to play a large part in the life of the United States—Theodore Roosevelt and Henry Cabot Lodge."[5]

In 1890 Mahan was convinced that latent and generally unforeseen dangers to the peace of the Western Hemisphere would attend the construction of an Isthmian canal. Not only would the canal have strategic value of the utmost importance, but every position in the Caribbean from both a commercial and military point of view would be immeasurably enhanced. Inevitably each nation would seek points of support and means of influence in this region, a region where the United States had been "jealously sensitive to the intrusion of European powers"; against such action the United States could allege but one right, "that of her reasonable policy supported by her might." Yet with no navy and no defense of the seaboard, and no interest to provide either, without the necessary bases in or on the borders of the Caribbean, and without even the beginnings of a navy

4 Mahan to Ashe, March 11, 1885, Flowers Collection.

5 Samuel G. Inman, "The Significance of the Caribbean," in Curtis A. Wilgus (ed.), The Caribbean Area, 23.

yard on the Gulf of Mexico which could serve as a base of operations, American interests in the Caribbean would be at the mercy of any strong maritime country. Wrote the naval strategist:

Militarily speaking and having reference to European complications only, the piercing of the Isthmus is nothing but a disaster to the United States, in the present state of her military and naval preparations. . . . Despite a certain original superiority conferred by our geographical nearness and immense resources . . . the United States is wofully unready, not only in fact but in purpose, to assert in the Caribbean and Central America a weight of influence proportionate to the extent of her interests.[6]

Moreover, in her present state of unpreparedness, quite aside from her Caribbean interests, a transisthmian canal would be a military disaster for the United States. The Atlantic seaboard, though no more or less exposed, would be confronted with "increased dangers of foreign complications with inadequate means to meet them." The problem of the Pacific states, however, would be fundamentally altered; so much as the distance between them and Europe would be lessened by a canal which a stronger maritime power could control, just so much would their safety, and consequently that of the nation as a whole, be imperiled.[7]

Mahan assumed that the United States would not readily acquiesce in a change of ownership in the Caribbean. But this was not enough; it should "be an inviolable resolution of our national policy that no foreign state would acquire a coaling position within 3,000 miles of San Francisco,—a distance which includes the Hawaiian and Galapagos Islands and the Coast of Central America." Adequate

6 Mahan, "The United States Looking Outward," *Atlantic Monthly,* December, 1890, reprinted in *The Interest of America in Sea Power, Present and Future,* 13–15, 20–21.

7 *Ibid.,* 20–23.

harbor and coast defense and a navy were also necessary to meet the military needs of the states west of the Rockies.

By way of conclusion to this critical essay, "The United States Looking Outward" (1890), Mahan publicly advocated, as "one of the first of our external interests," a "cordial understanding" with Great Britain. Because of her navy and her positions near our shores, she was our most formidable enemy. Formal alliance was definitely excluded, but a "cordial recognition of the similarity of character and ideas will give birth to sympathy, which in turn will facilitate a co-operation beneficial to both; for if sentimentality is weak, sentiment is strong."[8]

In thus presenting the military significance of the piercing of the Isthmus, Mahan did not desire to dampen in the least the rising American spirit of assertiveness; he sought rather to sober, rationalize, and direct it into channels of greater usefulness. He strove valiantly and forcefully to link the growing canal sentiment with the inadequate appreciation of the strategic implications involved.

One of Mahan's fellow officers was much pleased with the strength and soundness of this initial magazine article. He wrote Mahan: ". . . you so strongly put the case that I am sure it will do good, great good. The effect of such blows are often not strictly manifest but the *impression* remains. I hope you will deepen it by blow after blow."[9]

It should not be assumed that Mahan was the only writer who believed that the United States was "looking outward." Mr. Eddy, a member of a United States exporting firm, thought that the interest shown in the canal, in foreign markets, in the navy, and in the recent dispute with Germany and Great Britain over the Samoan Islands indicated an awakening in the United States. He predicted an aggressive commercial policy in the near future and dis-

8 *Ibid.*, 15, 21, 26, 27.
9 F. M. Bunce to Mahan, November 30, 1890, Mahan Papers.

cussed American resources for a program of this kind and the advantages to be gained. Mr. Jordan, a leader in the 1870 Cuban revolution and later editor of a mining journal in New York, stressed in good Mahanian fashion the strategic elements of Cuba. Though "just and generous," "mindful and considerate" of Spain, "all considerations urge us to this acquisition without regard to European opinion or antagonism."[10]

Nor should it be taken for granted that there were no critics of these expansion publicists. Most conspicuous among them was Carl Schurz, who raised his voice against giving heed to an appetite that would "grow with the eating." There will always be "more commercial advantages to be gained, the riches of more countries to be made our own, more strategical positions to be occupied to protect those already in our hands. Not only a taste for more, but interest, the logic of the situation would push us on and on." He illustrated the point: In case Cuba were acquired, it would lead, he said, to the acquisition of Puerto Rico, Haiti, Santo Domingo and "hardly a stopping place north of Gulf of Darien—and many reasons not to stop there."[11]

The Harrison administration was attentive to the rising expansive spirit of the country. The Maritime Canal Company of Nicaragua, chartered in 1889, had experienced financial difficulties. Amendments to the company's charter, providing for the guarantee of its bonds by the United States government and in turn giving the government a controlling voice in the management of the canal, were suggested by the Senate Committee on Foreign Relations in its report of January 10, 1891. The committee definitely stated that

10 Ulysses D. Eddy, "Our Chance for Commercial Supremacy," *Forum*, Vol. XI (June, 1891), 419–28; Thomas Jordan, "Why We Need Cuba," *Forum*, Vol. XI (June, 1891), 559–67. See also John Sherman, "The Nicaragua Canal," *Forum*, Vol. XI (March, 1891), 1–9.

11 " 'Manifest Destiny,' " *Harper's Monthly*, Vol. LXXXVII (November, 1893), 137–46.

it could be "justly affirmed" that the convention of 1850 had "become obsolete" and therefore did not need to be considered an obstacle to the passage of the measure.[12] In his annual message of December, 1891, President Harrison gave this scheme his sanction and stated that the completion of the canal was "a matter of the highest concern to the United States"; a year later he recommended that Congress give the Maritime Canal Company "prompt and adequate support."[13]

The administration was definitely in sympathy with Mahan's concern about the vital importance to the United States of the control of the canal approaches. Desirous of capitalizing upon certain supposed obligations to the United States, upon the chaotic political conditions, and upon the greed for gold, the government sought to secure leases for naval bases at Môle St. Nicholas in Haiti and Samana Bay in Santo Domingo. Neither endeavor was successful; the Haitian president openly repulsed the advances while the Dominican executive, once rumors of what was in the air were circulating, was forced to forego further negotiations.[14]

In the summer of 1891 the Danish government suggested the sale of St. Thomas and St. John islands to the United States. Secretary Blaine believed that their purchase should await American acquisition of the larger West Indies. He thought the Danish isles were too small to be of great commercial or strategic importance, and that they would be quite difficult to defend. They were "destined to become ours, but among the last of the West Indies that should be taken."[15] Secretary Foster, who succeeded Blaine,

---

[12] 51 Cong., 2 sess., *Senate Report, 1944.*

[13] James D. Richardson (ed.), *A Compilation of the Messages and Papers of the Presidents,* IX, 189, 317.

[14] Sumner Welles, *Naboth's Vineyard,* I, 468–95; Alice F. Tyler, *Foreign Policy of James G. Blaine,* 91–98.

[15] Blaine to Harrison, August 10, 1896, Harrison Papers, cited by Charles Tansill, *The Purchase of the Danish West Indies,* 191.

was more favorably disposed toward the project. "The question of the acquisition of the Islands is one of far-reaching and national importance, the extent of which is appreciated by no one more than the President," he wrote the United States minister at Copenhagen. "As his administration is, however, drawing to its close, he considers it inadvisable to express any views or indicate any policy, the consummation of which he could not effect."[16]

The overthrow of the royal government in the Hawaiian Islands in 1893 and the desire on the part of the new government for annexation to the United States brought the whole matter of the "outward view" to the fore, with attention to the Pacific. This was to Mahan's liking. It has already been indicated how closely related and interdependent he believed the whole program of the canal and the Pacific to be. "Hawaii and Our Future Sea Power" served to crystalize his views on the problem of the Pacific, to urge expansion and sea power upon a hesitant nation, and to emphasize again the broader aspect of the Isthmian problem. Said he:

The demands of our three great seaboards, the Atlantic, the Gulf, and the Pacific,—each for itself, and all for the strength that comes from drawing closer the ties between them—are calling for the extension through the Isthmian Canal of that broad sea common along which, and along which alone, in all ages, prosperity has moved. . . . So the Isthmian Canal is an inevitable part in the future of the United States; yet one that cannot be separated from other necessary incidents of a policy dependent upon it.[17]

The *Review of Reviews* called this article a "broad and comprehensive discussion" of our future sea power.[18]

16 Foster to Carr, December 20, 1892, MS, Dept. of State, *Denmark, Inst.*, Vol. 15, cited by Tansill, *op. cit.*, 195.
17 Mahan, "Hawaii and Our Future Sea Power," *Forum*, March, 1893, reprinted in *The Interest of America in Sea Power, Present and Future*, 51–52.
18 *Review of Reviews*, Vol. VII (April, 1893), 324–27.

In the *Atlantic Monthly*, September, 1893, Mahan discussed at length the canal problem in "The Isthmus and Sea Power." A sketch of the Caribbean and the Spanish Main from the time of Columbus through the heyday of Spanish greatness onward through the era of colonial wars and the disruption of the Spanish colonial empire made a colorful background. Ample opportunity was afforded for an exposition of the sea-power thesis in practice, for a hearty eulogy of British farsightedness, and for a few subtle, poignant thrusts at American provincialism. He embarked for the first time upon certain international aspects of the Isthmian problem. Because of her position upon two seas, the United States held predominant interest in the Isthmus and therefore in the Caribbean; this was a "reasonable, natural—it might almost be called a moral—claim." Other countries might have definite commercial interests at stake but the United States had political as well as commercial interests to be safeguarded. Though her own interests were overruling, Mahan recognized they were by no means exclusive; any settlement worthy of the name must effect "our preponderating influence, and at the same time insure the natural rights of other peoples."[19]

Her wide-flung empire and her position as a great sea carrier naturally made Great Britain, Mahan thought, "the exponent of foreign opposition to our own asserted interest in the Isthmus." Yet the British should not be obdurate, he reasoned, for only a small fraction of their existing trade would be unfavorably affected by competition introduced by a canal; nor would the problem of the integrity of the Empire be seriously involved, for nowhere had Great Britain "so little territory at stake." He added: "Concessions of principle over-eagerly made in 1850, in order to gain com-

---

[19] Mahan, "The Isthmus and Sea Power," *Atlantic Monthly*, September, 1893, reprinted in *The Interest of America in Sea Power, Present and Future*, 83, 98–99.

pensating advantages which our weakness could not extort otherwise" now caused us regret and resentment, and not until the United States took "steps to formulate a policy or develop a strength" that could give "shape and force to her pretensions" would British pre-eminence be displaced.[20]

The basic decision, Mahan asserted, rested not with Britain but with the United States. For a country "to which the control of the strait is a necessity, if not of existence, at least of its full development and of its national security, who can deny," asked Mahan, "the right to predominate in influence over a region so vital to it?" And the answer: "None can deny save its own people," and they, Iscariot-like, not in words but in acts, in "indolent drifting, in wilful blindness to the approaching moment when action must be taken."[21]

Mahan reiterated his belief in the certainty of the construction of a canal. Since the birth of the Republic, except for the mid-century flurry of interest due to special causes, suggestive but inadequate and resulting in the "paralyzing Clayton-Bulwer Treaty," the importance of the Isthmus had been merely "potential and dormant." The century had wrought changes. The peopling of the Far West, the increasing political and commercial importance of the Pacific Ocean, and the rapid growth of the productive forces of the nation calling for outlets to regions beyond were indicative of the approaching change. Both interest and dignity now demanded that the United States no longer let her rights depend upon another state; her predominance in the Carib-

20 *Ibid.*, 83, 86, 93–94. For British reaction to comments such as these, see G. S. Clarke, "Captain Mahan's Counsels to the United States," *Nineteenth Century*, Vol. XLIII (February, 1898), 292–300. Clarke's article is a review of Mahan's book, *The Interest of America in Sea Power, Present and Future.*

21 Mahan, "The Isthmus and Sea Power," *Atlantic Monthly*, September, 1893, reprinted in *The Interest of America in Sea Power, Present and Future,* 96–97.

bean was essential. Since he believed that the control of any maritime region rested upon a navy and suitably chosen bases, it is not strange to find Mahan writing:

At present the positions of the Caribbean are occupied by foreign powers, nor may we, however disposed to acquisition, obtain them by means other than righteous; but a distinct advance will have been made when public opinion is convinced that we need them, and should not exert our utmost ingenuity to dodge them when flung at our head.[22]

In the interim, no moral obligations stood in the way of the development of the navy.

In this article, Mahan's punches were not drawn as he attacked the indecision, drifting, and lack of a consciously chosen and vigorously followed foreign policy. To appreciate fully and interpret correctly the depth of his feelings and the sincerity of his remarks, it should be recalled that the change of administration in March had resulted in Cleveland's immediate withdrawal (March 9) from the Senate of the Hawaiian annexation treaty submitted the middle of the preceding month. Mahan was fully aware that in a democratic country such as the United States national policy was largely dependent upon public opinion, that consistent and well-proportioned action could not be a matter of party politics but must rest upon a well-settled conviction. Consequently, here was an occasion for attack by the sea-power advocate; here was an opportunity for the publicist to wield his influence; here was a duty for the strategist to fulfill.

Among the expansionists none was more eager than the young Lodge, to whom Mahan had sent a complimentary copy of *The Influence of Sea Power Upon History, 1660–1783*, and who had arduously endeavored to gain further land stay for Mahan so that he might pursue his important

22 *Ibid.,* 99–100, 103.

studies. In the opening chapter on foreign affairs in his life of Washington, Lodge wrote: "Our relations with foreign nations today [1889] fill but a slight place in American politics and excite generally only a languid interest. We have separated ourselves so completely from the affairs of other people that it is difficult to realize how large a place they occupied when the government was founded." As the decade advanced, however, this situation which Lodge found so lamentable rapidly changed, and numerous occasions arose which permitted the advocates of the larger and aggressive policy to express themselves. The Hawaiian problem, covering in its various phases over five years, released a torrent of expansion sentiment. The Venezuelan boundary dispute with England, naval appropriations, the plight of the Maritime Canal Company of Nicaragua, the fear of foreign acquisitions in the Caribbean, the insurrection in Cuba—these public questions gave repeated opportunities to spread-eagle and to twist the lion's tail, to worship at the altar of duty and to pay homage to manifest destiny.

Lodge, in particular, was most eloquent in his plea for the assumption of an "intelligent" foreign policy. He had not pursued Mahan's books for naught; "the sea power has been one of the controlling forces in history," he told his fellow senators in 1894, and added, "Without sea power no nation has been really great."[23] In the following year, to the larger audience of the Forum, in an article entitled "Our Blundering Foreign Policy," he contrasted Cleveland's policy of "retreat and surrender" with his own forward-looking policy of naval and territorial expansion. National honor, dignity, pride of country and of race urged America to look beyond her borders. "In the interests of our commerce and of our fullest development" the Nicaragua Canal should be American built and supplemented by the acquisition or control of the approaches in both oceans. Among the West In-

23 53 Cong., 3 sess., Cong. Rec., 3082.

dies "we should have . . . at least one strong naval station, and when the Nicaraguan Canal is built, the island of Cuba . . . will become to us a necessity."[24]

Neither Cleveland nor his secretaries of state, Gresham and Olney, displayed interest in the purchase of islands or in the acquisition of naval bases in the Caribbean; their sole interest was the enforcement of the Monroe Doctrine and the maintenance of the *status quo*. Secretary Olney discredited predecessor Frelinghuysen's attempts to escape from the paralyzing Clayton-Bulwer Treaty as unsound. Olney held that

if changed conditions now make stipulations which were once deemed advantageous, either inapplicable or injurious, the true remedy is not ingenious attempts to deny the existence of the treaty or to explain away its provisions, but in direct and straightforward application to Great Britain for a reconsideration of the whole matter.[25]

Cleveland's "small policy" obviously failed to please those dedicated to the "outward view." However, his firm and dogged handling of the Venezuelan–British Guiana episode generally evoked favorable comments, even from his political opponents. The Republican police commissioner of New York City could not forego a word of congratulation to Secretary Olney, who, upon the death of Gresham, had fallen heir to this South American imbroglio. These were Roosevelt's words: "I must write you a line to say how heartily I rejoiced at the Venezuela message. I earnestly hope our people won't back down in any way."[26]

The assertive spirit of Congress, evoked by the Vene-

[24] "Our Blundering Foreign Policy," *Forum*, Vol. XIX (March, 1895), 17.

[25] J. B. Moore, *Digest of International Law*, III, 208–209.

[26] Roosevelt to Olney, December 20, 1895, Olney Papers, cited by Tansill, *op. cit.*, 200.

zuelan incident, may be seen in the excerpt from the concurrent resolution, passed in January, 1896, upholding the Monroe Doctrine:

The United States of America reaffirms and confirms the doctrine and principles promulgated by President Monroe in his message . . . and declares that it will assert and maintain that doctrine and principles, and will regard any infringement thereof, and particularly any attempt by any European power to take or acquire any new or additional territory on the American continents, or any island adjacent thereto, or any right or sovereignty or dominion in the same in any case or instance as to which the United States shall deem such an attempt to be dangerous to its peace or safety by or through force, purchase, cession, occupation, pledge, colonization, protectorate, or by control of the easement in any canal or any other means of transit across the American Isthmus . . . as the manifestation of an unfriendly disposition toward the United States and as an interposition which it would be impossible in any form for the United States to regard with indifference.[27]

When the atmosphere had cleared somewhat from this highly charged condition, Mahan wrote in the March issue, 1897, of *Harper's* that he feared the position taken by the United States in the Venezuelan case might entail upon her "greater responsibilities, more serious action" than she had heretofore assumed or was now able to fulfill. In military metaphor, the United States had occupied "an advanced position, the logical result very likely of other steps in the past" but one which implied such organization of strength as would enable her to hold it.[28] Opportunity was also afforded again to discuss the degree and nature of naval preparedness demanded by the United States. A strong navy and a sufficient coast defense to permit the former its right-

27 54 Cong., 1 sess., *Cong. Rec.*, 783.
28 Mahan, "Preparedness for Naval War," *Harper's Monthly,* March, 1897, reprinted in *The Interest of America in Sea Power, Present and Future,* 186.

ful role of offense, supplemented by an adequate force of trained men, would be "preparedness for anything likely to occur."

It must not be assumed, however, that Mahan in the least opposed the spirit of American assertiveness in the Venezuelan dispute. He wrote a close British friend: "It indicates, as I believe and hope, the awakening of our countrymen to the fact that we must come out of our isolation, which a hundred years ago was wise and imperative, and take our share in the turmoil of the world."[29]

The Cuban insurrection, starting in February, 1895, was a continual source of trouble to Cleveland during his last two years in the White House. Cautious conservatism characterized his treatment of this perplexing problem. A man of profound conviction and downright sincerity, with unalterable faith in the might of justice, this President, who had not minced words with powerful Britain, now used infinite patience and persuasion with decadent Spain. Cleveland hoped that this new Cuban insurrection might be handled by pacific means as had the even more sanguinary struggle of a quarter of a century earlier. However, in the meantime a marked change in American temperament had taken place. The earlier insurrection had come at a period when the United States was opposed to further territorial expansion or further projection of national influence, when the American people had turned their faces inland; the latter came at a time when the United States felt destiny was beckoning from beyond the horizons and grew desirous of a larger national policy, when the American people had turned their faces outward from the continent.

Cleveland failed to sense the strength or declined to follow the lead of the expansionists who were urging a "looking outward." His view was that "the mission" of our nation was "to build up and make a greater country out of

[29] Mahan to James R. Thursfield, January 10, 1896, Mahan Papers.

what we have, instead of annexing islands."[30] Though in Congress and throughout the country there was a rising tide of sentiment favorable to the Cuban insurrectionists, the administration paid no heed. Many resolutions were introduced and eventually a concurrent resolution was passed by the two houses (the Senate in February and the House in April, 1896) which asked for the recognition of a status of belligerency, and further urged the President to offer Spain the good offices of the United States for a peace with Cuban independence.

As was his privilege, Cleveland largely ignored this resolution. His offer to co-operate with Spain in the restoration of peace in the war-torn island on the basis of home rule was politely refused, with the suggestion that the United States could better aid in more effectively preventing the departure of the unlawful filibustering expeditions. In his last annual message, after his party and program had been repudiated at the national elections in favor of the Republicans, who had declared openly for the "large policy" in their platform, Cleveland stated that the United States was not a nation to which peace was a "necessity" and that a situation could conceivably arise in which our obligations to the sovereignty of Spain would be "superseded by higher obligations," which we could "hardly hesitate to recognize and discharge."[31]

Cuba libre slightly modified Lodge's earlier view of Cuba as a necessity to the United States. "Cuba in our hands or in friendly hands, in hands of its own people, attached to us by ties of interest and gratitude," he informed his senatorial colleagues, "is a bulwark to the commerce, to the safety, and to the peace of the United States." Danger to American property, ruin of American commerce, the opening of an immense field to American capital, the securing of a vast

30 Allan Nevins (ed.), *Letters of Grover Cleveland*, 492.
31 Richardson, *op. cit.*, VIII, 6151.

market for American products, and the geographic and political importance of the island—these were "all weighty reasons for decisive action on our part," he told the readers of *Forum*. These reasons were "pecuniary, material, and interested"; that which makes "action imperative on the part of the United States in regard to Cuba, rests upon a higher ground than any of these. . . . The interests of humanity are the controlling interests." The underlying selfishness of Lodge's plea for our intervention in Cuba could not remain hidden:

If one Administration declines to meet our national responsibilities as they should be met, there will be put in power another administration which will neither neglect nor shun its plain duty to the United States and to the causes of freedom and humanity.[32]

It has been discerningly stated that the Massachusetts senator "apparently . . . thought our duty was to take it [Cuba], on grounds of humanity, from Spain because of its usefulness to the United States."[33]

The aggressive spirit of the foreign planks in the Republican platform of 1896 clearly showed the hand of Lodge and ably expressed the Mahanian philosophy. The Republicans advocated a reaffirmation of the Monroe Doctrine in its fullest extent, the creation of a navy commensurate with our new position and responsibility, the independence of Cuba, the construction of an American-owned and operated Nicaragua Canal, and the purchase of the Danish islands. The platform also called for the eventual withdrawal of European powers from the Western Hemisphere.[34]

The Hanna-managed campaign between the Eastern

[32] 54 Cong., 1 sess., *Cong. Rec.*, 1972; "Our Duty to Cuba," *Forum*, Vol. XXI (May, 1896), 286–87.

[33] S. F. Bemis and G. G. Griffin, *Guide to the Diplomatic History of the United States, 1775–1921*, 521.

[34] E. Stanwood, *History of the Presidency from 1788–1897*, I, 535–36.

bondholder and the Western plowman largely ignored matters of foreign policy. McKinley in his Canton front-porch speeches scarcely touched such themes; and shortly after he assumed the presidency, he assured Carl Schurz that there would be no "jingo nonsense" in his administration.[35] The party imperialists viewed matters differently. Just two weeks after the inauguration, Senator Lodge reintroduced his resolution of the preceding year (January 3, 1896) which called upon the Senate Committee on Foreign Relations to investigate the possible purchase of the three major Danish islands as provided for in the treaty of 1867.[36] Desirous of "testing public opinion," as he expressed it, McKinley sent a slightly altered Hawaiian annexation treaty to the Senate on June 16, 1897. Neither of these measures obtained favorable action, but they served to keep the issues before the public.

In the meantime, the erstwhile civil-service advocate and colorful New York police commissioner, having gained preferment largely through assistance marshaled by Lodge, had been called to Washington as assistant secretary of the navy. That McKinley was hesitant about this appointment is confirmed by the Roosevelt-Lodge correspondence; in an interview on December 2, 1896, at Canton, when Lodge was urging Roosevelt's appointment, the President-elect commented, "I hope he has no preconceived plans which he would wish to drive through the moment he got in."[37]

Without doubt, when he came to Washington in 1897, Roosevelt was still the junior member of the firm of Lodge and Roosevelt. He had expressed himself less upon foreign matters than either his senior partner or their mutual men-

35 C. M. Fuess, *Carl Schurz, Reformer,* 349.

36 55 Cong., 1 sess., *Cong. Rec.,* 52. For the earlier resolution see 54 Cong., 1 sess., *Cong. Rec.,* 782.

37 Lodge, *Selections from the Correspondence of Theodore Roosevelt and Henry Cabot Lodge, 1884–1918,* I, 241; see also 240–46, 252–55 for further indications of "strings" pulled for this appointment. Hereinafter cited as *Selections.*

tor, the expositor of the sea-power doctrine. Roosevelt, however, was no stranger to the "outward view" and the "large policy." To Lodge in October, 1894, he had signified his hope that the Republicans would annex Hawaii and "build an oceanic canal with the money of Uncle Sam"; later, when the aggressive spirit had gained incorporation in the Republican platform and McKinley had been elected, he wrote the Massachusetts senator, "I do hope he [McKinley] will take a strong stand about both Hawaii and Cuba."[38]

Roosevelt first met Mahan in 1888, while the latter was struggling with the establishment and preservation of the War College at Newport.[39] As has been previously stated, Roosevelt was deeply interested in and profoundly impressed by *The Influence of Sea Power upon History, 1660–1783,* and in a friendly note he offered Mahan congratulations and predicted for the book a place among the classics; he also was among those who sought to have the Navy Department grant Mahan in 1893 special permission to forego sea duty in order to continue his writing. Roosevelt frequently reviewed Mahan's books and always in laudatory terms;[40] he characterized some of his magazine contributions as "really noble articles."[41] He had the highest respect for Mahan and often publicly commented upon the value of his service to the nation. In speaking of the era when our national policy was one of "peace with insult," when "we wished to enjoy the incompatible luxuries of an unbridled tongue and an unready hand," Roosevelt added, "gradually a slight change for the better occurred. the writings of Cap-

[38] Lodge, *op. cit.,* I, 139, 243.

[39] Roosevelt, "A Great Public Servant," *Outlook,* Vol. CIX (January 13, 1915), 85–86.

[40] *Atlantic Monthly,* Vol. LXVI (October, 1890), 563–67; *ibid.,* Vol. LXXI (April, 1893), 556–59; *Political Science Quarterly* (March, 1894), Vol. IX, 171–73; *Bookman,* Vol. V (June, 1897), 331–34.

[41] Lodge, *op. cit.,* I, 274 (Roosevelt to Lodge, August 26, 1897); Roosevelt to Mahan, August 30, 1897, Roosevelt Papers.

tain Mahan playing no small part therein."[42] Their extant correspondence is considerable and indicates a close relationship and a frequent exchange of visits.

In Roosevelt, Mahan had a friend in the civil branch of the navy, a sympathizer who "wanted action and wanted it without delay."[43] Wrote the sea-power philosopher and propagandist to the new Assistant Secretary of the Navy very shortly after Roosevelt took office: "You will, I hope, allow me at times to write to you on service matters, without thinking that I am doing more than throw out ideas for consideration." The chief idea offered "for consideration" in this letter was the vital significance of American preparedness in the Pacific. The aspects of the canal in relation to the Pacific were brought to Roosevelt's attention in the following words:

I would suggest as bearing upon the general policy of the Administration, that the real significance of the Nicaragua Canal now is that it advances our Atlantic frontier by so much to the Pacific, and that in Asia, not in Europe, is now the greatest danger to our proximate interests.[44]

In reply to this letter, Roosevelt assured Mahan that the department was aware of the significance of the canal as a military measure but that Secretary Long was not so "decided as you and I are." Without minimizing the "immense importance of the Pacific Coast," Roosevelt reminded Mahan of "big problems" in the West Indies. "Until we definitely turn Spain out of those islands (and if I had my say that would be done tomorrow), we will always be menaced by trouble there." The expulsion of Spain, accompanied by the purchase of the Danish islands, would serve notice of the real position of the United States in Caribbean af-

42 Theodore Roosevelt, *Autobiography*, 225–26.
43 A. W. Dunn, *Harrison to Harding*, I, 261.
44 Mahan to Roosevelt, May 1, 1897, Roosevelt Papers.

Theodore Roosevelt (1858–1919). Twenty-fifth president of
the United States, 1901–1909. An ardent student of naval affairs
long before he met Mahan in 1888, he recognized mutuality of
interests and a close friendship developed. He frequently expressed admiration for and often acknowledged indebtedness
to Mahan. *Photograph by Underwood-Stratton*

U.S.S. *Congress*, the frigate on which Mahan sailed as passed midshipman.

U.S.S. *Chicago*, a cruiser, Captain Mahan's last sea command.
Official U.S. Navy photographs

fairs. Something of the intimacy of the Mahan-Roosevelt friendship may be gained from this further excerpt:

I need not say that this letter must be strictly private. I speak to you with the greatest freedom, for I sympathize with your views, and I have precisely the same idea of patriotism, and of belief in and love for our country. But to no one else excepting Lodge do I talk like this.[45]

Mahan answered immediately, assuring Roosevelt that he should fear no leakage because of him; "your letter has been read and destroyed." He reasserted the view formerly expressed concerning the nature of their correspondence: "you will believe that when I write to you it is only to suggest thoughts, or give information, not with any wish otherwise to influence action or to ask information." He added this telling self-analysis:

I have known myself too long not to know that I am the man of thought, not the man of action. Such a one may beneficially throw out ideas, the practical effect of which can rest only, and be duly shaped only, by practical men. The comparison may seem vain, but it may be questioned whether Adam Smith could have realized upon his own ideas as Pitt did.[46]

That Roosevelt correctly interpreted Mahan's inner desires is seen in his reply: "All I can do toward pressing our ideas into effect will be done. . . . Do write me from time to time, because there are many, many points which you will see that I should miss."[47]

There is no doubt that the sea-power exponent's "ideas for consideration" reached Roosevelt's hesitant superior. "I have shown that very remarkable letter to the Secretary," he told his friend.[48] Nor is there dearth of evidence of his

[45] Roosevelt to Mahan, May 3, 1897, *ibid.*
[46] Mahan to Roosevelt, May 6, 1897, *ibid.*
[47] Roosevelt to Mahan, May 17, 1897, *ibid.*
[48] Roosevelt to Mahan, June 9, 1897, *ibid.*

respect for and desire to profit from the judgment of the quiet, unassuming man who spoke in philosophic tone with mystical certainty and in language couched in moral and religious terms. "I wish very much I could get a chance to see you," Roosevelt wrote Mahan. "There are a number of things about which I want to get your advice, and a number of other things I would like to talk over with you."[49]

It is informative but scarcely surprising that the noted British author, James Bryce, answering negatively, in a request article for the *Forum,* concerning the wisdom of an annexation policy for the United States, singled out and characterized as the leading advocates of expansion his "valued friends," Mahan and Roosevelt.[50]

An ardent and loyal co-worker with Mahan, Lodge, and Roosevelt was Albert Shaw, editor of the newly created *Review of Reviews.* The pages of this magazine, in editorials, news comments, and article reviews, frequently bore witness of indebtedness to Mahan. It would appear that Dr. Shaw's personal contacts with Mahan were neither frequent nor intimate and such correspondence as he may have possessed was, through accident, unfortunately destroyed.[51]

How like Mahan's "The United States Looking Outward" are these lines:

The American nation for twenty-five years has turned its gaze inward, intent upon the development of a continent. . . . The times have changed somewhat; and there are unmistakable marks of a strong disposition to return to the sea.

Or again,

It is a great mistake to assume that our country has no more history to make, and that acquisitions, developments, and bold

[49] Roosevelt to Mahan, August 30, 1897, *ibid.*

[50] James Bryce, "The Policy of Annexation for the United States," *Forum,* Vol. XXIV (December, 1897), 388.

[51] Letter to author, March 24, 1937.

projects belong wholly to the past, while henceforth we must fossilize. We need a broad and masculine quality of statesmanship at Washington, which will disregard the timid plaints of those critics who are forever opposed to anything that involves a decisive attitude on the part of our government.[52]

For Shaw, as for Mahan, Hawaii was but the beginning; the United States should also construct and own the Nicaragua Canal and obtain "advantageous ports and coaling stations in the West Indies."[53]

An editorial in the June, 1894, issue of the *Review of Reviews* paid tribute to Mahan's reception in Europe and to the credit which his first sea-power study brought the United States Navy. The frontispiece of the following number was a large portrait of Captain Mahan with this subscript: "His enthusiastic reception in England has constituted an international event of agreeable character and considerable significance." Another picture and a short article of "this interpreter of naval history" appeared at the time of his appointment as a delegate to the Hague Peace Conference and the readers were informed that "American publishers alone have sold more than 50,000 copies of his books—an extraordinary number for works of that class."[54]

Mahan's articles and books were quite often reviewed in Shaw's magazine and in most commendatory terms. There can be no question but that the *Review of Reviews* was doing its part to fulfill its statement made in 1897 that "Captain A. T. Mahan, U. S. N., is as much in evidence these days, through his discussion of naval matters, as was

[52] Editorials in *Review of Reviews*, Vol. IV (September, 1891), 125, and in Vol. XV (May, 1897), 528.

[53] Editorial in *ibid.*, Vol. XVI (August, 1897), 135. Cf. *ibid.*, Vol. IX (May, 1894), 515–18; Vol. XVII (January, 1898), 13; Vol. XVII (February, 1898), 143.

[54] *Ibid.*, Vol. IX (June, 1894), 644; Vol. X (July, 1894), 2; Vol. X (November, 1894), 481; Vol. XIX (May, 1899), 553–54.

ever Perry or John Paul Jones through naval victories."[55]

Mahan realized that he was a man of thought whose opportunity for influence lay in the power of ideas masterfully expressed. He appreciated the value of men like Lodge and Roosevelt, who were in a position where action was possible; yet he likewise appreciated the power of public opinion in the formation and execution of policy. Lodge and Roosevelt were so situated that they could urge the President to "look at things our way" and in other respects do all that could be done "toward pressing our ideas into effect"; yet Mahan was uniquely qualified in aptitude, position, and prestige to call public attention to the demands of the hour as these expansionists saw the needs.

The scant attention paid to Lodge's resolutions relative to the Danish islands and the failure of the Hawaiian annexation treaty to come up for vote were indicative of the task ahead. Mahan, therefore, renewed his attack upon the "small Americans." Duty called for and destiny pointed toward the assumption of a greater role, by the United States. While the "large policy" was being accorded an adverse decision in the "test of public opinion," Mahan was replenishing the arsenal for his fellow expansionists and seeking to enlighten the American public by two significant articles which urged anew the "outward view."

The first of these articles, "A Twentieth-Century Outlook," was written in May, 1897, and carried the same trend of thought that he was contemporaneously expressing by letter to Roosevelt. In view of the unstable conditions in general in the Far East and in light of the vigor and energy displayed by the Japanese in their war with China in particular, Mahan predicted a stupendous struggle between

55 Ibid., Vol. XV (March, 1897), 331–32. In addition to certain citations previously noted, see for reviews of articles and books ibid., Vol. VII (April, 1893), 324–27; Vol. XVII (January, 1898), 71–72; Vol. XVII (June, 1898), 719–21; Vol. XXVI (November, 1902), 613–14; Vol. XXX (October, 1904), 470–72.

the East and the West. It was essential to our own good, he believed, yet it was more essential as part of our duty to the commonwealth of peoples to which we racially belong, for us dispassionately yet resolutely to recognize that there was a rapid closing together of vastly different civilizations. While the European armies safeguarded the land frontiers, the United States, occupying one of the front lines of Western culture, must prepare herself to battle on the side of the Lord in the day of Armageddon with a navy and with a canal whose approaches were firmly secured in both the Pacific and the Caribbean. This political fact rather than any mere commercial advantage, maintained Mahan, was the truly significant aspect of a future canal.[56]

In the Caribbean archipelago with its cluster of island fortresses—"the very domain of sea power if ever region could be called so"—existed the influence by which a maritime canal could be controlled. It was, however, "to be regretted that so serious a portion of them" was in hands which not only never had given, but to all appearance never could give, "the development" which was "required by the general interest." Toward this region, which was "one of the greatest nerve centers of the whole body of European civilization," to the preservation of which civilization Mahan now dedicated the twentieth century, the United States had evinced a particular and peculiar sensitiveness. And, he concluded, "Where we thus exclude others, we accept for ourselves responsibility for that which is due to the general family of our civilization."[57]

Here was subtle subordination of self-interest; here was the challenge of high duty in defense of what was great and good; here was the crusader's lure of glory in the service

---

[56] Mahan, "A Twentieth-Century Outlook," *Harper's Monthly*, September, 1897. reprinted in *The Interest of America in Sea Power, Present and Future*, 263–64.

[57] *Ibid.*, 260–61; 265. *The Literary Digest*, Vol. XV (September 11, 1897), 571–72, gave three columns to excerpts from this article.

of Western Christianity. How fortunate that this call should come to a knight who was growing ever more anxious to don the shining armor; how appropriate that it should embrace a region at once incapable of self-government and self-development, one in which the United States had long asserted her definite right of special interest and privilege. In majestic tones one seemed to hear, as at Clermont in days long past, *Deus vult*. Is it any wonder that Roosevelt thought this "a really noble article"!

As has been seen in the foregoing discussion, from his first sea-power lectures on through the various magazine articles, Mahan had commented frequently upon the interest in and the right of American dominance in the Caribbean and had intimated in a general way the prerequisites of that control. But nowhere had he carefully, scientifically, and in detail analyzed the highly important problem of military or naval positions in that region. This obvious need was now filled by "The Strategic Features of the Gulf of Mexico and the Caribbean Sea," written in June of 1897 and published in the October issue of *Harper's*. It is worth noting that this article alone of those which Mahan wrote in the nineties relative to American national and foreign policy was unsolicited by an editor.[58] In light of Cuban affairs it was an extremely timely article.

In each of these bodies of water Mahan found one position of pre-eminent importance; in the Gulf it was the mouth of the Mississippi and in the Caribbean, the indeterminate Isthmus. Four principal water routes eastward which connected these points with others were specified: first, the Yucatan Channel between the Isthmus and the Mississippi; second, the Strait of Florida connecting the Gulf of Mexico with the North American coast; third, the Windward Passage joining the Isthmus with the North American coast; and fourth, the Anegada Passage linking

[58] Mahan, *Retrospect and Prospect*, 24.

the Isthmus with Europe. Mahan proceeded to analyze the relative strategic importance of the principal naval strongholds, actual or potential, in the Gulf and the Caribbean. In this evaluation the strategic significance of any position was considered: first, from point of situation, with reference chiefly to lines of communication; second, from view of strength, inherent or acquired; and finally, from angle of resources, natural or stored. Inasmuch as strength and resources were capable of alteration, primary attention naturally rested upon situation.[59] Thinking in these terms, with emphasis upon entrance to and transit across the Caribbean to the Isthmus—the two prime essentials to the enjoyment of the advantages of the latter—and viewing in a similar manner the Gulf and the Mississippi, Mahan one by one indicated the individual and relative importance of the various military positions in these regions. The written word was effectively reinforced by a map which gave graphic reality to an otherwise somewhat elusive topic.

Cuba was accorded first place, for she was without a "possible rival in her command of the Yucatan Passage" and had "no competitor . . . for the control of the Florida Strait." Though she shared with Jamaica the control of the Windward Passage and though the latter was blessed with a singularly central position within the Caribbean proper, yet all in all "the advantages of situation, strength, and resources" were "greatly and decisively in favor of Cuba." Cuba was "not so much an island as a continent," virtually capable of self-sufficiency; "the extent of coast-line, the numerous harbors, and the many directions from which approach" could be made, minimized the dangers of total blockade, to which all islands were more or less subject.[60]

---

[59] Mahan, "The Strategic Features of the Gulf of Mexico and the Caribbean Sea," *Harper's Monthly*, October, 1897, reprinted in *The Interest of America in Sea Power, Present and Future*, 283.

[60] *Ibid.*, 289, 305–13.

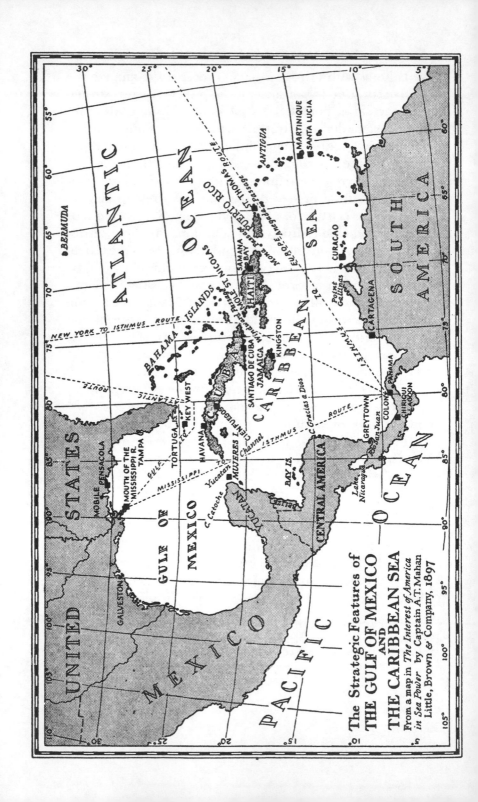

The Strategic Features of
THE GULF OF MEXICO
AND
THE CARIBBEAN SEA

From a map in *The Interest of America in Sea Power* by Captain A.T. Mahan
Little, Brown & Company, 1897

Samana Bay and the island of St. Thomas likewise were given favorable consideration, for they represented "efficiently and better than other positions, the control of two principal passages into the Caribbean Sea from the Atlantic." Neither could boast of much natural strength or of resources, yet their potential importance in the hands of a progressive government was great.[61]

That Mahan had the United States definitely, even centrally in mind in writing this article cannot be gainsaid; yet nowhere did he suggest that the United States should seize Cuba or acquire Samana Bay or the island of St. Thomas. He may well have thought it unnecessary to point the moral so openly, for both he and his reading public were aware that he had been repeating for nearly a decade the necessity of American acquisitions in that area, and he had just written "A Twentieth-Century Outlook," which maintained that the preservation of Western civilization was dependent upon American control of the Caribbean. He might also have thought such advice both unwise and unnecessary in light of the highly charged nature of the Cuban question.

The various magazine articles which Mahan had been writing during the decade relative to American national and foreign policy—"The United States Looking Outward," "Hawaii and our Future Sea Power," "The Isthmus and Sea Power," "Possibilities of an Anglo American Reunion," "The Future in Relation to American Sea Power," "Preparedness for a Naval War," "A Twentieth Century Outlook," "The Strategic Features of the Caribbean Sea and the Gulf of Mexico"—were now brought, at this crucial moment (1897), to a larger reading public in book form in *The Interest of America in Sea Power, Present and Future*.

The book by no means met with uniform approval, yet even its critics sensed correctly its purpose and implication.

[61] *Ibid.*, 297–99.

An Englishman, generally a great admirer of Mahan, was definitely nonplussed. He thought no great nation ever needed guidance "more than did the United States today"; and though no one was "as well qualified as Captain Mahan to render this service to his country," he had failed in this instance. From these articles

readers will gather that expansion of some kind is necessary; that Great Britain is, in some unexplained way, seeking to oppose the annexation of Hawaii and to create difficulties in relation to the trans-isthmian canal; that the Atlantic Seaboard is in grave peril; and that the existence of coal within 3,000 miles of San Francisco would be a National danger.[62]

Despite the disparaging tone of these words, Colonel George Sydenham Clarke had not missed the import of Mahan's counsels!

An American reviewer wrote:

The spirit of the book is so plain that he who runs may read. Military glory and far reaching domination are the great ends of man's aspiration. To give opportunity for these, the United States must have numerous distant, outlying possessions, each sticking out like a sore thumb to be hurt by whatever passes, each wanting its impregnable fortifications and its great garrison to defend it, each demanding its fleet to scour the adjacent seas, and great reserve armies and navies at home besides, to overpower every possible antagonist.[63]

In prospect, this fellow countryman in 1898 predicted, "When the people's 'sober second thought' is spoken, we do not believe it will be the adoption of such a policy for our twentieth century programme"; in retrospect, four years later, a Frenchman stated, "The author would not have to write them today; for the majority of the questions which

[62] G. S. Clarke, loc. cit., 293–96.
[63] The Nation, Vol. LXVII (July 14, 1898), 34–36.

are there put are actually resolved, and have received exactly the solutions which he held desirable."[64]

Cleveland had conceded in his annual message of December, 1896, that open hostility to Spain was not inconceivable. McKinley and many of his party leaders ardently hoped that the Cuban crisis would break one way or another under Cleveland. Their wishes were not fulfilled, and, with its ever increasing complexities, the problem was turned over to new hands for solution. Though there was little immediate visible shift in policy toward Cuban affairs, the change in administration was significant. It brought to the presidency a man content to follow public opinion rather than one bent on directing it; it called to Washington a new assistant secretary of the navy eager for action and imbued with the sea-power doctrine; it gave additional opportunity for Lodge to press for the fulfillment of those demands of expansion, based upon commercial and patriotic grounds, which weighed so heavily with him.

During the month in which the subscribers of *Harper's* were reading Mahan's "really noble article," McKinley was offering Spain the good services of the United States as mediator and Roosevelt was talking with the President, sketching what he thought ought to be done in case of possible war with Spain over the Cuban question. The plan embraced action in the Caribbean, against the Spanish coast, and in the Philippines. The advisability of the last scheme was suggested also to his superior in the Navy Department.[65] Mahan, in the meantime, had been urging Roosevelt to see that the "best admiral" be in the Pacific for "much more initiative *may* be thrown on him than *can* be on the Atlantic man."[66] Dewey was the man found, and

[64] Moireau, "La Maîtresse de la Mer," *Revue des deux Mondes*, Vol. XI (October, 1902), 681–708.

[65] Lodge, *op. cit.*, I, 278 (Roosevelt to Lodge, September 21, 1897) ; J. B. Bishop, *Theodore Roosevelt and His Times*, I, 83.

[66] Mahan to Roosevelt, May 1, 1897, Roosevelt Papers.

Roosevelt engineered his appointment to the Asiatic squadron, persuading the Commodore to use the necessary political influence.[67]

Before Dewey reached Hong Kong not only had Lodge written Henry White that "there may be an explosion any day in Cuba which would settle a great many things," but the explosion itself, probably of a more catastrophic nature than the Senator had had in mind, was greatly complicating an already intricate and highly charged situation.[68] Ten days after the *Maine* disaster, Secretary Long, seeking respite from the tension of the event, turned over to Roosevelt for a Saturday half-day the direction of the department. The acting secretary came "very near causing more of an explosion than happened to the *Maine*," subsequently complained his superior. "The very devil seemed to possess him"; he went at the issuance of orders "like a bull in a China shop." Just the species of the demon which possessed Roosevelt that fateful afternoon has never been determined, but it is known that friend Lodge was his guest and colaborer.[69] One telegram, important in its implications and results, was the subsequently famous cable to Dewey, to "keep full of coal and in event of declaration of war . . . to see that the Spanish squadron does not leave the Asiatic Coast and then to begin offensive operations in Philippine Islands."[70] This much has been ascertained about how Mahan, Roosevelt, Lodge, and Dewey prepared for Manila.

The time seemed propitious, thought Lodge, to try once more for the Danish islands. Success nearly crowned his effort. On March 31, 1898, on behalf of the Senate Foreign

67 Walter Millis, *The Martial Spirit*, 85–86.

68 Lodge to White, January 31, 1898, cited by Allan Nevins, *Henry White, Thirty Years of Diplomacy*, 130.

69 L. S. Mayo (ed.), *America of Yesterday, Diary of John D. Long*, 169–70; Lodge, *op. cit.*, I, 349.

70 George Dewey, *The Autobiography of George Dewey, Admiral of the Navy*, 179.

Relations Committee, he presented a bill which authorized the President to negotiate the purchase of these islands and provide him with five million dollars, or as much as necessary thereof, for that purpose. In an accompanying report he traced briefly the story of the islands and placed emphasis upon the advantages of American ownership. As long as they remained on the market, there was danger of their purchase by some European power, with consequent infraction of the Monroe Doctrine and resulting foreign complications. Moreover, because of their position, they were of "incalculable value to the United States"; his argument was buttressed by reference to Mahan, who viewed St. Thomas as "one of the greatest strategic points in the West Indies."[71]

Prior to the Lodge resolution the virtual consent of the Danish government had been gained, a price of five million dollars agreed upon, and the approval of naval officials and McKinley's cabinet assured. However, because of the rapidly increasing Spanish-American tension, the Danish government refused to conclude negotiations on the ground that it might be "a diplomatic discourtesy to Spain."[72] Undoubtedly the imminence of the war between Spain and the United States foiled this attempt of Lodge, but it must have been a defeat easy to accept, for that conflict quickly brought consummation to a considerable part of the "large policy" and the "outward view."

[71] 57 Cong., 1 sess., *Senate Executive Report 1*, Appendix A; 57 Cong., 2 sess., *Senate Doc. 284*. For introduction of resolution see 55 Cong., 2 sess., *Cong. Rec.*, 3409.

[72] Tansill, *op. cit.*, 212–17.

VII

THE CARIBBEAN—FULFILLMENT

I T SEEMS WELL-NIGH INEVITABLE that many of the aspirations to which Mahan had given such eloquent voice in his essays should sooner or later have taken active form. Economic, political, and psychological forces were at work which were slowly yet surely shaping American policy along the lines which he and other expansionists were indicating. By the nineties the old frontier was gone, the continent was largely settled, the most lucrative fields for exploitation seemed to be closing, and capital was casting its glance outward for avenues of investment. The home market was approaching satiation in the "extensive sense" and "at a price," qualifications which should always be borne in mind when speaking of capitalist economics. American foreign commerce had more than doubled between 1880 and 1898, increasing from around $93,000,000 to about $223,000,000. Without doubt "the movement of the country from an undeveloped, agricultural, debtor nation, exporting raw materials and borrowing capital for improvements, to a developed, manufacturing, creditor nation, exporting manufactured goods and capital, and importing raw materials" was a movement gathering momentum as the nation became more and more exploited. This trend was in full swing as the century drew to a close.[1] Yet it must not be forgotten that the United States was still overwhelmingly a debtor nation in the last decade of the nineteenth century, owning abroad only about $500,000,000 while

1 Scott Nearing and Joseph Freeman, *Dollar Diplomacy*, 1–2.

owing over $3,000,000,000. The full force of commercial imperialism did not motivate American policy in the nineteenth century; "the need of colonial markets was discovered not by business men but by historians and other intellectuals, by journalists and politicians."[2]

Psychological factors are significant in an explanation of the increasing tendency of America to look outward. The United States was no stranger to the aggressive spirit; behind her lay a story of expansion—half by war, half by negotiation—of the richest portions of a major and virgin continent. "In the United States a spirit of imperialism—a demand to expand at the expense of other nations, a disregard for the rights of backward peoples—had existed since the beginning of the nineteenth century."[3] During the nineties there was a general quickening of the American pulse, a resurgence, as it were, of that militant aggressiveness of the mid-century. A strong feeling was arising in many quarters that the United States had reached her majority, politically speaking, and was ready to imitate the European countries in taking on new responsibilities. A leading American editor trenchantly commented upon this expansive tendency of mankind in the following words:

The scramble has never ceased, except when treaties are arranged to give the combatants breathing-spells, and it goes on today wherever there is any possession or trade that is coveted by anybody. To a supernatural being looking down upon the earth the sight must be pathetically humorous. Wherever there is a fishing station, or a coffee ranch, or a palm tree island, or an elephant jungle, or a desert roamed by nomads, or a peaceful community unable to defend itself, or a Naboth's vineyard (on the Rhine or elsewhere) contiguous to a great man's estate, there

[2] Pratt, *Expansionists of 1898*, 22; see also John Carter, *Conquest: America's Painless Imperialism*, 88; Louis Hacker, "The Holy War of 1898," *American Mercury*, Vol. XXI (November, 1930), 316–26.

[3] Tansill, *The Purchase of the Danish West Indies*, 386.

is somebody advancing on it and planting a flag, in the name of civilization and the Great Jehovah.[4]

Few expressed this spirit of expansion in more eloquent or more stirring language couched in terms to arouse enthusiasm for answering the call of self-interest and duty than the sea-power exponent. As previously quoted, Mahan early stated, "In our infancy we bordered upon the Atlantic only, our youth carried our boundary to the Gulf of Mexico; today maturity sees us upon the Pacific." Then came the lesson in the form of a rhetorical appeal:

Have we no right or no call to progress in any direction? Are there for us beyond the sea horizon none of those essential interests, of those evident dangers, which impose a policy or confer rights?[5]

The sense of destiny, in respect to both territory and peculiar function, had been an attribute of the United States from her inception as an independent nation. Throughout her history there had been a conviction and an assertion that her form of government was superior and that her people enjoyed happiness to an extraordinary degree. Coupled with this belief, at times, was the desire for new territory, contiguously or strategically located, and the eager willingness for the responsibility, if need be, of bestowing upon others the benefits which had been vouchsafed her. In this sense of manifest destiny, which has rightly been interpreted as primarily an emotion, "there was a golden ideal . . . but there was also an alloy of baser metals."[6]

As the nineteenth century drew to a close, the United States had ceased to be "bound and swathed in the tradition of the eighteenth century"; she was "looking outward"; in-

[4] Editorial in *Harper's Monthly*, Vol. LXXXVII (November, 1893), 962–63.

[5] Mahan, "Hawaii and Our Sea Power," *Forum*, March, 1893, reprinted in *The Interest of America in Sea Power, Present and Future*, 35–36.

[6] E. D. Adams, *The Power of Ideals in American History*, 93.

deed, she was ready and waiting to take a "twentieth-century outlook." The affairs in Cuba fatefully, kindly, offered the nation an unusual opportunity by which more quickly to achieve and more dramatically to proclaim the assumption of a place among world powers. The renewed struggle for independence, the concentration camps, the De Lome letter, and the sinking of the *Maine* raised the fever in the body politic which was to be allayed only by the drawing of blood.

The Spanish-American War was provoked by a variety of forces.[7] The call of duty made its strong appeal to religion. The organized church, except the Quakers and Unitarians, intrigued by humanitarian issues, offered less opposition than encouragement to intervention; and, after war was declared, justified and supported it. Playing upon humanitarian sympathies, an irresponsible, self-interested, and sensational journalism fed the flames of hatred, bigotry, and irrationality. For the benefit of the impressionable mind, the unfavorable elements of Spanish history—the barbarous Inquisition, the bloody Alva, the avaricious Pizarro, the cunning Cortez, the proverbial, procrastinating "tomorrow"—were called afresh, in their traditional garb, as testimony of age-long Spanish cruelty, vindictiveness, duplicity, and colonial unfitness. Senator Cullom expressed the perversion of truth by the press when he stated that it made "a mole hill of fact a mountain of falsehood."[8] Popular reaction, whipped to a frenzy by the yellow journalism, was supported by eager politicians who sought personal promi-

[7] Walter Millis offers the best lengthy analysis of the national psychology of the war in *The Martial Spirit*. Julius Pratt, *op. cit.*, has two able chapters on the points of view of religious and business groups. Cf. Mark Sullivan, *Our Times*, I, 302 ff. For the role of the press in greater detail, see M. M. Wilkerson, *Public Opinion and the Spanish-American War, a Study in War Propaganda*; J. E. Wisan, *The Cuban Crisis as Reflected in the New York Press, 1895–98*.

[8] 55 Cong., 2 sess., *Cong. Rec.*, 3877.

nence or party security through advocacy of new adventurous issues in foreign policy.

Business in early 1898, except that dealing directly or indirectly with Cuban sugar, was reluctant to engage in hostility, fearing a cessation of the rising tide of returning prosperity after the panic of the early nineties; but once in the fray and with Manila so quickly proffered as a possible base for Eastern trade, it no longer feared but welcomed all colonial responsibilities that the war might bring.

The appeal to defense on the ground of strategy, to which Mahan and Lodge had already given voice, now was brought again to Congressional attention. The inalienable right of self-preservation—the highest of all rights—gave us the moral right to possess or to control possession by others of Cuba, which, in language strangely like Mahan's, was described as standing sentinel over the Gulf of Mexico, the entrance to the Mississippi River, and as lying in the direct course of our commerce via the Isthmus of Panama.[9]

President McKinley, declaring that he had "exhausted every effort to relieve the intolerable condition of affairs," on April 11 placed the issue arising from the Cuban situation in the hands of Congress.[10] Within a fortnight diplomatic relations were severed. The war marked the emergence of America as a world power; to view it as an isolated and sudden phenomenon is to ignore the fact that the American outlook had altered in the decade which had just closed. Though a turning point for the United States, the war was less a revolution than a revelation; it disclosed those ideals and made manifest those forces which had been at work in the preceding years. An important contemporary state official saw the war as synchronous with America's

[9] 55 Cong., 2 sess., *Senate Report 885, Part II,* 1; 55 Cong., 2 sess., *Cong. Rec.,* 3844.

[10] *Papers Relating to the Foreign Relations of the United States, 1898,* 760.

THE JOURNAL WILL CELEBRATE OUR FIRST AMERICAN VICTORY TO-NIGHT AT MADISON SQUARE AT 8 O'CLOCK. ALL FRIENDS OF AGGRESSIVE AMERICANISM ARE INVITED. MUSIC AND FIREWORKS,

EDITION FOR GREATER NEW YORK

WAR SECTION. | # NEW YORK JOURNAL | *WAR SECTION.*

AND ADVERTISER

NO. 4,646. | NEW YORK, MONDAY, MAY 2, 1898.—16 PAGES. | PRICE ONE CENT

VICTORY!!

Complete! Glorious!

Spanish Fleet in the Philippines Destroyed.

Forced Passage at Night, Battle Begun at Dawn.

Olympia and Raleigh Dashed Into the Harbor.

All Their Ships Burned, Blown Up and Sunk.

Spaniards in Despair Scuttled Their Own Vessels.

Madrid in a Tumult. Troops Suppress Revolution.

THE MAINE IS AVENGED.

MADRID, MAY 1, 8 P. M.--The following is the text of the official dispatch from the Governor-General of the Philippines to the Minister of War, Lieutenant-General Correa, as to the engagement off Manila:

"Last night, April 30, the batteries at the entrance to the fort announced the arrival of the enemy's squadron.

"They forced a passage under the obscurity of the night.

"At daybreak the enemy took up position and began firing.

"They opened up with a strong fire against Fort Cavite and the Arsenal.

"Our fleet was protected by the Cavite and Manila forts.

"They engaged the enemy in a brilliant combat.

"Our fleet obliged the enemy, with heavy loss, to manoeuvre repeatedly.

Front page of the *New York Journal*, reprinted in *Literary Digest*, June, 1898.

CAPT. ALFRED T. MAHAN.   REAR-ADMIRAL MONTGOMERY SICARD.
CAPT. A. S. CROWNINSHIELD.

THE NAVAL BOARD OF STRATEGY.

An emergency board created by Secretary of the Navy John D. Long for advice during the Spanish-American War, from *Literary Digest*, July, 1898.

abandonment of isolation; the struggle was not the cause and at most only hastened the process by an inconsiderable period; the change was inevitable, had been long preparing and could not have been long delayed.[11] Another competent authority thought that, in our stage of political and economic development, territorial expansion was "as certain as the advent of spring after winter" and that to oppose it would be as futile as to offer "opposition to the trade winds or the storms."[12]

While the tension between Spain and the United States had been growing following the untoward events of February, the Assistant Secretary of the Navy had been in very close touch with Mahan. The details of strategy, then interesting them, are now subordinate in importance to the close friendship, to the high esteem of Roosevelt for Mahan, and to the acknowledged obligation of this influential man of action to the quiet expositor of the sea-power thesis repeatedly manifested in their correspondence. "I earnestly wish that my chief would get you on here to consult in the present crisis,"[13] Roosevelt wrote him the day after the House had passed (311 to 0) the famous "Fifty Million Bill" defense measure, which McKinley personally had requested "Uncle Joe" Cannon to introduce. Mahan sent his advice about procedure in case of war; it was passed on to Secretary Long and to certain naval officers.[14] When the plan of campaign was shortly drawn up by the department, it was submitted by Roosevelt to Mahan for comments, which were accordingly given and elicited in response this eulogistic letter:

There is no question that you stand head and shoulders

11 Richard Olney, "Growth of Our Foreign Policy," *Atlantic Monthly,* Vol. LXXXV (March, 1900), 290.

12 F. H. Giddings. "Imperialism?," *Political Science Quarterly,* Vol. XIII (December, 1898), 586.

13 Roosevelt to Mahan, March 10, 1898, Roosevelt Papers.

14 Roosevelt to Mahan, March 14, 1898, *ibid.*

above the rest of us! You have given us just the suggestions we want, I am going to show your letter to the Secretary first, and then get some members of the Board to go over it. . . .

You probably don't know how much your letter has really helped me clearly to formulate certain things which I had only vaguely in mind. I think I have studied your books to pretty good purpose.[15]

Still further "very valuable" suggestions were received, and Mahan was informed that all his recent letters were being sent to Captain Sampson for him to examine and return. Once again the man who wanted action expressed his indebtedness to the man of thought for what he had learned from the sea-power books "long before" he had had "any practical experience."[16]

Mahan, who had been contemplating a European trip, was advised by the department to continue with his plans and was assured that he would be notified in event of need. The prospect for war seemed doubtful to Roosevelt, who deprecatingly wrote: ". . . I fear the President does not intend that we shall have war if we can possibly avoid it."[17]

In view of the high regard which Roosevelt had for Mahan, it is not surprising that the outbreak of hostilities brought orders for his return from Italy to serve as a member of the Naval War Board along with Admiral Sicard and Captain Crowinshield. In light of the closeness of their friendship, it is not astonishing to learn that, upon volunteering for duty, Roosevelt placed his Washington home at the disposition of his friend as long as service on the War Board should necessitate his residence in the capital. That Secretary Long may have been more skeptical than his assistant concerning the importance of the sea-power author's

[15] Roosevelt to Mahan, March 16, 1898; Roosevelt to Mahan, March 21, 1898: *ibid.*

[16] Roosevelt to Mahan, March 24, 1898, *ibid.*

[17] Roosevelt to Mahan, March 14, 1898, *ibid.*

contributions to the war effort may be read into these lines which he wrote in his diary at the time:

He [Mahan] has achieved great distinction as a writer of naval history, and has made a very thorough study of naval strategy, no naval officer stands higher today. Yet I doubt very much whether he will be of much value practically. He may be or he may not. That remains to be seen.[18]

An examination of the activities of the Board during the period of Mahan's association with it is unnecessary. One or two items which particularly show his views and indicate his contribution will suffice. In a letter to Long the last of July, Mahan strongly urged against a *general* armistice but suggested a local armistice for Spanish European possessions, with the consequent postponement or cancellation of the expedition of the United States Fleet to the Spanish coast. Relying upon a confidential dispatch of the secret service, he argued that the effect of the sailing of the fleet "upon the susceptibilities of the Spanish people would be unfavorable to the attainment of peace." Shown to President McKinley, the letter evoked the postscript to the Secretary: "There are some good suggestions in the foregoing. Think of them."[19]

Mahan proposed the solution accepted in the evacuation of Santiago. The majority of professional opinion in a special meeting of cabinet members, army men, and the Naval Board, considering the surrender of the Spanish at Santiago, favored, as did Generals Shafter and Miles, the acceptance of the Spanish Army's offer to surrender if permitted to march out and go anywhere it chose. The President "vehemently" opposed the offer, and it was rejected. Mahan suggested as an alternative that the enemy might surrender and return to Spain, a plan which met with the approval of all

[18] Mayo, *America of Yesterday, Diary of John D. Long*, 191.
[19] Mahan to Long, July 28 [1898]; July 29 [1898]; August 5, 1898; August 7, 1898: Long Papers.

and was accordingly followed. Mahan did not care to have his role made public but did "object to credit, if such there be, being attributed to another by the public and in history," especially to Secretary Alger who "was a monument of incapacity."[20]

Throughout the war Mahan was strongly of the belief that official responsibility in way of professional advice to the Secretary should be individual; he thought a chief of staff should consult with others but maintained that the final determination of advice submitted should rest with the single officer. He wrote the Secretary accordingly and discussed the matter with the board. Secretary Long was not pleased; he stated: "Captain Mahan is on the rampage again. He is very frank and manly; does not go around Robin Hood's barn, but blurts out his entire dissatisfaction with the entire Naval War Board." Though Long did not agree with Mahan's views about the nature or organization of the board, he did not continue to hold his former doubts whether the sea-power strategist would be of "much value practically." In retrospect he wrote that "the Board possessed high intelligence and excellent judgment, and its service was invaluable in connection with the successful conduct of the war."[21]

Because of his position as a naval officer and writer, quite aside from any official connection with the war, Mahan took sides in the famous Schley-Sampson controversy. This dispute arose over the respective roles by these two naval leaders in blockade activities in the Caribbean and in the battle of Santiago de Cuba on July 3 with Admiral Cervera's fleet. As Rear Admiral Sampson was absent on official business at the moment of battle and Commodore Schley was in actual command, many minimized the role of the superior

20 Mahan to Long, August 21, 1899; April 25, 1901; June 17, 1901: *ibid.*
21 Mayo, *op. cit.,* 194; John D. Long, *The Rise of the New Navy,* I, 163.

officer. Mahan, however, favored Sampson and opposed any official recognition to Schley.[22]

Despite gross sins of omission and glaring sins of commission in the conduct of the war on the part of the United States, hostilities were over by midsummer. Advocates of the "large policy" and the "outward view" were at no loss how to capitalize on their war-given opportunities. The sense of destiny, territorially and governmentally, the urge for defense, strategically for our own bulwarks as well as for the possible Armageddon of the future, the requirements of development, politically and commercially, were now given fulfillment when the call of duty to ourselves and the Cubans was answered. Some of the expansionists "deeply regretted" the self-denying Teller Amendment by which Congress had declared that the United States would claim no sovereignty, jurisdiction, or control over Cuba except for its pacification, and, when that was accomplished, would leave the government and control of the island to its people. None of the expansionists, however, considered this resolution as applicable to territory other than Cuba.[23] The anti-imperialists thought quite differently; to them "it was idle to say that we meant the Teller resolution to apply only to Cuba."[24]

Though Roosevelt may have been "motivated by adolescence rather than shrewdness"[25] in leaving the Navy Department to become lieutenant colonel of the cowboy regiment, he did not lose contact with Washington nor did he lessen his expansionist desires. With the war scarcely started, he wrote from his camp in Texas to Lodge at the capital

[22] Mahan to Lodge, July 29, 1898; Mahan to Lodge, February 19, [1901?]; Lodge to Mahan, February 21, 1901: Lodge Papers. Mahan to Long, November 16, 1898; Mahan to Long, December 12, 1899: Long Papers. Mahan to Luce, October 17, 1911, Luce Papers.

[23] Whitelaw Reid to McKinley, April 19, 1898, cited by Royal Cortissoz, *The Life of Whitelaw Reid*, II, 222–23.

[24] F. H. Gillett, *George Frisbie Hoar*, 206; George F. Hoar, *Autobiography of Seventy Years*, II, 310–11.

[25] H. F. Pringle, *Theodore Roosevelt, a Biography*, 182.

urging that no peace be made until Puerto Rico was ours and Cuba was independent. Lodge in reply assured him that

Porto Rico is not forgotten and we mean to have it. Unless I am utterly and profoundly mistaken the Administration is now fully committed to the large policy that we both desire.[26]

By the middle of June, over a month before the expeditionary force was to begin the conquest of the island, Lodge wrote his restless, eager soldier friend that the Secretary of State, Judge Day, had told him there was no longer any question about the United States' getting and keeping Puerto Rico. Lodge frequently talked with McKinley; toward the end of July he informed Roosevelt that the President seemed "very clear and strong" about both Cuba and Puerto Rico. With the signing of the protocol of August 12 guaranteeing the relinquishment of all Spanish claims in the Caribbean, it was no wonder that our expansionist senator thought that "so far as the West Indies is concerned all is right."[27] And yet it should be added that he would have been willing for more; in exchange for the Philippines, excepting Luzon, he thought the British might give us the Bahamas and Jamaica and buy us the Danish West Indies for good measure![28]

Before the drafting of the treaty of peace with Spain, the Naval War Board, at the request of the Senate Naval Affairs Committee, submitted a report to the Navy Department about "what coaling stations should be acquired by the United States outside their own territorial limits." Judging from its broad strategic reasoning and unmistakable

26 Lodge, *Selections*, I, 299, (Roosevelt to Lodge, May 19, 1898); *ibid.*, I, 299–300 (Lodge to Roosevelt, May 24, 1898). Similar views are also expressed on 301, 302, and 309.

27 *Ibid.*, I, 311 (Lodge to Roosevelt, June 15, 1898); *ibid.*, I, 330 (Lodge to Roosevelt, July 23, 1898); see also 323 (Lodge to Roosevelt [July 12?], 1898; *ibid.*, I, 337 (Lodge to Roosevelt, August 15, 1898).

28 Lodge to Day, August 11, 1898, Lodge Papers.

literary style, the report was written by Captain Mahan. This report urgently called attention to the importance of the Windward Passage between Cuba and Haiti as being

the great direct commercial route between the whole North Atlantic Coast and the Isthmus. No solution of the problem of coaling and naval stations can be considered satisfactory which does not provide for military safety upon that route. The most available ports for that purpose are Santiago and Guantanamo, on the south shore of Cuba. To those may be added the Bay of Nipe on the north. . . . Santiago or Guantanamo is preferable in strategic position to Nipe.[29]

The general provision as incorporated in the Platt Amendment of 1901 for the sale or lease to the United States of coaling or naval stations in Cuba at specified points, to be determined later by the President of the United States, was given more definite form by an agreement of 1903. By this agreement the United States received Guantánamo in eastern Cuba and Bahía Honda in the northwestern part of the island.[30] The latter was given up in 1912 in return for an enlargement of the area at Guantánamo.

Mahan, discussing the strategic features of the Gulf of Mexico and the Caribbean Sea in his timely article in 1897, had not placed emphasis upon the significance of Puerto Rico; the control of the Mona and the Anegada passages was better assured by Samana Bay and St. Thomas. The "professed motives" of the war "prevented pre-eminence" being given to Puerto Rico in the campaign strategy.[31] Once the possibility of its acquisition loomed on the horizon, it is

[29] 58 Cong., 3 sess., *Hearings Before the House Committee on Naval Affairs*, 504–505.

[30] W. M. Malloy, *Treaties, Conventions, International Acts, Protocols, and Agreements between the United States of America and Other Powers, 1706–1909*, I, 358 ff.

[31] Mahan, "Lessons of the War with Spain," *McClure's Magazine*, December, 1898, reprinted in *Lessons of the War with Spain and Other Articles*, 26–28; see also Roosevelt to Mahan, March 14, 1898, Roosevelt Papers.

certain that Mahan favored it, especially when taken in its wider setting. In the aforementioned report of the Naval War Board, Puerto Rico was viewed as being advantageously situated on the circumference or entrance to the Caribbean, and the mutually supporting relation of Puerto Rico and Culebra was pointed out. In a magazine article, before the treaty was signed, Mahan wrote, "Porto Rico considered militarily is to Cuba, to the future Isthmian canal, and to our Pacific Coast, what Malta is, or may be, to Egypt and the beyond." The necessity to hold and strengthen it "in its entirety and in its immediate surroundings" was strongly urged. "It would be very difficult for a trans-Atlantic state to maintain operations in the western Caribbean with a United States fleet based upon Porto Rico and the adjacent islands."[32]

In light of what Mahan had written before the war started, there can be comparatively little doubt what he had in mind when speaking of Puerto Rico and "the adjacent islands," or of Puerto Rico "in its entirety and in its immediate surroundings." Even prior to the signing of the protocol which brought cessation to hostilities, Mahan had communicated with Lodge about matters in the Caribbean. He wrote:

Assuming, as seems pretty certain, that the United States is to acquire Porto Rico, may I suggest the advisability as a corollary to this step, *after peace is signed,* the purchase of St. Thomas.

Puerto Rico and these small Danish islands, he added,

form a compact strategic entity, yielding mutual support. St. Cruz is immaterial . . . the harbor of St. Maria is very fine. . . . the port of St. Thomas, reasonably fortified, would be a distinct

32 Mahan, "Lessons of the War with Spain," *McClure's Magazine,* December, 1898, reprinted in *Lessons of the War with Spain and Other Articles,* 29.

Henry Cabot Lodge (1850–1924). United States representative
and senator from Massachusetts. Leading exponent of "the
large policy," he found in Mahan kindred spirit and drew from
him clarification and support for his nationalist programs. *From
a photograph by Histed; courtesy Henry Cabot Lodge, Jr.*

U.S.S. *Mahan*, destroyer, 1,190 tons, commissioned in 1918, designed speed of 35 knots.

U.S.S. *Mahan*, destroyer, 1,500 tons, commissioned in 1936, designed speed of 36.5 knots. *Official U.S. Navy photographs*

addition to the military strength of Porto Rico, considered as a naval base.[33]

In light of Lodge's utilization of the strategist as support in earlier attempts to push through an annexation treaty for the Danish West Indies, it is interesting to find Mahan here informing the Senator that he had never favored the acquisition of St. Thomas as an isolated possession, believing it too small and too distant.

Negotiations looking toward the acquisition of these islands were shortly initiated by Secretary Hay, but quarrels between the American consul and the minister at Copenhagen, a change in the Danish ministry, price dickering, and modifications of one sort or another in Hay's first rough draft impeded rapid progress. It was not until January 24, 1902, three years after the inception of official negotiations, that the American secretary of state signed the treaty. The Senate Committee on Foreign Relations reported favorably upon the treaty, commenting that these islands, together with Puerto Rico, were of "great importance in a strategic way, whether the strategy be military or commercial." Appended thereto was the report which Senator Lodge had submitted with his bill of 1898, in which, as already noted, Mahan had been called to testify that St. Thomas was "one of the greatest strategic points in the West Indies."[34]

The treaty was ratified by the United States Senate after only an hour's consideration but failed in the Danish Landsthing. Several contemporary statesmen, including Hay, Lodge, White, and Roosevelt, believed German intrigues had defeated the treaty. Some historians, as Allan Nevins and A. L. P. Dennis, give credence to this supposition.[35]

33 Mahan to Lodge, August 4, 1898, Lodge Papers.

34 57 Cong., 1 sess., *Senate Executive Report 1;* or 57 Cong., 2 sess., *Senate Doc. 284.*

35 A. L. P. Dennis, *Adventures in American Diplomacy, 1896–1906,* 271–75; Nevins, *Henry White, Thirty Years of Diplomacy,* 203–205.

However, Charles Tansill in his able monograph on the Danish West Indies, after careful scrutiny of German interests in the Caribbean, repudiates any German influence in the matter of the rejection of this treaty. He concludes that "in face of the proofs . . . adduced from the foreign office archives of both Denmark and Germany, it will be difficult for any future historian to conjure up again the old bogey of 'perfidious Allemagne.' "[36] Alfred Vagts, in his two-volume study, substantiates Tansill's position. It must not be assumed, however, that the German Admiralty did not repeatedly urge the Foreign Office, as previously noted, to secure Caribbean bases, including St. Thomas.[37]

In 1905 Senator Lodge suggested reopening negotiations with Denmark, this time including Greenland in the deal; his friend Roosevelt, now president, thought other problems were more important and the matter was dropped.[38]

The failure to secure the Danish West Indies was no major blow to the expansionists; as Mahan had well stated, they were but a "corollary" to the acquisition of Puerto Rico, and both they and Puerto Rico in entirety were subsidiary to the larger problem which he and others had in mind. The central proposition upon which all else rested was American dominance in the Caribbean Sea. This dominance was essential for strategic and defensive purposes, not only for the Atlantic and Gulf coasts of the United States but for her Pacific frontier as well. The central link in this defensive chain was the projected Isthmian canal, and the primary fact affecting the diplomacy of the United States regarding Latin America from the Spanish-American War to World War I was the desire and the determination to

[36] Tansill, op. cit., 373–453.

[37] Alfred Vagts, Deutchland und die Vereinigten Staaten in der Weltpolitik, II, 1410ff.

[38] Lodge, op. cit., 119–20 (Lodge to Roosevelt, May 12, 1905); ibid., 125 (Roosevelt to Lodge. May 24, 1905).

dig, own, and control this inter-oceanic canal. Much of Roosevelt's "high type of opportunism"—the taking of Panama, intercession for Venezuela, preservation of order in Cuba, mediation in Central America, and intervention in Santo Domingo—"was guided or dominated by his devotion to the cause of national defense" and not by concern for economic exploitation.[39] Nor did the successors of Roosevelt prior to World War I vitally depart from the pursuance of this strategic, benevolent, imperialistic tutelage. As one competent authority has said, "What generally is referred to as the Caribbean policy of the United States more appropriately might be called the Panama policy."[40]

The nature and degree of support which Mahan gave these various manifestations of the "Panama Policy" cannot be fully determined. Allusion has been made to his *desire* for St. Thomas, his *eagerness* for and *approval* of Puerto Rico, and his *insistence* upon bases in Cuba. As for other naval positions in the Caribbean, Mahan had written favorably, prior to the war, of Samana Bay in Santo Domingo; in the report made by the Naval War Board, however, it received no mention, St. Thomas evidently having been given preference. Similarly, Môle St. Nicholas in Haiti, given only a passing comment in 1897, now received no mention. In fact, the report specifically cautioned against too many bases; except in the immediate neighborhood of the Isthmus, the positions in Cuba, Puerto Rico, and St. Thomas were deemed sufficient. Every naval station, "while affording facilities for naval operations, on the other hand imposes upon the fleet a burden of support and communica-

[39] H. C. Hill, *Roosevelt and the Caribbean*, 200. Cf. Nearing and Freeman, *op. cit.*, 264; J. W. Pratt, "The Collapse of American Imperialism," *American Mercury*, Vol. XXXI (March, 1934), 270.

[40] S. F. Bemis, *A Diplomatic History of the United States*, 519. See Carter, *op. cit.*, 95; Dennis, *op. cit.*, 309; Dudley Knox, *A History of the United States Navy*, 374–75; S. G. Inman, "The Significance of the Caribbean," in Wilgus (ed.), *The Caribbean Area*, 24.

tion. The just balance between too few and too many should therefore be carefully struck."[41]

In light of these facts and in view of Mahan's general naval policy, it would seem quite doubtful whether the desire for additional bases in Santo Domingo and Haiti was shared by him. On the other hand, with his unqualified opposition to encroachment by European powers in the Caribbean, there is no doubt that Mahan shared the anxiety lest financial difficulties in Venezuela and Santo Domingo lead to European control of outposts of the canal. Ultimately, from this angle he was glad to see, as the basis of American policy in the Caribbean, the displacement of "watchful vigilance" by the doctrine of "international police power" with its emphasis upon preventive action.[42] But not until confronted with an actual case in which the previous interpretation seemed potentially dangerous, did Mahan favor the extension of American responsibility which this enlarged version of the Monroe Doctrine necessitated. Writing in an English magazine shortly after the 1902 Venezuela episode had passed the crisis, he stated:

Not to invade the rights of an American state is to the United States an obligation with the force of law; to permit no European State to infringe them is a matter of policy; but as she will not acquiesce in any assault upon their independence or territorial integrity, so she will not countenance by her support any shirking of their international responsibility.

41 58 Cong., 3 sess., *Hearings before the House Committee on Naval Affairs*, 505.

42 In an address at Chicago in 1903, Roosevelt termed his attitude on the Venezuela crisis of the preceding year as "watchful vigilance." The interpretation of the Monroe Doctrine as one requiring the United States to play the role of "international police power," growing out of the Santo Domingo imbroglio, came in his annual message of December 6, 1904. The division of power and responsibility, inherent in the generally accepted view of the Monroe Doctrine, Roosevelt contended, was "incompatible with international equity."

SOMETHING IN THE SMOKE.

Cartoon from Detroit *News-Tribune,* reprinted in the *American Monthly Review of Reviews,* spring, 1903.

THE NEWS REACHES BOGOTA.—From the *Herald* (New York).

Cartoon from the New York *Herald,* reprinted in the *American Monthly Review of Reviews,* December, 1903.

JOHN BULL: "I quit; you dig."

Cartoon from Philadelphia *North American*, reprinted in the
American Monthly Review of Reviews, November, 1902.

Yet he was not ready to involve the United States further, for he added:

Neither will she undertake to compel them to observe their international obligations to others than herself. To do so, which has been by some argued a necessary corollary of the Monroe Doctrine, would encroach on the very independence which that political dogma defends.[43]

During the Santo Domingo affair Mahan altered his views; despite his previous unmistakable statement to the contrary, he now favored the incorporation of the "international police power" idea. Unmindful of the obvious contradiction with his earlier utterances, he stated that this "species of development" was inherent from the beginning —"evident, logical, and irresistible." Conditions which tended toward European intervention, justifiable morally and internationally, "must by American nations be remedied; if not by the state responsible, then by others."[44] It should be pointed out that this did not necessarily mean unilateral action by the United States as became the prevailing policy for the next quarter of a century.

This change in interpretation was welcomed by Mahan not only because of its safeguarding feature, but also because it gave indication that the Monroe Doctrine was a vital principle, a living and growing policy. This aspect of vitality accorded with previously expressed views on the matter.[45] Almost immediately after the Treaty of Paris, which definitely strengthened the position of the United States in the Caribbean and gave her possessions in the far-

[43] Mahan, "The Monroe Doctrine," *National Review*, February, 1903, reprinted in *Naval Administration and Warfare*, 395–96.

[44] Mahan, *Naval Administration and Warfare*, 406, 409. This is from a subscript to "The Monroe Doctrine" essay and written at the time of its reprint in book form (1908).

[45] Mahan, "The Monroe Doctrine," *National Review*, February, 1903, reprinted in *Naval Administration and Warfare*, 407–409.

ther Pacific, Mahan had advocated a re-examination of the Monroe Doctrine. During a lifetime of several generations this serviceable, working theory had acquired the added force of tradition, which tended to invest an accepted policy with the attribute of permanency. He wrote:

> The principles upon which an idea rests may conform to essential, and therefore permanent, truth; but application continually varies, and maxims, rules, doctrines, not being the living breath of principles, but only their embodiment—the temporary application of them to conditions not necessarily permanent—can claim no exemption from the ebb and flow of mundane things. We should not make of even this revered doctrine a fetich, nor persuade ourselves that a modification is under no circumstances admissible.[46]

Now in 1900, as a decade earlier when he had been strongly urging the United States to take the "outward view," Mahan was suggesting that time might make "the ancient good uncouth."

He early sensed that whatever our outward adherence to the Doctrine might be, we would have to readjust our views about "our apartness" from European complications. Thought he:

It is not, indeed, likely . . . that we should find reason for intervention in a dispute localized in Europe; but it is nevertheless most probable that we can never again see with indifference, and with the sense of security which characterized our past, a substantial, and still less a radical, change in the balance of power there. . . . From this follows the obvious necessity of appreciating the relations to ourselves of the power inherent in the various countries, due to their available strength and to their position; what also their attitude toward us resultant from the temper of the people, and the intelligent control of the latter

46 Mahan, "The Problem of Asia." *Harper's Monthly*, March, 1900, reprinted in *The Problem of Asia*, 16–17.

by the government—two very different things, even in democratic communities.[47]

He likewise sensed the shift of world interest to the Pacific. In light of the changed conditions in Europe and the Far East, he thought a partial retrenchment of responsibility under the Monroe Doctrine ought to follow. He advocated a very considerable delimitation, yet under no circumstances should the Caribbean Sea be neglected. In this region were the outworks of the Central American Isthmus; here, more than ever before,

all indications of political change affecting it even remotely must be sedulously watched; but on the American continent, south of points where influence can be effectually exerted upon the isthmus, the Monroe Doctrine loses much of its primacy. ... and for American communities beyond that range [Amazon] our professed political concern is to us a waste of strength, as it is to them distasteful.[48]

A withdrawal such as this of a pledge of political and military protection to "states that bear us no love," Mahan argued, would not only strengthen our position in the Caribbean but would also leave us at much greater liberty to engage in the rich, large and imminent opportunities opening in Asia.

In this idea of retrenchment of responsibility under the Monroe Doctrine via the limitation of area, Mahan met with no success; even Lodge and presumably Roosevelt, his close political and personal friends, did not follow him.[49] In the larger and more important matter of the construc-

47 Ibid., 17–18. Cf. Mahan, The Interest of America in International Conditions, 81, 118, 149–51, 163–64, 178–79.

48 Mahan, "The Problem of Asia," Harper's Monthly, April, 1900, reprinted in The Problem of Asia, 85–86; Mahan, "Effect of Asiatic Conditions upon World Policies," North American Review, November, 1900, reprinted in ibid., 202.

49 Lodge, op. cit., I, 487 (Lodge to Roosevelt, March 30, 1901).

tion, purpose, and utilization of a canal, there was no vital disagreement between these men of action and their intellectual mentor. The wave of sentiment, which had been rising in the years prior to the war, for an American-dug, American-owned, and American-controlled canal became an irresistible flood which coursed onward through the labyrinth of diplomacy, through the maze of dissension and intrigue over the choice of routes, and did not subside until it had violated the sovereignty of one nation and destroyed much of the good will which another nation had heretofore enjoyed among its neighbors in the Western Hemisphere.

The embarrassments to American naval strategy and defense resulting from the possession of coast lines so remote from one another brought forcibly home by the voyage of the *Oregon* of fourteen thousand miles from San Francisco around South America to the Atlantic coast of the United States, the growth of trade with China and western South America, the new acquisitions in the Pacific, and the advance into the Caribbean—all of these called for an early building of an interoceanic canal. As editor Shaw, an ardent advocate of the "large policy," wrote shortly after the war:

Perhaps we were rash in buying the wagon, and perhaps we ought not to have bought the horse; but having made these investments for better or for worse, let us not now hesitate about buying a set of harness. The way to justify expansion is to make the most effective possible use of what we have acquired. . . . Viewed from the material standpoint (commercial) and tested as a business proposition (by doubling the efficiency of the navy), the Nicaragua Canal is as necessary to the completion of our new territorial, commercial, and strategical policies as the harness is necessary to the utilization of the horse and wagon.[50]

Diplomatic negotiations relative to the canal fell largely

[50] *Review of Reviews,* Vol. XXI (February, 1900), 134.

to Secretary Hay, who had behind him an uncompromising Senate, an aroused nationalism, and better than ordinary good luck in the conjunction of events beyond his control.[51] The first treaty, delayed by the Alaskan boundary difficulty, was not submitted to the Senate until February, 1900. It contained the principle of neutralization which denied the right of the United States to fortify a canal; it also called for the adherence of other states to the treaty subsequent to its ratification by the United States and Great Britain.[52] A storm of criticism immediately greeted both these features. At Albany, Roosevelt publicly and privately declared his opposition to the treaty. In a personal letter to Hay, he told him that the failure to permit fortification by the United States strengthened against us "every nation" whose fleet was "larger than ours," and that the acceptance of any provision inviting a joint guarantee was a contravention of the Monroe Doctrine.[53]

The reaction toward this treaty was so unfavorable that Secretary Hay sought to resign. His annoyance and disgust took the form of petulant and witty comments to his friends. "When I sent in the Canal Convention," he wrote, "I felt sure that no one out of a mad house could fail to see that the advantages were all on our side. But I underrated the power of ignorance and spite, acting upon cowardice." And again, "It is as if you should offer Yale College a million dollars and the trustees should refuse the gift on the ground that they wanted a million and a half."[54] Among the Hay letters there is a note of February 12, 1900, without salutation, which Professor Dennett thinks was written to New

51 Tyler Dennett, *John Hay*, 212.

52 *Papers Relating to the Foreign Relations of the United States, 1901*, 241–43.

53 Roosevelt to Hay, February 18, 1900, cited by W. R. Thayer, *Life and Letters of John Hay*, II, 339–40.

54 Hay to J. J. McCook, April 22, 1900, cited by Dennis, *op. cit.*, 168; Hay to Whitelaw Reid, February 7, 1900, cited by Thayer, *op. cit.*, II, 224.

York's "war governor" after his declaration of opposition and evoked in reply the explanatory letter previously cited. The note reads:

Et tu! Cannot you leave a few things to the President and the Senate who are charged with them by the constitution!

As to "sea power" and the Monroe Doctrine, we did not act without consulting the best living authorities on those subjects.

Do you really think the Clayton-Bulwer Treaty preferable to the one now before the Senate? There is no third, except dishonor. Elkins and Pettigrew say, "Dishonor be damned!" I hardly think you will.

Please do not answer this—but think about it awhile.[55]

Mahan surely merited inclusion among "the best living authorities" on sea power, but no evidence has been found to show that his views were sought. Consultation with Admiral Dewey, president of the General Board, who believed fortification of the canal would make the Isthmus a battleground in case of war and hence undesirable, may be considered as giving some validity to the Secretary's statement.[56] Mahan's reaction to the treaty cannot be positively stated. Roosevelt expressed his views to Mahan by letter, but there is no indication in this of the latter's view.[57] His previous outlook on the matter of the exclusion of European powers from the Caribbean and the Isthmus, his earlier attitude about the value of fortifications in relation to the fleet, and his subsequent definitely expressed views on these specific topics in relation to the canal lead one to think that Mahan did not give his approval to the treaty. Moreover, one may assume that if Mahan had been in favor, Hay and other friends of the convention would probably have sought his support.

55 Hay to [?], February 12, 1900, cited in *ibid.*, II, 225; see also Dennett, *John Hay*, 339.

56 63 Cong., 2 sess., *Senate Doc. 471*.

57 Roosevelt to Mahan, February 14, 1900, Roosevelt Papers.

Mahan's firm conviction of the closeness of English and American policies may have had something to do with his *absence* of *opposition*. In an article written in August, 1900, though not published until November, he noted that Great Britain had manifested a disposition to acquiesce in our naval predominance in the Caribbean. Mahan predicted that this disposition would increase since Great Britain's interests elsewhere were so great that she needed to unload herself of responsibilitiy in the Caribbean; and, too, there was a decided similarity between the major interests of the two powers which would consequently necessitate the same general line of policy. It was to Britain's interest that we remain strong, and since an essential element of our strength was in the Caribbean, we might prudently reckon upon the moral support of that country in any political clash with other nations there, unless we assumed a position morally indefensible.[58]

The Senate ratified the treaty only after three amendments, which so seriously altered it that the British refused to accept it.[59] The second Hay-Pauncefote Treaty, signed in November of 1901, and ratified the following February, met the objections which an assertive, sensitive nationalism had found in the first. The Clayton-Bulwer Treaty of 1850, which had called for a neutral and unfortified canal under international guarantee, was now expressly abrogated; and the United States was given exclusive control over any canal that might be constructed, with specific grant of the right to maintain military police adequate for its protection. British acquiescence to American demands in this canal treaty was one of many steps in British diplomacy away from the policy of "Splendid Isolation" which she had proudly pur-

[58] Mahan, "Effect of Asiatic Conditions upon World Policies," *North American Review*, November, 1900, reprinted in *The Problem of Asia*, 180–86.

[59] W. S. Holt, *Treaties Defeated by the Senate*, 184–94.

sued in the latter nineteenth century; the Hay-Pauncefote Treaty was not only a demonstration of British policy to cultivate American good will but also proof positive of British decision to surrender, for good or for worse, the Caribbean and western Atlantic to the United States.

The new canal treaty cleared the way for negotiations with an Isthmian country for an American-owned and American-controlled canal. The fight over routes ensued. Mahan did not take sides in the Nicaragua-Panama controversy; consequently, neither a consideration of the dissension over the choice of routes nor a discussion of the diplomatic negotiations concerning the acquisition of a right of way is within the purview of this study. In dealing with the strategic implications of the canal, he wrote in 1893, "Whether the canal of the Central Isthmus be eventually at Panama or at Nicaragua matters little to the question now in hand, although, in common with most Americans who have thought upon the subject, I believe it surely will be at the latter point." Four years later in his more careful analytical article, "The Strategic Features of the Gulf of Mexico and the Caribbean Sea," he discussed the positions of strength controlling each.[60] In personal correspondence, as late as 1902, Mahan called himself "a Nicaragua man," though adding that he was "without personal knowledge of the merits of the case."[61]

Mahan did not consider Roosevelt's handling of Panama "a chapter in dishonor." He complimented Hay upon his conduct of diplomatic matters relative to the canal. In reply to a letter from Mahan of November 20, 1904, Hay stated:

I am greatly obliged to you for your kind references to our

[60] Mahan, "Hawaii and Our Future Sea Power," *Forum*, March, 1893, reprinted in *The Interest of America in Sea Power, Present and Future*, 44; Mahan, "The Strategic Features of the Gulf of Mexico and the Caribbean Sea," *Harper's Monthly*, October, 1897, reprinted in *ibid.*, 293–94.

[61] Mahan to Admiral Bouverie Clark, February 8, 1902, Mahan Papers.

work in the State Department. I receive so many compliments which I know I do not deserve, from people who have no capacity for judging, that when I occasionally get a generous word of support from the highest possible authority, like yourself, I am extremely grateful for it, and begin to doubt my own distrust.[62]

In 1912 Mahan came to a defense of Roosevelt's policy toward Colombia. He did not consider it censurable from point of either natural law or natural equity. Man was not made for law; law should be viewed as an instrument or means and not as a principle or end. Yet he held that no advantage to the United States, Panama, or to general welfare would justify the 1903 action if it had been done in *certain contravention* of treaty rights. From his point of view this had not been the case; he maintained that the 1846 treaty—which granted American citizens open and free right of passage across the Isthmus, on condition that the United States guaranteed the perfect neutrality of the Isthmus and Colombia's rights of sovereignty and property in the Isthmus—was inapplicable to the 1903 uprising and consequently the right of forcible intervention remained.[63]

After the war with Spain, as before, Mahan consistently stressed the naval and strategical significance of the canal rather than its economic and commercial importance. He again spoke of the "community of interests and duty to the world's future, centering about China" as obligations which could be cared for only by a strong grip upon the canal— "the essential link" in our line of communications. To safeguard this line, and especially this link, the United States must have available for immediate action in the Caribbean

62 Hay to Mahan, November 23, 1904, *ibid.*

63 Mahan, "Was Panama 'A Chapter of Dishonor'?," *North American Review*, October, 1912, reprinted in *Armaments and Arbitration*, 218–50. This article was a reply to Dr. Leander Chamberlain, "A Chapter in National Dishonor," *North American Review*, Vol. CXCV (February, 1912), 145–74.

a fleet with power great enough "to make it evidently in-expedient, politically, for the greatest navy to contest our predominance" in that region.[64] With definite indebtedness to Mahan, W. V. Judson likewise called attention to the reciprocal influence existent between the navy and the canal supplemented by bases, the former being dependent upon the latter, yet the latter useless without the former.[65]

As the construction of the Panama Canal neared completion, it was necessary that Congress pass measures for its regulation and control. Mahan anticipated one vital phase of this problem; in several forceful articles he pleaded for adequate fortification of the canal by the United States.[66] Even prior to these magazine contributions, Mahan had been consulted by the joint army and navy board charged with planning land defenses of the canal.[67]

Mahan consistently opposed neutralization and urged adequate fortifications. He appealed to pride, tradition, and necessity. As the Canal Zone, except for specific limitations in Colon and Panama, was definitely American soil, he claimed the United States would be constituting over herself a kind of protectorate if she sought from foreign states a guarantee of the Zone's neutrality. An invitation to non-American states to assume American responsibility would also contravene the traditional American policy.

[64] Mahan, "Effect of Asiatic Conditions upon World Policies," *North American Review*, November, 1900, reprinted in *The Problem of Asia*, 181–84.

[65] W. V. Judson, "Strategic Value of Her West Indian Possessions to the United States," *Annals of the American Academy of Political and Social Science*, Vol. XIX (May, 1902), 383–91.

[66] Mahan, "Why Fortify the Panama Canal?," *North American Review*, March, 1911, reprinted in *Armaments and Arbitration*, 181–95; "The Panama Canal and Sea Power in the Pacific," *Century*, June, 1911, reprinted in *ibid.*, 155–80; "The Importance of the Command of the Sea," *Scientific American*, Vol. CV (December 9, 1911), 512. Additional strategical aspects were developed in "The Panama Canal and the Distribution of the Fleet," *North American Review*, Vol. CC (September, 1914), 406–17.

[67] Crozier, War Department, Office of the Chief of Ordnance, to Mahan, April 23, 1910, Mahan Papers.

THE MAN BEHIND THE EGG.—From the *Times* (New York).

Cartoon from the *New York Times*, reprinted in the *American Monthly Review of Reviews*, December, 1903.

JOHN BULL: "It's really most extraordinary what training will do. Why, only the other day I thought that man unable to support himself."
—*The Inquirer, Philadelphia.*

Cartoon from the New York *Herald*, reprinted in the *American Digest*, August, 1898.

Surely memory of the difficulties experienced under the co-partnership of the Clayton-Bulwer Treaty would suffice to prevent a similar but worse recurrence.[68]

Once it was granted that the United States intended to make use of the canal in time of war, Mahan left no doubt about the necessity of fortifications. Fortifications would limit the number of battleships needed. The strategist reasoned in these words:

> It is precisely in order that a constant guard of battleships may not be necessary that fortifications are requisite. Fortifications liberate a fleet for action, whenever elsewhere required; and by preserving the canal for use as a bridge between the two oceans, render unnecessary the maintenance of a big fleet in both.[69]

Moreover, a properly fortified canal would give a greater degree of success to an inferior navy in an attempt to defend the canal by permitting the navy to operate at the strategic point of Guantánamo rather than at the Isthmus. This thought, thrown in for argumentative purposes, was dangerous in its implications and was followed by words more in keeping with the concern of the author. "If the United States desires peace with security, it must have a navy second to none but that of Great Britain."

Fortifications would assure the use of the canal in wartime not only more cheaply than warships but also more certainly, as structures could not be moved in moments of real or panicky pressure. Too, if duly fortified, the canal not only would be a defensive provision, serving to liberate the offensive arm by permitting the American fleet to leave

[68] Mahan, "Why Fortify the Panama Canal?," *North American Review*, March, 1911, reprinted in *Armaments and Arbitration*, 181–82.

[69] Mahan, "The Panama Canal and Sea Power in the Pacific," *Century*, June, 1911, reprinted in *Armaments and Arbitration*, 157. Cf. Mahan, "Importance of the Command of the Sea," *Scientific American*, Vol. CV (December 9, 1911), 512.

for a measurable period of time unconcerned about the safety of this "most important link in the line of our communications," but also would enable the fleet to issue upon either ocean in effective order. Defenses should exist for the canal and not vice-versa, for its value was not its impregnability of position but "its usefulness to the Navy as the offensive defender of the whole national coast-line—Atlantic, Gulf, and Pacific."[70]

In the last major article which Mahan published, only three months prior to his death, he again discussed the relation of the canal to the navy. Once more the canal was spoken of as the "decisive link in a most important line of communications," giving advantage in fewer ships and in less time; yet now, as often before, a word of warning was added: "that the Canal may so serve, it must be fortified, and able to stand by itself without battleship help against attack. . . . In the matter of defense, regarded as a question of mere fighting, the fleet and Canal have no essential connection with each other."[71]

To the very last Mahan labored to make more certain the fulfillment of his first and foremost concern, predominance of the United States in the Caribbean Sea.

[70] Mahan, "Why Fortify the Panama Canal?," *North American Review,* March, 1911, reprinted in *Armaments and Arbitration,* 186–90; 193–95.

[71] Mahan, "The Panama Canal and the Distribution of the Fleet," *North American Review,* Vol. CC (September, 1914), 416–17.

VIII

HAWAII

WHEREAS Mahan's desire for dominance of the United States in the Caribbean was marked by a clear certainty of statement and by a high degree of fulfillment before his death, his solution for American interests in the Pacific was not characterized by a similar degree of conviction or success. The vastness of area involved, the multiplicity of interests at stake, the rapidity of change on the international horizon, the extent and suddenness of territorial involvements by the United States in the Far East prevented any single or easy solution. From Mahan's point of view the American objective in the Pacific was usually stated as one of influence and not of supremacy; his policy for the United States in that region may be said to have been one primarily of co-operation. Nevertheless, the possessions of the United States and the approaches to them demanded assured supremacy, and at times he maintained that our duties in the Pacific were of such a nature that in case of disputes "the presence of a naval force adequate to command" was essential. Varying aspects of his thought may be seen in the eager determination with which he sought Hawaii, in the dutiful and reluctant willingness with which he accepted the Philippines as a manifestation of providential design, and in his conviction of the righteousness and efficacy of insistence on the free exchange of thought and trade in the rich, lucrative, and politically unstable region on either side of the Yangtze.

Hawaii, or the Sandwich Islands, had long been an emporium successively for fur traders, sandalwood buyers, whalers, and transpacific navigators. As early as 1842 the United States had formally recognized the independence of Hawaii and had declared that because of "the volume of trade and its special interest in the islands, it would consider as an unfriendly act the attempt on the part of any European power to interfere with this independence."[1] Subsequently, not only was this position reaffirmed but endeavors were numerous to bring the islands more closely within the American orbit. Several American statesmen, from Marcy onward, planned annexation or sought reciprocity treaties. The growing importance of the Pacific coast, the increase in transpacific commerce, and the improvement of steam navigation tended to focus attention on the islands from point of commercial and naval strategy. The desirability of a naval base in Oahu was forcibly brought out in a report submitted in 1873 by General J. M. Schofield and Lieutenant Colonel B. S. Alexander.[2]

Eventually, in 1875, a reciprocity treaty was ratified which granted exclusive trading privileges to both nations and guaranteed the independence of the islands against any third party; nine years later another treaty renewed these privileges and granted the United States the right to Pearl Harbor as a naval base.[3] These treaties brought Hawaii within the American commercial system and definitely precluded intervention by other powers. American capital poured in, sugar production increased fivefold in a decade, and by 1890 virtually all of the twenty million dollars of exports went to the United States. The day of "Hawaii for Hawaiians" was swiftly drawing to a close. The native pop-

[1] W. R. Castle, "John W. Foster," in S. F. Bemis (ed.), *The American Secretaries of State and Their Diplomacy*, IX, 210.

[2] The Schofield-Alexander report may be conveniently found in the *American Historical Review*, XXX (1925), 561–65.

[3] *Papers Relating to the Foreign Relations of the United States, 1894*, Appendix II, 164–67.

ulation, declining rapidly throughout the century, was scarcely more than a fifth of what it had been sixty years earlier in 1830.

Economic and political factors combined in the early nineties to create a crisis which marked the death of the independent Hawaiian monarchy. Island prosperity was suddenly disrupted by the McKinley tariff of 1890. While this measure encouraged Cuban production by placing sugar on the free list and protected domestic output by a two-cent bounty, it had the effect of halving the price of Hawaiian sugar. Annexation offered the Hawaiian capitalists their best hope of economic security. The political situation was drastically altered by the death in 1891 of King Kalakaua, puppet of American settlers, and by the ascension of his sister, Liliuokalani, who shortly inaugurated a policy looking to the curtailment of American influence and the restoration of autocracy. A stable white government was essential for economic and political reasons; a counteroffensive was taken.

Knowledge of the peaceful revolution of January 17, 1893, of the connivance of the American minister, of the activities of the United States Marines, of the abdication of the Queen under protest, of her appeal to the President of the United States, and of the establishment of a Provisional Government, was brought to the United States on January 28 by the diplomatic commission of "white Hawaiians" —four Americans and one Englishman—sent by the new government to negotiate a treaty of annexation. This treaty was quickly arranged by Secretary Foster and signed on February 14; on the following day the Senate received the treaty with a report by the Secretary and a message from the President urging prompt and favorable action.[4]

In 1890 in his essay, "The United States Looking Outward," Mahan had alluded to the political instability of

4 *Ibid.*, 197–202.

175

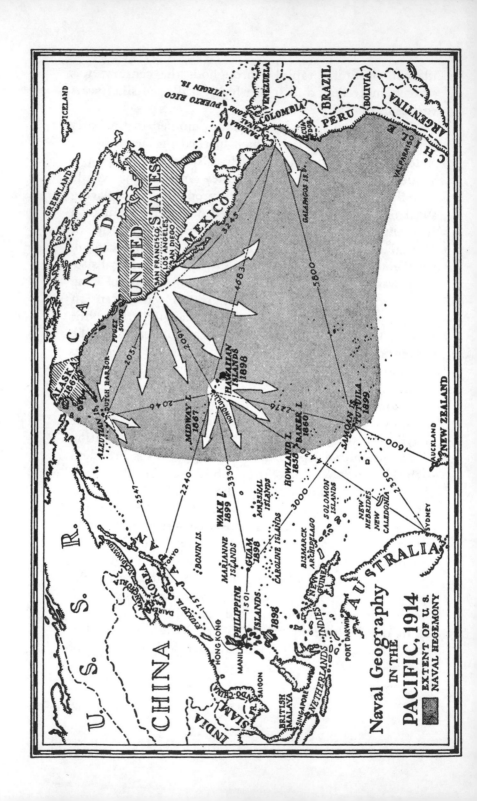

Naval Geography IN THE PACIFIC, 1914

■ EXTENT OF U.S.
NAVAL HEGEMONY

the Hawaiian Islands and to their military and commercial importance to the United States.[5] News of the revolution brought immediate public utterance from him. In a letter to the New York *Times,* appearing on January 31, he called attention to the relatively great number of Chinese living in Hawaii and to the consequent close relation of the islands to China as well as to American and European countries. This was a vital aspect of the Hawaiian problem which he thought others had neglected and one to which he frequently returned. Fear that the vast mass of now inert China might "yield to one of those impulses which have in past ages buried civilization under a wave of barbaric invasion," a movement which might break eastward across the Pacific as well as westward toward Europe, led Mahan to think that "it would be impossible to exaggerate the momentous issues dependent upon a firm hold of the Sandwich Islands by a great, civilized, maritime power." The United States with its nearness to the scene was naturally the proper guardian or custodian.[6]

At the request of Walter H. Page, editor of the *Forum,* who happened to read this letter, Mahan wrote for the March, 1893, issue of that magazine his most influential article. In this essay, "Hawaii and Our Future Sea Power," he discussed the general military or naval value of the islands in their control of the North Pacific, appraised the relative claims upon them, and placed their annexation as an incident in a larger whole. The central position of the Hawaiian Islands, the absence of alternatives for a wide area, and their singular location upon the more important trade routes of the Pacific gave them outstanding advan-

[5] Mahan, "The United States Looking Outward," *Atlantic Monthly,* December, 1890, reprinted in *The Interest of America in Sea Power, Present and Future,* 7–8, 26.

[6] Letter by Mahan to the New York *Times,* January 31, 1893, reprinted in *The Interest of America in Sea Power, Present and Future,* 31–32.

tages, whether viewed from point of commercial security or naval control. The defense of the whole Pacific coast and of the future Isthmian canal was vitally and intimately tied up with these islands. Mahan disposed of the rights of other nations to Hawaii (British Canada was specifically mentioned) on the ground that the United States, "by far the greatest, in numbers, interests, and power, of the communities bordering upon the North Pacific," would have and actually did have relations with Hawaii "more numerous and more important" than any other power could have.[7]

The need of the United States for the islands was indeed great; her claims upon them were pre-eminent; she could noway see them in the possession of another nation; the problem of annexation was at hand and the issue could not be dodged; now was the time for the decision, a decision "not unlike and not less momentous than that required of the Roman Senate, when the Mamertine garrison invited it to occupy Messina, and so to abandon the hitherto traditional policy which had confined the expansion of Rome to the Italian peninsula." It was in this wider setting that Mahan sought to place Hawaiian annexation; it was not so much a matter of a "particular action as a question of principle pregnant of great consequences in one direction or in the other." The real question was one of growth and development. Was the United States to recede or advance; was she to rest content with the phenomenal growth from the Atlantic colonies to a great continental power bordering on the Gulf and on the Pacific; or was she to heed the call and find across the sea those interests which would lead her to continued development, to still greater achievements?

7 Mahan, "Hawaii and Our Future Sea Power," *Forum*, March, 1893, reprinted in *The Interest of America in Sea Power, Present and Future*, 43–47. For British reaction see G. S. Clarke, "Captain Mahan's Counsels to the United States," *Nineteenth Century*, Vol. XLIII (February, 1898), 294–95, and P. H. Colomb, "The United States Navy under New Conditions of National Life," *North American Review*, Vol. CLXVII (October, 1898), 434–44.

For the sea-power expansionist the question was valid and the answer clear. The annexation of Hawaii was to be

but a first fruit[8] and a token that the nation in its evolution has aroused itself to the necessity of carrying its life . . . beyond the borders which heretofore have sufficed for its activities. . . . It is rarely that so important a factor in the attack or defense of a coast-line—of a sea frontier—is concentrated in a single position; and the circumstance renders doubly imperative upon us to secure it, if we righteously can. It is to be hoped . . . that the opportunity thus thrust upon us may not be viewed narrowly.[9]

However anxious for the "first fruit," Mahan did not leave his plea for expansion without a word of warning, a word designed to implement further the sea power of the United States. Too often did people speak as if a given island or harbor rendered control of a given body of water; this was "an utter, deplorable, ruinous mistake," he thought. He cautioned that "the confidence of our nation in its native strength, and its indifference to the defence of its ports and the sufficiency of its fleet, give reason to fear that the full consequences of a forward step may not be weighed soberly." Here, as in the case of the construction of the canal, Mahan did not wish to dampen but to temper and direct the spirit of aggressiveness.

Time was too short under the Harrison administration

8 There is no certainty that Mahan had seen the cartoon carried on the first page of the San Francisco *Call* of January 29, 1893, entitled "Uncle Sam Catches the Ripe Fruit." This pictured Uncle Sam seated under an apple tree, with Hawaii in the form of an apple dropping into his hat, while Canada, Mexico, Haiti, Cuba, and Samoa were still on the tree, evidently not ripe but ripening. Secretary Bayard, during Cleveland's first administration, had suggested that, "It was simply a matter of waiting until the apple should fall." Minister Stevens varied the fruit but kept the figure when he cabled his government on February 1, 1893, "The Hawaiian pear is now fully ripe, and this is the golden hour for the United States to pluck it."

9 Mahan, "Hawaii and Our Future Sea Power," *Forum*, March, 1893, reprinted in *The Interest of America in Sea Power, Present and Future*, 33–36, 48–49, 53.

for the consummation of the Foster treaty of annexation. Cleveland withdrew the treaty, sent Commissioner Blount to investigate, vainly sought to restore the deposed queen, and, dismissing the ethical questions that formerly had troubled him, eventually recognized the independence of the Hawaiian Republic which the revolutionists, despairing of immediate annexation, had set up. These various phases of the Hawaiian problem gave abundant opportunity for an expression of attitude relative to our foreign policy. Though often more specific about details, the views of the expansionist writers and speakers in the press and in Congress[10] were essentially those presented by Mahan: first, the primacy of American right to the islands; second, their urgent necessity to the United States from point of naval strategy in the defense of the Pacific coast and the future canal; third, their prime importance as giving commercial control over a region which seemed to offer the greatest promise for the future of American trade; and finally, their annexation was but a turning point in American policy, the initial manifestation that the "outward view" was being taken. In thus summarizing the voluminous expansionist material on this subject, I make no subtle pretense that it stemmed wholly from Mahan. It is certain, however, that he occupied a most important role in influencing the public opinion of the United States on the matter of American policy toward Hawaii. A contemporary writer in 1900 said that it was "upon Captain Mahan more than any other single person that the nation relied in its annexation of Hawaii." At a somewhat later date, Admiral Luce wrote:

The cogent arguments advanced by the eminent author showing the great advantages, from a strategic point of view, of the possession of those islands, served to crystallize current thought

10 For further development of these views, see Pratt, *Expansionists of 1898*, 146 ff.

of the past sixty years on the subject, and matters finally began to take definite shape.[11]

Indications are not wanting to show that Mahan had followers in Congress. "Hawaii and Our Future Sea Power" was incorporated in the report of the Senate Committee on Foreign Relations, to which had been given the task of "seeing what, if any, irregularities there had been relative to the Hawaiian revolution."[12] Quite early in the Hawaiian question, Senator Lodge emphasized the strategical importance of the islands viewed from both military and commercial aspects; he sought to reinforce his remarks with a little patriotic tail-twisting of the British lion by exhibiting a map of the world upon which were marked the naval stations of Great Britain, showing the relative naval strength of Great Britain and the United States in the Atlantic and the Pacific. "In the heart of the Pacific where I am now pointing, lie the Sandwich Islands. They are the key of the Pacific." The United States now had the opportunity to strengthen herself in that region against her old rival, said Lodge, and further expounded the Mahanian doctrine in these words:

Without sea power no nation has been really great. Sea power consists, in the first place of a proper navy and a proper fleet; but in order to sustain a navy we must have suitable posts for naval stations, strong places where a navy can be protected and refurnished.[13]

11 Wallace Rice, "Some Current Fallacies of Captain Mahan," *Dial*, Vol. XXVIII (March 16, 1900), 198–200; Stephen B. Luce, "Naval Strategy," United States Naval Institute *Proceedings*, XXXV (1909), III.

12 53 Cong., 2 sess., *Senate Report 227*, 113–20.

13 53 Cong., 3 sess., *Cong. Rec.*, 3082. See also Lodge in *ibid.*, 622, 1211. Lodge also presented his views on Hawaii, as well as on expansion in general, to a different and wider audience in "Our Blundering Foreign Policy," *Forum*, Vol. XIX (March, 1895), 8–17. Representative Draper (Massachusetts) was also a most ardent enthusiast for the extension of our sea frontier and for a strong navy. See 53 Cong., 2 sess., *Cong. Rec.*, 1844–49.

Expansion publicists outside of Congress also came to Mahan for ideas of support. The former minister of Hawaii, John L. Stevens, wrote:

It should not be forgotten that contiguity of water is sometimes more important than contiguity of land. It would be well if some of our public men would carefully study the remarkable work of Captain Mahan on "Sea Power." . . . To say that we do not need the Hawaiian Islands as a security to our immense future interests . . . is blindly and recklessly to ignore the logic of irresistible circumstances and to scoff at the plainest teachings of history.[14]

The *Review of Reviews*, by a careful résumé of the *Forum* essay on Hawaii, carried to a still wider audience the views of that article, which this magazine termed "a broad and comprehensive discussion" of our future sea power. Editor Shaw frequently urged Hawaiian annexation, usually linking it in the approved sea-power fashion with the canal, Caribbean bases, and a navy.[15]

The "first fruit," unplucked, had fallen to the ground, where it lay sedulously watched until it might be picked up after the hostility of the "little Americans," epitomized in Cleveland, was withdrawn. In the December interview with the President-elect in which Lodge urged Roosevelt's appointment to the Navy Department, he "first talked with him about Hawaii" and obtained McKinley's permission to have Mr. Cooper, the Hawaiian secretary of state, call on him in Canton.[16] The President's assurance to Schurz that there would be no "jingo nonsense" under his administration gave way, before the attacks of annexation lobbyists and "yellow perilists," to a "desire to test public opinion."

[14] J. L. Stevens, "A Plea for Annexation," *North American Review*, Vol. CLVII (December, 1893), 744–45. See also Lieutenant F. L. Winn, U. S. A., "Nicaragua Canal," *Overland Monthly*, Vol. XXXIII (May, 1894), 496.

[15] *Review of Reviews*, Vol. VII (1893), 325, 131–36; 731–36; *ibid.*, Vol. IX (1894), 515–18.

[16] Lodge, *Selections*, I, 240 (Lodge to Roosevelt, December 2, 1896).

UNCLE SAM CATCHES THE RIPE FRUIT.

Cartoon from San Francisco *Call*, January 29, 1893.

"LIL" TO "AGGY:" "Say, chile, if my fren' Grover wa
jus' President you'd hab a cinch."
From the *Journal* (Minneapolis).

DONE GONE EXPANDED
George Washington Dewey to
George Frisbie Hoar: "I cannot tell
a lie, gran'ther. I took them with my
little cruiser. We've already got
them. The question is, What are we
going to do with them? Don't think
you mentioned that." Cartoon from
Minneapolis *Journal,* reprinted in the
American Monthly Review of Reviews,
February, 1899.

Cartoon from Minneapolis *Journal,*
reprinted in the *American Monthly
Review of Reviews,* February, 1899.

THE WHITE (?) MAN'S
BURDEN
Cartoon from New York *Life,* re-
printed in the *American Monthly
Review of Reviews,* April, 1899.

McKinley submitted a new treaty of annexation to the Senate on June 16, 1897. This time the "peril" was Japan, who had just emerged from a victorious war with China and now felt that she was a power to be reckoned with in any Pacific question. The Hawaiian government in an attempt to curtail Oriental immigration had run into difficulty with Japan, and as the tension increased between the two governments, the United States became somewhat apprehensive lest Japan had ulterior designs on Hawaii. This fear seemed partially justified when the signing of the new Hawaiian annexation treaty brought a protest to the United States from the Island Empire—no objection had been made against the Foster treaty in 1893—on the ground that the consummation of such a project would disturb the international balance in the Pacific and would further jeopardize the treaty rights of Japanese subjects in Hawaii. Though a cordial settlement of the matter of immigration was shortly arranged and the protest withdrawn, Japan unwittingly had provided another incentive for action on the part of the United States.[17]

Keenly aware of the Japanese-Hawaiian dispute, Mahan sent his friend and admirer, the Assistant Secretary of the Navy, information relative to the Japanese naval program, urging that appropriate consideration be given it; for the immediate present, he advised the strengthening of the Pacific squadron and the appointment of a man of initiative and ability to be in charge. He was fearful that Roosevelt's chief would view the annexation of the Hawaiian Islands by the United States as a difficult political problem. "To this, in my mind," he wrote, "the only reply is: Do nothing unrighteous; but as regards the problem, take the islands

[17] T. A. Bailey gives a good account of this episode in "Japan's Protest Against the Annexation of Hawaii," *Journal of Modern History*, Vol. III (April, 1893), 46–61.

first and solve afterwards." Roosevelt replied in language which must have been pleasing to Mahan:

> As regards Hawaii I take your views absolutely, as indeed I do in foreign policy generally. If I had my way we would annex those islands tomorrow. . . . I believe we should build the Nicaragua Canal at once and . . . should build a dozen new battleships, half of them on the Pacific Coast. . . . I am fully alive to the danger from Japan. . . . I have been getting matters in shape on the Pacific Coast just as fast as I have been allowed. . . . My own belief is that we should act instantly before the two new Japanese warships leave England . . . and hoist our flag over the island, leaving all details for after action. I shall press these views upon my chief just so far as he will let me; more I cannot do. . . . I earnestly hope we can make the President look at things our way. Last Saturday night Lodge pressed his views upon him with all his strength.[18]

The sea-power advocate was impressed by Roosevelt's desire to act prior to the sailing of the Japanese warships from England. Mahan was fearful of immediate and serious trouble in the Pacific and was caustic in his criticism of the nonannexationists. In a recent lecture, he told Roosevelt, he had said, "The decision not to bring under the authority of one's own government some external position, when just occasion offers, may by future generations be bewailed in tears of blood." Recalling his letter published more than four years earlier in the New York *Times* in which he had stated that the question of the future of Hawaii was Mongolian rather than European, he now assailed the "crass blindness" of the Cleveland administration, to which was due the "very real present danger of war, easily foreseen then."[19]

Mahan did not rest content with these words of caution,

[18] Mahan to Roosevelt, May 1, 1897; Roosevelt to Mahan, May 3, 1897: Roosevelt Papers.
[19] Mahan to Roosevelt, May 6, 1897, *ibid.*

encouragement, and advice to Roosevelt. It was during May of 1897—contemporaneous with this correspondence and shortly after the inauguration of a government committed by its platform to a more aggressive foreign policy—that Mahan, coupling the increasing seriousness of the Japanese danger with the destructive Cuban insurrection entering its third year, wrote "A Twentieth-Century Outlook." This article developed in a much wider setting and at greater length the neglected aspect of the Hawaiian question which he had mentioned in his open letter in the New York *Times* of January 30, 1893. Looking forward into the twentieth century, Mahan foresaw a gigantic struggle between the East and the West. While the European armies, perhaps providentially intended for this noble mission, were holding safe the citadel of Christian civilization in Europe, the United States by her power on the sea should be ready to protect the western outposts of Euro-American culture.

This self-appointed task required by way of preparation the construction of a canal, the creation of a navy, and the acquisition of bases in the Caribbean and of outposts in the Pacific—among the latter, none comparable to Hawaii. The only safeguard against "the teeming multitudes of central and northern Asia," Mahan had written in 1894, was "the warlike spirit of the representatives of civilization. What'er betide, Sea Power will play in those days the leading part which it has in all history, and the United States by her position must be one of the frontiers from which, as from a base of operations, the Sea Power of the civilized world will energize."[20]

The McKinley treaty for annexation, submitted to the Senate the middle of June, was reported back from the

20 Mahan, "A Twentieth-Century Outlook," *Harper's Monthly*, September, 1897, reprinted in *The Interest of America in Sea Power, Present and Future*, 217–18; Mahan, "Possibilities of an Anglo-American Reunion," *North American Review*, November, 1894, reprinted in *ibid.*, 123–24.

Committee on Foreign Relations a month later but received no further attention before the adjournment of Congress. Early in the new session, Roosevelt informed Mahan that there was "serious danger of Congress not backing up the President" in the Hawaiian matter and told him that Senator Hoar was one of the doubtful members. Roosevelt urged Mahan to communicate with Hoar immediately about annexation, suggesting first a letter and then, "after consultation with Lodge and one or two others of the friends of Hawaii," a telegram. Mahan did as he was advised.[21] By January Roosevelt thought "the Hawaiian matter touch-and-go," with fair certainty of solid Republican support and some prospect of scattered Democratic assistance.[22] In this prediction he was mistaken, for not even the tireless efforts of the annexationists, aided by the Japanese menace, were able to win sufficient support from hesitant Democrats, anti-expansionist Republicans, and sugar-interested senators of both parties, to gain the necessary two-thirds vote.

While the treaty thus lagged, the President, resorting to the Texas precedent, urged annexation by joint resolution of Congress. The Committee on Foreign Relations forthwith (March 16, 1898) introduced into the Senate a joint resolution accompanied by a favorable report for annexation;[23] but here the measure languished because of lack of interest and preoccupation with more urgent matters in the Caribbean. In the House the procedure for joint action ran into the powerful opposition of Speaker Reed, who held out for three weeks before he permitted a rule for its consideration.[24] It was not until May 4, three days after Dewey's victory at Manila, that an annexation resolution was intro-

21 Roosevelt to Mahan, December 9, 1897; December 11, 1897; telegram of same date; December 13, 1897: Roosevelt Papers.

22 Roosevelt to Mahan, January 3, 1898, ibid.

23 55 Cong., 2 sess., Senate Report 681.

24 William A. Robinson, Thomas B. Reed, Parliamentarian, 366–67.

duced in the House, referred to the Committee on Foreign Affairs, and shortly (on May 17) given a majority endorsement by that committee.[25]

The reports of both the Senate and House committees played up the Japanese menace; in light of the rapidly increasing Japanese population in the islands, they maintained that any delay involved an unwarranted risk and would eventuate in the assimilation, domination, and incorporation of the islands by a foreign power. Mahan could no longer think, as he had in 1893, that the Mongolian aspect was neglected. In words echoing Mahan, the Senate committee said:

The present Hawaiian-Japanese controversy is the preliminary skirmish in the great coming struggle between the civilization of the awakening forces in the East and the civilization of the West. The issue is whether, in that inevitable struggle, Asia or America shall have the vantage ground of the control of the naval "Key of the Pacific," the commercial "Crossroads of the Pacific."[26]

In both these reports, the strategical significance of the islands was thoroughly discussed and received primary emphasis. The views of military and naval experts were given, and none so frequently as Mahan's. In these comparatively short reports, covering with appended material only a trifle over one hundred pages, Mahan was cited five times.[27] Lengthy excerpts from "Hawaii and Our Future Sea Power" were included, as was the exchange of letters between Mahan and Senator James H. Kyle of South Dakota. This senatorial friend of Hawaiian annexation, writing

25 55 Cong., 2 sess., *House Report 1355, Part I; Part II* includes the Democratic minority report.

26 55 Cong., 2 sess., *Senate Report 681,* 30–31; 55 Cong., 2 sess., *House Report 1355,* 30–31.

27 55 Cong., 2 sess., *Senate Report 681,* 39, 51, 53, 86–87, 98–99; 55 Cong., 2 sess., *House Report 1355,* same pages.

Mahan on February 3, 1898, first informed him that "many quotations" had been made from his "valuable and highly interesting contribution to literature in regard to these islands," and then proceeded to ask him four specific questions of a military nature relative to the Hawaiian Islands. He queried whether their possession would strengthen or weaken the United States from a military point of view, whether in case of war a larger navy would be required to defend the Pacific coast with or without the possession of Hawaii, whether it would be practicable for any transpacific country to attack our western coast without Hawaii as a base, and whether such an attack relying upon colliers and sea transference of coal would be feasible. It scarcely need be stated that Mahan's reply was phrased in terms favorable to annexation. This correspondence was utilized by Senator Teller in an executive session of the Senate and published in the New York *Journal* (February 10, 1898) before its reprint in the House and Senate reports.

In a separate memorandum on the Pacific and its defense, George Melville, chief engineer of the navy, also buttressed his case by reference to Mahan.[28]

The debates in both the Senate and the House brought repeated, almost continuous, references to the sea-power expansionist.[29] Congressmen from Kentucky to Oregon, from California to New York, called upon "the great naval expert and author," "the most distinguished writer and authority of our time on the history of sea power," "the greatest of our naval authorities," to testify that the Hawaiian Islands were essential to the United States on the ground of naval strategy. The *Forum* article and the Kyle-Mahan correspondence served as the arsenal for the annexa-

---

28 55 Cong., 2 sess., *Senate Doc. 188.*

29 55 Cong., 2 sess., *Cong Rec.,* 2868, 2872, 2896, 5771, 5834, 5835, 5846–47, 5876–77, 5895, 5905, 5908, 5916, 5918, 5927–28, 5931, 6003, 6191; and also in Appendix, 499, 531, 583, 649, 659.

tionists with verbatim extracts frequent. A revealing comment was made by Representative Dolliver of Iowa, "There is one thing about Captain Mahan's reasoning that I like, and that is that, notwithstanding my meagre technical knowledge, I can understand this man."[30] It is indicative of the weight Mahan carried that the opponents of annexation who alluded to the strategical argument for expansion almost invariably singled out the sea-power publicist as its primary advocate and author.[31]

As in 1893, advocates of expansion outside the halls of Congress went to Mahan as a high witness who was not "smitten with the microbe of incompetence" nor "sordidly seeking his own selfish aggrandizement." On what grounds, indeed, could the opposition rest their case when one of "the most distinguished living experts" generally "acknowledged in all countries as the highest authority in such matters" was "strenuously, ardently, advocating annexation?" These publicists urged that the nation should no longer wait for Democrats who were motivated by fealty for Cleveland or for Republicans who clung to outworn traditions.[32]

The added impetus necessary to shove the joint resolution of annexation through Congress was furnished by the Spanish-American War, especially by Dewey's gift of Manila.[33] The resolution was passed by the House on June 15

30 55 Cong., 2 sess., *Cong. Rec.*, 6003.

31 *Ibid.*, 5897; also Appendix, 570, 603, 618.

32 Extracts from address by L. A. Thurston before Hamilton Club of Chicago, January 11, 1898, cited by Mr. Mann (Illinois) in 55 Cong., 2 sess., *Cong. Rec.*, 5846–47; excerpts from report of the Republican Club of New York, quoted by Mr. Grosvenor (Ohio) in *ibid.*, 5876; *Public Opinion*, Vol. XXIV (June 9, 1898), 707; see also John Proctor, "Hawaii and the Changing Front of the World," *Forum*, Vol. XXIV (September, 1897), 34–35; John W. Foster, "The Annexation of Hawaii," in address before the National Geographic Society (1897).

33 Thomas A. Bailey, "The United States and Hawaii during the Spanish-American War," *American Historical Review*, Vol. XXXVI (April, 1931), 560.

(209 to 91), by the Senate on July 7 (42 to 21),[34] and signed by the President the following day. On August 12 the islands were formally transferred to the United States.[35] This naval position of the Pacific which Mahan saw standing alone, "having no rival, and admitting of no rival," had been secured; the "first fruit" had been gathered.

[34] 55 Cong., 2 sess., *Cong. Rec.*, 6019, 6712.

[35] On the matter of subsequent fortification of Pearl Harbor, Mahan again was called to testify to the commanding importance of the "Key to the Pacific." 60 Cong., 1 sess., *Hearings before the House Committee on Naval Affairs*, 496; and in that committee's report to the House in 60 Cong., 1 sess., *House Report 1132*.

IX

THE PHILIPPINES

THE "FIRST FRUIT" once tasted was as wine to the expansionists already growing giddy with visions of world power. Prior to the war with Spain there had been no demand for the Philippine archipelago; in fact, relatively few Americans knew of the existence of these Spanish-controlled islands on the other side of the world, or at least of their exact location. President McKinley, after Dewey's victory, had to look them up on a map; "I could not have told," Kohlsaat remembered his saying, "where those darned islands were within 2,000 miles!"[1] Fewer knew that the Filipinos had been in incipient or open revolution for more than a decade; to be sure, some word of the conditions reached Americans through magazines such as the *Literary Digest,* but rarely in articles such as "The Cuba of the Far East" in the *North American Review.*[2] Still fewer Americans were aware of the plans being made by Commodore George Dewey, commander of the Far Eastern Squadron, yet the United States consul in the Philippines for some time had been sending data to Dewey at Hong Kong relative to general conditions in Luzon as well as to the nature and extent of defenses at Manila.[3] Very few, indeed, were those who knew of the orders, issued by

---

1 H. H. Kohlsaat, *From McKinley to Harding,* 68.

2 *Literary Digest,* Vol. XIV (1896), 22, 342, 407, 681, 743; Vol. XV (1897), 759; John Barrett, "The Cuba of the Far East," *North American Review,* Vol. CLXIV (February, 1897), 173–80.

3 55 Cong., 3 sess., *Senate Doc. 62,* 320 ff.

"the bull in the China shop," which Dewey had received
ten days after the destruction of the U. S. S. *Maine;* nor has
evidence yet been disclosed to prove that even these directing few had more in mind than an effective means of waging
war by a bold stroke against the menace of the Spanish fleet
in the Pacific.[4] Though most of the advocates of the "large
policy" and the "outward view" held the belief that the Pacific Ocean was to be "the theatre of the great events of the
coming century" and though they were cognizant of "the
beginning of momentous issues in China and Japan," their
"vision reached not past Hawaii, which also, as touching the
United States, they regarded from point of view of defence"
rather than as the singularly important means to "any farther influence in the world."[5]

Dewey's victory on the first of May brought the Philippines to the fore, fired the Fourth of July spirit, and fanned
the flame of imperialist sentiment. It was not long before
the press, at first•only speculative, became fascinated by the
sudden intrusion of American dominion over the Philippines. A *Literary Digest* poll covering nearly two hundred
newspaper editors revealed the growing sentiment toward
acquisition.[6] The great preponderance of vocal religious
sentiment in the summer and fall of 1898 likewise favored
American possession. Business leaders who had been hostile
to war with Spain now saw the Philippines as a gateway to
the markets of eastern Asia, just recently and seriously jeop-

4 *Supra,* Chapter VI, 125–26; see also Pratt, *Expansionists of 1898,* 222 n.;
L. M. Hacker, "The Holy War of 1898," *American Mercury,* Vol. XXXI
(November, 1930), 320; Pringle, *Theodore Roosevelt,* 178; Tyler Dennett,
Americans in Eastern Asia, 616; Bishop, *Theodore Roosevelt and His Times,*
I, 83; Lodge, *Selections,* I, 278.

5 Mahan, "The Problem of Asia," *Harper's Monthly,* March, 1900, reprinted in *The Problem of Asia,* 7. See also editorial in *Review of Reviews,*
Vol. XVII (February, 1898), 143; and Commodore G. W. Melville, "Our Future on the Pacific—What We Have There to Hold and Win," *North American Review,* Vol. CLXVI (March, 1898), 281–96.

6 *Literary Digest,* Vol. XVII (September 10, 1898), 307–308.

ardized by the threatened partition of China as signalized by the advent of various European leases.[7]

As to the disposition of Dewey's gift, complicated by the sending of an army to invest Manila, McKinley, as usual, followed rather than directed public opinion. Sometime during May, he and his advisers became convinced that at least Manila would be desirable as a commercial and naval base.[8] As late as June 3 the President personally was expecting to permit Spain to keep the Philippines except "a port and necessary appurtenances." By the middle of June he was less certain and thought that the future status of the islands could not then be determined.[9] The postponement of the ultimate "control, disposition, and government of the Philippines" to the treaty of peace, as provided for in the peace stipulations of July 30 and approved in the protocol signed on August 12, was a manifestation of the President's continued indecision, and was due partly to a difference of opinion among the President's advisers.[10]

A month later, when instructions were given the peace commissioners, there still was no certainty or unanimity; the call of humanity and duty and the dictates of commercial opportunity demanded that "the United States accept no less than the cession of the full right and sovereignty of the island of Luzon." Finally, on October 26, the Secretary of State cabled the commissioners that information which the President had received since their departure had convinced him that it would be a political and commercial mistake to divide the islands, and that they should therefore demand the whole archipelago.[11] The President's additional

7 Pratt, op. cit., 273, 314; Dennett, Americans in Eastern Asia, 603–505.

8 Ibid., 627.

9 Day to Hay, June 3, 1898, Hay Papers; Day to Hay, June 14, 1898, cited by Dennett, John Hay, 190–91.

10 C. S. Olcott, The Life of William McKinley, II, 61–63.

11 56 Cong., 2 sess., Senate Doc. 148. 7–8, 35.

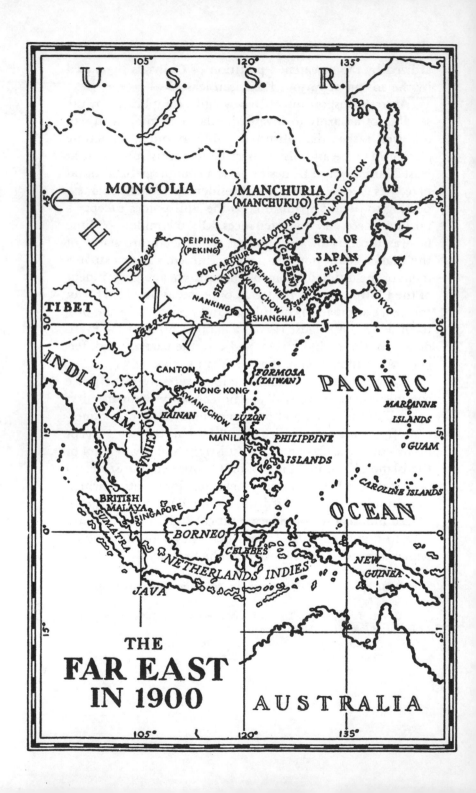

THE
FAR EAST
IN 1900

information, in part, "would appear to have been gathered from reports of American military and naval authorities and from diplomatic correspondence from the various foreign capitals in both the East and the West."[12] Without doubt European and Asiatic interest in the islands was great and exercised a very considerable influence in the formation of American policy; however, it should not be overlooked that American sentiment was strongly expansionist. Some scholars believe that McKinley's western trip, which he completed just prior to the demand for the whole archipelago, was quite significant, convincing him that the West was in favor of such a course.[13]

The President's own well-known explanation of how the decision came to him through a religious experience, though causing interesting speculation about the validity of his interpretation of the source of the answer, clearly depicted the possible alternatives with their pros and cons. Democratic and Republican counsels had helped but little, he told a missionary committee of the Methodist Episcopa' church, so he turned to Almighty God and prayed

for light and guidance more than one night. And one night late, it came to me this way—I don't know how it was, but it came: (1) That we could not give them back to Spain—that would be cowardly and dishonorable; (2) that we could not turn them over to France or Germany—our commercial rivals in the Orient—that would be bad business and discreditable; (3) that we could not leave them to themselves—they were unfit for self-government—and they would soon have anarchy and misrule over there worse than Spain's was; and (4) that there was nothing left for us to do but to take them, and by God's grace do the very best we could by them, as our fellowmen for

[12] Dennett, *Americans in Eastern Asia*, 623; James K. Eyre, Jr., "Russia and the American Acquisition of the Philippines," *Mississippi Valley Historical Review*, Vol. XXVIII (March, 1942), 539–62.

[13] Dunn, *From Harrison to Harding*, II, 279; L. W. Busbey, *Uncle Joe Cannon*, 194.

whom Christ also died. And then I went to bed, and to sleep and slept soundly.[14]

There was a sharp division of opinion in the Senate and in the country at large concerning the wisdom of the annexation of the Philippines as provided in the Treaty of Paris. Though feeling ran high, wit and satire often found their way into the discussions. Secretary Hay professed to be unable to understand the attitude of the anti-imperialists who wished the United States to give the Philippines to some other nation; this point of view seemed to him much like that of the old maid who, having come to the belief that " 'her jewels were dragging her down to Hell, . . . immediately gave them to her sister,' "[15] Senator Mason of Illinois begged his fellow legislators:

Will you tell me, please, how grand larceny and criminal aggression [expressions used by McKinley previous to the war in respect to American annexation of Cuba] becomes high Christian civilization in the Philippines? Is there some place in the Pacific Ocean where we change the code of ethics and good morals as we change the calendar and the ship's clock in crossing?[16]

The Anti-Imperialist League, with Hoar, Carnegie, Schurz, Storey, and others, was organized and offered concerted opposition.[17] On the grounds of legality, morality, and general expediency, this group argued that territorial expansion in the Far East, resulting in inevitable involvement in world affairs and in dominion over alien peoples whose consent had not been gained, was at once unwise and

[14] *Christian Advocate*, January 22, 1903, cited by Olcott, *op. cit.*, II, 110–11.

[15] J. B. Bishop, *Notes and Anecdotes of Many Years*, 64–65.

[16] 55 Cong., 3 sess., *Cong. Rec.*, 531.

[17] F. H. Harrington, "The Anti-Imperialist Movement in the United States, 1898–1900," *Mississippi Valley Historical Review*, Vol. XXII (September, 1935), 211–30.

un-American. The imperialists called upon duty, humanity, morality, and trade as reasons for annexation. The presence of some 15,000 American soldiers and the existence of the formidable Aquinaldo insurrection were motives of a peculiarly patriotic sort which influenced some votes for forthright ownership.

Oddly enough, it was an anti-imperialist who probably saved the treaty from defeat. Convinced that free silver was dead and that the battle over imperialism was the one chance for Democratic success in 1900, William Jennings Bryan brought pressure on wavering Democrats and Populists to accept the treaty with the expectation that Philippine independence would be the election issue.[18] Ten Democrats and eight Populists voted with thirty-nine Republicans on February 6, 1899, to give the treaty one more than the two-thirds majority required for ratification.[19]

What was Mahan's attitude and role in the American acquisition of the Philippines? No categorical answer can be given, but from such evidence as is available it seems safe to conclude that the sea-power expositor was more a follower than a leader—that at first he viewed with doubt the acceptance of even Luzon when considered from a strictly selfish basis, but that at last he hesitatingly rose to the defense of the policy pursued.

Extant correspondence, some undated, indicates that Mahan was a frequent guest at the Lodge home during his stay in Washington while serving on the Naval War Board. In one letter he expressed appreciation of "the privilege of calling in the evenings"; in another he extended thanks for "the kind attention" shown him while in town. Lodge replied, "You conferred very great pleasure on Mrs. Lodge

[18] Hoar, *Autobiography of Seventy Years*, II, 322–23. Cf. Paxton Hibben, *The Peerless Leader: William Jennings Bryan*, 220–22; M. E. Curti, *Bryan and World Peace*, 129–32.

[19] 55 Cong., *Journal of the Executive Proceedings of the Senate*, 1284; Holt, *Treaties Defeated by the Senate*, 169.

and myself by coming to our house during those hot and anxious days."[20] Secretary Day, as well as Mahan, dined with the Lodges on one occasion; the host subsequently informed Roosevelt: "Mahan and I talked the Philippines with him for two hours. He said that he thought we could not escape our destiny there."[21] It would be interesting and informative to know the nature of this conversation. Either Secretary Day's interpretation of "our destiny there" was quite different from the probable Lodge-Roosevelt view, or his conversion was of short duration. The Secretary's draft of a reply some days later to the Spanish note for peace terms called only for a port as a naval base; furthermore, at the time of his appointment as one of the peace commissioners, he even had some doubts about a coaling station, and to the very last he definitely opposed more than Luzon and one or two other islands.[22]

The part which Mahan took in the conversation is problematical, for it is unlikely that he himself was within the imperialist fold at this time, if the faith of the true convert called for more than the occupation of Luzon. Over a month later he wrote Lodge relative to suggestions for peace and alluded to the President as one "more disposed to follow public opinion than to lead, or even guide, it." He continued:

Public opinion I assume will insist that Spain quit America forever. But feeling as to the Philippines is much more doubtful. *I myself, though rather an expansionist, have not fully adjusted myself to the idea of taking them, from our own standpoint of advantage.* It does seem to me, however, that the heavy force, army and navy, we have put in Luzon, has encouraged

20 Mahan to Mrs. Lodge, June 23 [1898?]; Mahan to Lodge, July 12, 1898; Lodge to Mahan, July 23, 1898: Lodge Papers.

21 Lodge, *op. cit.*, I, 313 (June 24, 1898). See also Mahan to L. J. Maxse, August 17, 1898, Mahan Papers.

22 Olcott, *op. cit.*, II, 61; Cortissoz, *The Life of Whitelaw Reid*, II, 247–48; 56 Cong., 2 sess., *Senate Doc. 148*, 33–35.

the revolutionists to an extent for which we are responsible. Can we ignore the responsibility and give them back to Spain? I think not. Spain cannot observe a pledge to govern justly, because she neither knows what good government is, nor could she practice it if she knew. As to an agreement with other Powers, I hope no entangling alliances for us. But we have done nothing in the other islands of the group. Might it not be a wise compromise to take only the Ladrones and Luzon; yielding to the "honor" and exigencies of Spain the Carolines and the rest of the Philippines.[23]

In reply Lodge cautiously omitted his own probably larger view. The Philippines, he admitted, were a difficult question and much would depend upon the character of the peace commission. The President was inclined, he thought, to hold Manila in any event and likely Luzon, but was doubtful about more.[24] Just what Lodge's "large policy" for the Far East was is not certain; it can be assumed that ultimately it was not quite so large as at first. Only three days after Dewey's victory at Manila, he wrote Henry White that the Philippines were now ours and were of inestimable value to the country; "they must be ours under the treaty of peace."[25]

By August his zeal had slackened. Three days after the rather noncommittal letter to Mahan, Lodge urged upon Secretary Day the acquisition of all the Ladrones, and seeing "very plainly the enormous difficulties of dealing with the Philippines," he stated that he was "by no means anxious to assume the burden of possession outside of Luzon." He added that consideration would have to be given to public sentiment and he believed there was "a strong reluctance" on the part of the people to return the Philippines to Spain. The "only practical solution" as he saw it was "that we

23 Mahan to Lodge, July 27, 1898, Lodge Papers. The italics are mine.
24 Lodge to Mahan, August 8, 1898, ibid.
25 Nevins, Henry White, 146.

should take the whole group as an indemnity for the war, and then cede all the islands except Luzon to England in exchange for the Bahamas, and Jamaica and the Danish Islands, which I think we should be entitled to ask her to buy and turn over to us." Almost contemporaneously he wrote Roosevelt that the administration seemed a little hesitant about the Philippines, but added that he hoped they would at least keep Manila, "which is the great prize, and the thing which will give us the Eastern trade."[26]

So far as is known, Mahan was not called upon for his opinion nor did he seek to impress his views of limited acquisition upon others than Lodge. He did give some support to the administration in its endeavor to secure approval of its policy. In the documents accompanying the treaty of peace, he permitted the publication of a personal letter from his English friend, Colonel George Sydenham Clarke. This "earnest well-wisher" of the United States, cognizant of the gravity of the decision for Great Britain as well as for America, urged Mahan to call the President's attention to the British success in the Malay States—a close parallel, he thought, to the Philippines. Lord Sydenham expressed appreciation of the hesitancy of the Americans to assume responsibility for the future of the alien Filipinos, but added that the only alternative to American ownership was "anarchy first, with considerable annexation following." He suggested, "Have your naval stations and try this political experiment. The results will surprise you, and they will be beneficial to the world."[27]

Mahan's only magazine contribution, prior to the ratification of the treaty, which bore in the least on the Philippine question appeared in the *Engineering Magazine* (January, 1899) under the title "The Relations of the United

26 Lodge to Day, August 11, 1898, Lodge Papers; Lodge, *op. cit.*, I, 337 (August 15, 1898).
27 55 Cong.; 3 sess., *Senate Doc. 62, Part III*, 631–32.

States to Their New Dependencies." In this short article, probably written after the terms of the treaty were rather definitely fixed, no mention was made of particular possessions. Nevertheless it is obvious that the Philippines were in mind, though not necessarily more than Luzon, as he wrote:

> Enlightened self-interest demands us to recognize not merely, and in general, the imminence of the great question of the farther East, which is rising so rapidly before us, but also, specifically the importance to us of a strong and beneficent occupation of adjacent territory. . . . Sea power, as a national interest, commercial and military, rests not upon fleets only but also upon local territorial bases in distant commercial regions. It rests upon them most securely when they are extensive, and when they have a numerous population bound to the sovereign country by those ties of interest which rest upon the beneficence of the ruler.[28]

Upon ratification of the treaty, Mahan sent Lodge a note congratulating him upon his able efforts.[29] He now expressed himself more explicitly in regard to the Philippines. To Long he stated his vehement opposition to the withdrawal of troops or even any suspension of hostilities during the insurrection.[30] In a magazine article he definitely asserted the superiority, from a naval point of view, of the treaty provisions which gave considerable supporting territory in comparison with a mere navy yard as some individuals had preferred.[31] Again there is no assurance but that Luzon alone would have met this requirement.

Mahan viewed the islands both from the angle of self-

28 Mahan, "The Relations of the United States to Their New Dependencies," *Engineering Magazine*, January, 1899, reprinted in *Lessons of the War with Spain and Other Articles*, 245–46, 249.
29 Mahan to Lodge, February 7, 1899, Lodge Papers.
30 Mahan to Long, June 7, 1899, Long Papers.
31 Mahan, "Conditions Determining the Naval Expansion of the United States," *Leslie's Weekly*, October 2, 1902, reprinted in *Retrospect and Prospect*, 44–45.

interest and responsibility, but the former was subjugated to the latter. He wrote:

The great question before us is one of responsibility and duty. We have received a charge; something has to be done with it. . . . The task is troublesome, the issue perhaps doubtful; but the charge of a great opportunity having been committed to us, are we by our action to say, practically to Him who gave it, "Lord, I know thee, thou art an austere man; so I have buried thy talent in the earth. Lo! there thou hast that is thine!"[32]

This concept of the Philippines as a charge Mahan held throughout his life; from point of innate value he asserted in 1911 they might be missed by the United States no more than a "joint of a little finger."[33]

Though Mahan deprecated giving self-interest precedence over beneficence, whether by advocates or by opponents of expansion, he did not ignore self-interest. He shared with his contemporaries the belief that the future lay in the Pacific Ocean. In accordance with the sea-power doctrine, Mahan viewed all the acquisitions at the close of the century from both a naval and commercial angle. Serving as bases, these new possessions lessened the burden of purely naval increase, "for by tenure of them and due development of their resources," the navy received "an accession of strength, augmented facility of movement," making it more able to defend the manifold interests the nation had abroad even prior to its possession of "a square foot of territory without its borders."[34] Specifically "in the problem of East-

[32] Mahan, "The Transvaal and the Philippines," *Independent*, Vol. LII (February 1, 1900), 290. See also "The Philippines and the Future," *ibid.* (March 22, 1900), 697–98.

[33] Mahan, "Why Fortify the Panama Canal?," *North American Review*, March, 1911, reprinted in *Armaments and Arbitration*, 182.

[34] Mahan, "Conditions Determining the Naval Expansion of the United States," *Leslie's Weekly*, October 2, 1902, reprinted in *Retrospect and Prospect*, 41–42; "Current Fallacies upon Naval Subjects," *Harper's Monthly*, June, 1898, reprinted in *Lessons of the War with Spain and Other Articles*, 301–308.

ern Asia, still in an early stage of its solution and of doubtful issue," the Philippines, Hawaii, and the proposed canal were important "as facilitating our access to the seas of China and the valley of the Yangtze, and as furnishing territorial support to our action there."[35] With China on the brink of partition, the Philippines offered a well-nigh miraculous opportunity for the United States to prevent her own exclusion from the spoils of the rich man's estate. Indeed for Mahan the island archipelago appeared to be the gift of Providence, a gift valuable for what it might lead to rather than for any intrinsic worth.

[35] Mahan, "Retrospect and Prospect," *World's Work*, February, 1902, reprinted in *Retrospect and Prospect*, 34.

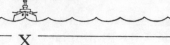

X

THE FAR EAST

EW PERIODS in the history of the Far East have been filled with happenings of greater significance for that area than the decade which closed the nineteenth and opened the twentieth century. The Sino-Japanese War of 1894–95 publicized to the world the impotence of China and forced her to grant to Japan valuable territorial concessions in the Pacific and on the continent. Though certain of the European powers prevented Japan from capitalizing upon her continental gains, these powers were not in the least adverse to profit from Chinese helplessness themselves. There ensued a scramble for naval bases, leased territories, and spheres of influence at China's expense by which not only monopolistic trade rights but frequently exclusive privileges in rail and mining developments were secured. In 1898, for example, Germany obtained Kiaochow in Shantung Peninsula in North China; Russia gained the warm water harbor of Port Arthur in Liaotung Peninsula in southern Manchuria; Great Britain established herself at Weihaiwei, lying between the German and Russian acquisitions; and France set herself up in southeastern China at Kwangchowan.

Such activities, if not halted, foreshadowed the partition of China, and from the point of view of the United States, newly entrenched in the Philippines, foredoomed the hopes of any increase of American trade with China. In view of these developments and in light of the fact that the traditional policy of the United States in the Orient called for equality of commercial opportunity for all nations, Secretary of State John Hay, in September, 1899, addressed a circular note to the powers concerned asking them to subscribe to the doctrine of equal trading opportunities, including equality in tariffs, harbor dues, and railroad rates in the areas they respectively controlled. Though some of the replies were evasive, Hay stated that the nations had accepted the "Open Door" for China.

The following year brought new difficulties for Hay and his program. A Boxer antiforeign uprising reached such serious proportions in Peking that an international relief expedition was organized. Fearful that the presence of foreign armies might result in the forthright dismemberment of China, Secretary Hay issued the second Open Door note which sought a multilateral guarantee of the territorial and administrative integrity of China. The powers accepted this proposal, and after some negotiations concerning terms, peace with China was arranged in 1901. Contrary to the peace terms, Russia retained troops in Manchuria; the Russian threat in the Far East, coupled with the mounting tension in Europe, caused Great Britain and Japan to form a defensive alliance in 1902, which provided not only for the protection of their respective interests in Asia and the Pacific but also permitted Britain to concentrate further her naval strength in European waters. Supported by this alliance, Japan moved for a showdown with Russia; peaceful negotiations gave way to the Russo-Japanese War of 1904–1905. By the Treaty of Portsmouth Japan obtained important territorial concessions, including the cession of Russian privileges in Liaotung Peninsula and the Russian withdrawal from Korea. For the Japanese, the Treaty of Portsmouth helped to offset the ignominy which she had suffered when her continental gains won from the Chinese a decade earlier had been denied her by Russia and other powers.

As has been seen in the preceding chapter, Mahan's

views on American policy in China and in the Philippines were closely interrelated. He was thoroughly cognizant of the politico-commercial rivalry centering in China, and it was this decadent empire of the Far East that elicited his greater interest. In conversation with certain of the British delegation at the Hague Conference, he said that American interests now lay in the East and the West and that the United States proposed to look after her Chinese markets.[1] American interposition near the scene of action as a result of the Spanish-American War was but one of several events, nearly simultaneous, as has been noted, which might demand, as Mahan said, a "readjustment of ideas as well as of national policies and affiliations."

The sea-power commentator accordingly analyzed Asiatic conditions and their effect upon world politics in a series of magazine articles. Three of these were written in the fall and winter of 1899 after his return from The Hague via London and a fourth in the following August; all were immediately reprinted and published as *The Problem of Asia* (1900). It should be borne in mind that these essays were written during a period crowded with happenings important to China—the Hay Open Door notes of September, 1899, and of July, 1900, the Boxer Rebellion, the siege and relief of the legations at Peking. John Hay's able biographer, Professor Tyler Dennett, has suggested:

Though there is little documentary evidence to support the assertion, it seems probable that Mahan was seeing Secretary of State John Hay rather frequently during the period in which these essays were in course of preparation. . . . Many paragraphs recall sentiments which Hay was contemporaneously writing to Henry Adams, Joseph Choate, Henry White, Alvey A. Adee, and others. Indeed we probably do no one an injustice in regarding *The Problem of Asia* as a summary of the views re-

[1] G. P. Gooch and Harold Temperley, *British Documents on the Origins of the War, 1898–1914*, I, 230–31.

garding the Far East current in the best-informed official circles in Washington during the first part of the year 1900.[2]

The Problem of Asia was both a diagnosis and a remedy. To Mahan at the time, it was his "swan song" on contemporary politics; to Professor Dennett thirty-five years later, it possessed "the attributes of an intellectual land mark."[3] Mahan essayed to select and expose the permanent facts and forces implicit in the problem of Asia and then to note the influence exerted by these factors upon political events in the Far East and elsewhere. The important portion of Asia, politically and geographically, was the middle belt roughly between the thirtieth and fortieth degrees of north latitude and extending from the Mediterranean to the China Sea. With Australasia and Africa partitioned, this was the only large region politically unstable and therefore open to serious change by foreign influences. Key positions were held on either side of this area by Great Britain and Russia; between them was "debated and debatable ground," a no man's land which Mahan saw as destined to be the battleground between two essentially differing civilizations, English and Russian.[4]

The struggle was enlarged to include nations with interests similar to those of these major contestants. The duel thus took the form of a contest between land power and sea power with Russia in opposition to Great Britain, Germany, the United States, and Japan. He thought it safe to assume that these four sea powers would follow "a common line of action" should necessity arise. None alone was able to exert predominance in China, and none alone was able

2 "The Future in Retrospect, Mahan's *The Problem of Asia*," *Foreign Affairs*, Vol. XIII (April, 1935), 464.

3 Mahan to Roosevelt, May 12, 1900, Roosevelt Papers; Dennett, *loc. cit.*, 464.

4 Mahan, "The Problem of Asia," *Harper's Monthly*, March, 1900, reprinted in *The Problem of Asia*, 21 ff.

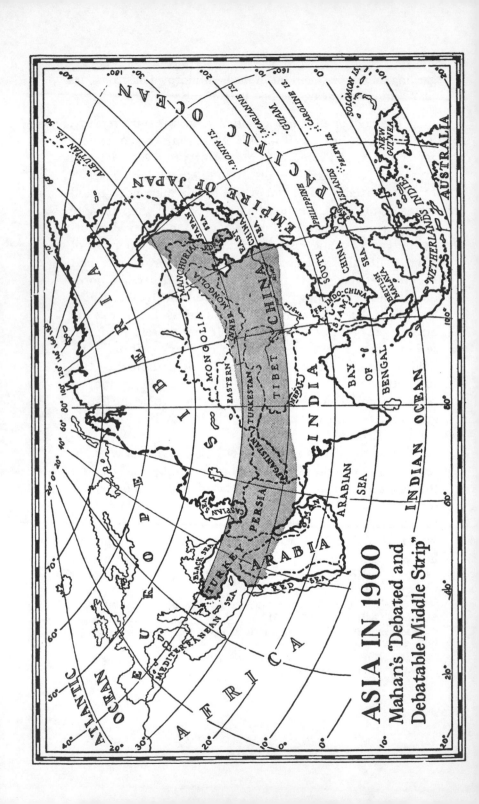

ASIA IN 1900
Mahan's "Debated and
Debatable Middle Strip"

to prevent the extension of Russian progress from the north, while all were anxious as trading nations to preserve peace and all were dependent upon naval might to enforce their wishes. Each sea power was strategically placed: Japan was protected by her insular position, Germany had Kiaochow, England had Hong Kong, the United States now had in the Philippines, which were almost "forced upon her," a base similarly secure.[5]

This analyst of power politics further complicated the contest by injecting the problem of race. He thought the Asiatic was culturally static and the Slavonic, as a regenerative force, he considered much inferior to the Teutonic. Oddly enough Japan was classed not among the Asiatic but with the Teutonic; though racially the former, adoptively she had become the latter. Because of her restricted area and limited population and wealth, despite propinquity, Japan was unable to contribute weight to the Asiatic; therefore, she was forced to choose between the other two contending races which was by "'character and ambitions most favorable, both to her immediate interests and the free ultimate development of Asia in the line of its natural capacities.[6] In 1900, Mahan was pleased that this only "willing convert" to Westernization in the Far East had adopted not only the more obvious material improvements but had shown herself open as well to the influence of intellectual and moral ideals. Subsequent events would scarcely substantiate the thoughts of this seer who expressed his views in Biblical phraseology as follows:

It is well worthy of consideration whether we may not see in Japan the prepared soil, whence the grain of mustard seed,

5 Mahan, "The Problem of Asia," *Harper's Monthly*, April, 1900, reprinted in *ibid.*, 62–64; "The Problem of Asia," *Harper's Monthly*, May, 1900, reprinted in *ibid.*, 133–34; "Effect of Asiatic Conditions upon World Policies," *North American Review*, November, 1900, reprinted in *ibid.*, 154.

6 Mahan, "The Problem of Asia," *Harper's Monthly*, May, 1900, reprinted in *ibid.*, 106, 114.

having taken root may spring up and grow to the great tree, the view of which may move the continental communities of Asia to seek the same regenerating force for their own renewal.[7]

Mahan's solution to the problem of Asia was the establishment of a political equilibrium in which both the interests of the natives and the ambitions of the major powers were reconciled. The inhabitants of the middle zone of debatable ground were definitely not to be considered as sheep to be bought and sold but as lambs without a shepherd. The Western Christian nations, bringing the spiritual as well as the material aspects of their culture, were to be the good shepherds leading the lambs not to fleecing or slaughter but to the fold of regenerated Christian souls.

Mahan was convinced that any Russian advance into the Near and Middle East could not be permitted; but in the Far East, by way of compensation, Manchuria was granted this Slavic state as her particular sphere of influence. The Teutonic powers, the sea powers, were allotted China proper, especially the Yangtze Valley. Within this relatively little known and slightly exploited field lay, purportedly at least, lucrative, even fabulous opportunities for trade. Whether considered from a commercial, political, or missionary point of view, seed sown in the Yangtze would yield a hundredfold as compared with thirtyfold elsewhere. In this restricted area Mahan advocated co-operation among the powers and due regard for the uplift of the natives. The accomplishment of this program demanded: first, "The prevention of preponderant political control by any external state, or group of states; and, second, insistence upon the open door . . . open not only for commerce, but also for the entrance of European thought."[8]

7 Mahan, "Effect of Asiatic Conditions upon World Policies," *North American Review*, November, 1900, reprinted in *ibid.*, 148.
8 *Ibid.*, 164–65, 167.

Here was an endorsement of the Hay Open Door policy; an appeal for popular support followed. Political movements in China were at a turning point determinative of great future issues; it was "essential to the United States that her individual citizens should seriously consider, and within themselves settle, the part the country ought to play and the preparation necessary to that part." Many Americans thought China possessed limitless fields for exploitation. Our export trade with her had grown fourfold between 1890 and 1897, though still less than $12,000,000 at the latter date; to critics who thought this amount insignificant, the reply was that the increase was indicative and that far greater possibilities lay ahead.[9] As might be expected, Mahan based his case not only upon these commercial opportunities, small yet promising, but also upon Christian duty which inescapably fell upon the United States. Divine sanction was ours, with opportunity marked and responsibility grave:

The part offered us is great, the urgency is immediate, and the preparation made for us, rather than by us, in the unwilling acquisition of the Philippines, is so obvious as to embolden even the least presumptuous to see in it the hand of Providence.[10]

In Mahan's solution to the problem of Asia, policy and power were interrelated; it was necessary that the United States be prepared, with "physical weight" as well as with "moral influence" to do her share in warding off Russia and in controlling China. Physical weight capable of use at a distance naturally took the form of naval power; hence a larger navy and an Isthmian canal thoroughly secured were obviously required.

This naval preparation, though essential, was subordi-

9 John Barrett, "Our Interests in China—A Question of the Hour," *Review of Reviews*, Vol. XXI (January, 1900), 42–45.

10 Mahan, "Effect of Asiatic Conditions upon World Policies," *North American Review*, November, 1900, reprinted in *The Problem of Asia*, 175.

nate to the central contention of a policy of co-operation. America could no longer escape recognition of her irrevocable entry into world politics. Of all the nations which the United States would meet in the Far East, Great Britain was the one with whom she had by far the most in common. Similarity though not identity of interests in China, basic likeness in standards of law and justice, community of language and of political standards—all these pointed toward Anglo-American co-operation. Britain's attitude toward the United States during the war with Spain and her willingness to concede to American desires in the Caribbean, as witnessed in the canal treaty, indicated that she was ready to do her share. What was the attitude of mind in the United States? Previously on many occasions, Mahan had stated his belief in the desirability of a cordial understanding between the branches of the Anglo-Saxon race. Aware of the seriousness of the problem of Asia for his own and other peoples, he once again made a powerful plea to his fellow-Americans: he urged them to dismiss all prepossessions, to cast aside old animosities, to sink racial prejudices, and to forego ancient grudges in whole-hearted support of a program which seemed to him pregnant with great good for all concerned.[11]

This definite appeal, soliciting general support for a united front of the sea powers, especially of the United States and Great Britain, against the relentless Russian on-

[11] *Ibid.*, 177–79, 186–91. Mahan discussed his views on Anglo-American relations at greatest length in "Possibilities of an Anglo-American Reunion," *North American Review,* November, 1894, reprinted in *The Interest of America in Sea Power, Present and Future,* 107–34. For other expressions, see the following: "The United States Looking Outward," *Atlantic Monthly,* December, 1890, reprinted in *ibid.,* 27; "Hawaii and Our Future Sea Power," *Forum,* March, 1893, reprinted in *ibid.,* 55; "A Twentieth-Century Outlook," *Harper's Monthly,* September, 1897, reprinted in *ibid.,* 257–59; "Motives to Imperial Federation," *National Review,* May, 1902, reprinted in *Retrospect and Prospect,* 134–35; *The Interest of America in International Conditions,* 81 ff.; "The Panama Canal and Sea Power in the Pacific," *Century,* June, 1911, reprinted in *Armaments and Arbitration,* 167 ff.

slaughts Mahan supplemented by letters to men of marked influence. "Filled with consternation" upon hearing of America's withdrawal from the hitherto joint enterprise against the Boxers, Mahan wrote President McKinley warning him of Russian motives: "She is not only playing her own game—all states do that—but playing it with the unscrupulous craft of the Asiatic."[12] He sent Lodge a copy of *The Problem of Asia* which the latter read "with the utmost care," found "profoundly interesting," and reported he had been "much instructed by it." Mahan predicted for Lodge, in light of the "distinguished public service" he had already rendered, that he was to be "one of the determining factors" in the country's future. "I am rejoiced, consequently, to know that your opinion coincides in general outline with my own concerning the community of interest between ourselves and Great Britain in some of the great questions of the future."[13] Mahan also wrote Whitelaw Reid thanking him for having shown the public, through the *Tribune,* that there was a British as well as a Boer side to the Transvaal controversy. "A temperate and full presentment of the whole truth of this matter by a paper of the *Tribune's* influence" was most desirable and helpful; under no circumstances should the Transvaal issue be permitted to breed discord between Great Britain and the United States in their pursuit of the vitally essential policy of "cordial understanding" in "the very great impending Eastern question."[14]

To Roosevelt, temporarily "shelved" as vice president, Mahan expressed his belief that neither the United States nor Great Britain, singly or jointly, could "check Russia by main force in Northern China." The only "true counter

[12] Mahan to McKinley, September 2, 1900, McKinley Papers.
[13] Lodge to Mahan, December 6, 1900; Mahan to Lodge, December 8, 1900: Lodge Papers.
[14] Mahan to Reid, October 20, 1899, cited by Cortissoz, *The Life of Whitelaw Reid,* II, 269–70.

check" was the establishment of naval power in the Yangtze Valley—"the very heart of China in every sense of the word" —which would render the necessary physical and moral support to the Chinese. And if, in addition, "the Sea Powers . . . will require of China . . . liberty of entrance for European thought as well as European commerce, China will . . . be saved. . . . Such is my swan-song," added the sea-power advocate, who had been for a decade the frequent and timely counselor of Roosevelt, and now feared as he neared threescore years that he would lag behind. "I cannot but hope that this idea may enter, for whatever it is worth, into the grasp of one who . . . has still much activity and growth before him."[15]

In reply Roosevelt told Mahan that he was in essential agreement with him concerning China and that he considered his views "eminently sound"; but he added that public officials could "go *somewhat,* though not very much, farther than public opinion" had prepared the way, and as yet American public opinion was "dull on the question of China." As for Mahan's ceasing his activities, Roosevelt begged him not to talk even of such a course; "we must rely upon you as one of our foremost educators of public thought, and I trust for many years to come. . . . I greatly wish to see you and have a long talk with you."[16]

At the turn of the century Mahan was not certain about the policy of upholding the integrity of China which Hay had enunciated in July of 1900; nor is it clear that he (or Hay) appreciated that the European spheres of influence in China were carved out not for trading purposes primarily but as outlets for capitalistic exploitation. A decade later he was positive on both points. Integrity was essential to the Open Door, a doctrine which opposed "territorial control, however exerted or disguised." Leases almost always re-

15 Mahan to Roosevelt, March 12, 1901, Roosevelt Papers.
16 Roosevelt to Mahan. March 18, 1901, *ibid.*

sulted in "closing the Open Door in part or wholly" and not infrequently resulted in annexation, as seemed near at hand by the Japanese in Korea. The Open Door applied not only to commerce per se but equally to the development of China. Evidently with the 1910 consortium and allied negotiations in mind, Mahan noted with pleasure that the United States had firmly and successfully met the attempt to exclude her from development projects. Within the next generation "very many railroads will have to be built in China," he asserted, and he saw no reason why American capital should not profit thereby.[17]

For Mahan, the Open Door policy was merely another expression for balance of power in eastern Asia. He had no faith in the temporary truce recently arranged between Russia and Japan; he likened them to a quarreling couple who had for the moment joined hands against outsiders but whose causes of variance still remained. Manchuria was not only a common point of contact for China, Japan, and Russia but also the center of intersecting and clashing interests. "For some time to come," he predicted, it would be "to the Farther East what Belgium in the seventeenth and eighteenth centuries was to Western Europe."[18]

Mahan was keenly aware of the interrelation of power politics in Asia, America, and Europe; he was thoroughly apprehensive of the resultant dangers for the United States. Despite our professed abstention from the affairs of Europe as proclaimed by the Monroe Doctrine, he vehemently insisted that the United States could not escape the repercussions of events on that continent. He believed it was highly probable that the exigencies of the alliance system in Europe would neutralize or greatly reduce European influence in the Far East. The result, he predicted, would be

17 Mahan, *The Interest of America in International Conditions*, 84, 144–47, 182–84.
18 *Ibid.*, 211, 135.

that the balance of power in China, if it were maintained, would rest upon the two chief Pacific nations, the United States and Japan. This situation presented very real difficulties. The Japanese-American relations, despite the brief Hawaiian episode, had been friendly and cordial up to 1905. The blame for Japan's failure to secure in the Treaty of Portsmouth all that was hoped for was largely and unfairly placed upon the United States. Several factors accentuated this bitterness. Japan resented the Open Door policy as a hindrance to fullest exploitation of the fruits of the war with Russia. As she felt obliged to extend her naval policy, hitherto confined to the Yellow Sea and the Sea of Japan, so as to bring the Pacific Ocean into her field of strategy, she shortly ran into American opposition.

The feeling of hostility in Japan toward the United States was further sharpened by the treatment of her nationals in California. The Japanese-American relations became tense, the "1897 peril" of Mahan and Roosevelt flared into the "war scare of 1907" and the World Cruise of the American fleet.[19] Mahan favored this action and was in frequent correspondence with Roosevelt during the cruise; he wrote an apology and defense for it prior to the departure of the fleet as well as after its return to San Francisco. He rejected the element of threat as a motive; the need for practice was sufficient. Meanwhile, the "Gentlemen's Agreement" had set to rest, temporarily at least, the school discrimination and immigration difficulties which had immediately provoked the flare-up. Mahan personally thought the Asiatic unassimilable, though not on the ground of in-

[19] Thomas A. Bailey, *Theodore Roosevelt and the Japanese-American Crisis.*

[20] Roosevelt to Mahan, June 8, July 10, October 1, 1908, Roosevelt Papers; Mahan, "The Value of the Pacific Cruise of the United States Fleet, 1908, Prospect," *Scientific American*, December 7, 1907; "The Value of the Pacific Cruise of the United States Fleet, 1908, Retrospect," *Collier's Weekly*, August 29, 1908, reprinted together in *Naval Administration and Warfare*, 309–53.

Cartoon from the Duluth *News-Tribune,* reprinted in *Literary Digest,* April, 1908.

Cartoon from Detroit *Journal,* reprinted in the *American Monthly Review of Reviews,* October, 1907.

The Great White Fleet enters Sydney Heads, Australia, August 20, 1908, on a world cruise. *Official U.S. Navy photograph*

HAPPY AFTERTHOUGHTS.

JAPAN (to American Eagle)—" But how sweet of you to come all this way on purpose to see me!"

EAGLE—" Why, yes, I thought you'd be pleased!"

—*Punch.*

Reprinted in the *American Monthly Review of Reviews*, April, 1908.

A DUTCH VIEW OF THE SENDING OF THE AMERICAN FLEET TO THE PACIFIC.

UNCLE SAM (to the Mikado): "My good friend, my ships are bent on the friendliest of missions. Come, now, let us smoke the pipe of peace together." MIKADO: "My good brother, nothing would please me more."

MIKADO: "Great heavens! There is gunpowder in that tobacco!"

UNCLE SAM: "Great Scott! Who would have believed it! That tobacco was probably grown in Manila."

From the *Amsterdammer* (Amsterdam).

Reprinted in the *American Monthly Review of Reviews*, September, 1907.

feriority, and favored exclusion as preferable to immigration without citizenship.[20]

In 1910, as he surveyed the foreign affairs of the United States in *The Interest of America in International Conditions*, Japan was indeed the "problem state." This Far Eastern power had successfully engaged in war with Russia and could no longer be viewed, as in 1900, "unable to contribute weight"; in fact, her very nearness, her low transportation costs, her cheap labor when coupled with "the mingled weakness and perverseness" of Chinese negotiators "breed that sense of proprietorship which, in dealing with ill-organized states, easily glides into the attempt at political control that ultimately means control by force."[21]

Confronted with these positive Japanese advantages and the strong possibility of European preoccupations, Mahan was less inclined to push for American rights in the Far East than he had been ten years earlier. His whole trend of thought, he said, rejected the idea of any claim to supremacy in the Pacific on the part of the United States; it was "not to the interest of the United States to propose to herself the object of supremacy in the Pacific. . . . An assured supremacy over her own possessions, and over the approaches to them" was a legitimate aim menacing none. Attention should be called to the fact that, in speaking of the right of assured supremacy over our possessions, Mahan probably did not have in mind the Philippines; these islands he always regarded as a responsibility or obligation rather than as a possession. "America in the Philippines has in the Pacific that which she may not call her own possession but

21 Mahan, *The Interest of America in International Conditions*, 149–51, 196–201. Mahan evidently was never pleased with the Anglo-Japanese Alliance. He wrote Admiral Bouverie Clark in 1909, "I fear, and have from the first believed, that your Government backed the 'wrong horse in the Alliance with Japan." The alliance was a distinct handicap to friendly Anglo-American relations and also alienated Australia, he thought. Mahan to Clarke, July 23, 1909, Mahan Papers.

has recognized as her especial charge."[22] Despite this concession in interpretation, Mahan, at times, came very near advocating the supremacy which he professed to disclaim; on one occasion he wrote that the United States did have duties in the Pacific, which, in case of disputes, would require "the presence of naval force adequate to command."[23]

Thus, in the course of the decade, though still claiming the beneficence, wisdom, and value of the Open Door, Mahan had definitely altered his view concerning the ultimate disposition of the Eastern middle belt and its surrounding waters. The "unregenerative" Asiatic was now accorded the western Pacific, while the European and the American were granted the eastern Pacific. "The question awaiting and approaching solution is the line of demarcation between the Asiatic and European elements in the Pacific." Mahan predicted this division would follow a line running through Hawaii and Samoa joining Pacific America to Australia. There would be European and American positions north and west of that line, just as European possessions still existed in the Caribbean as remnants of past conditions. A period of adjustment was ahead; naval power, the military representative of sea power, was to be determinative; because of this "the American Navy should be second to none but the British."[24]

It was in this fashion that Mahan in 1911 read the future of the Pacific, a future probably less distant than he thought and a future certainly less bright for Japan. Mahan's analysis in 1900 of the Far East as a scene of conflict between the Teutonic and the Asiatic, with China playing a critical role

[22] Mahan, *The Interest of America in International Conditions,* 192; Mahan, "The Panama Canal and Sea Power in the Pacific," June, 1911, reprinted in *Armaments and Arbitrations,* 177.

[23] Mahan, "The Importance of the Command of the Sea," *Scientific American,* Vol. CV (December 9, 1911), 512.

[24] Mahan, "The Panama Canal and Sea Power in the Pacific," *Century,* June, 1911, reprinted in *Armaments and Arbitration,* 179–80.

and Manchuria as the center of intersecting and clashing interests, elicits amazement as prognostication of development nearly fifty years later; his solution to the problem of Asia as one of balance of power resting upon a composite of mutual concession and stark might with similarity of Anglo-American interests calling for joint effort against the Asiatic sounds strangely familiar and still claims many supporters.

XI

THE UNITED STATES NAVY

THE SEA-POWER DOCTRINE viewed naval and commercial development as concomitant with overseas territorial expansion. In the preceding discussion of the emergence of the United States as a world power with her claim to predominance in the Caribbean vindicated and her right to a position of influence on the basis of co-operation in the Pacific established, repeated reference has been made to Mahan's emphasis upon the urgency of naval development for the United States. Mahan was concerned not only with the growth of the navy but with the manner of its employment. His views materially affected the development of both American naval power and policy.

Sweeping technological improvements revolutionized naval art and science in the middle and later nineteenth century. Conspicuous in this transformation was the slow victory of steam over sail, the substitution of the breech-loading, rifled gun for the smooth-bored, muzzle-loading cannon, the ever increasing utilization of armor on side and deck totally outmoding the wooden walls of former years, and the beginning of a rapid differentiation of types caused by the practical impossibility of combining in maximum in any single vessel the qualities of speed, armor protection, and gun power.

Until the eighties the United States was either oblivious or indifferent to these highly important changes. Possessing no significant merchant marine or colonial possessions, determined to avoid interference in European affairs, and convinced of the improbability of attack from abroad, the country bent her whole energy upon internal development. The United States Navy succumbed to rot, rust, and obsolescence. The first steps in its rehabilitation were taken in 1881.[1] Garfield's secretaries of state and navy, Blaine and Hunt, were men of ability, energy, and action. An early exponent of militant nationalism and resurgent mercantilism, Blaine called the attention of his fellow-Americans to the world which lay outside their own boundaries—southward to the Isthmus and beyond as well as on the Pacific coast and westward to the Hawaiian Islands. Hunt organized a naval advisory board of fifteen officers, who carefully determined naval requirements; on the basis of their report, the Secretary made a most urgent plea for an immediate consideration of the very real needs of the navy. He supplemented this formal appeal by conversations with individual senators and representatives and by joint conferences of important Congressional and naval leaders for discussion of naval policy.[2]

Congressional action was forthcoming. Designed to write off the obsolete vessels more rapidly, limitations upon expenditures in repair of existing vessels were incorporated in the naval appropriation bill of 1882 and were made more drastic in the 1883 bill. It was here provided that no wooden ship was to receive repairs amounting to more than 20 per cent of the estimated cost of a new vessel of the same size.[3] The latter bill also authorized the construction of four steel

[1] The two most recent studies of the rise of the navy, Harold and Margaret Sprout, *The Rise of American Naval Power, 1776–1918*, and George T. Davis, *A Navy Second to None*, largely supplant previous efforts. The best analysis of Mahan's strategical principles and their implications for modern triphibian war is Bernard Brodie, *A Guide to Naval Strategy*.

[2] Thomas Hunt, *Life of Wm. H. Hunt*, 216 ff.; Davis, *op. cit.*, 37; Sprout and Sprout, *op. cit.*, 186–87.

[3] *Statutes at Large*, XXII, 291; *ibid.*, 476.

vessels in American yards, "said vessels to be provided with full sail power and full steam power." These ships, completed by 1887, were the initial vessels of the new navy; they were small, unarmored craft varying in size from 1,500 to 4,500 tons.

Though limited in nature and extent, an auspicious beginning had been made, and during the first Cleveland administration thirty vessels aggregating nearly 100,000 tons were authorized with the stipulation that the armor and armament must be of "domestic manufacture." A government gun factory was built, and the Bethlehem Iron Company and the Carnegie Steel Company were "persuaded" to erect the necessary plants for the demands of the naval program, present and potential. Vested interests thus created were destined to be active lobbyists and propagandists for continuous and progressive naval expansion. The Naval War College was opened at Newport, Rhode Island, in 1884 for advanced training in strategy, international law, naval history, and tactics. A middle-aged officer "drifting on lines of simple respectability" was called by President Luce to lecture in naval history, tactics, and strategy.

Before this call Mahan had been one of many, out of the service as well as in the service, who deplored "Grantism" in the navy. From the Boston Navy Yard he wrote his friend Ashe fully and frequently of his reaction to conditions and sought advice and assistance. He believed Grant was "personally upright," but had the "unfortunate habit of shutting his eyes to his friends' shortcomings."[4] Nor was he content to give vent to his views merely to Ashe; he wrote senators and others in positions of influence. Since his last letter, he told Ashe, "I have been very busy . . . writing to everyone I could think of that would be likely to feel an interest, or a duty, in seeing justice done in and by the

4 Mahan to Ashe, May 21, 1875; December 27, 1875; January 27, 1876; February 1, 1876; March 28, 1876: Flowers Collection.

navy."[5] The "dishonesty and indifference" of Secretary Robeson and the "rascality" of Chief Constructor Hanscom were repeatedly mentioned. He even admitted that his "convictions about these two" were so strong that they possibly hampered his "reason."[6] Mahan was of the belief "that much money might be spared if politics could be exiled from the management of the Yards"; and he advocated as a remedy greatly increased power to the commandant, with an accompanying decrease in the authority of the constructor. Aware of the necessity of the yards in war and regretful of any move to abolish them, Mahan stated that, "if they are to continue, however, a football for local politicians," he would be reconciled to their discontinuance.[7]

Shortly after Secretary Hunt's assumption of office, Mahan called his attention to the great numbers of midshipmen and cadet midshipmen yearly graduated for whom no advancements were possible; he believed that the British system of retirements and promotions offered a possible solution and urged the Secretary to give the matter fair consideration.[8]

In these post–Civil War years Mahan was not an advocate of a large navy. He recognized that "immersed" as the people were "in peaceful and material pursuits," the military establishment was "necessarily one of our lesser interests" and "the country, and the navy too, have looked on [its disintegration] with some unconcern for the prospect of foreign entanglement seemed so remote; and few of us favored an attempt to compete with the iron-clad navies of foreign powers."

In 1880 Mahan was content with a small navy of swift

---

[5] Mahan to Ashe, January 27, 1876, Flowers Collection.

[6] Mahan to Ashe, March 12, 1880, ibid.; see also letters in n. 4.

[7] Mahan to Ashe, January 27, 1876; February 1, 1876: ibid.

[8] Mahan to Secretary Hunt, April 20, 1881, Navy Department, Commander's Letters, Navy Department Archives.

commerce destroying cruisers unless we followed an aggressive policy in Central America. He wrote:

Now the canal at the Isthmus *may* bring our interests and those of foreign nations in collision and in that case—which is for statesmen to forecast—we must without any delay begin to build a navy which will at least equal that of England when the canal shall have become a fact. . . . That this will be done I don't for a moment hope; but unless it is we may as well shut up about the Monroe Doctrine at once.[9]

Five years later, after the beginning of the new navy, similar views were expressed:

As regards the type of ships, opinions are very divergent. I give you mine. The surest way to maintain peace is to occupy a position of menace. I think that our geographical position will make war with us unlikely but the surest deterrent will be a fleet of swift cruisers to prey on the enemy commerce . . . particularly if coupled with adequate defense of our principal ports.[10]

These views, he added, were based upon the supposition that the United States had no interests beyond her own borders. If an Isthmian policy were to be adopted, "nothing short of a numerous and thoroughly first-class, iron-clad navy equal either to England or France" would suffice to meet our needs.

Mahan's studies of the commerce, politics, and wars of the seventeenth and eighteenth centuries not only transformed him into a forthright imperialist but also profoundly altered his concepts of naval needs and naval policy. Mahan's studies of these years of mercantilistic imperialism, witnessing as they did the decline of the French and the Dutch in power politics and the simultaneous rise of the British Navy and the British Empire, offered ample oppor-

[9] Mahan to Ashe, March 12, 1880; December 21, 1882: Flowers Collection.
[10] Mahan to Ashe, March 11, 1885, *ibid.*

tunity for illustrative substantiation of his views that national power, national security, and national prosperity were dependent upon foreign commerce, which in turn called for a marine, bases, and naval protection. The sea became "a link, a bridge, a highway"; and to the navy able to occupy it in adequate force, it conferred the all-important military attributes of interior lines, central position, and assured communications.

History, at least for Mahan, abounded with words of admonition, and the sea-power exponent passed these on with the fervent hope that they would be heeded by his fellow countrymen. History bore abundant evidence concerning such widely scattered naval topics as the stupidity of unpreparedness, the impossibility of preparation on the spur of the moment, the importance of a thoroughly trained personnel, the prime necessity of a number of ships of the line, the inadequacies of other vessels (torpedo, submarine, etc.), the futility of privateering as more than a secondary factor, the ruinous consequences of nonconcentration of the fleet, the values as well as the limitations of the blockade, the necessity of adequate coast defenses, the deplorable consequences of a navy for defense only, and the absurdity of granting immunity to seizure of private property at sea.

Mahan surveyed the naval needs and policies of the United States in *The Influence of Sea Power upon History, 1660–1783*. Her present development and future welfare, when viewed upon the world stage and in light of his historical studies, called for the creation of a naval force adequate to insure her an opportunity for commercial expansion and to safeguard her against the dangers of commercial competitors. He sorrowfully acknowledged the serious limitations in merchant shipping and overseas bases and strongly urged that these deficiencies be remedied. In the meantime it was essential to have naval power of such a character as to insure foreign neutral shipping free access to our harbors in time of war and peace as well as to guarantee the unhampered use of our ports for our naval vessels. Other interests and obligations also existed. In his master work he publicly expressed views comparable in import to those he had earlier expressed to Ashe relative to the impending crisis developing at the Isthmus and the consequent necessity of revamping our naval policy. In his first important magazine article, "The United States Looking Outward," written in 1890, he stated that he thought the United States would not willingly acquiesce in an infringement of her rights as she saw them whether in Central America, South America, Hawaii, Bering Sea, or Samoa; yet obviously she did not have the power which could weigh "seriously when inevitable discussions" arose.

For nearly a quarter of a century the same refrain was sounded: the United States had "neither the tradition nor the design to act aggressively beyond the seas"; yet she did have very important transmarine interests which needed protection, two widely separated coasts to be defended, and openly asserted policies in the Caribbean which demanded force that would make itself felt politically as well as militarily. Was the country willing, queried Mahan in 1911, to concede on points such as these "because unready to maintain them by organized force?" To the sea-power philosopher, the reply was negative and the answer was one of an "annual increase of the navy."[11] Throughout the years subsequent to his first lectures at the War College, Mahan sought to link national policy and national defense. He did not advise a contraction of obligations, except in the application of the Monroe Doctrine in southern South America; rather he advocated the creation of force which would be

11 Mahan, "Navies as International Factors," *North American Review*, September, 1911, reprinted in *Armaments and Arbitration*, 67; Mahan, "The Importance of the Command of the Sea," *Scientific American*, Vol. CV (December 9, 1911), 512.

U.S.S. *Oregon* (1890), battleship, 10,288 tons; carried four 13″, eight 8″, and four 6″ guns; designed horsepower and speed, 25,000 and 21 knots.

U.S.S. *Delaware* (1906), dreadnought, 20,000 tons; carried ten 12″ and fourteen 5″ guns; designed horsepower and speed, 25,000 and 21 knots.

U.S.S. *Missouri* (1940), superdreadnought, 45,000 tons; carried nine 16″ and twenty 5″ guns, as well as smaller antiaircraft guns; designed horsepower and speed, 212,000 and 33 knots. The *Missouri* was the last superdreadnought to be commissioned.
EVOLUTION OF THE MODERN SHIPS OF THE LINE
Official U.S. Navy photographs

THE THIRD FLEET, 1945
Admiral William F. Halsey's Third Fleet maneuvers off the coast of the Japanese Empire on August 17, 1945, following news of Japan's offer to surrender. *Official U.S. Navy photograph*

sufficient to meet these obligations. The solution was naval preparedness. Said he:

Every danger of a military character to which the United States is exposed can be met best outside her own territory—at sea. Preparedness for naval war—preparedness against naval attack and for naval offence—is preparedness for anything that is likely to occur.[12]

What was the nature and degree of preparedness which the United States required? Mahan's answer to this question hinged on both military and political factors. From a military point of view it turned on his interpretation of the word "defence." Mere coast defense with a navy that could "only await attack and defend its own, leaving the enemy at ease as regards his interests, and at liberty to choose his own time, and manner of fighting" was absurd when viewed from logic and ruinous when put to the test.[13] If the United States had interests, rights, and obligations beyond the sea "which a navy may have to protect, it plainly follows that the navy has more to do, even in war, than to defend the coast." A "navy for defence only" was "a wholly misleading phrase," Mahan told his readers,

unless defence be construed to include *all* national interests, and not only national territory; and further unless it be understood that the best defence of one's own interest is power to injure those of his enemy.[14]

[12] Mahan, "Preparedness for Naval War," *Harper's Monthly*, October, 1895, reprinted in *The Interest of America in Sea Power, Present and Future*, 214.

[13] Mahan, "Current Fallacies upon Naval Subjects," *Harper's Monthly*, June, 1898, reprinted in *Lessons of the War with Spain and Other Articles*, 286.

[14] Mahan, "The Future in Relation to American Naval Power," *Harper's Monthly*, October, 1895, reprinted in *The Interest of America in Sea Power, Present and Future*, 156–57; Mahan, "Current Fallacies upon Naval Subjects," *Harper's Monthly*, June, 1898, reprinted in *Lessons of the War with Spain and Other Articles*, 299–300.

It was definitely not sufficient to keep the enemy out of our ports; the least that should be anticipated was to keep him "far away from our coasts." One should possess "a military force afloat" able at all times so to endanger a blockading fleet operating at distances far removed from the shores that it could "by no means keep its place." What really was needed was to be strong enough to "go out and assail the enemy and hurt him in his vital interests," crush him "by depriving him of the use of the sea."[15] Effective defense, hence, did not consist primarily of power to protect but of power to injure. Maintained the sea-power strategist:

however defensive in origin or in political character a war may be, the assumption of simple defensive in war is ruin. War once declared, must be waged offensively, aggressively. The enemy must not be fended off, but smitten down. You may then spare him every exaction, relinquish every gain; but till down he must be struck incessantly and remorselessly.[16]

This interpretation of "defence" did not eliminate coast defenses, but it totally discarded as foolish and suicidal the concept of passive coastal defense prevalent in American naval strategy of the day. Coast defenses were necessary so that the navy might be permitted offensive action. Stationary fortification was essential, yet there should exist an "element of offensive power, local in character, distinct from the offensive navy" of which, nevertheless, it formed a part; for this mobile aspect of coast defense, "the torpedo boat, in its various developments" was admittedly suited.[17]

15 Mahan, *The Influence of Sea Power upon History, 1660–1783*, 86–87; Mahan, "Current Fallacies upon Naval Subjects," *Harper's Monthly*, June, 1898, reprinted in *Lessons of the War with Spain and Other Articles*, 286, 301. See also Mahan, *Retrospect and Prospect*, 151–54.

16 Mahan, "Current Fallacies upon Naval Subjects," *Harper's Monthly*, June, 1898, reprinted in *Lessons of the War with Spain and Other Articles*, 302; and "Preparedness for Naval War," *Harper's Monthly*, March, 1897, reprinted in *The Interest of America in Sea Power, Present and Future*, 192–93.

17 Mahan, *ibid.*, 194–96.

Nor did this interpretation of "defence" completely discard commerce raiding, yet it also relegated this prevalent and contemporary concept of the navy's function in war to a definitely subsidiary role. The *guerre de course* was an important "secondary operation"; it was, however, only overbearing power on the sea that struck down the enemy and allowed him to appear on the great common solely as a fugitive. "This overbearing power," wrote Mahan after an analysis of a century and a quarter crowded with naval wars, "can only be exercised by great navies." Cruisers would not suffice for this purpose; ships of the line, capital ships, not too large but numerous and well manned were required. These vessels must operate as a fleet and not in detached units; almost without exception history had shown grievous effects from division of naval forces. Inasmuch as the sea was all one and no part could be fenced off and defended by itself, for one's own safety the opponent must be driven from the whole. Commerce raiding could not achieve this objective; only the destruction or neutralization of the organized force of the enemy afloat could assure this result. Hence "the proper main objective" of the navy was the enemy's navy either in battle or in blockade.[18]

Mahan was aware of the grave defects and serious limitations of the blockade, of the tremendous strain upon the blockaders and the intense relief brought by each decisive engagement; but failing the good fortune to achieve the forthright elimination of the enemy's fleet, the blockade was strategically wise. Mahan viewed the blockade as both offensive and defensive; it was both "sword and shield." The blockading fleet not only protected home coasts, overseas territories, and trade communications, but also cut the sinews of the enemy's power by depriving him of sea-borne

18 Mahan, *The Influence of Sea Power upon History, 1660–1783*, 138; Mahan, *Naval Strategy, Compared and Contrasted with the Principles of Military Operations on Land*, 6–9, 115–18, 199.

commerce, promoted the reduction of his colonies, and conferred the power to detract and interfere with his action on land all the way from diversionary landings to real invasions. In Mahan's essay on "Blockade in Relation to Naval Strategy," he wrote:

Whatever the number of ships needed to watch those in an enemy's port they are fewer by far than those that will be required to protect the scattered interests imperilled by the enemy's escape. Whatever the difficulty of compelling the enemy to fight near the port, it is less than that of finding him and bringing him into action when he has got far away. Whatever the force within, it is less than it will be when joined to that, which may at or near the same time escape from another. Whatever the tactical difficulties involved, the strategic necessities compel a diligent study of how to meet them.[19]

The essence of Mahan's strategy lay in this concept of the command of the sea, this doctrine of concentration of power. In the final analysis, his interpretation of "defence" called ideally for a fleet of capital ships capable of destroying the enemy's naval forces or of driving them to hiding, of blockading their ports and so disrupting their maritime communications, and of denying the enemy access to areas where they might seriously endanger the free flow of one's own merchant shipping. Mahan was doubtful, however, whether one power could ever again control the sea as England had in the eighteenth and nineteenth centuries.[20]

It is only fair to point out that Mahan did not attribute England's successful challenge of the naval power of Spain,

[19] Mahan, "Blockade in Relation to Naval Strategy," United States Naval Institute Proceedings, Vol. XXI (December, 1895), 856, 864–65 (Reprinted from Journal of the Royal United Service Institution, Vol. XXXIX, November, 1895); Mahan, "Considerations Governing the Disposition of Navies," National Review, July, 1902, reprinted in Retrospect and Prospect, 153–54.

[20] Mahan, The Influence of Sea Power upon History, 1660–1783, 138; see also "Possibilities of an Anglo-American Reunion," North American Review, November, 1894, reprinted in The Interest of America in Sea Power, Present and Future, 124–25.

Holland, and France wholly to superior fleets and sounder strategy. He repeatedly emphasized the very great and, so far as her European rivals were concerned, the unique advantage of her insularity which made it possible for her to concentrate virtually her whole military effort on naval development.[21] Geographical position also favored England, giving her the advantage of interior lines; and, furthermore, until the appearance of modern fleets in the Western Hemisphere and the Far East, her position when coupled with Gibraltar gave her virtual global command of the sea, chiefly because of her ability to assert successfully control over the narrows of the English Channel, the North Sea, and the Mediterranean.[22]

Political considerations supplemented, even perhaps partially altered, Mahan's view of naval preparedness for the United States which a military approach alone seemed to dictate. "Preparation, like most things," said he, was "a question of both kind and degree." And he continued:

The measure of degree is the estimated force which the strongest *probable* enemy can bring against you, allowance being made for clear drawbacks upon his total force, imposed by his own embarrassments and responsibilities in other parts of the world. The calculation is partly military, partly political, the latter, however, being the dominant factor in the premises.[23]

[21] Mahan, *The Influence of Sea Power upon History, 1660–1783*, 140–41, 170; *The Influence of Sea Power upon the French Revolution and Empire, 1793–1812*, II, 17; "Considerations Governing the Disposition of Navies," *National Review*, July, 1902, reprinted in *Retrospect and Prospect*, 163–64, 169; "The Persian Gulf and International Relations," *National Review*, September, 1902, reprinted in *ibid.*, 247.

[22] Mahan, *The Influence of Sea Power upon History, 1660–1783*, 31–32; *The Influence of Sea Power upon the French Revolution and Empire, 1793–1812*, I, 10; *The Interest of America in International Conditions*, 53 ff., 192, 195–96; *Naval Strategy*, 73–74, 128–30, 177; "Considerations Governing the Disposition of Navies," *National Review*, July, 1902, reprinted in *Retrospect and Prospect*, 165–68.

[23] Mahan, "Preparedness for Naval War," *Harper's Monthly*, March, 1897, reprinted in *The Interest of America in Sea Power, Present and Future*, 193; *ibid.*, 180.

Though the emphasis placed upon "probable" is Mahan's, yet attention should be called to the other qualifying word, "strongest." Earlier in the same article he stated: "It is not the most probable of dangers but the most formidable that must be selected as measuring the degree of military precaution to be embodied in the military preparations henceforth to be maintained."

Political considerations as they affected the American naval situation were discussed at length in the sea-power advocate's first major magazine article. It was "perfectly reasonable and legitimate" when calculating our military needs to take into account "the remoteness of the chief naval and military nations" and the consequent difficulty of maintaining operations at a distance. It was also proper to keep in mind "the jealousies of the European family of states," their unwillingness to incur the enmity of the United States with fear of revenge in the future, and their inability to detach more than a portion of their forces to American shores without losing weight in European councils. Yet the strategist immediately cautioned that however "undeniable and just" as elements in the calculation of the statesmen were these advantages of a political nature accruing to the United States because of her position and status among the nations, they were after all "mere defensive factors and partial at that" and much more needed "to be cast into the scale that it may incline in favor of our strength."[24]

It was in such tones and along these lines that Mahan considered the nature and the degree of naval preparedness required for the United States; naval growth and naval strategy were part and parcel of his "outward view," implicit in the sea-power doctrine. Sometimes in magazine articles and sometimes in books, sometimes in the classroom and sometimes in committee hearings, sometimes to the

[24] Mahan, "The United States Looking Outward," *Atlantic Monthly*, December, 1890, reprinted in *ibid.*, 16–18.

Secretary of the Navy and sometimes to the President of the United States, sometimes subtly by insinuation but more often openly, in season and out of season, for a quarter of a century this great navalist and strategist preached these views to an audience well-nigh incalculable in numbers.

Mahan's writings came at a critical moment in American naval development. To be sure, the corner had been turned in the matter of naval development with the adoption of the program calling for the gradual scrapping of the anti-quated remnants of the Civil War navy and the replacement of these obsolete crafts with modern vessels embodying some of the revolutionary advances in naval technology, yet no first-class battleships had been authorized. Furthermore American naval policy, except for a few voices crying in the wilderness, was still dominated by the belief that commerce raiding and passive coast defense were the basic functions of the navy in war.

Naval development in the United States entered a decidedly new phase in 1889–90. Circumstances were propitious for the inauguration of "modern navalism" patterned basically upon the Mahanian thesis. Harrison's secretaries of state and navy contributed materially. Blaine's return to his former position in the cabinet presaged an aggressive foreign policy. Benjamin F. Tracy, a man of outstanding ability, brought to the secretaryship of the navy talents of energy and initiative. His annual report of 1889 gave official endorsement to the capital-ship theory of naval defense and emphasized the prime necessity of a fighting fleet. The secondary role of cruiser commerce destruction and the utter inadequacy of passive coast defense were also set forth.[25] Harold and Margaret Sprout in their able and carefully developed account of *The Rise of American Naval Power* assert: "Whether Mahan drafted certain passages, whether Tracy had access to Mahan's manuscript [of his

25 51 Cong., 1 sess., *House Executive Doc. 1, Part III*, 3–4.

magnum opus], or whether he merely consulted him, it is difficult to say, but the ideas were indubitably Mahan's."[26]

Circumstances in the Southwest Pacific lent support to Tracy's plea for an enlarged and improved navy. The Anglo-German-American interests in Samoa reaching a climax in the early months of 1889 brought forcibly home our naval deficiencies. The hurricane in Apia put out of commission three American warships, whose "old fashioned engines and defective steampower" prevented their reaching the open sea where they could ride out the storm. This loss served as tragic proof of the need for modern vessels and left us with virtually no warships worthy of the name in the Pacific.

Certain factors much closer geographically than the Samoan Islands also contributed to the partial adoption of the Tracy report. By 1889 the legislative proviso in the previous naval appropriation bills calling for materials of "domestic manufacture" had given the necessary stimulation to manufacturing interests whose capacity for producing the plate, ordnance, and machinery for battleships of the largest size and power was shortly to equal their already eager desire for increased orders.

Some six weeks after the publication of Mahan's book, *The Influence of Sea Power upon History, 1660–1783*, Congress on June 30, 1890, authorized the construction of three "sea-going, coast-line battleships" with fuel endurance for five thousand nautical miles. Granted the coast-line qualification was designed partly to gain votes, the fuel stipulation clearly indicated that the American bid for command of the sea was quite restricted in scope. No specific references to Mahan were made in the debates in the House in early April or in the Senate the latter part of May. Only a few of the advocates of the bill sensed the significance of their actions. Charles A. Boutelle of Maine, chairman of the

26 Sprout and Sprout, *op. cit.*, 207.

House Naval Affairs Committee, strongly backed the report of Navy Secretary Tracy. He argued that commerce raiders and blockade-runners were not sufficient; numerous ships of the line operating aggressively as a fleet were demanded. He quoted with approval the Secretary's statement couched in Mahan's phraseology that our navy "must be able to divert an enemy's force from our coast by threatening his own, for a war, though defensive in principle may be conducted most effectively by being offensive in its operations."[27] ations."[27]

Lodge, second ranking member of the House committee, paradoxically maintained that the battleship clause was "strictly" in the line of previous policy. More accurately and more in keeping with the changing strategical ideology, he added that this construction of ships of the highest speed and fighting capacity was the "next step" in our naval program and that it would enable our fleet to meet the enemy "on the high seas" before they reached our coast.[28] However, most of the debate on the proposed legislation, favorable as well as unfavorable, was still in the traditional terms of commerce destruction and passive coast defense.[29]

Naval development made steady advances during the nineties. No name is more closely correlated with this progress than Mahan's. Tracy's successor, Hilary A. Herbert, chairman of the House Naval Affairs Committee in the Forty-ninth, Fiftieth, and Fifty-second Congresses, recorded his indebtedness to Mahan in the following letter of October 4, 1893. He wrote:

Permit me to thank you for your kind letter and to tell you of my change of opinion as to the War College, after inspecting the War College building personally and carefully reading the

27 51 Cong., 1 sess., *Cong. Rec.*, 3163, 3170.
28 *Ibid.*, 3170.
29 For debates on the battleship clause in the House, *ibid.*, 3161–71, 3216–23, 3256–71; in the Senate, *ibid.*, 5173–82, 5236–38, 5276–97.

241

two articles by you upon the subject, and also your two volumes upon *The Influence of Sea Power on the French Revolution.* . . . I . . . am particularly struck with your citations from history of the comparatively little effect of commerce destroyers in bringing the war to a successful conclusion, and expect to use in my forthcoming report the information you have therein set forth in my arguments for the building of battleships.[30]

Herbert's report incorporated these points in forceful language with substantiation obviously drawn from Mahan's studies. The Secretary's unqualified endorsement of the capital-ship theory of naval defense clearly indicates that the strategist's theory of naval policy was gaining strong and able adherents. His forthright assertion that the navy was more than a defensive guardian of the home shores in war, that it was a powerful agency in the advancement and protection of American commerce and a significant factor in the re-enforcement of American diplomacy in all parts of the globe likewise suggests the growing support given to Mahan's philosophy of politico-naval imperialism.[31]

Though not always specifically recognizing the indebtedness, senators and representatives showed an increasing knowledge of Mahan and a growing appreciation of his ideas. As the discussions on American policy in the Pacific and in the Caribbean afforded opportunities for congressmen to utilize the expansionist doctrines of Mahan, so did the debates upon naval appropriations offer occasions to consider the wisdom of his views upon naval growth and strategy. "Sea power" became a familiar phrase; it was frequently eulogized as "essential to the greatness of every great people," as that without which no nation could "be great or complete."[32] Mahan must surely have been pleased

30 Cited by Taylor, *Life of Admiral Mahan*, 34–35.

31 Navy Department, *Annual Report*, 1893. See 53 Cong., 2 sess., *House Executive Doc. 1, Part III*, 37–38, 40–41.

32 53 Cong., 3 sess., *Cong. Rec.*, 2260, 3084, 3106.

when national legislators talked of the limited role of commerce raiding, of the inadequacy of the "monitor and harbor defense" strategy, and of the vital need for "real seagoing battle ships."[33] Battleships were called "the first line of defense" and "the backbone of the modern navy"; they permitted the employment of "the offensive-defensive system"; they were essential to "the command of the sea."[34] Strategical concepts had passed beyond passive coast defense and commerce destruction when congressmen viewed it imperative to have a "formidable fighting force" that was "able to go out and meet the enemy upon the high seas," based on the strategy that "the best defense in the world is the means of offense."[35] That the broader implications of Mahan's teachings had been grasped is apparent in the following comments of Senator Proctor of Vermont, an adherent of coastal defense:

The Senator from Delaware referred to the great work of Captain Mahan, but its one great fundamental idea is that to build up a great navy a country must own colonial possessions across the sea in different parts of the world; . . . that a navy is necessary for colonies and that colonies are necessary for a navy. Captain Mahan's book is generally accepted as the best authority. . . . That being the case, and we not having during this session annexed any of the outlying Islands, I certainly think we ought to go slowly in the matter of this increase of battleships.[36]

The failure to have annexed any outlying territories cannot be blamed upon Mahan, Lodge, and other exponents of the "large policy" who were doing everything in their

[33] 52 Cong., 1 sess., *Cong. Rec.*, 4357; 55 Cong., 2 sess., *Cong. Rec.*, 3183.

[34] 52 Cong., 1 sess., *Cong. Rec.*, 4357; 53 Cong., 3 sess., *Cong. Rec.*, 2251–57, 2307, 3107–3108, 3109–12; 54 Cong., 1 sess., *Cong. Rec.*, 3193; 55 Cong., 2 sess., *Cong. Rec.*, 3461, 3462, 3463, 3467.

[35] 52 Cong., 1 sess., *Cong. Rec.*, 4357; 54 Cong., 1 sess., *Cong. Rec.*, 3195; 55 Cong., 2 sess., *Cong. Rec.*, 3197.

[36] 53 Cong., 3 sess., *Cong. Rec.*, 3113.

power in the last decade of the century to persuade their country to take the "outward view." It was in these years that Mahan as the skillful publicist was seeking to indoctrinate his fellow countrymen with the politico-economic imperialism of his sea-power philosophy. Always opportunely, and at times amazingly synchronized with the march of events, he sought to focus public attention upon the Isthmus and the Caribbean, upon Hawaii and the future of the Pacific. The persistence of difficulty in Samoa, the Hawaiian imbroglio with all its perplexities, the ever present fisheries controversy in the Bering Sea, the Sino-Japanese War with its repercussions in world politics, the growing interest in an American-controlled canal, the acutely disrupting Venezuelan crisis, and the Cuban revolution furnished what additional impetus was necessary to secure the continuance of naval appropriations. By 1894 cruising stations also were reorganized, and arrangements made for all vessels of each station to assemble periodically for exercises and maneuvers.[37] As time passed, there gradually emerged Mahan's "fighting fleet," designed and built to wage the offensive, guided in policy by concentration of power, and posited on the conviction that though there was no necessity to equal European fleets, our safety and interest demanded the indisputable command of all strategic approaches to the continental United States.

The Spanish-American War confirmed the value of the battleship program and vindicated the command of the sea concept. However, the hysterical anxiety of the Atlantic coast, occasioned by the totally ungrounded fear of attack by Cervera's fleet, bore evidence that Mahan's views concerning the functions of the navy had not spread sufficiently widely nor sunk deeply enough. The brief struggle strikingly demonstrated the rigid limitations which the

37 Navy Department, *Annual Report*, 1894. See 53 Cong., 2 sess., *House Executive Doc. 1, Part III*, 23.

problems of fuel, service, and repairs imposed upon the radius of operation of modern naval vessels. The war with Spain renewed and increased the sense of national pride in the navy. It brought consummation to the Mahanian program of manifest destiny far more quickly and far more extensively than its ardent advocates could have dreamed of a short decade earlier.

The lessons of the war with Spain did not go unheeded by Mahan; he wrote a series of essays on the topic in 1898–99 which were published in book form in the latter year. Mahan affirmed that the command of the sea had won the day and made possible the successful military invasion of Cuba and Puerto Rico. The policy of concentration had proved itself, and this despite the hysteria of the coastal regions. This embarrassment "should be pondered" as an "object lesson"; to avoid the repetition of "the preposterous and humiliating terror of the past months," Mahan suggested the improvement of the nation's coast defenses. Furthermore, he strongly urged that all views which envisaged the primary function of the navy as coastal defense be completely scrapped; he stated once again that history had shown without exception that the offense, not the defense, determined issues. He advocated that our future naval construction program be planned in light of these lessons. Primarily this demanded more and better battleships, somewhat larger and more powerful with coal capacity greatly increased to permit wider cruising range. He cautioned against excessive size; he thought that ten to twelve thousand tons was the best vessel and recommended that they be similar in construction so that they could maneuver and fight together in squadrons.

Mahan did not slacken his endeavors with the achievements so dramatically accorded in 1898–99, but rather doubled his efforts that these victories might be secured and yet others gained. Nearly threescore articles definitely pertaining to contemporary problems and covering such topics as "Current Fallacies upon Naval Subjects," "Considerations Governing the Disposition of Navies," "Conditions Determining the Naval Expansion of the United States," "The United States Navy Department," "Retrospect upon War between Japan and Russia," "The Panama Canal and Sea Power in the Pacific," "The Place of Force in International Relations," "Germany's Naval Ambitions," and "Sea Power in the Present European War" came in almost never ending succession. Approximately four-fifths of these articles appeared in American magazines and about the same number were reprinted, forming in total seven volumes. In addition, six other studies of a politico-naval import were published. *The Interest of America in International Conditions* was exclusively concerned with contemporary happenings, while most of the others, such as *Sea Power in the Relation to the War of 1812*, were replete with "lessons" for the present and the future. Moreover, much that had been previously written about the Caribbean and the Pacific took on fresh interest.

Mahan's approach in these years was not essentially different from that previously indicated. The close correlation between international affairs and naval requirements was repeatedly pointed out. Now definitely a world power, the United States could no longer be merely an indifferent observer in the political evolution of Europe and Asia. Political considerations determined the nature of our military preparations and as international situations altered corresponding adjustments in our naval program became essential, he argued.

Nor, in general, did Mahan's views undergo drastic change. The doctrine of sea power and the principles of naval strategy were further elaborated and substantiated. Vistas widened, phraseology varied, former concepts were further developed and buttressed by new proofs when op-

United States naval airship and a convoy in World War I.
Official U.S. Navy photograph

Convoy off Brest, November 1, 1918. Twenty-five ships seen from *Rambler*, a yacht armed as a convoy ship.

The *Leviathan* in camouflage as she served as troop transport during World War I carrying 12,000 on board. *Official U.S. Navy photographs*

portunities, such as the Russo-Japanese War, permitted. For example, Mahan utilized the Russian fleet disaster as a striking example of the validity of the capital-ship theory. He wrote:

To an instructed, thoughtful, naval mind in the United States, there is no contingency affecting the country, as interested in the navy, so menacing as the fear of popular clamor influencing an irresolute, or militarily ignorant, administration to divide the battleship force into two divisions, the Atlantic and the Pacific. . . . Concentration protects both coasts, division exposes both. *It is of vital consequence to the nation of the United States, that its people, contemplating the Russo-Japanese naval war, substitute therein, in their apprehension, Atlantic for Baltic, and Pacific for Port Arthur. So they will comprehend as well as apprehend.*[38]

The growing strength and the expanding ambitions of the German Empire in these years caused Mahan to be more and more apprehensive of the future. Though he recognized German commercial and naval activities as "legitimate expressions" of sovereign rights, he viewed them as grave menaces to American interests. Friendly relations with Great Britain were essential; in the maintenance of British sea power he saw not only the security of the British Empire but the safety of the United States as well. At times he thought it not even beyond the bounds of possibility for Germany to defeat successively the British and American navies, to protect her two land fronts on the continent and yet, despite the obvious difficulties in waging war across the ocean with no naval bases on this continent, to "spare a large expeditionary force for overseas operations."[39]

The horizon of naval perspectives and strategic responsi-

38 Mahan, "Retrospect upon the War between Japan and Russia," *National Review*, May, 1906, reprinted in *Naval Administration and Warfare*, 168, 173. The italics are Mahan's.

39 Mahan, *America's Interest in International Conditions*, 36, 75-78, 162–63; *Naval Strategy*, 104 ff.

bilities was greatly expanded by the Spanish-American War. The nation's naval policies in the decade following were recast in an enlarged and bolder form. Modern navalism, visible in Secretary Tracy's report, became forthrightly avowed and openly pursued. The acquisition of outlying dependencies coupled with the psychological factors incidental to a victorious war gave a rational and persuasive tone for a more aggressive policy. The General Board in 1903, adopting a long-range program designed to give the country what the navy thought would be a well-balanced fleet, took into consideration "an estimate and forecast of the future as to what would be the development of foreign countries with which conflict might be probable and what our own development should be to insure peace."[40] The American naval program was no longer content with merely a bigger and better navy designed to give us the command of a wide zone extending outward a thousand miles from our continental. seaboards; in light of increased frontiers and growing international complications, it became geared to naval rivalries of Europe and the Far East. The goal now was "a Navy second to none but that of Great Britain."

In these years following the turn of the century, the influence of Mahan in the growth of United States naval policy and power was perhaps second only to that of his eager student and close friend, Theodore Roosevelt. At the close of the Spanish-American War, Senator Lodge reasserted his indebtedness to Mahan; he wrote that he considered him the "greatest authority living or dead on naval warfare"; and added, "I venture to hope that I have not studied your teaching upon this subject wholly in vain." Over a decade later, in 1912, he told Mahan in response to his letter just received:

It gives me a number of new points admirably stated, which I very much want when I come to discuss battleships in the Sen-

[40] Navy Department, *Annual Report*, 1915, 3–4.

ate. .... I shall rob you in a perfectly conscienceless way and use all your suggestions freely for the benefit of my speech.[41]

Other congressmen called upon the historian-philosopher as "one of the ablest of modern writers" both to bear witness that "the glory and security of a people" lay in sea power and to testify in behalf of increased appropriations for further ships of the line.[42] The capital-ship theory of strategy was widely if not universally endorsed.[43] His "Reflections, Historic and Otherwise, Suggested by the Battle of the Japan Sea" was incorporated in the debates; in another case a representative supported his arguments upon various naval topics by seven selections from Mahan's books and magazine articles.[44]

The chairman of the House Naval Affairs Committee in 1911 sought the views of this "most distinguished naval strategist living" as regards the necessity for a strong battleship fleet in the Pacific to meet the demands of the West Coast states. Mahan's reply might well be surmised: the concentration of the fleet was essential and under no circumstances should it be divided; as to whether the fleet should be in the Atlantic or Pacific, he thought that beyond his province to state.[45]

The construction during and immediately following the war with Spain raised the United States Navy from a lowly and insignificant place in 1889 to the second strongest. Unsupported by an indifferent Congress and confronted with renewed naval rivalry abroad, the United States shortly fell

41 Lodge to Mahan, October 19, 1898; Lodge to Mahan, April 9, 1912: Mahan Papers.

42 56 Cong., 1 sess., *Cong. Rec.*, 4319; 56 Cong., 2 sess., *Cong. Rec.*, 1421; 58 Cong., 2 sess., *Cong. Rec.*, 2075–77; 59 Cong., 1 sess., *Cong. Rec.*, 6979.

43 56 Cong., 1 sess., *Cong. Rec.*, 4319; 56 Cong., 2 sess., *Cong. Rec.*, 1419; 58 Cong., 2 sess., *Cong. Rec.*, 2368–69; 50 Cong., 1 sess., *Cong. Rec.*, 4576.

44 59 Cong., 2 sess., *Cong. Rec.*, 1051–56; 58 Cong., 2 sess., *Cong. Rec.*, 2095–2101.

45 George W. Perkins to Mahan, January 7, 1911; Mahan to Perkins, January 11, 1911: Mahan Papers.

behind. Her failure to maintain the pace cannot be placed upon the lack of advice, warnings, and pleas of the publicist-propagandist, Alfred Thayer Mahan, nor upon the lack of enthusiasm, initiative, and showmanship of the Mahanian-indoctrinated Theodore Roosevelt.

In the discussion of Mahan's connection with the navy during the Spanish-American War, allusion was made to his belief that responsibility in way of professional advice to the civilian secretary of the navy should be individual rather than corporate, as was the case in the emergency Naval War Board. He made this suggestion to Secretary Long at once upon his appointment to the board before any difference with his colleagues had arisen or could arise. He added, "Resting, as my opinion does, upon a wide study of military history, it is not liable to change, and at present it has the advantage of absolute impersonality."[46] He repeated his views but without success. He told Luce:

I have written and talked and stormed for three months before the Board, the Secretary, and the President, and I feel now very much like the teacher who after laborious explanations, receives from one of his boys one of those answers we see in the funny columns of a newspaper.[47]

In 1900 this body, which had been created during the war to serve as a board of strategy, was reconstituted and designated as the "General Board," but without Congressional enactment. There was considerable agitation in and out of the service that the board be given a status of permanency and that its powers be enlarged so as to be comparable to the general staffs of European pattern. This problem of reorganization of the Navy Department elicited Roosevelt's attention when he became president. Mahan was eager for reform and wrote the President that there was

46 Mahan to Long, May 10, 1898, Long Papers.
47 Mahan to Luce [1898?], Luce Papers.

urgent need for an organized body which could "impart accuracy, clearness and fixity, lasting from administration to administration."[48] He appropriately contributed two articles to magazines upon the matter of 'naval organization: "The United States Navy Department" and "The Principles of Naval Administration, Historically Considered: The American and British Systems Compared." Along with certain other essays, these immediately appeared in *Naval Administration and Warfare*. Mahan maintained:

> The utility of a steadying factor, of a body of digested professional knowledge, continuously applied to the problems of naval advance is evident. . . . The essence of their [General Board] utility will consist in their embodying a policy which they can only do by permanence. Such policy . . . will ever be subject to the Secretary's alteration . . . but there can be no more doubt of the utility of such an embodied policy than there can be of a settled national tradition like those about entangling alliances, or against European interference in this hemisphere.[49]

The consideration of departmental organization was forced upon Congress by Roosevelt in 1904. Mahan's approval of a continuous staff and of single responsibility in war was brought out in the hearings before the House Naval Affairs Committee.[50] Congressmen, fearful that the creation of such a naval staff might establish an institution that would ultimately not only dominate the civilian secretary but deprive them of their policy-determining function as well, refused to give their sanction.

Mahan did not let the matter drop. He submitted an account of the activities of the Naval War Board to the Gen-

48 Mahan to Roosevelt, September 7, 1903, Roosevelt Papers.

49 Mahan, "The United States Navy Department," *Scribner's*, May, 1903, reprinted in *Naval A dministration and Warfare*, 84–85.

50 58 Cong., 2 sess., *Hearings before the House Naval Affairs Committee, 146*, 843.

eral Board, which report forcefully emphasized the necessity of a continuous body concerned with the preparation of
war plans and naval policy.[51] Nor did Roosevelt cease to
agitate for a revamping of the Navy Department. It is probable that he was "a sympathetic observer, if not actually a
conspirator" in the Reuterdahl criticisms of 1908 of the
navy which provoked a senatorial investigation and "set
the stage for another drive to create a general staff."[52]

Mahan and Roosevelt again corresponded at some length
upon the matter. Mahan proposed a general staff, "continuous in existence and gradual in change," as the "only means"
by which "consecutive knowledge" essential for the formation of sound policy and action could be achieved. Allud-
ing to his historical studies and his experiences with the
Naval War Board in 1898, he reiterated, as his "particular
point," his belief that "advice must be single, not corporate"; that though the knowledge must be in the General
Staff at large the chief must be solely responsible for all information and advice to the Secretary, whose position must
remain unweakened with power "to overrule and upset, if
necessary, every one beneath him, from the Chief of Staff
down." Roosevelt appointed Mahan as one of the commission to study the problem.[53] Acting upon the recommendation of this group, the President appointed a joint commission of naval and military men charged with the task of giving consideration to matters vital to national defense; he
made Mahan chairman of this commission.[54] Nothing in
way of reorganization was accomplished; the General Board,
as a creature of the Secretary, remained in existence.

[51] Navy Department, Bureau of Naval Personnel, General File, No. 2473—14.

[52] Sprout and Sprout, *op. cit.*, 275–76.

[53] Roosevelt to Mahan, January 8, 1909; Mahan to Roosevelt, January 13, 1909; Roosevelt to Mahan, January 29, 1909: Roosevelt Papers. For re-port of this commission see 60 Cong., 2 sess., *Senate Doc. 693*.

[54] Roosevelt to Mahan, February 25, 1909, Roosevelt Papers.

Roosevelt consulted Mahan on technical problems such as size and speed of ships and types of battery. Mahan continued to advocate, as he had in 1898, gun power rather than speed, numbers rather than size, and he opposed all-big-gun ships. He conceded that his former maximum size of twelve thousand tons might need modification in light of the twenty-thousand-ton dreadnoughts. He said: "While I deplore the present tendency, in size as in speed, I admit that no one nation can wholly resist it. . . . it does not therefore follow, however, that no modification of a tendency, no brake, is possible." Mahan was fearful that too large ships would result in too few ships. Numbers permitted increased combination, and combined action was the particular force of fleets. Offensive power was more important than speed, for the latter fell within the province of evading the enemy while the former within that of crushing him. He also contended that a competitive race in big ships would result in the "willful, premature antiquating of good vessels."[55] In this instance Mahan led a losing fight. Among his naval colleagues, Sims, Dewey, and Fiske disagreed with him;[56] and Roosevelt threw his influence to the "big-ship" group.

Roosevelt turned to Mahan for support and advice in other matters. It was the Assistant Secretary of the Navy who had written him in 1898, "I think I have studied your books to pretty good purpose," and who had expressed indebtedness for "what I learned from your books long before I had any practical experience." It was now the President of the United States who was telling him that he was "rereading" his sea-power books and was writing, "I wish you could get

[55] Roosevelt to Mahan, October 25, 1902; September 2, 1906; Mahan to Roosevelt, October 3, 1906; October 22, 1906: Roosevelt Papers. Mahan's views are also found in 59 Cong., 2 sess., *Senate Doc. 213*. See also 59 Cong., 2 sess., *Cong. Rec.*, 1051–56.

[56] *Ibid.*; E. E. Morison, *Admiral Sims and the Modern American Navy*, 164–72.

on here. There are so many things I should like to speak to you about."[57]

On one occasion Roosevelt wrote the sea-power mentor, "I believe you will like what I said of the Navy in my [first] message." On another occasion, this time in October of 1906, he wrote:

In my message to Congress my present intention is to take the rather unusual course of commending your "War of 1812" for general reading. In any event I want to use several sentences that are contained in your book, weaving them in with my own in such a way that would make it inadvisable to try to give credit for them to you. Do you object?[58]

Mahan replied that he would be "only too glad" for the President to use any of his writings "in any manner that may be serviceable to you or that you may think serviceable to the country. The question of credit in such connection is to me quite immaterial."[59] The "unusual course" was followed, and in his message of December 3 Roosevelt called attention to the navy as "the surest guarantee of peace" which the country possessed. The teachings of history should be heeded;

a strong and a wise people will study its own failures no less than its triumphs, for there is wisdom to be learned from the study of both, of the mistake as well as of the success. For this purpose nothing could be more instructive than a rational study of the War of 1812, as it is told, for instance, by Captain Mahan.[60]

Then followed a sermon on unpreparedness, in true Mahanian style, and the "selections" which Roosevelt had hoped to weave into his message were included.

[57] Roosevelt to Mahan, March 21, 1898; March 24, 1898; Roosevelt to Mahan, September 1, 1903; November 21, 1904: Roosevelt Papers.

[58] Roosevelt to Mahan, December 11, 1901; Roosevelt to Mahan, October 22, 1906: *ibid.*

[59] Mahan to Roosevelt, October 24, 1906, *ibid.*

Noting in the press, during the 1907 difficulty with Japan arising from discriminatory action against Japanese by certain California school boards, that four battleships were to be sent to the Pacific, Mahan was filled "with dismay" and immediately wrote Roosevelt. This obvious lack of trust was too much for Roosevelt's equanimity. He replied:

don't you know me well enough to believe that I am quite incapable of such an act of utter folly as dividing our fighting fleet? I have no more thought of sending four battleships to the Pacific while there is the least possible friction with Japan than I have of going thither in a rowboat myself. On the contrary, if there should come the most remote danger of war I should at once withdraw every fighting craft from the Pacific until our whole Navy could be gathered and sent there in a body.[61]

Continued clamors from the West coast for a portion of the battleships in the Pacific drew from Roosevelt in his annual message a public appeal for a united fighting fleet. Based on sound Mahanian strategy, his message told Congress and the nation that any dispersion of the fleet to defend seacoast cities must be avoided "under penalty of terrible disaster"; the true function of the navy must ever be to attack and crush the enemy's naval forces and this end could be achieved only by the principle of concentration of power.[62]

In the very closing days of the Roosevelt administration, Mahan asked the President if he would give a "last earnest recommendation" to Taft requesting that "on no account" should he divide the fleet between the two coasts. The Chief Executive replied that he had "already warned" Taft on the

60 Richardson (ed.), *Messages and Papers of the Presidents*, X, 7445–47.

61 Mahan to Roosevelt, January 10, 1907; Roosevelt to Mahan, January 12, 1907: Roosevelt Papers.

62 Richardson, *op. cit.*, XIV, 7114.

March 2, 1909

Dear Mr. President:

Will it be in any wise improper that you should put a suggestion that you should recommend to Mr. Taft on no account to divide the battleship fleet between the two coasts?

As a matter of between out cry, this is a right sure I was. With all his presidency eminent qualifications for the Presidency, I do not know whether Mr. Taft

has a strong military sense; and as I see it, this is one of the most evident external dangers threatening the country.

Pardon the intrusion

Sincerely Yours

N. L. Wilson

President Roosevelt.

March 3, 1909.

My dear Admiral:

I had already warned Mr. Taft on the subject of
dividing the battle fleet, and had shown him my letter
to Mr. Foss of the House Naval Committee, the paragraph
of which that deals with the subject I enclose for your
information.   I shall send him in writing one final
protest.   I am sure *the fleet* will never be divided.   We got
the mischievous proposition struck out of the bill.

Faithfully yours,

Theodore Roosevelt

Rear Admiral A. T. Mahan, U.S.N.retired
    Lawrence, L.I., N.Y.

    P.S.   I enclose you a copy of my final letter to Taft.

Enclosure

March 3, 1909.

Dear Will:

One closing legacy.   Under no circumstances divide the battleship fleet between the Atlantic and Pacific Oceans prior to the finishing of the Panama Canal.   Malevolent enemies of the navy, like
Hale; timid fools, like Perkins; and conscienceless scoundrels, like
Tillman, will try to lead public opinion in a matter like this without regard to the dreadful harm they may do the country; and good,
but entirely ignorant,men may be thus misled.   I should obey no direction of Congress and pay heed to no popular sentiment, no matter
how strong, ~~of it went wrong~~ in such a vital matter as this.   When I sent the fleet
around the world there was a wild clamor that some of it should be
sent to the Pacific, and an equally mad clamor that some of it should
be left in the Atlantic.   I disregarded both.   At first it seemed
as if popular feeling was nearly a unit against me.   It is now nearly a unit in favor of what I'did.

It is now nearly four years since the close of the Russian-
Japanese war.   There were various factors that brought about Russia's defeat; but most important by all odds was her having divided
her fleet between the Baltic and the Pacific,and, furthermore, splitting
up her Pacific fleet into three utterly unequal divisions.   The entire
Japanese force was always used to smash some fraction of the Russian

'orce.   The knaves and fools who advise the separation of our fleet
ιowadays and the honest, misguided creatures who think so little
,hat they are misled by such advice, ought to take into account this
ιtriking lesson furnished by actual experience in a great war but
'our years ago.   Keep the battle fleet either in one ocean or the
ither and have the armed cruisers always in trim, as they are now,
ιo that they can be at once sent to join the battle fleet if the need
ιhould arise.

                    Faithfully yours,

                        Theodore Roosevelt

ιon. William H. Taft,
      Washington, D.C.

subject but agreed to send him "in writing one final protest" and enclosed a copy of it with his reply to Mahan.[63]

Mahan's services of a public nature continued after Roosevelt's retirement from office. In 1911 he was consulted by the Secretary of the Navy, George von Lengerke Meyer, for his views upon the proposed Council of National Defense. The Secretary found the reply "very interesting" and thought it contained "some valuable suggestions"; he sent it to a member of the House Naval Affairs Committee with the suggestion that it might be "useful" in argument before the committee.[64] Mahan was later ordered by the Navy Department to appear before the committee when hearings were held upon the matter.[65] The phase of the proposed measure that appealed most to Mahan was the close correlation of the navy, army, and diplomacy which would result. Mahan reiterated his view that "after all, our military and naval policy depends substantially upon what we conceive our relations to be with foreign countries, a forecast of the future, and what the probabilities of the future are."[66] A statement of Mahan's appearance before the committee and selections from his letter to the Secretary were incorporated in the committee's reports.[67]

Acting under instructions from the Navy Department, Mahan was a frequent lecturer at the Naval War College. He was detached from all official duty in June, 1912, after having spent fifty-six years either on the active or retired

[63] Mahan to Roosevelt, March 2, 1909; Roosevelt to Mahan, March 3, 1909: Roosevelt Papers.

[64] Meyer to Foss, January 27, 1911; Mahan to Meyer, February 1, 1911; Meyer to Hobson, February 2, 1911: cited in 61 Cong., 3 sess., *Hearings before the House Naval Affairs Committee, 51,* 669–70.

[65] Meyer to Mahan, May 17, 1911, Navy Department, Bureau of Naval Personnel, General File, No. 2473—50.

[66] 62 Cong., 2 sess., *Hearings before the House Naval Affairs Committee, 35,* 1547–48.

[67] 61 Cong., 3 sess., *House Report 2078;* 62 Cong., 2 sess., *House Report 584.*

list of the navy. During the major portion of this more than a half-century of association with the navy, he labored diligently, first for eradication of corruption and improvement of the service, then for its enlargement and increased efficiency. His activity bore witness to a passion and a sincerity, to an abiding conviction and an unfailing certainty of the validity and urgency of his message.

Mahan entered the navy in time to serve inconspicuously during its heyday of the Civil War; he was a living witness of the depths to which it sank in the years which followed; he saw it rise slowly, steadily from the nadir of the early eighties until by 1894 it ranked sixth among the powers; he served on the board of strategy in the brief and victorious war which brought new possessions to defend and which gave release to the growing desire to cut a figure on the world-stage; he observed with satisfaction in 1904 that the fleet of the United States, built or projected, was surpassed only by that of Great Britain; he was a member of the General Board and saw incorporated as the official naval policy one that looked beyond simple coastal protection to the defense of American interests wherever they might be found; he was heart and soul behind the Rooseveltian "big-navyism" and witnessed the birth of the Navy League in 1903; he lived to see his cry for "a Navy second to England only" defeated by the combined forces of an apathetic Congress and a European naval race; he saw the opening of the European holocaust which was to spread to all parts of the earth; he did not live to see the repercussions of that event upon the naval policy of his own country; he did not live to see his "second to Britain" discarded for a "second to none"; nor did he live to see what was written by his friend and admirer, Roosevelt, whose qualifications for judgment on this issue were surpassed by none. Wrote Roosevelt in 1914:

in the vitally important task of convincing the masters of us all
—the people as a whole—of the importance of a true understanding of naval needs, Mahan stood alone. There was no one
else in his class, or anywhere near it.[68]

[68] Roosevelt, "A Great Public Servant," *Outlook*, Vol. CIX (January 13, 1915), 85–86.

XII

MERCHANT MARINE AND RULES REGULATING WARFARE

AHAN'S ACTIVITIES in behalf of a program for adequate national defense were not limited to persistent pleas for naval preparedness or to repeated discussions on the intelligent employment of the navy along sound strategical principles. Sometimes in magazine articles, often in private letters, and frequently in an official or semiofficial capacity, he seized the opportunity to present his views to others upon such widely scattered topics as the relation of the merchant marine to the navy, the use of asphyxiating gases, the problem of exemption from capture of private property at sea, the wisdom of arbitration, motivating factors of national policy, and the place of force in international relations.

In 1890 the virtual nonexistence of peaceful shipping under the American flag greatly perturbed Mahan. His initial study of sea power had convinced him of the close relation between the navy and the merchant marine; the latter not only supplied in times of crisis the needed reserves but offered the surest means of constant support to a program of naval development. "In a representative government," he said, "any military expenditure must have a strongly represented interest behind it, convinced of its necessity."[1]

Mahan did not return to this theme of merchant shipping nearly so often as he did to territorial expansion, naval development, and naval strategy. This may have been due in part to the continuance of his belief, expressed in his

[1] Mahan, *The Influence of Sea Power upon History, 1660–1783*, 87–88.

265

master study, that even though the United States developed a great national shipping, she was so well protected by her distance from other great powers that it was "doubtful whether a sufficient navy would follow." The reason may have been in part his realization of the lack of the value of merchant seamen for the modern navy with its increasing technological developments. At least, in 1900 he stated that the merchant seamen were of doubtful value in the handling of a modern warship; they could supply not over one-third, at most, of the personnel needed by such a vessel.[2] Or perhaps the explanation lies in the fact that he followed the lines of attack which he thought would most likely accomplish his primary objectives.

However, it must not be assumed that Mahan ceased to desire a strong merchant marine. He was called to testify in 1904 before the specially created Merchant Marine Commission.[3] He reiterated the "obvious view," as he called it, that the greater the seafaring group, the larger the naval reserves. He told the commission that, as concerned carrying trade, when England in 1650 had been in exactly the same plight as the United States now found herself, she then adopted the Navigation Acts. "The effect was to develop the carrying trade of the nation, to largely develop their resources of seamen, and that to that, largely" was due the British supremacy of the seas which followed. He added "a bit of warning," "an important qualification": The United States must be on her guard "not to expect too much" in the form of available reserves.[4] Some pertinent excerpts from *The Influence of Sea Power upon History, 1660–1783* were

[2] Mahan, "Effect of Asiatic Conditions upon World Policies," *North American Review*, November, 1900, reprinted in *The Problem of Asia*, 199–201.

[3] Secretary of the Navy to Mahan, November 23, 1904, Navy Department, Bureau of Naval Personnel, General File, No. 2473—50.

[4] 58 Cong., 3 sess., *Hearings before the Merchant Marine Commission*, 1745–48.

BE IT PEACE OR WAR, UNCLE SAM WILL BE WELL REPRESENTED AT THE HAGUE.—From the *Journal* (Minneapolis).

Cartoon from the Minneapolis *Journal*, reprinted in the *American Monthly Review of Reviews*, May, 1899.

The Naval War College today. *Official U.S. Navy photograph*

The "Mahan corner" of the Naval War College Library. *Official U.S. Navy photograph by Lt. Commander C. Black (W), USNR*

incorporated in the commission's report to Congress the following year.[5]

Advocates of the commercial development of the United States frequently buttressed their pleas by reference to Mahan.[6] His views on the close interdependence of navy and merchant marine were utilized in the Naval Academy's prize-winning essay of 1910 which was published in the United States Naval Institute *Proceedings* and reprinted by Senate order for incorporation in Congressional documents.[7] Mahan's views along these lines were also brought out in hearings before a special subcommittee of the House Naval Affairs Committee in 1914.[8]

Mahan was a militarist, and thus it was only natural and perhaps logical that he should look askance at all measures which might tend to limit the effectiveness of war (i. e., immunity of private property at sea), to lessen its rigors (i. e., abolition of asphyxiating gases), or to decrease its frequency (i. e., arbitration). Mahan's views on these topics are most clearly seen against the background of the Hague Peace Conferences of 1899 and 1907 and attendant developments.

Mahan was a member of the American delegation to the First Hague Conference[9] and played an important, though not a conspicuous role. His colleagues were Seth Low, Stanford Newel, William Crozier, and Andrew White, who acted as chairman; Frederick Holls served as secretary to the delegation. It is now generally agreed that Russia's motive in

5 58 Cong., 3 sess., *Senate Report, 6291.*

6 53 Cong., 3 sess., *Cong. Rec.*, 2249; 55 Cong., 2 sess., *Cong. Rec.*, 3196; 56 Cong., 2 sess., *Cong. Rec.*, 1421; 58 Cong., 2 sess., *Cong. Rec.*, 2076, 2093, 2096.

7 61 Cong., 2 sess., *Senate Doc. 466*, (bound in *Reports of House Committee on Naval Affairs*).

8 63 Cong., 2 sess., *Hearings before the House Naval Affairs Committee*, II, 114.

9 Evidently John Hay had a hand in Mahan's appointment. See letters from Hay to Mahan and Hay to McKinley, November 9, 1898, and April 4, 1899, Hay Papers.

calling the conference was basically financial, a subtle ruse to relieve her overburdened exchequer. At the time, however, speculation was rife.[10] Mahan was perhaps as near the truth as any of his contemporaries; in a letter to Ashe after his return from The Hague, he suggested as the immediate cause

the shock of our late war [Spanish-American] resulting in the *rapprochement* of the United States and Great Britain and our sudden appearance in Asia as a result of a successful war. . . . the prospect of America and England side by side, demanding China be kept open for trade, means either a change in her [Russian] policy or war. Hence she wishes peace—by pledge.[11]

Mahan's reaction to The Hague gathering and its activities was realistic in the Bismarckian sense. "The Conference itself was very well for a time," he wrote Ashe in the same letter, "and interesting in a way; but ten weeks of it was rather too much." It can be said in all fairness that he was not in great sympathy with the purported purposes of the conference. He had made known his views concerning arbitration, armaments, and kindred topics during the decade of the nineties. It would have been strange if he had now changed front—indeed, it was not expected that he should.

Mahan believed that though "arbitration should always be a nation's first thought . . . it should never pledge itself by treaty, or otherwise, to arbitrate before it knows what the subject of dispute is. Needless to say, I have no sympathy with those who hold that war is never imperative."[12] At the Hague Conference, it was Captain Mahan who "threw in a bomb," as Andrew White termed it, relative to the convention (Article 27) regulating the peaceable settlement of international conflicts as an infringement of the Monroe Doc-

10 E. J. Dillon, *The Eclipse of Russia*, 296 ff.; *Die Grosse Politik der Europaischen Kabinette, 1871–1914*, XV, 146 ff., and G. P. Gooch and H. Temperley, *British Documents on the Origins of the War, 1898–1914*, I, 216 ff.
11 Mahan to Ashe, September 23, 1899, Flowers Collection.
12 Mahan to Ashe, September 23, 1898, *ibid.*

trine.[13] A resultant declaration was drawn up to meet his contention and was incorporated in the official proceedings. Mahan thought it "difficult to exaggerate the actual importance" to the United States of this qualifying declaration and wrote of it to Lodge and alluded to it in an article in the *Independent*.[14] In the drafting of the declaration he claimed no part, but he did seek to have the "records" straight about his contribution. He thought Secretary Holls in his story of *The Peace Conference at The Hague* gave the impression that he, rather than Mahan, had been responsible for this qualification. Mahan took the matter seriously, though privately, and wrote not only to Holls but to several other persons.[15]

Mahan frequently informed his British and American audiences of his views on arbitration. He considered arbitration limited both in scope and effectiveness, and as a basis for justice faulty and dangerous. Law was "artificial and often of long date" and "frequently inapplicable to a present dispute." The settlement, therefore, was insecure for its foundations were not solid; "in the long run the play of natural forces" reached "an adjustment corresponding to the fundamental facts of the case."[16] "National honor" and "vital interests" represented sentiments and determinations which defied "every argument but force," and "equity which cannot be had by law must be had by force."[17]

13 Andrew White, *Autobiography*, II, 338 ff.

14 Mahan, "The Boer Republics and the Monroe Doctrine," *Independent*, Vol. LII (May 10, 1900), 1102; Lodge to Mahan, May 14, 1900, Lodge Papers.

15 There are thirty-five letters from March, 1901, through March, 1902, on this controversy in the Mahan Papers. Correspondents include J. B. Moore in addition to members of the American delegation. See also Mahan to Long, April 25, 1901, Long Papers.

16 Mahan, *Armaments and Arbitration*, 12.

17 Mahan, "The Panama Canal and Sea Power," *Century*, June, 1911, reprinted in *ibid.*, 171; Mahan, "A Twentieth-Century Outlook," *Harper's Monthly*, September, 1897, reprinted in *The Interest of America in Sea Power, Present and Future*, 228.

Mahan, indeed, put the question of arbitration upon a high level of morality. He wrote in 1899:

The great danger of undiscriminating advocacy of arbitration, which threatens even the cause it seeks to maintain, is that it may lead men to tamper with equity, to compromise with unrighteousness, soothing their conscience with the belief that war is so entirely wrong that beside it no other tolerated evil is wrong.[18]

A half-dozen years later he said:

In these days of glorified arbitration it cannot be affirmed too distinctly that bodies of men—nations—have convictions binding on their consciences, as well as interests which are vital in character; and that nations, no more than individuals may surrender conscience to another's keeping. Still less may they rightfully pre-engage so to do. Nor is this conclusion invalidated by a triumph of the unjust war. Subjugation to wrong is not acquiescence in wrong. A beaten nation is not necessarily a disgraced nation; but the nation or man is disgraced who shirks an obligation to defend right.[19]

Roosevelt drew material from this quotation, both verbatim and in context, for his 1906 annual message to Congress.[20]

At the conference, Mahan vigorously objected to the outlawry of projectiles, the sole purpose of which was to

---

[18] Mahan, "The Peace Conference and the Moral Aspect of War," *North American Review*, October, 1899, reprinted in *Lessons of the War with Spain and Other Articles*, 236–37.

[19] Mahan, *Sea Power in Its Relation to the War of 1812*, viii.

[20] Richardson (ed.), *Messages and Papers of the Presidents*, X, 7445–46. Mahan and Roosevelt frequently exchanged ideas on arbitration. Most of the fifteen letters in the last six months of 1911 mention this subject. See especially the four letters in August, Mahan Papers. Four letters of the Mahan-Lodge correspondence in January and February, 1912, also deal with arbitration, Lodge Papers. The inadvisability of arbitration treaties was frequently mentioned in correspondence with Englishmen; for example: Mahan to Colonel J. B. Sterling, February 13, 1896, April 27, 1897, and May 31, 1897; Mahan to Admiral Bouverie Clarke, September 6, 1907, July 23, 1909: Mahan Papers.

spread asphyxiating or deleterious gases. His reasons for opposition were: first, that too little was known of the matter to warrant intelligent action; secondly, that, granted the existence of such shells, the mere charge of cruelty was equally valid when used against the torpedoes and firearms, both of which now were used without scruples; thirdly, that being asphyxiated by gases might be no worse than being choked by water, which was the result for many, if not most, sailors when ships were sunk by a torpedo boat.[21] His views resulted in the United States delegation's gaining the distinction of casting the only negative vote to this proposal, though Great Britain, having qualified her vote with the proviso that there should be unanimity, remained a nonsignatory until 1907. Chairman White was dissatisfied with the course of the United States but pleaded helpless, "What can a layman do when he has against him the foremost contemporary military and naval experts?"[22]

The conference formulated and adopted ten articles which looked toward the adaptation of the Geneva Convention of 1864 to maritime war. They were left unsigned by the American delegation, again chiefly through the influence of Mahan. Upon his return, he twice wrote Secretary Long of the Navy Department suggesting close scrutiny of the articles by the legal staff of his department. "I formulated certain objections to them and proposed amendments, for which I could obtain no support; but I am quite sure I was right, and, I should regret to think that our government should accept this work . . . without careful consideration of the articles themselves and of my arguments upon them."[23]

[21] J. B. Scott (ed.), *The Proceedings of the Hague Peace Conference,* 283 ff.; White, *op. cit.,* II, 282–83, 319–20.

[22] *Ibid.,* II, 319–20.

[23] Mahan to Long, August 21, 1899; September 27, 1899: Long Papers. Cf. Scott, *op. cit.,* 391 ff.

Mahan likewise strenuously attacked the view held by his government and the rest of his fellow delegates on the matter of immunity of private property at sea. The absurdity of granting immunity for private property was one of the lessons which Mahan had gained from his study of naval history. The "freedom of the seas" was in violation of his "command of the seas," and he had long ridiculed the folly of America's official position upon this subject. The object of war was to smite the enemy "incessantly and remorselessly" and crush him by "depriving him of the use of the sea"; this meant strangling him into submission by cutting off his trade, including of course the neutral's right to trade with him. Property in transit, by land or sea, in neutral or belligerent vessel, privately or publicly owned, was the lifeblood of national prosperity on which war depended, and as such was national in its employment and only in ownership private. It sustained the well-being and endurance of a nation at war, and "two contending armies might as well agree to respect each other's communications as two belligerent states to guarantee immunity to hostile commerce."[24]

Though willing, under instructions from Washington, to join in signing a memorial to the conference on the topic, Mahan let it be known that it was in nowise a personal belief with him to grant such immunity. In the consideration of the final draft of this memorial by the American delegation, "various passages were stricken out, some of them—and indeed one of the best," said White, "in deference to the ideas of Captain Mahan." He thought that if Mahan's ideas of doing all that one could to weaken and worry the enemy were logically carried out, one would return to the marauding and atrocities of the Thirty Years War.[25]

24 Mahan, "Possibilities of an Anglo-American Reunion," *North American Review*, November, 1894, reprinted in *The Interest of America in Sea Power, Present and Future*, 134; see also *ibid.*, 126 ff.

25 White, *op. cit.*, II, 316–17.

From what has been said of Mahan's attitude and action during the ten weeks at The Hague, it is not surprising that the chairman, in writing the delegation's report for the State Department, was especially embarrassed by the fact that

the wording of it must be suited to the scruples of my colleague Captain Mahan. He is a man of the highest character and of great ability, whom I respect and greatly like; but . . . he has had very little, if any sympathy with the main purpose of the Conference, and has not hesitated to declare his disbelief in some of the measures which we were especially instructed to press.

Then Dr. White added this provocative thought:

Still his views have been an excellent tonic; they have effectively prevented any lapse into sentimentality. When he speaks the millenium fades and this stern, severe, actual world appears.[26]

In 1904 Roosevelt suggested the meeting of a second conference, and in the foreground of the subjects for consideration he placed the exemption of private property from capture at sea. This drew from Mahan a long letter of "concern" with a seven-page enclosure of the portion of his forthcoming story of the War of 1812 dealing with immunity of private property. The very fact that the American view was "traditional" demanded consideration

as to whether it may not have lost the fitness it possibly once had to national conditions. . . . There is no more moral wrong in taking "private" property than in taking "private" lives; and I think my point incontestable, that property employed in commerce is no more private, in uses, than lives employed on the firing lines are private. . . . The question of limiting armaments

26 *Ibid.*, II, 346. The "Report of the American Commission to the First International Peace Conference at The Hague," including Mahan's special report, is on file in the State Department Archives.

is a very thorny one; it will not be helped I think, by allaying fears that commerce, men's pockets, will suffer in war.[27]

Roosevelt expressed interest in Mahan's letter and enclosure and agreed to take the matter up with Hay. "You open a big subject for discussion," he wrote Mahan, "I shall have to think over the matter before I could answer you at all definitely on this proposition."[28]

The Russo-Japanese War intervened, and the second gathering at The Hague was postponed. Sometime prior to the actual opening of this conference, Mahan renewed his attempt to gain official reconsideration of America's position on the subject of immunity of private property at sea. This time he approached the Secretary of State, Elihu Root. He apologized for writing and added that he "ought perhaps to accept as final the adverse reply of the President" but that the matter was too vitally important for an irrevocable stand to be taken until given "careful consideration in light of *present* conditions." Why, he inquired, should not the General Board be consulted about the military aspects? Three enclosures and references to the appropriate discussions in his "War of 1812" accompanied this lengthy appeal to the Secretary of State.[29] Root did ask the Secretary of the Navy to call upon the General Board for its views on the matter and enclosed Mahan's letter for its use. In his reply to Mahan, he stated that he personally "had already entertained and in private expressed serious doubts" concerning the wisdom of continuing to grant immunity for private property at sea; but, he added:

the subject is no longer an open one for us. The United States has advocated the immunity of private property at sea so long

27 Mahan to Roosevelt, December 27, 1904, Roosevelt Papers.

28 Roosevelt to Mahan, December 29, 1904, *ibid.*

29 Mahan to Root, April 20, 1906, Department of State, Miscellaneous Letters, Part III, 1906. See also Mahan to General Board, June 20, 1906, with enclosures, Mahan Papers.

and so positively that I cannot see how it is possible to make a *volte face* at The Hague.[30]

In a personal interview with Roosevelt at Oyster Bay in 1906, Mahan discussed the question of exemption of private property from maritime capture, and especially the possibility of his being excused from the naval regulation which forbade officers to discuss publicly matters of policy on which the government was embarked. The discussion was continued by letter. He pointed out the close correlation of British and American interests and continued:

Exempt it [maritime commerce] and you remove the strongest hook in the jaw of Germany that the English-speaking people have—a principal gage for peace. . . . When to Germany are added the unsolved questions of the Pacific, it may be said truly that the political future is without form and void. Darkness is upon the face of the deep. We will have to walk very warily in matters affecting future ability to employ national force.[31]

The plea for permission to write on the matter was also renewed by letter. This request was granted; Roosevelt wrote:

Your position is a peculiar one.'. . . You have a deserved reputation as a publicist which makes this proper from the public standpoint. Indeed I think it important for you to write just what you think of the matter.[32]

The publicist capitalized upon his privilege, and two articles, well synchronized with the meeting of the Second Hague Conference, appeared in both English and American magazines. They were "The Hague Conference; the Question of Immunity of Belligerent Merchant Shipping" and "The Hague Conference and the Political Aspects of

30 Root to Mahan, May 21, 1906, Department of State, Domestic Letters, CCXC, 628–29.
31 Mahan to Roosevelt, August 14, 1906, Roosevelt Papers.
32 Roosevelt to Mahan, August 16, 1906, *ibid.*

War."[33] The propagandist had a very definite reason for wishing the articles published in English journals. He was fearful that the existent British government, "with its huge heterogeneous majority to keep placated," might yield on the historic British stand. This lack of confidence in the Liberal government was a further reason why he thought the United States should alter her position; with a Conservative government in England we might safely continue in our traditional policy, knowing that it would not be accepted; but with the present government, he told Roosevelt, "you will on military questions be playing with fire."[34]

Mahan's definition of national interest and his philosophical justification of war will be considered at some length in the following chapter.

33 Mahan, "The Hague Conference; the Question of Immunity of Belligerent Merchant Shipping," *National Review*, June, 1907 (and in *Living Age*, July 6, 1907), reprinted in *Some Neglected Aspects of War*, 157–93; "The Hague Conference and the Practical Aspects of War," *National Review*, July, 1907 (and in *Living Age*, July 27, 1907), reprinted in *ibid.*, 57–93.

34 Mahan to Roosevelt, August 14, 1906, Roosevelt Papers.

XIII

CONCEPT OF NATIONAL INTEREST
AND JUSTIFICATION OF WAR

IN NO SINGLE ONE of his twenty-odd volumes from *The Influence of Sea Power upon History, 1660–1783* in 1890 to *Armaments and Arbitration* in 1912, and in but few of his hundred-odd magazine articles from "The United States Looking Outward" in 1890 to "The Panama Canal and the Distribution of the Fleet" in 1914, did Mahan fail to deal in one way or another with the doctrine of power. Sometimes it was an analysis of the basic interests of the state and the need of organized force for the defense of these interests that received attention, at other times it was the most profitable manner of utilization of this force that was considered, while at still other times it was the moral and philosophical justification of the employment of force that was developed. Nowhere, however, did Mahan prepare a full statement of his philosophy of force; his views are scattered here and there in his voluminous writings. And though he was perhaps the most thorough-going systematist on war that the United States has produced, one cannot claim for Mahan any marked degree of consistency; sometimes so-called realism loomed uppermost, at other times moral sentiment, bordering on sentimentality, was primary.

It must not be assumed that this problem with which Mahan dealt was merely a speculative one nor that a solution could be certain, simple, or easy; philosophers and statesmen in all ages, from Aristotle and Alexander to Marx and Stalin, have given their most earnest consideration to this problem of power, its basis, its use, and its defense. Stated simply, Mahan analyzed the motivation behind national action; he found basic interests of a moral and political nature; he saw that the interests of one nation conflicted with those of another nation; he believed that in certain cases compromise was impossible and that under no circumstances could a state pre-engage to arbitrate concerning its interests; he was convinced that the barbarian hordes without and the destructive chaotic elements within the pale of civilized Christian states presented problems which could be settled only by war or being so ready that the opponent would not fight.

Mahan's solution to the problem of conflicting national interests as one of war or preparedness for war was supplemented by a moral and philosophical vindication of such action. Again stated simply, believing that national interests necessitated defense by the armed might of the individual state, Mahan sought moral justification of war; consciously or unconsciously, though very largely the latter, Mahan drew from the philosophical milieu of his day; he marshaled Christian moral sentiment and Kantian categorical imperative to support his views; he summoned Darwinism and nineteenth-century utilitarianism to sustain his concepts; he called forth military nationalism to defend his beliefs.

Mahan was keenly aware of the chaotic turbulence in international life, and he valiantly endeavored to justify the political obligations which he believed the great Christian powers could assume or neglect at their peril. In a world of sovereign states and power rivalries, Mahan sought moral bases for war; the resultant justification was a curious mixture of Christian and moral sentiments clearly produced by the necessity of circumstances as Mahan saw them, a veritable hodgepodge of philosophical views possessing for the student of political and moral philosophy greater interest about their origin than admiration of their consistency of principle.[1]

Nations operated, Mahan thought, according to national interests and moral sentiments. In depicting national interest as the prime consideration of foreign policy, he wrote:

Self-interest is not only a legitimate but a fundamental cause for national policy; one which needs no cloak of hypocrisy.[2] . . . Governments are corporations, and as corporations have not souls. Governments moreover are trustees, not principals; and as such must put first the lawful interests of their wards, their own people.[3] . . . it is vain to expect governments to act continuously on any other ground than national interest. They have no right to do so, being agents and not principals.[4]

Mahan's concept of national interest was practically epitomized by his concept of "command of the sea." He declared: "Control of the sea, by maritime commerce and naval supremacy means predominant influence in the

---

1 Some conception of the hostile criticism anent his views on the doctrine of force to which Mahan was subjected during his lifetime may be gathered from an examination of the following: Norman Angell, *The Great Illusion;* Mahan, "The Great Illusion," *North American Review*, March, 1912, reprinted in *Armaments and Arbitration*, 121–54; Angell, "The Great Illusion" (a reply to Admiral Mahan), *North American Review*, Vol. CXCV (June, 1912), 754–72; George W. Nasmyth, *Organized Insanity;* Lucia Ames Mead, "Some Fallacies of Captain Mahan," *Arena*, Vol. XL (September, 1908), 163–70. See also the following book reviews: *Nation*, Vol. LXVII (July 14, 1898), 34–36 (a review of *The Interest of America in Sea Power, Present and Future*); *ibid.*, Vol. LXX (January 18, 1900), 55–56 (a review of *Lessons of the War with Spain and Other Articles*); Wallace Rice, "Some Current Fallacies of Captain Mahan," *Dial*, Vol. XXVIII (March 16, 1900), 198–200 (a review of *Lessons of the War with Spain and Other Articles*). For more recent criticisms dealing with these aspects, see Charles Beard, *The Navy: Defense or Portent?;* Beard, *The Idea of National Interest;* Mauritz Hallgren, *The Tragic Fallacy;* Albert Weinberg, *Manifest Destiny;* Louis Hacker, "Incendiary Mahan—A Biography," *Scribner's*, Vol. XCV (April, 1934), 316–17; Puleston, *Mahan.*

2 Mahan, "The Problem of Asia," *Harper's Monthly*, May, 1900, reprinted in *The Problem of Asia*, 97.

3 Mahan, *The Interest of America in International Conditions*, 42.

4 Mahan, "Effect of Asiatic Conditions upon World Policies," *North American Review*, November, 1900, reprinted in *The Problem of Asia*, 187.

world.[5] . . . [and] is the chief among the merely material elements in the power and prosperity of nations."[6] He recognized that the wealth and strength resulting from such control would cause competition, even war. As early as 1890 his survey of the story of sea power in the seventeenth and eighteenth centuries had taught him that to secure for "one's own people a disproportionate share of such benefits [wealth and strength], every effort was made to exclude others, either by peaceful legislative methods of monopoly or prohibitory regulations, or, when these failed, by direct violence."[7] A similar appraisal of the primacy of economic motives and of their impact upon society was expressed in 1912 when war clouds were gathering in Europe:

> The armaments of European states are not so much for protection against conquest as to secure to themselves the utmost possible share of the unexploited or imperfectly exploited regions of the world—the outlying markets, or storehouses of raw material, which under national control shall minister to national emolument.[8]

These economic advantages or interests were not attached to any territorial area of fixed boundaries; they were subject to change; their development was dependent upon the necessity of the state. Mahan maintained:

> The first law of states, as of men, is self-preservation—a term which cannot be narrowed to the bare tenure of a stationary round of existence. Growth is a property of healthful life, which does not . . . necessarily imply increase in size of nations . . . but

---

[5] Mahan, "Possibilities of an Anglo-American Reunion," *North American Review*, November, 1894, reprinted in *The Interest of America in Sea Power, Present and Future*, 124.

[6] Mahan, "Hawaii and Our Future Sea Power," *Forum*, March, 1893, reprinted in *ibid.*, 52.

[7] Mahan, *The Influence of Sea Power upon History, 1660–1783*, 1.

[8] Mahan, "The Place of Force in International Relations," *North American Review*, January, 1912, reprinted in *Armaments and Arbitration*, 113.

it does imply the right to insure by just means whatsoever contributes to national progress.[9]

This transference of the biological law of natural growth to national life served neatly as a basis for imperialism, whether viewed as territorial acquisition or merely as financial penetration and exploitation.

With "national progress" interpreted in terms of "control of the sea," it necessarily followed that, "as subsidiary to such control, it is imperative to take possession, when it can righteously be done, of such maritime positions as contribute to secure command."[10] Propinquity justified paramount interest in commercial, strategic, and political affairs. Acquisition of "natural outposts" was essential for American naval and commercial purposes; it might also serve as a preventive measure against their hostile use by other countries. Thus self-preservation and defensive expansion became virtually synonymous. It must be pointed out, in interpreting self-defense, that Mahan included therein not merely national territory but all national *interests;* the word "defense" had applications "at points far away from our own coast."[11]

National interest asserted itself in many ways and paraded under many banners; it was couched in a variety of terms, such as "self-defense," "self-interest," "self-development," "natural growth," and "paramount interest." Translated into a program of action for the United States, national interest demanded predominance in the Caribbean, preference in Hawaii, and equality in the Far East; it asserted

9 Mahan, "The Problem of Asia," *Harper's Monthly*, March, 1900, reprinted in *The Problem of Asia*, 29–30.

10 Mahan, "Hawaii and Our Future Sea Power," *Forum*, March, 1893, reprinted in *The Interest of America in Sea Power, Present and Future*, 52.

11 Mahan, "The Isthmus and Sea Power," *Atlantic Monthly*, September, 1893, reprinted in *ibid.*, 104. Also Mahan, "Current Fallacies upon Naval Subjects," *Harper's Monthly*, June, 1898, reprinted in *Lessons of the War with Spain and Other Articles*, 299.

the right of acquisition of strategic bases at certain points and the protection of American interests in all quarters; it necessitated the maintenance of the Monroe Doctrine, the promotion of American commerce, and the defense of national territory.

At no time, however, did Mahan emphasize national interests as the sole motivating factor in national policy to the exclusion of moral sentiments. The primacy given to national interests, as depicted in the preceding paragraphs, in certain respects was definitely contradicted in 1911 when confronted with Norman Angell's contention in *The Great Illusion* that modern war was ruinous and futile to victor as well as to vanquished. Said Mahan:

Nations are under no illusion as to the unprofitableness of war. . . . A mature consideration of the wars of the past sixty years . . . will show that the motives to war have not often been "aggression for the sake of increasing power, and consequently prosperity and financial well-being." The impulses . . . have risen above mere self-interest to feelings of convictions which the argument of *The Great Illusion* does not so much as touch. . . . To regard the world as governed by self-interest alone is to live in a nonexistent world, an ideal world, a world possessed by an idea much less worthy than those which mankind, to do it bare justice, persistently entertains. . . . The inciting causes of war in our day are moral. . . . Even where material self-interest is at the bottom of the trouble, as possibly in the present state of feeling between Germany and Great Britain, it is less the loss endured than sense of injustice done, or apprehended, that keeps alive the flame.[12]

The role of moral sentiments and moral obligations is further clarified in the following:

The sentiment of a people is the most energetic element in national action. Even when material interests are the original

[12] Mahan, "The Great Illusion," *North American Review*, March, 1912, reprinted in *Armaments and Arbitration*, 126, 153–54.

exciting cause, it is the sentiment to which they give rise, the moral tone which emotion takes, that constitutes the greater force. Whatever individual rulers may do, masses of men are aroused to effective action—other than spasmodic—only by the sense of wrong done, or of right to be vindicated. For this reason governments are careful to obtain for their contentions an aspect of right which will keep their people at their backs.[13]

Though the paths along which "conscience" leads its followers are frequently devious, and though the view that "moral sentiment profoundly influences national behavior may at first thought seem ironical to those who hold that certain national policies tend to be morally questionable if not unquestionably immoral,"[14] it cannot be denied that "governments are careful to obtain for their contentions an aspect of right."

Mahan bolstered his plea for national interest with appeals to conscience, to right, and to duty. The welfare of the world outweighed individual or even national well-being. Possession was no longer nine points in the law of nations as Mahan enunciated it. Wise utilization and not mere technical possession of territory was the criterion by which right of ownership was determined. Startling and definitely challenging are his views:

The claim of an indigenous population to retain indefinitely control of territory depends not upon a natural right, but upon political fitness, shown in the political work of governing, administering, and developing, in such manner as to insure the natural right of the world at large that resources should not be left idle, but be utilized for the general good.[15]

On another occasion Mahan discussed this point of view in these words:

There is no inalienable right in any community to control

13 Mahan, The Interest of America in International Conditions, 167–68.
14 Weinberg, op. cit., 3.
15 Mahan, "The Problem of Asia," Harper's Monthly, May, 1900, reprinted in The Problem of Asia, 98.

the use of a region when it does so to the detriment of the world at large, of its neighbors in particular, or even at times of its own subjects. . . . the right is inalienable only until its misuse brings ruin or a stronger force appears to dispossess it. . . . In questions of great import to nations or to the world, the wishes, or interests, or technical rights, of minorities must yield, and there is no more injustice in this than in their yielding to a majority at the polls.[16]

In light of these statements is it surprising that imperialists everywhere acclaimed Mahan their champion? A philosophy such as this was certainly as "threatening to the backward peoples logically" as was the "imperialist's weapon of force physically." World interest, or the interest of a large section of mankind, as well as self-interest, urged the United States to secure Hawaii, gain bases in the Caribbean, build a canal, construct a navy, and be prepared for the arduous role of defending Western civilization against the hordes of Asia. World interest became the vehicle in which national interest rode to victory.

It was a short step from this philosophical imperialism to the humanitarian imperialism involved in the concept of the "white man's burden." Mahan emphasized beneficence to the subject people. "Materially," he said, "the interest of the nation is one with its beneficence; but if the ideas get inverted, and the nation sees in its new responsibilities, first of all, markets and profits, with incidental resultant benefit to the natives, it will go wrong."[17]

This Christian expansionist saw involved in the nation's answer to the call to assume the burden of beneficent imperialism, its possible growth or decadence. Said he: "To

[16] Mahan, "The Future in Relation to American Naval Power," *Harper's Monthly*, October, 1895, reprinted in *The Interest of America in Sea Power, Present and Future*, 167–68.

[17] Mahan, "The Relations of the United States to Their New Dependencies," *Engineering Magazine*, January, 1899, reprinted in *Lessons of the War with Spain and Other Articles*, 250.

right what is amiss, to convert, to improve, to develop, is of the very essence of the Christian ideal; . . . comparative religion teaches that creeds which reject missionary enterprise are foredoomed to decay. May it not be so with nations?"[18] After the signal acquisitions by the United States at the turn of the century, Mahan wrote, "What the nation has gained in expansion is a regenerating idea, an uplifting of the heart, a seed of future beneficent activity, a going out of self into the world to communicate the gift it has so bountifully received."[19]

Closely allied in thought with the philosophical and humanitarian rationalizations of imperialism was the belief that Providence leads and guides a nation in its path of beneficence. To Mahan the American acquisition of the Philippines was an example of such divine overruling; the growth of much of the British Empire was similarly viewed.[20] Mahan recognized that the recipients of these divinely ordained trusteeships might not appreciate the benefits so graciously bestowed upon them by their Christian stewards in the employment of their "talents," yet the "sense of duty achieved, and the security of tenure," were the rewards of the ruler.[21]

Given the call of world interest, the duty to the brown

18 Mahan, "The Place of Force in International Relations," *North American Review*, January, 1912, reprinted in *Armaments and Arbitration*, 117; Mahan, "Hawaii and Our Future Sea Power," *Forum*, March, 1893, reprinted in *The Interest of America in Sea Power, Present and Future*, 50.

19 Mahan, "Growth of Our National Feeling," *World's Work*, February, 1902, reprinted as "Retrospect and Prospect," in *Retrospect and Prospect*, 17.

20 Mahan, "The Transvaal and the Philippines," *Independent*, Vol. LII (February 1, 1900), 290; "The Philippines and the Future," *Independent*, Vol. LII (March 22, 1900), 698; "Effect of Asiatic Conditions upon World Politics," *North American Review*, November, 1900, reprinted in *The Problem of Asia*, 175; "Strategic Features of the Gulf of Mexico and the Caribbean Sea," *Harper's Monthly*, October, 1897, reprinted in *The Interest of the United States in Sea Power, Present and Future*, 307–308.

21 Mahan, "The Relations of the United States to Their New Dependencies," *Engineering Magazine*, January, 1899, reprinted in *Lessons of the War with Spain and Other Articles*, 247.

brethren, and the mandate of God, it would seem that more was not needed; but Mahan added a strain of determinism, a certain fatalism. "Whether they will or no, Americans must now begin to look outward." American expansion was "natural, necessary, irrepressible."[22]

In light of these various motivating forces it would not be strange, either in theory or in practice, to find Divine destiny and manifest destiny, world interest and national interest, and self-sacrifice and self-aggrandizement becoming confused and losing their respective identities. Observe this intertwining of motives to which appeal was made relative to American acquisition and retention of the Philippines:

Upon us has *devolved,* by an *inevitable* sequence of causes, *responsibility* to our *conscience* for an assemblage of peoples in *moral* and *political childhood;* and *responsibility* further to the *world at large,* and to *history,*—the supreme earthly judge of men's actions,—for our course in the *emergency thrust upon us.* As such the United States has accepted the *burden.* Its *duties* are not to be discharged by throwing them overboard, or by wrapping our *political talent* in a napkin for *our own national security* and *ease.*[23]

These national interests and moral sentiments according to which nations operated demanded organized force, Mahan believed, for their satisfaction and fulfillment. He argued, as most militarists have done, that military preparedness was in nowise a threat to peace; indeed "the most beneficial use of a military force is not to wage war, however successfully, but to *prevent* war."[24] Continued he:

22 Mahan, "The United States Looking Outward," *Atlantic Monthly,* December, 1890, reprinted in *The Interest of America in Sea Power, Present and Future,* 21, 36.

23 Mahan, "Motives to Imperial Federation," *National Review,* May, 1902, reprinted in *Retrospect and Prospect,* 95–96. The italics are mine.

24 Mahan, "Current Fallacies upon Naval Subjects," *Harper's Monthly,* June, 1898, reprinted in *Lessons of the War with Spain and Other Articles,* 286.

That the organization of military strength involves provocation to war is a fallacy, which the experience of each succeeding year [writing in 1893] now refutes. The immense armaments of Europe are onerous; but nevertheless, by the mutual respect and caution they enforce they represent a cheap alternative, certainly in misery, probably in money, to the frequent devastating wars which preceded the era of general military preparation.[25]

On the eve of World War I Mahan still saw the immense armaments "as institutions maintaining peace, which they have done effectually for forty years in Europe."[26] Had he lived to witness the aftermath of that war, the coming of a second world holocaust, and the chaos subsequent thereto, would Mahan still have subscribed to these lines penned in 1897?

Is it nothing that wars are less frequent, peace better secured, by the mutual respect of nations for each other's strength; and that, when a convulsion does come, it passes rapidly, leaving the ordinary course of events to resume sooner, and therefore more easily? War now not only occurs more rarely, but has rather the character of an occasional excess, from which recovery is easy.[27]

It was perhaps inevitable that Mahan should be led to a reasoned defense of militarism, not as a necessary evil but as a moral system. The protection of national interests and the preservation of peace were not the only functions of force. Organized force manifesting itself in war became an ethical and moral necessity, not only serving as a means to suppress objective evil and to thwart subversive natural

25 Mahan, "The Isthmus and Sea Power," *Atlantic Monthly*, September, 1893, reprinted in *The Interest of America in Sea Power, Present and Future*, 104.
26 Mahan, *Armaments and Arbitration*, 13.
27 Mahan, "A Twentieth-Century Outlook," *Harper's Monthly*, September, 1897, reprinted in *The Interest of America in Sea Power, Present and Future*, 233.

impulses, but also acting as the advance agent of morality to clear the way for Christian progress and make possible the attainment of moral ends not otherwise attainable. War satisfied the righteous dictates of a nation's conscience. Mahan rationalized this view as follows:

A state, when it goes to war, should do so not to test the rightfulness of its claims, but because being convinced in its conscience of that rightfulness, no other means of overpowering evil remains. . . . It is not accuracy of the decision, but faithfulness to conviction, that constitutes the moral worth of the action, national or individual. . . . Even if mistaken, the moral wrong of acting against conviction works a deeper injury . . . than can merely material disasters that may follow upon obedience. Even the material evils of war are less than the moral evils of compliance with wrong.[28]

Mahan believed that in public disputes, as in private, there was "not uncommonly on both sides, an element of right, real or really believed," which prevented either party from yielding, as in the United States Civil War; under such circumstances war was the only alternative to wrongdoing. As he expressed it:

on questions of merely material interest men may yield; on matters of principle they may be honestly in the wrong; but a conviction of right, even though mistaken, if yielded without contention, entails a deterioration of character, except in the presence of force demonstrably irresistible—and sometimes even then.[29]

War, Mahan declared, was "the regulator and adjuster"

[28] Mahan, "The Peace Conference and the Moral Aspect of War," *North American Review*, October, 1899, reprinted in *Lessons of the War with Spain and Other Articles*, 214–16; also reprinted in *Some Neglected Aspects of War*, 30–32.

[29] Mahan, "Preparedness for Naval War," *Harper's Monthly*, March, 1897, reprinted in *The Interest of America in Sea Power, Present and Future*, 177–78.

of human actions. By war man could "measurably control, guide, delay, otherwise beneficially modify results which threaten to be disastrous in their extent, tendency or suddenness."[30] To hold that war was wicked and unchristian amounted to saying that it was "wicked for society to organize and utilize force for the control of evil."[31] Mahan argued that war served as the "true antidote" to what was bad in socialism. The elimination of armament races might result, he feared, in "a socialistic community of states in which the powers of individual initiative, of nations and of men, the greatest achievements of our civilization so far," would be atrophied. Mahan was certain that demoralization of the nations would follow if the sums now spent on armaments were released to a strictly "beneficiary system" of social organization.[32]

Thus, in Mahan's reasoning, war was remedial and preventive; it was at once a cleansing agent by means of which objective evil was suppressed and an immunizing agent by which nations were saved from their baser passions. But war was more than a negative force, more than remedial and preventive; war was a positive force, war was productive of great good. Peace was not adequate to all progress.[33] Wrote Mahan:

> Time and staying power must be secured for ourselves by that rude and imperfect, but not ignoble arbiter, force,—force potential and force organized—which so far has won, and still secures, the greatest triumphs of good in the checkered story of

30 Mahan, "The Practical Aspects of War," *National Review*, June, 1907, reprinted in *Some Neglected Aspects of War*, 92.

31 *Ibid., viii.* ◆

32 Mahan, "Possibilities of an Anglo-American Reunion," *North American Review*, November, 1894, reprinted in *The Interest of America in Sea Power, Present and Future*, 122; Mahan, *Armaments and Arbitration*, 13.

33 Mahan, "The Peace Conference and the Moral Aspect of War," *North American Review*, October, 1899, reprinted in *Lessons of the War with Spain and Other Articles*, 231; reprinted also in *Some Neglected Aspects of War*, 46.

mankind.[34] . . . Force has been the instrument by which ideas have lifted the European world to the plane on which it now is, and it supports our political systems, national and international, as well as our social organization.[35]

Mahan carefully considered the use of force in the past to show that its employment had been motivated by high purpose and had eventuated in good. He felt that "what the sword, and it supremely tempered only by the stern demands of justice and of conscience, and the loving voice of charity" had done for India and for Egypt was "at once a tale too long and too well known" to need repetition.[36] Wrote Mahan on another occasion:

Whether the original enterprise or the continued presence of Great Britain in Egypt is entirely clear of technical wrongs, open to the criticism of the pure moralist, is as little to the point as the morality of an earthquake; the general action was justified by broad considerations of moral expediency, being to the benefit of the world at large, and of the people of Egypt in particular—however they might have voted in the matter.[37]

In 1912 Mahan surveyed the wars of the past half-century; he found moral purpose and moral good in all. The southern slaves were freed from their masters in the United States War of Secession; the Prussian wars against Denmark, Austria, and France "embraced a conception of German racial unity consolidated into political unity" and were "fol-

[34] Mahan, "A Twentieth-Century Outlook," *Harper's Monthly*, September, 1897, reprinted in *The Interest of America in Sea Power, Present and Future*, 245.

[35] Mahan, "The Problem of Asia," *Harper's Monthly*, May, 1900, reprinted in *The Problem of Asia*, 122.

[36] Mahan, "The Peace Conference and the Moral Aspect of War," *North American Review*, October, 1899, reprinted in *Lessons of the War with Spain and Other Articles*, 231; reprinted also in *Some Neglected Aspects of War*, 46.

[37] Mahan, "The Future in Relation to American Naval Power," *Harper's Monthly*, March, 1897, reprinted in *The Interest of America in Sea Power, Present and Future*, 166–67.

lowed by great industrial and economic advance"; the Russo-Turkish War of 1877 was primarily motivated by "popular sentiment inflamed by sympathy with the oppression of nearby peoples"; the call of humanity demanded the end of Spanish rule in the Caribbean and the Philippines; the establishment of "fair treatment," "union and equality," justified British action in South Africa; Japan "not without reason" had been forced to fight Russia to guarantee her "national self-preservation."[38]

History, for Mahan, proved that war was justified by what it had accomplished, and it confirmed his belief that what had been beneficial in the past would be beneficial in the present and foreseeable future. At the time of the First Hague Peace Conference, he wrote:

Step by step in the past, man has ascended by means of the sword, and his more recent gains, as well as present conditions, show that the time has not yet come to kick down the ladder, which has so far served him.[39]

On another occasion he stated:

Ease unbroken, trade uninterrupted. hardship done away with, all roughness removed from life—these are our modern gods; but can they deliver us, should we succeed in setting them up to worship? Fortunately, as yet we cannot do so. We may, if we will, shut our eyes to the vast outside masses of aliens to our civilization, now powerless because we still, with a higher material development, retain the masculine combative virtues which are their chief possession; but, even if we disregard them, the ground already shakes beneath our feet with physical men-

[38] Mahan, "The Place of Force in International Relations," *North American Review*, January, 1912, reprinted in *Armaments and Arbitration*, 109–12.

[39] Mahan, "The Peace Conference and the Moral Aspect of War," *North American Review*, October, 1899, reprinted in *Lessons of the War with Spain and Other Articles*, 230; reprinted also in *Some Neglected Aspects of War*, 45.

ace of destruction from within, against which the only security is in constant readiness to contend.[40]

Moreover, it was "not in universal harmony, nor in fond dreams of unbroken peace," continued Mahan, that rested "the best hopes of the world"; it was "in the rivalries of nations, in the accentuation of differences, in the conflict of ambitions" that lay the preservation of the martial spirit which alone was "capable of coping finally with the destructive forces that from outside and from within threaten to submerge all the centuries have gained."

Power or force was Christian; Mahan considered it "one of the talents committed to nations by God" that could not be "carelessly or lightly abjured, without incurring the responsibility of one who buries in the earth that which was intrusted to him for use." Continuing in Biblical language, he maintained:

> Much is required of those to whom much is given. So viewed, the ability speedily to put forth the nation's power . . . is one of the clear duties involved in the Christian word "watchfulness,"—readiness for the call that may come, whether expectedly or not.[41]

And, said Mahan, "Without man's responsive effort, God himself is not powerless but deprived of the instrument through which he wills to work."[42]

Though peace was Mahan's professed goal, he hedged with numerous qualifications. He wrote:

[40] Mahan, "Possibilities of an Anglo-American Reunion," *North American Review*, November, 1894, reprinted in *The Interest of America in Sea Power, Present and Future*, 121–22.

[41] Mahan, "The Peace Conference and the Moral Aspect of War," *North American Review*, October, 1899, reprinted in *Lessons of the War with Spain and Other Articles*, 232–33; reprinted also in *Some Neglected Aspects of War*, 47–48. Cf. Mahan, "Armaments and Arbitration," *North American Review*, May, 1911, reprinted in *Armaments and Arbitration*, 30.

[42] Mahan, "The Place of Force in International Relations," *North American Review*, January, 1912, reprinted in *ibid.*, 117.

Let us worship peace, indeed, as the goal at which humanity must hope to arrive; but let us not fancy that peace is to be had as a boy wrenches an unripe fruit from a tree. Nor will peace be reached by ignoring the conditions that confront us, or by exaggerating the charms of quiet, of prosperity, of ease, and by contrasting these exclusively with the alarms and horrors of war. Merely utilitarian arguments have never convinced nor converted mankind, and they never will; for mankind knows that there is something better.[43]

He thought peace, "that alluring, albeit somewhat ignoble, ideal," was "not to be attained by the representatives of civilization dropping their arms, relaxing the tension of their moral muscle, and from fighting animals become fattened cattle fit only for slaughter."[44] The goal was peace but the means, "during a future far beyond our present foresight," depended upon the due organization of force.[45]

It was along the lines here depicted that Mahan defined his concept of national interest and evolved his justification of war. His philosophy of power has evoked responses ranging from warmest flattery to bitterest denunciation. However much one admires Mahan, one cannot unreservedly praise his logic or his lucidity; however much one condemns Mahan, one cannot rightly question his sincerity or his integrity. A study of few individuals will more forcefully delineate the basic conflict between the desirability of the national and international approaches to the handling of the foreign relations of nations. Mahan ably represents that group which holds to the untrammeled exercise of national

[43] Mahan, "A Twentieth-Century Outlook," *Harper's Monthly*, September, 1897, reprinted in *The Interest of America in Sea Power, Present and Future*, 267.

[44] Mahan, "Possibilities of an Anglo-American Reunion," *North American Review*, November, 1894, reprinted in *ibid.*, 120.

[45] Mahan, "The Relations of the United States to Their Dependencies," *Engineering Magazine*, January, 1899, reprinted in *Lessons of the War with Spain and Other Articles*, 251.

sovereignty; he was too honest to his convictions to give lip service to schemes of international organization qualified with "buts" and "ifs." If Alfred Thayer Mahan did not deify force, glorify expansion, and make war moral and beneficent, his expressions on these topics bring him very close to such views. The New York *Post,* at the time of his death, referred to him as "about the nearest type we had to the German glorifiers of war on high and mystic grounds."

XIV

MAHAN YESTERDAY AND TODAY

MAHAN LIVED in an age of dynamic power politics. In his lifetime Germany, Italy, Japan, and the United States emerged as world powers; the older world powers of France, Britain, Austria-Hungary, and Russia aggressively asserted their rights to increased roles of influence. Mahan was both product and spokesman of this era. As ardent navalist, forthright imperialist, and frank nationalist, Mahan interpreted his age to itself and that age of competitive navalism, rampant imperialism, virulent nationalism, and lawless militarism acclaimed him seer and champion.

In the decades since his death in 1914, two world wars have vastly modified the status of the major powers; technological developments have greatly changed the manner of warfare, naval and military, and have altered the equation of power relations of nations; domestic revolutions of major consequence have occurred and totalitarian ideologies of fascism, naziism, and communism have arisen. Surely there is no comparable period in history in which have transpired so many vitally significant and far-reaching events. The world today is a vastly altered world from that which Mahan knew, yet it is a world in which nations still strive for power and still seek their own advantage. It is a world in which Mahan and Mahanism continue to be significant.

An evaluation of the role of Mahan in history must take into account the influence exerted not only during his lifetime but also in subsequent years. An appraisal of his significance must reckon not only with the indoctrination of his fellow countrymen, which was his primary concern, but also with the wider repercussions of his activities on other nations. A consideration of his importance must take cognizance of the many ways through which his influence was widely manifested.

He was a navalist who was interested in the size, nature, and use of naval forces; he was an expositor of the significance which the sea played in the course of human history and as such affected the concepts and expressions of power politics, in the form of geopolitics as well as in the doctrine of sea power; he was a philosopher of power politics who justified and approved the struggle for power and evolved a defense for nationally organized force; he was a historian whose points of view were sufficiently new and original to challenge the serious attention of fellow scholars; he was an expansionist who believed the greatest good to the greatest number came from a policy of beneficent imperialism; he was a publicist-propagandist whose many books and articles sought to give public demonstration of his theories and their applicability to contemporary problems. In the following pages we shall seek to summarize his influence upon his contemporary world and endeavor to appraise his position in the present day in his roles as navalist, expositor of sea power, philosopher of force, historian, expansionist, and publicist-propagandist.

As navalist, Mahan contributed materially to both the growth and the use of naval forces, and though more symptomatic of his age in the former than in the latter, his influence in both was great in Britain, Germany, France, Japan, and the United States. Few individuals spoke more effectively on naval subjects and none stated the issues more clearly and forcibly, nor was any appealed to more frequently as arbiter. In the United States, his immediate influence upon his fellow officers was probably less than that of the older, farsighted Luce or of the younger, insurgent Sims, yet in the formation of public opinion he had no peer.

In the correct utilization or employment of naval forces, Mahan shortly came to occupy a position comparable to that held by Jomini and Clausewitz among students of land operations. This theorist's lessons of history relative to the overwhelming importance of capital ships, to the utmost significance of the concentration of the fleet, to the tremendous value of the blockade, and to the secondary role of commerce raiding very decidedly affected the naval policies of all major countries of the world.

The wide acceptance of Mahan's strategic principles does not necessarily prove their universal validity. It should also be observed that Mahan frequently has been misinterpreted. His strategic ideas often have been narrowly viewed as precepts of universal application and utility, without qualification of time or place. Mahan never equated sea power and naval power as so frequently do his critics, friendly or unfriendly, in their interpretation of his doctrine. Nations have been eclectic, choosing that which fits their interests, ignoring that which they found unpleasant or antithetical to their ambitions. Hohenzollern Germany adopted a crude version of Mahanism, a falsely narrow concept of sea power which ignored important qualifying factors of geography and resources. Mahan's command of the sea called for superior power on the sea; Germany's disadvantage of position and numerical inferiority in naval forces virtually doomed from the start any successful challenge by the High Seas Fleet to the British control of the sea. From a Mahanian point of view, Tirpitz' risk theory was a weak second choice; it was indeed a poor substitute which at times became a mere subterfuge for the German Admiralty. The future of Western civilization might have been markedly altered had William II and von Tirpitz created a great fleet of submarines instead of "literally devouring" Mahan and ruinously embarking upon the futile one and one-half billion dollar capital-ship race with Britain. Nor can justification for objection, British or American, to submarine warfare be found in Mahan, that militarist who would not outlaw the use of asphyxiating gases, that strategist who would rigorously and remorselessly hunt out, smite down, utterly crush the enemy and drive him from the sea.

Beyond doubt Mahan was so intrigued with the capital-ship theory of securing the command of the sea that he was overly contemptuous of other craft, most conspicuously the submarine. In activity and by disposition Mahan largely looked to the past; he gained his lessons from a study of the past and used the past for analogies. There can be no doubt that Mahan was so absorbed with the past that he often failed to appreciate future trends in naval warfare. He was not sufficiently alive to the fact that history frequently does not repeat itself and that the shape of things to come may not always follow the pattern of the past; to be sure, he studied contemporary events, but because of misinformation, as in the Battle of Tsushima, or because of the general human inclination to seek proofs for existing theories, Mahan was slow to alter his views.

With the appearance of each major technological development, there have been those who sought to decry, either in theory or practice, Mahan's doctrine of concentration. On three occasions within the past century, certain naval leaders have sought to prove the primacy of commerce destruction, but without success. With the shift from sail to steam, the French hoped that the superiority of the English capital-ship navy might be reduced by French steam frigates functioning as commerce raiders. Their hopes did not materialize.

In 1916 the Germans were confident they could reduce Great Britain by the unrestricted use of the submarine. This comparatively new weapon with an element of surprise tem-

U.S.S. *Holland* (1900), considered first modern submarine, 54′ long with 75 tons displacement. *Official U.S. Navy photograph*

U.S.S. *Triton* (1959), made first submerged circumnavigation of globe (26,723 nautical miles), February 16 to April 25, 1960. Length 447′ and 5,940 tons displacement. *Official U.S. Navy photograph*

Underwater firing of the Polaris A-3 missile by unidentified submarine. *Official U.S. Navy photograph*

porarily gave promise of success; until countermeasures were found and antisubmarine defenses strengthened, allied victory hung in the balance. In an examination of the extent to which Mahan's theories were confirmed in World War I, it must be borne in mind that though the British Navy did not prevent an occasional bombardment of the East coast, and though the Grand Fleet did not win at Jutland and was thereby kept tied down in the North Sea by the German fleet-in-being, the British were able to limit seriously the activities of the High Seas Fleet and to prevent it from breaking the stranglehold of the blockade. It must furthermore be recalled that the command of the surface gained by the capital-ship strategy enabled the Allies ultimately to find the measures to defeat the submarine menace.

In World War II another attempt was made to win in defiance of the capital-ship theory. The Nazis with greatly improved submarines, vastly superior bases from which to operate, and considerably altered techniques in fighting made the battle of the Atlantic most severe and carried the struggle to the Caribbean and to the Mediterranean; yet commerce destruction again failed to achieve the victory sought.

Mahan's failure to grant the submarine the place which it has won for itself was not wholly because of its comparative lack of development and its limited testing under battle conditions. Other forces operated. Partially because of his comparative indifference to commerce destruction and partially because of his belief that as naval craft the submarine would be employed against warships, Mahan never fully envisaged the possibility of its widespread use against merchant shipping.

Time has proved beyond doubt that the submarine is an important weapon.[1] It can operate successfully for long periods in waters essentially controlled by the enemy. It

1 The most helpful appraisals of naval strategy at the close of World

necessitates patrol craft and escort vessels above and beyond those otherwise required. Improvements in design and construction are continually giving it superior range, greater resistance to depth bombs, increased depth-diving possibilities, and other desirable characteristics. Though the submarine lessens, it by no conceivable means obviates, surface superiority. The submarine remains essentially a raider with potentialities more limited than those which can be brought against it; detection devices, for example, offset to a considerable degree the reasons for its submersibility. The submarine has twice imperiled and may again endanger the control of the seas; it did not secure, and at present, there is not sufficient evidence to show that it is likely to secure, the coveted command of the sea.[2]

There is no reason to suppose that Mahan would not have welcomed the airplane as a weapon in naval warfare; yet in light of his overweening confidence in the capital ship with resulting hesitancy to accord sufficient roles to torpedo or submarine craft, one may well question whether he would not have been slow to acknowledge the true potentialities of the air arm. Undoubtedly he would forcefully call attention to the importance of the older weapons; sure-

---

War II are found in the writings of Bernard Brodie and Herbert Rosinski. The former has an exceptionally able study entitled *A Guide to Naval Strategy* (1944) which is a completely revised edition of *A Layman's Guide to Naval Strategy* (1942) . Brodie has two short, valuable articles in "War at Sea: Changing Techniques and Unchanging Fundamentals," *Virginia Quarterly Review*, Vol. XIX (Winter, 1943) , 1–19, and "New Tactics in Naval Warfare," *Foreign Affairs*, Vol. XXIV (January, 1946) , 210–23. There is also pertinent information in his *Sea Power in the Machine Age* (1941) . In addition to the two articles by Herbert Rosinski cited in Chapter IV, see his "Command of the Sea," in Rear Admiral H. G. Thursfield (ed.) , *Brassey's Naval Annual, 1939*, 85–100. Assistance at times may be gained from the articles by Theodore Ropp and Margaret Sprout cited in Chapter IV. Notice should be given to Admiral Raoul Castex's monumental study on strategical theories noted in the same chapter; see also his article "The Weapon of the Weak," *Journal of the Royal United Service Institution*, Vol. LXXVII (November, 1932) , 737–43.

ly he would never permit the military air enthusiasts to scoff at naval vessels without calling it high sacrilege, or without pointing out that they ignore a long chain of circumstances which permit the plane its function. It is safe to assume that he would seek to prove that local air superiority is frequently dependent upon sea power; that strategic airfields are often made available by ship-transported troops; that conveyance of maintenance crew, fuel, and other supplies, and at times even the plane, is by ship; and furthermore, that Britain's whole military effort, including her Royal Air Force, is utterly dependent upon the comparative command of the sea approaches in the Atlantic.

For Mahan, sea power was the sum total of forces and factors, tools and geographical circumstances, which operated to gain command of the sea, to secure its use for oneself and to deny that use to the enemy. Consequently, from this point of view, the assertion made by some that the airplane antiquates the doctrine of sea power largely confuses the aims of military power with the weapons of execution. Protagonists of Mahan strongly assert that the sea-power thesis will not cease to have meaning until the transport plane carries the major burden of the transfer of men and equipment and displaces the freighter, whether it be a Liberty or a Victory ship, a nondescript tanker or barge matters not at all for the point in discussion. As keenly aware as Mahan was of the need of bases for the ships of the sea, he might well be among the advocates who stress the even greater need of bases for the ships of the air; as strongly

2 Some statements in this chapter, perhaps a bit traditional in viewpoint even when written, clearly call for revision. Rather than to mix new and old, or to appear to profit from hindsight, I have made no changes other than to correct four or five sentences that proved misleading or were erroneous at the time. The dated or outdated statements are rectified, I believe, as Mahan is revisited in the following chapter in which the impact of recent technological advances, the insight of new scholarship, and my own increased perspective are discussed.

convinced as he was of the close correlation of the diplomatic, military, and naval arms of the government, he probably would insist upon joint plans and integrated action by all branches of the service.

The airplane has opened vastly large horizons in military and naval operations; its utilization as a fighting weapon has caused many persons to think that the basic principles of strategy which survived the revolutionary changes of the nineteenth century are now completely outmoded. Obviously the plane has points both of weakness and of strength. The limitations imposed by weather, endurance, and fragility, so conspicuous in earlier planes, are constantly being reduced. The limitations that remain are offset by speed, by elusiveness as a target, and by ability to attack otherwise inaccessible objectives, such as well-fortified harbors and vital seas closed even to submarines. The demand for the tactically desirable features of speed, maneuverability, rate of climb, range, armament load, and invulnerability, rate of climb, range, armament load, and invulnerability have brought about a specialization in the aircraft as did the desire for the maximum in speed, armor, and ordnance in surface vessels.

The plane is valuable to naval forces as both a scouting agent and a weapon of attack. In spotting submarines, in bringing together scattered convoy whose radios are necessarily silenced, in noting major movements of the enemy fleet, and in general liaison activity, the airplane has proved virtually indispensable. In these reconnaissance capacities the plane tends to tip the scales in favor of the superior fleet and hence strengthens rather than weakens the traditional patterns of strategy.

In an offensive capacity, as a weapon of attack, however, the plane has had more serious and far-reaching repercussions. The aircraft has proved its offensive merit in many critical battles and defensively a fleet is seldom secure without adequate air cover. The ship-based plane is highly valuable. In this respect, it should be pointed out that the aircraft carrier is a warship like other warships with its function fully specialized and its weapons planes instead of guns. For considerations of naval strategy, land-based planes present a somewhat different problem. These planes have wreaked havoc on shipping in coastal waters, on docks and repair facilities, on ports and industries which form the substructure of naval power, and at times, especially in narrow waters, on the fleet itself. Used in sufficient numbers from favorably situated bases, the plane can exercise at least tenuous control over narrow seas.

Beyond dispute, the impact of the land-based plane on naval warfare has been most important; it does not follow, however, that naval craft are obsolete or have lost ascendancy, nor that sea power has been overthrown. The *Luftwaffe,* based on the French and Norwegian coast in World War II was superior for two years to the Royal Air Force, and yet the Germans did not wrest the control of the Atlantic from the Allies. One dislikes to contemplate what the results might have been had the German Navy been superior to the Grand Fleet. The land-based plane in the Pacific theater in the earlier days of the war took its toll on Allied naval strength and limited naval operations; however, the concentration of carrier-borne forces and the incorporation of antiaircraft artillery coupled with additional vessels reduced the losses to our navy and largely restored its former freedom of action.

In commerce destruction the land-based plane in World War II was roughly analogous to the submarine in the great struggle a quarter of a century earlier. Shipping losses in each instance were particularly heavy until countermeasures were established; until defense caught up with offense, the danger was real and the threat serious. In a correct evaluation of the military plane as a commerce destroyer, one must keep in mind not merely the terminal areas where sinkings most frequently occur but the extent and significance of the whole sea lane as well. Unless the destructive violence toward the end of the run assumes such proportion that a successful ocean voyage becomes unimportant, it seems most improbable that the land-based plane can dominate the sea.

Irrespective of the extent to which Mahan would welcome the airplane to the arsenal of naval warfare and irrespective of the altered evaluation which time might force him to accord the submarine, it is doubtful whether he would greatly revise the basic principles of strategy which he enunciated. While he was preparing in 1885–86 his lectures for the strategy courses at the War College, he was repeatedly confronted with and much perplexed by the question, "Under all the changed conditions of naval warfare of what use is knowledge of the bygone days?" He received encouragement from the great military strategist, Jomini, who maintained that though changes in weapons often affected the practices of military warfare the principles remained unchanged.[3]

Mahan's own detailed studies of the naval wars from the middle of the seventeenth century to the close of the Napoleonic upheaval convinced him of a similar permanency in the fundamentals of naval warfare. In his great work on sea power he affirmed that the teachings of the past have in the field of naval strategy "a value which is in no degree lessened" by the passage of time. He recognized that "the unresting progress of mankind causes a continual change in the weapons" and, consequently, "a continual change" in the handling and disposition of ships in battle, yet "considerations and principles" which enter into strategical dis-

3 Mahan to Luce, January 22, 1886, Luce Papers; Mahan, *Naval Strategy*, 4.

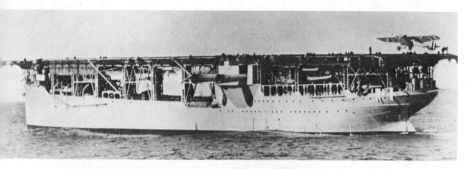

U.S.S. *Langley* (1922), converted collier, first U.S. aircraft carrier to land planes. Deck area less than ⅘ acres.

U.S.S. *Enterprise* (South China Sea, 1969), nuclear- powered attack aircraft carrier; 4½ acres of flight deck. She carries 70 to 100 planes and launches four A-3J Vigilante jets per minute. *Official U.S. Navy photographs*

One of the earliest planes operated by the navy.

Formation of F4U-5 Corsairs (c. 1950).

F-48 Phantom II, from aircraft carrier U.S.S. *John F. Kennedy* (Mediterranean Sea, 1970), launching a target drone. *Official U.S. Navy photographs*

cussions "belong to the unchangeable, or unchanging, order of things, remaining the same, in cause and effect, from age to age. . . . From time to time the superstructure of tactics has to be altered or wholly torn down; but the old foundations of strategy so far remain, as though laid upon a rock."[4]

An examination of the naval wars of the nineteenth and twentieth centuries re-enforced Mahan's convictions that, though technological developments might alter tactics, the principles of strategy remained constant. In 1895 in his "Blockade in Relation to Naval Strategy," he stated that the advent of steam, steel, and the torpedo had definitely changed the problem of the close blockade of earlier times, yet the alterations affected practices, not principles; the new weapons, he said, had "simply widened the question, not changed its nature."[5] In 1911 when he finally reworked his War College and Annapolis lectures and case studies on naval warfare, bringing them together in book form (*Naval Strategy, Compared and Contrasted with the Principles of Military Operations on Land*), these opinions concerning the impact of steam, steel, and torpedo on naval practices and principles were reaffirmed. Similar views about the probable effects of the submarine on naval warfare were now expressed. Mahan freely predicted that the undersea craft would modify tactics by placing "far greater strain on the blockaders" and by compelling "them to keep at a much greater distance"; he asserted, however, that the fundamental principles of strategy would remain intact.[6]

As the Nazis laid plans for the approaching conflict, they

[4] Mahan, *The Influence of Sea Power upon History, 1660–1783*, 7–10, 21–22, 88.

[5] Mahan, "Blockade in Relation to Naval Strategy," United States Naval Institute *Proceedings*, Vol. XXI (December, 1895), 851–66 (Reprinted from *Journal of the Royal United Service Institution*, Vol. XXXIX (November, 1895). See also Mahan, "Considerations Governing the Disposition of Navies," *National Review*, July, 1902, reprinted in *Retrospect and Prospect*, 173–74.

[6] Mahan, *Naval Strategy*, 2–4.

discarded the Mahan-Tirpitz theory of battle-fleet supremacy. Seeking to profit from the lessons of World War I and
hoping to take advantage of improved submarines, powerful pocket battleships, and unmatched air power, the German High Command attempted to by-pass the basic principle of the command of the sea and to resolve naval warfare
into mutual attack and defense of trade by means of the
convoy system and cruiser warfare. Their hopes were
dashed; their endeavors fell short of achievement; their
plans went awry; the Allies refused to abandon the time-
proved strategy of concentration of power. Though significant naval engagements were infrequent in the Atlantic
and Mediterranean theaters, though the blockade was restricted by extenuating circumstances, and though shipping
losses were heavy, the Allies largely enjoyed the fruits of
command.

The war in the Pacific presented well-nigh unprecedent-
ed difficulties. The main resources of strength were on opposite sides of the widest ocean in the world; nor were there
two or three areas, such as the exits on either side of the
British Isles and the Strait of Gibraltar in the Atlantic,
which if dominated would automatically, at least for surface
vessels, give command of the whole. So widely scattered were
the island archipelagoes that neither side, in the earlier days
of the war, had strength to assert supremacy in all regions
which might become critical. These geographical factors
plus the utilization of new instruments of warfare, especially the airplane, caused both sides in the early months of the
war to abandon, at times, the principle of fleet concentration.

This "task force" strategy, adopted in part because of the
exigencies of the time, had serious limitations, and its practice proved slow and costly, a fact nowhere more clearly
seen than at Guadalcanal. As soon as the United States Navy
had secured plane and ship superiority and had thoroughly

revamped its aerial tactics in both defense and offense, it returned to the classical principles of Mahanian strategy. From the Gilbert Islands campaign of November, 1943, onward—in the assaults upon the Marshalls, the Carolines, the Marianas, and the inner defenses of the Japanese Empire—our fleet activities, though they continued to be spoken of as task forces, usually involved entire battle fleets capable of engaging and defeating the whole enemy fleet. The principle of obtaining and retaining a decided command around any land area invaded now replaced the tactics of attrition employed at Guadalcanal. The concentration of the major ships into a unified battle fleet which was able to assert and maintain dominance gave victory to the United States. In the Pacific, even more strikingly than in the Atlantic, the principles of strategy which Mahan had so ably elucidated and popularized two generations earlier proved valid.

The maintenance of communications for the Allies in the Pacific and in the Atlantic seemed at times surrounded by almost insuperable difficulties, yet they never lost sight of the fact that only by the unremitting possession of command could truly defensive measures to their shipping be provided. They recognized that without this fundamental cover every individual convoy ran the risk of being overwhelmed by superior power. In light of the records of this war, there is no reason to believe that Mahan's thesis of the innate dependence of communications upon command has been overthrown by the new weapons; it is indeed no exaggeration to state that without the constant support of the battle squadrons the whole complicated system of Allied sea power would have at once collapsed.

Not only were the Allies able to carry on their own vital communications behind this protective shield, but they seriously disrupted those of the enemy, preying alike upon his raiders and his shipping. Mahan foresaw that the disruption of enemy communications was restricted by the cessation of the continuous and close blockade. He did not foresee that the effectiveness of the blockade might be as greatly reduced as it was by the Nazis and the Japanese by precautionary stock piles, synthetic substitutes, and the acquisition of important resources from subjugated peoples.

Obviously the former major advantages of command—immunity to invasion, maintenance of one's own communications, the disruption of the enemy's lines, and the power to distract and to interfere with the opponent's action on land—have been modified. Fleet supremacy alone is no longer adequate to insure against invasion in this day of the paratrooper; the assistance of a land-based air arm and the presence of a considerable home force are essential. The advantage accruing to the possessor of the command of the sea to interfere with enemy action on land has been modified by long range artillery, torpedo craft, air might, and the increased mobility of land forces, yet World War II again proved conclusively that successful military invasions are absolutely contingent upon this fundamental principle of strategy as expounded by Mahan.

So gigantic and significant were the land battles in World War II, so spectacular and important was the air war, that not infrequently has the magnitude of naval operations and the degree to which these operations contributed to final victory been slighted. In this truly global war the pooling of resources and the transport of men and material to all quarters required for success comparative command of the seas. On no previous occasion have the difficulties been greater in the achievement of that control; never before had the very existence of navies been so threatened; never in the life of mankind has the influence of sea power upon history been more marked.

It cannot be denied that the phenomenal advances in military and naval technology in the past century in the fields of propulsion, armor, ordnance, and weapons have had far-reaching repercussions. As for the United States, she has ceased to be a continent and has become an island—with its strengths and weaknesses—as once was Britain. Distance and the oceans still remain important factors in American defense, but distance and the oceans and the best military and naval defense that can be devised can no longer guarantee, as once they did, to keep war from American shores.

These technological developments as affecting naval warfare have modified tactics immeasurably. They have greatly circumscribed the operations of the fleet; its offensive power has been weakened in range, space, and time. Nevertheless, unless the submarine and the airplane can drive from the sea the surface warship and eliminate its previous ascendancy and even its entire utility, there is little to justify the belief that naval strategy as enunciated by Mahan will be basically altered. This statement does not overlook the possibility that in an atomic war the very sinews of national life might be so crippled as to make useless the naval strength of the nation even if that arm of defense escaped intact; obviously, in that eventuality, a discussion of naval strategy becomes purely academic.

History thus far confirms Mahan's thesis that the primary objective of the navy, as a necessary preliminary to any and all other activities, is to search out the enemy's forces and to destroy or drive them from the seas. The extent to which this goal, this command of the sea, can be achieved certainly varies; the value accorded this achievement by most present-day strategists does not differ from that which the dean of modern strategists gave it. The means by which this goal, this command of the sea, can be achieved may vary; the value accorded the fleet action of capital ships in this achievement by some modern strategists differs markedly from that which the great sea-power strategist gave it.

Granted that Mahan might be slow in appreciating the merits of the airplane and the modern submarine, he would probably recognize them as valuable adjuncts to the surface fleet and emphatically insist upon the doctrine of concentration of naval might, whatever its composition. Mahan might go so far as to agree with the view that air power and sea power are really one and indivisible; that together they perform the function which neither alone can accomplish—to control the sea. It is logical to conclude that Mahan would calmly yet repeatedly assert that only by concentration of power can the command of the sea be secured; that he would quietly yet forcefully insist that the control of sea communications whether achieved under, above, or on the surface is still the cardinal, elemental prerequisite for success.

As expositor of sea power, Mahan was a geopolitical thinker long before that expression was coined; as espouser of sea power, Mahan was the precursor of Halford Mackinder, analyst exceptional of the forthcoming role of land power; as exponent of sea power, Mahan was the preceptor of Karl Haushofer, advocate extraordinary of depth in space, *lebensraum,* and land empire. Mahan's sea-power doctrine polarized a set of historical data concerning the role of the sea in its relation to national well-being. As he viewed the constituent elements affecting power on the sea, he discussed geographical position, physical conformation, extent of territory, number of population, character of people, and character of government. In the creation of national greatness as connected with sea power, he saw industry, markets, marine, navy, and bases closely related and theoretically, at least, in that sequence.

Regardless of the extent to which technology has affected naval strategy, scientific and political developments have adversely affected the comparative relation of sea power and land power. Naturally sea power enjoys less secure tenure because of the various restrictions previously noted which limit the advantages formerly enjoyed by the command of the sea. There are other factors, however, which have been undermining more seriously the fundamentals upon which power on the sea rests.

Prior to the present century sea power had the very great advantage over land power in its superior mobility and ubiquity. Yet in comparison to sea power whose characteristics have been but slightly altered by the advent of steam and oil, the mobility of land power has been immeasurably increased by the successive utilization of the railroad, automotive power, and aircraft. Topographical barriers which were formidable obstacles, to expansion and integration have been surmounted. Land power has overcome its age-old handicap of not being able to command effectively and control adequately huge land blocks. As horse and camel mobility have been superseded, land power with its new-found mobility can think in terms of the organization of continents and in the creation of nonoceanic economic systems.

Mahan was aware of some of the new forces and factors and qualified his doctrine in light of them.[7] He repeatedly called attention to the fact that British sea power was closely tied up with the unique geographical position of the home base, and, furthermore, that the appearance of sea power outside the continent of Europe lessened the hold of Britain on the sea. In the development of commerce he recognized that there were "numerous alternatives" to sea transport and suggested that the role of the sea might grow relatively less important, especially in light of air developments. Unquestionably he underemphasized the railroad and automotive power; he maintained that "unless we succeed in ex-

[7] *Supra*, 219–20; also Mahan, *The Problem of Asia*, 125–26, and Mahan, *Some Neglected Aspects of War*, 174 ff.

ploiting the air, water remains, and must always remain, the great medium of transportation."

Sir Halford Mackinder, the outstanding British geographer and one-time director of the London School of Economics, developed at greater length these restrictive features of sea power. As early as 1902, in *Britain and the British Seas,* he called attention to the temporary aspects of empires, reminding his readers that "other empires have had their day, and so may Britain." He agreed with Mahan that the location of Great Britain in relation to her adversaries, as long as their bases had been in Europe, had given the British a powerful leverage; indeed, geographical position had given "Britain a unique part in the world's drama," but neither central position nor insularity could continue to give "indefeasible title to marine sovereignty." Continued he, "In the presence of vast powers, broad-based on the resources of half continents, Britain could not again become the mistress of the seas."[8]

Two years later in a remarkable address before the Royal Geographical Society, entitled "The Geographical Pivot of History," Sir Halford stated his belief that the Columbian epoch of four hundred years of discovery and colonization of non-European regions was drawing to a close, and that this cessation of world-wide explorations signalized the establishment of a closed political system in which the railroad and other mechanical transport were already definitely altering the relative strength of land and sea power.

Mackinder saw history in great movements and read its meaning in broad terms; he saw history as the story of the movement of the landlocked peoples in the plains of Eastern Europe, Western and Central Asia against the inhabitants of the littoral of the Eurasian mass. As a network of railroads supplanted horse communications in this central re-

[8] Sir Halford J. Mackinder, *Britain and the British Seas,* 350, 358.

gion, the British geographer envisaged the creation of a great land power, a pivot state, which he termed the "Eurasian Heartland." He feared that the new mobility of these landlocked peoples would permit them to expand to and incorporate the marginal lands of Eurasia, and that with these vast continental resources for fleet construction a world empire was in sight.[9] It should be observed that Mackinder did not deprecate sea power; he merely held that sea power could not prevent the control by one state of the pivot region of the Heartland, and that, once that initial achievement had been made, the Heartland power could move on to control the continents of Europe, Asia, and Africa—the "World Island," as he called it—and with these unmatched resources could become the indisputable master of the seas and totally dominate the world.

With the reorganization of Europe fully in mind, Mackinder elaborated these views in 1919 in *Democratic Ideals and Reality: A Study in the Politics of Reconstruction*. He reaffirmed his belief in the key significance of the Heartland and its invulnerability to sea power. He recognized the predominant role which sea power had again played in winning a war, but he warned against thinking that sea power inevitably had "the last word in the rivalry with land power." Such complacency failed to take into consideration what might have been the case had the Heartland presented a united front and what might be the adverse effects on the relative strengths of land and sea power with the improvement of the aircraft, which he termed "the amphibious cavalry of the future." It mattered little whether it was Russia, Germany, Japan, or an entente of these powers that controlled this pivot state; the effects would be disastrous. He urged that in the politics of reconstruction the forces of

[9] "The Geographical Pivot of History," *The Geographical Journal*, Vol. XXIII (April, 1904), 421–44.

demography and geography be given careful consideration.[10]

The German geopoliticians, drawing their inspiration largely from Mahan and their ideas chiefly from Mackinder, evolved a theory of growth and empire built on expanding land power roughly analogous to Mahan's philosophy of sea power.[11] The most important of the German geopoliticians was Doctor Karl Haushofer, erstwhile major general in the Kaiser's army, who became professor of geography and military science at the University of Munich in 1919. Haushofer's teacher, Frederick Ratzel, definitely one of the more important intellectual figures in German life at the turn of the century, had been much impressed with Mahan's views, and undoubtedly influenced the outlook of his pupil. Haushofer greeted Mahan as a seer and frequently expressed great admiration for him. In Mahan he found one who thought in terms of world power and greater space; in him he discovered a kindred spirit and received inspiration and guidance. This German geopolitician called Mackinder's article on "The Geographical Pivot of History" a truly "grandiose description of world policy compressed into a few pages." The eclectic Haushofer and his followers capitalized on the Britisher's fears; with suitable modification, they accepted his views as a heaven-sent solution to Germany's world political dilemma. To a people who had just lost to sea power and were resentful of defeat and longed for a second trial of strength, Haushofer's land-power interpretation of history seemed more nearly to fit the potentialities of the German state and more surely to promise success than did another bid at sea power.

Beyond doubt Haushofer and his aides perverted geopolitical thought and frequently acted with little regard for historical accuracy, yet their impact was most important.

10 Pages 77 ff., 134 ff., 191 ff.

11 Robert Strausz-Hupé, *Geo-Politics: The Struggle for Space and Power*, 44 ff., 243 ff.

Sir Halford Mackinder (1861–1947). Outstanding British geographer widely known as the formulator of the Heartland concept in geopolitics. *National Portrait Gallery*

Dr. Karl Haushofer (1869–1946), professor of geography and director of the Institute of Geopolitics in the University of Munich, closely associated with the doctrine of *Lebensraum*. *United Press International photograph*

Without question Nazi leadership failed to follow fully the pattern of empire designed by the geopoliticians, but their philosophy of empire profoundly influenced national and international politics. Central in Nazi ideology was the concept of physically and politically dominated space. *Lebensraum* became the slogan, at once the reason for the conquest of space and the pretext to demand space in order to conquer yet more space. Political geography thus became the crucible into which imperial ambitions were poured, and over which were breathed the inarticulate aspirations of a great yet frustrated people, and from which was drawn, for at least a considerable majority of the German state, a seemingly valid, rationalized, and scientific dogma which proclaimed expansion of the Reich and its master race as natural, necessary, and inevitable. It is one of those ironies of history that the American advocate of sea power should have served to inspire a philosophy of power so antithetical to his own and to contribute even indirectly in the creation of a force that could be crushed only by the sustained efforts and the combined action of his own beloved country, his highly esteemed British Commonwealth and Empire, and their many powerful allies.

Time and technology have qualified beyond dispute the political and military significance of sea power as an instrument in world politics. So far as one may judge, sea power has been more circumscribed by these factors than Mahan anticipated. This is not surprising. Foresight is limited even among the greatest, and strides in scientific developments since Mahan's death have exceeded the expectations of virtually all. Mackinder's views on the rapidly increasing significance of land power have been largely confirmed. During the first two decades of the century, rail developments in Russia and Turkey endangered British life lines in Afghanistan, Persia, and Egypt. In World War I the threat to Egypt and India forced the creation of land power on the part of Great Britain and robbed her of the economic advantage which insularity had once given her. Comparable developments in subsequent decades have accentuated the comparative recession of sea power before land power. The full weight of automotive transportation and the growing power of aircraft have struck with force. World War II confirmed the fact that the relation of sea-power bases to land power is a most important consideration. The rapidity with which Singapore and Hong Kong fell show that defense in depth is essential. Geographical, demographical, and industrial resources and capacity, in the modern day, are the great political realities affecting the development of states. Without huge production, comparative self-sufficiency in resources, abundant man power, and space in depth, a state feels insecure and often seeks to improve its status in these respects. Mackinder's fears concerning the role of a pivot state in the Eurasian Heartland have not as yet materialized; world events, however, may now be shaping in such a fashion that history will proclaim him a prophet in this respect. In any case, despite Mahan's own prudent qualifications, Mackinder more fully and accurately perceived the limitations of sea power than did the American historian-analyst.

As philosopher, Mahan was a formulator and expositor of a doctrine of unregulated national power. The sea-power concept, basically a philosophy of empire, was an analysis of the fundamental and persisting factors behind world power and imperial dominion. Though ingenious and contradictory at times, this advocate of power politics nevertheless presented a persuasive rationalization of the imperialist struggle. Dominant influence was cloaked under national interest and moral right. The use of force as an instrument of national policy was glorified and hallowed; war was viewed as a moral and ethical necessity. The very essence of progress required the continuance of struggle; it was by the elimination of the weakest and the survival of

324

the fittest that the world had progressed in the past and would progress in the future. War was natural and beneficial; war was productive of great good for the state and for civilization; war served as an excellent tonic for the individual, calling out his noblest virtues.

This doctrine of power was not new. Mahan's concepts of force potential and force competitively organized, of peace ignoble and force not ignoble, of the best interests of mankind lying not in universal harmony nor in fond dreams of unbroken peace but in the rivalries of nations and the conflict of ambitions which preserve the martial spirit, of ownership of territory dependent not upon technical possession but upon wise utilization or upon the absence of a power strong enough to dispossess, of justification of British acquisition and occupation of Egypt on grounds of moral expediency (irrespective of the wishes of the inhabitants), of Divine approval of the Anglo-Saxon position of world dominance bear striking similarity to concepts and practices before, during, and since his day as characterized by such phrases as the "big stick," a "place in the sun," an "empire upon which the sun never sets," the "master race," the "superman and the superstate," the "world revolution," the "co-prosperity sphere," "lebensraum," and "security." "security."

No, Mahan did not originate but assiduously propagated the doctrine of force. He disclaimed the thesis that force begets force; he acclaimed that the ever increasing armaments of Europe not only preserved the peace but prevented the demoralization of the European peoples by preventing a flood of socialistic measures which would follow with the release of the sums then spent on armaments. For Mahan force was the only reliable solvent of international rivalries, rivalries which beyond question his doctrine inculcated. He was quick to see the weaknesses of internationally achieved arbitration and disarmament; for him war was the lesser danger. For him arbitration and disarmament did not appear in the least essential for the preservation of that for which his nationally organized force was predicated to defend.

As historian, from point of treatment and resulting creation of interest, Mahan occupies an important place in modern naval historiography; from content and interpretation, he presented a new philosophy of history. Salutarily, naval history in his hands, as has been seen, was something more than a mere chronicle of events; it became an analysis of the meaning and significance of those events with a deduction of their governing principles. However, in the development of his thesis that the rise and fall of modern nations rested upon the command of the sea, Mahan not infrequently slighted or totally missed other contributing factors. He virtually ignored the influence of the rise of the English middle class and the impact of the head start of the English industrial revolution as factors in his explanation of that nation's pre-eminence. Similarly, his preoccupation with maritime issues caused him to overlook the agrarian discontent and land hunger of the frontier as causes of the second war between the United States and England.

Mahan's emphasis upon the power element in international economic competition obscured the fact that peaceful utilization of the sea was not dependent upon military command. For perhaps similar reasons, the conquest and retention of overseas markets were viewed as resting upon the power of the state to open and retain them to the virtual exclusion of the economic abilities of the manufacturer and merchant. Mahan surely never claimed that sea power was the sole determinant in history, but he did claim for it a predominant role. The rise of Russia as a great nation, and potentially a greater nation, without sea power, stands conspicuously as an exception to the Mahanian thesis.

Finally, Mahan's sea-power idea, arising out of his study

of the commerce, politics, and wars of the seventeenth and eighteenth centuries, bears the unmistakable imprint of eighteenth-century mercantilism and contains the weaknesses as well as the strengths of that doctrine. Eighteenth-century mercantilism held that a nation's prosperity, power, and security depended upon an accumulation of the precious metals. The fulfillment of this objective called for a favorable balance of trade in the form of increased exports and decreased imports, the creation of a merchant marine which would limit carrying charges for freight and seamen's wages to one's own nationals, and the formation of foreign trading monopolies, preferably the establishment of colonies whose trade was so supervised that the colonies furnished the mother country with her essential raw materials and served as the outlet for her surplus of manufactured goods. Mercantilism, or bullionism as it may be called, largely ignored other factors in the creation and maintenance of national wealth, falsely assumed that profit does not accrue to the buyer as well as to the seller of goods in the international market, and overlooked the fact that not colonies but other great powers constitute a nation's best customers. It can readily be seen how close to mercantilism of the eighteenth century was Mahan's doctrine of sea power, with its emphasis upon industry, marine, colonies, and navy. Only gradually, if at all, did Mahan sense the difference between the overseas commercial activities of mercantilism and the imperialism of modern finance capitalism.

Despite the prominence gained in his day, Mahan can scarcely be placed among the great historians; and despite the prestige accorded him, one cannot classify him as a great thinker. His interpretation of history was both too simple and too inclusive and often misleading. Behind the philosopher-historian stood the Christian moralist, who was at once interpreter and prophet, publicist and propagandist. It is in this role of propagandist-publicist that Mahan's chief significance lay, at least for the United States. Preoccupation with his influence upon foreign naval and imperial rivalry, an influence not to be minimized, must not preclude consideration of his primary concern which was the indoctrination of his fellow countrymen. No claim can be made that Mahan was the central figure on the American public stage during the quarter of a century following his rise to fame in 1890 to his death in 1914. Rather he must be viewed as one of many who played a part in shaping the policies of the United States as she came of age.

True and abiding national greatness rested upon sea power—this was Mahan's thesis. The power and wealth of England were associated with her dependence upon and her command of the sea—this was his ever recurring text. Proper military mastery of the sea depended upon certain well-established laws of strategy—this was his sermon derived from lessons of the past. The United States, he believed, could rise to her full stature among the nations of the world if she would only adequately appreciate the close relation of distant markets to her immense powers of production, for in the wake of such a realization would follow the establishment of a merchant marine with a navy to protect it and colonies to serve as trading and military bases— this was his moral and his teaching, this was his central hope and abiding prayer.

The Mahanian message translated into action called for predominance in the Caribbean with an American-owned and American-controlled canal and bases on either side of the Isthmus, acquisition of Hawaii, equality in the Far East, a navy adequate to defend all national interests, the employment of sound strategic principles, and the justification of expansion and of war.

Mahan, according to his own correct analysis, was a man of ideas and not of action, but he saw to it that his ideas were made known to the public. By spoken word, by direct appeal to presidents, cabinet members, senators, representatives, newspaper and magazine editors, and other individuals of influence, by letters to the press, by numerous periodical articles and by many books, he gained a hearing before the arbiter, public opinion. Nor was public opinion as a whole adverse to such views and activities. In messages to Congress, presidents alluded to him by name and made verbatim extracts from his writings; secretaries in the Cabinet forthrightly acknowledged their indebtedness to him; various Congressional committees in their hearings received his personal testimony; senators and representatives repeatedly referred to his articles and books; Senate and House reports likewise cited or quoted him; expansionist publicists and big navy men throughout the country went to him for ideas and support; men of marked influence were his intimate friends and were periodically in correspondence with him; his magazine articles and his books were widely reviewed. In light of these facts, Mahan no longer can be considered a prophet without honor in his own country.

Living at an opportune moment, Mahan formulated and expounded a somewhat novel interpretation of national power based upon a philosophy of history which adroitly linked patriotism, politics, and economics. These views, based upon a broad foundation and presented in a straightforward manner, had a strong appeal and gained a wide audience. Beyond question Mahan contributed greatly to the history of his time and his influence is still felt. He not only recorded history but created history. Contribution and influence, however, may be malevolent as well as benevolent. Basically, aside from his views on naval strategy, an evaluative analysis of Mahan's role rests upon the validity accorded his general philosophy of history as seen in his seapower thesis and his doctrine of power. The final estimate awarded Mahan largely depends upon answers given to certain broad questions of policy. In the first place: Is national interest so inextricably associated with the command of the sea as Mahan maintained? Is the partial and tenuous control worth the huge and essentially nonproductive expenditures which an effort of this magnitude demands? In the second place: Does the overall balance sheet of imperialism actually show the profits which the expansionist exponent claimed? Must a nation exploit backward peoples in order to have a flourishing industry and foreign commerce? Are colonies essential as outlets for the investment of surplus capital? Do nations have to "conquer" their supply of raw materials? And finally: Have competitive armaments proved the security against wars and have wars advanced world progress as Mahan asserted they would? Should Ishmaelitish nationalism and rampant sovereignty be given still further trials? Is there no alternative, no means by which nations can form a truly co-operative world community, whether it be termed a league, a united nations, or a federation?

The answers which the great exponent of sea power gave to these questions found many supporters in his day and still find many adherents today. There was in his day, in the United States and in the world, a small group, which has grown in size and influence with the years, who view quite differently the lessons of history and whose answers would vary greatly from his. To the latter group freedom from war is the *sine qua non* for all other freedoms, be they four or forty, and without the achievement of which present civilization will perish. To them imperialism, nationalism, and militarism have proved their baneful nature in two terrible holocausts within a generation. These individuals are under no great illusion concerning the difficulties inherent in the achievement of collective security, and vigorously maintain that international co-operation is not the idle dream of the impractical visionary.

Realism as well as idealism motivates the conviction. It is not the specious realism of the Tiger who quipped concerning the Fourteen Points that God Almighty had been satisfied with ten; the world has had enough of that kind of realism. Nor is it the pseudo realism of the shortsighted isolationist of the twenties who feared that the participation of the United States in co-operative endeavors to enforce the peace would lead to the dispatch of American doughboys to quell the quarrels of a quarrelsome world; Anzio and Tarawa, Okinawa and Ardennes Bulge have proved the fallacy of that kind of realism. Nor is it the false realism of the ostrich-like, nationalistic neutrality-seeker of the thirties who hoped to dispel the gathering storm clouds and to escape the destructive fury of the coming hurricane by ignoring foreign affairs and concentrating upon domestic activities; the dismemberment of Czechoslovakia and the collapse of Poland, the fall of France and the attack on Pearl Harbor have shown all too clearly the stupidity of that kind of realism.

In this day of shrinking distances, sound realism knows that unrestrained sovereignty for nations leads to world chaos as surely as unregulated liberty of action for the individual brings community anarchy. In this day of increasing interdependence, true realism affirms that no nation, as no individual, can live a self-contained existence. In this day of interpenetrating purposes, sound realism demands that the laissez-faire philosophy be modified in international affairs as it has already been largely abandoned in national life. In this day of the airplane, the rocket, and the atomic bomb, intelligent realism calls for recognition of the global aspect of peace as of war, that concerted action for a stable world order is as necessary as it is for victory against a common enemy. In this day of broadening horizons, real realism recognizes that self-interest and world interest not only are not incompatible but are essentially interdependent. Clear vision and courageous action are necessary in these days as we plan and work for a new world. How much better the new world will be depends in no small measure upon the extent to which enlightened, robust realism operates. Certainly such realism cannot recognize for any power the potential world dominance inherent in the control of the Heartland as envisaged by Mackinder; yet also most surely the world will be neither newer nor better than in the past, if recourse to rival blocs·of powers be employed as the pattern of world order.

The doctrines of power and empire as enunciated by Mahan and his school of thought have not proved sound as a basis for international action. The adherents of power politics have led the world to the brink of disaster; the proponents of unrestricted national sovereignty have brought civilization to near destruction; the exponents of empire, whether their concept·be that of master race or white man's burden, have half the world seething in revolt. The atomic age has shown conclusively that the only guarantee of civilization is a society of nations. That is the stark, tragic reality of our day, though to judge the world by its conduct, it is a reality of which it is only dimly conscious.

The Greek world of the fifth-fourth centuries B. C. failed to achieve a working political concept greater than the city-state; the problem confronting mankind over two thousand years later is to achieve a working political concept greater than the nation-state. The task is not easy, but its accomplishment is urgent. As we face it, we need seek for no more applicable counsel than that given by Mahan to the problem of blockade in naval warfare: "Whatever the tactical difficulties involved, the strategic necessities compel a diligent study of how to meet them."

XV

MAHAN REVISITED

In March 1913, some eighteen months before his death, Mahan wrote his long-time English friend, Bouverie F. Clarke: "My vogue is largely over—I am no longer in demand." Although written in the context of interest in or demand for his writings, was this perhaps symptomatic of something more basic? Had time passed him by? Was his vogue really largely over? Or was Mahan unduly deprecating his status? Was he perhaps assuming overmuch as to his popularity in earlier years? And closely related, how well grounded was whatever popularity he may have had?

Contemporaries gave thought to these and related questions, and students of history, politics, and strategy have given much attention to both the merits and shortcomings of Mahan's writings and to their influence in his own lifetime and subsequently. Seven dissertations written during the 1960's are listed under the heading of Alfred Thayer Mahan, some deal only limitedly with him, others give him central place; three have appeared with modifications in book form.[1] Since World War II, national news weeklies have had articles touching on Mahan, two with photographs.[2] Historical and naval journals continue to publish

---

[1] Warren F. Kuehl, *Dissertations in History*, 2 vols. The basis for classification or quality of reporting may have varied between the two volumes, but it is instructive to note that only one, my own, was listed in volume one covering 1873–1960 in contrast to the seven in volume two covering 1961 to June, 1970. Some dissertations do not get reported—two pertinent ones written during the sixties are not listed in volume two.

[2] *Time*, LXIII (Feb. 8, 1954), 18, cites a quotation from Mahan pre-

articles about Mahan and at least twenty important studies on the foundations of national power, the history of expansion, the rise of new navies, and the development of changing strategy, written since my first edition, have important references, if not chapters, concerned with Mahan's thought and influence. A three-volume collection of his more important letters and papers has recently been published.[3]

These several scholarly activities confirm that Mahan was an important and in certain respects a controversial individual. It is a real boon to have most of the widely scattered letters, along with selected miscellaneous papers, so conveniently available and so ably edited.[4] The new studies on navy strategy and expansion, often presented in depth, make valuable contributions to an understanding of Mahan and his times. Those interested in the problem of expansion and the rise of the navy usually limit themselves to the period of Mahan's life or often even stop at the close of the century. Those concerned with the broader implications of the sea-power doctrine and naval strategy generally carry their analysis and appraisal through the intervening years since his death.

Without exception, recent scholarship supports the pri-

---

ceding an article on "Armed Forces" under National Affairs and also a photograph; *Time*, LXXII (August 4, 1958), 10 and 7, has a quotation and photograph plus lead note in "A Letter from the Publisher"; Raymond Moley, "Mahan's Long Shadow," *Newsweek*, LXVIII (July 18, 1966), 100.

3 Mahan, *Letters and Papers*. 3 vols. ed. Robert Seager II and Doris D. Maguire. The publishers state that Professor Seager is preparing a biography of the man and his letters.

4 Although these letters represent only the Mahan side of the correspondence and "probably no more than 20 or 25 percent of the letters he wrote," despite "several years of assiduous search," one can agree with the editors that those recovered "can be taken to comprise a representative sampling." (I, *vii*). Should additional correspondence be found, it is not likely to greatly alter the present picture—in fact the "new" material here presented, while giving additional touches especially on the personal side, does not appear to modify significantly the previously received record.

mary thesis I advanced thirty years ago that though Mahan was interested in and did affect foreign naval and imperial rivalry and did influence their strategic concepts, his primary concern was the indoctrination of his fellow countrymen with the importance and significance of sea power for the United States. This scholarship likewise supports the second major emphasis I then made that Mahan must be seen in perspective as one of several individuals who helped shape public opinion. He was both product of and spokesman for his age and he is to be viewed as neither a glorified hero nor as a despicable villain. Basically he was a publicist-propagandist presenting an intriguing and captivating interpretation of the important role and correct use of sea power. Timeliness was a critical feature whether seen from the foreign or domestic viewpoint. Had Mahan written a quarter of a century earlier, his message would undoubtedly have fallen on barren soil, and a quarter of a century later he would have had little reason to write as he did.[5] As it was, Mahan lived in the period of what Walter Langer calls "preclusive imperialism"—"a concomitant of the onrushing industrial revolution."[6] This period witnessed a resurgence of nationalism, the emergence of four new world powers, the collapse of the Ottoman and Spanish empires, the partitioning of Africa and the opening of China, the appearance of new naval rivalries, a race for overseas trade, raw materials, and empire, and the extension of Social Darwinism to the field of international politics.

The recent studies recognize that Mahan's writings were

[5] Writing in 1900, Mahan stated that one of the most interesting aspects about the reception of certain ideas that he had advanced was the "almost instantaneous readiness with which a seed of thought germinates when it falls upon mental soil prepared already to receive it." *The Problem of Asia and Its Effect upon International Politics*, 8–9.

[6] Walter L. Langer, "Farewell to Empire," *Foreign Affairs*, XLI (October, 1962), 120.

not responsible for initiating naval expansion and imperial rivalry abroad, but that they did give re-enforcement to Great Britain and encouragement to Germany and Japan in these respects. Mahan is best seen as a catalyst offering justification for policies already adopted or contemplated. He clarified strategic concepts and though offering little that was essentially new, he was more "creative" in this aspect than in the building programs.[7]

The situation was quite comparable on the domestic scene as regards both the navy and expansion. The new navy was clearly under way before Mahan's first sea-power book appeared in 1890, though this does not imply that he exercised no influence in this respect prior to that date. The decade of the 1880's was "characterized by vascillation, indecision and frustration," yet it was a period of preparation for the real turn which came in 1889–90. Ideas expressed were the "thought reservoir from which Mahan, the members of Congress, and others drew."[8] Admiral Stephen B. Luce has at long last received deserved recognition, if only briefly in a single chapter. He is ably portrayed as "the admiral in politics," playing a vital role in all naval affairs and, less convincingly, he is given the title of "father of the modern navy," an appellation that will not be uniformly accepted. This account gives Tracy and Luce "chief credit for America's naval renaissance," while another account written the same year broadens the scope by including with Luce, Mahan, and Professor Soley, "the scholarly workhorse," as the trio who "supplied the theoretical component

7 Captain Ronald B. St. John, "European Naval Expansion and Mahan, 1889–1906," *Naval War College Review*, XXIII (March, 1971), 74–83; Arthur J. Marder, *From Dreadnought to Scapa Flow: The Royal Navy in the Fisher Era, 1904–1919*, I, various.

8 Robert Seager II, "Ten Years Before Mahan: The Unofficial Case for the New Navy, 1880–1890," *Mississippi Valley Historical Review*, XL (December, 1953), 491 and 512.

of Tracy's new policy."[9] Secretary Tracy, as can be seen, remains the key figure in the rise of the new navy for this author, as he does for the biographer of the recently released life of Tracy which is subtitled "Father of the Modern American Fighting Navy."[10] Double parentage seems a bit difficult to comprehend but wisely no one is promoting Mahan for that honor! In fact, the scholars who advance Luce's role as primary in the rise of the new navy make a strong case that he, not Mahan, was likely the naval officer who most influenced Secretary Tracy in drafting his revolutionary annual report of 1889.[11]

In attempting to place men and events in perspective in the rise and growth of the new navy, it should perhaps be stated once again that Mahan's significance lies not in his being the first to express new or different ideas on the value and use of navies, but that he wrote more cogently and persuasively and that his views gained a wider audience. This fact is not fully appreciated by some scholars. One author, in examining the ideological roots of modern navalism in his study of United States naval officers active from the 1840's to the 1920's—covering a half generation on either side of Mahan's active years—gives a good historical sketch of sea power. He points out, as others have before, but more specifically and extensively, that most of the basic ideas of Mahan's doctrine of sea power had been earlier advanced by some of Mahan's contemporaries, by pre-Civil War officers, by the Founding Fathers, by contemporary British naval historians and officers, by earlier Englishmen as far back as Sir Walter Raleigh, and indeed by certain of the

---

9 John A. S. Grenville and George Young, *Politics, Strategy, and American Diplomacy*, 1 and 11; Walter R. Herrick, Jr., *The American Naval Revolution*, 51.

10 Benjamin Franklin Cooling, *Benjamin Franklin Tracy: Father of the Modern American Fighting Navy*, 46 ff:

11 Grenville and Young, *op. cit.*, 33–37. See *supra*, 239–40.

Greek statesmen.[12] Sketches such as this confirm what I wrote earlier that the "idea of sea power, if not the term itself, is as old as history."[13] These accounts are interesting as well as valuable in placing events and ideas in a correct and helpful setting, but unless care is exercised in interpretation they may obscure what I believe is crucial to an accurate understanding of Mahan. No careful student of Mahan has ever claimed Mahan discovered sea power, nor did he himself. He was fully aware that he was not the first to write about sea power; he evaluated his contribution as one who helped in clarifying, substantiating, popularizing, and making effective the doctrine. And no one can rightly quarrel with that appraisal.

One scholar has well observed that to discount Mahan, as two authors recently have, as one who "appeared relatively late on the scene" and that "his doctrine was not original," misses the point. Writes this critic: "That 'the concepts had been discussed for two decades by Congressmen and naval officers' is not very startling. They had been discussed by Drake, Raleigh and the elder Pitt two or three centuries before Mahan." He goes on to state that the few congressmen who anticipated Mahan were definitely in the minority and that "a careful reading of the complete Congressional debate of the 1880's will show a remarkable confusion about the uses and purposes of a navy." He concludes:

> In a period when most statesmen and many naval officers held vague and incorrect notions about the potentialities of sea power, he [Mahan] provided a clear and persuasive text on the subject. This and not its "originality" is the most important aspect of Mahan's work.[14]

12 Peter Karsten, *The Naval Aristocracy: The Golden Age of Annapolis and the Emergence of Modern Navalism*, 310–17.

13 *Supra*, 47–48.

14 Ronald Spector, "Professors of War: The United States Naval War College and the Modern American Navy, 1885–1915" (Ph.D. diss., Yale Uni-

Without doubt, Mahan's "clear and persuasive text" greatly helped displace "the vascillation, indecision and frustrations" of the 1880s. As one author correctly states, Mahan "defined a purpose, a mission for the New Navy," and adds that now most "naval officers viewed the world scene through the lens of Captain Alfred Thayer Mahan."[15] Indeed, one scholar states that at least so far as strategy was concerned "American naval thought took on a hagiolatrous

versity, 1967), 80, n. 16. His reference is to a statement by Grenville and Young, *op. cit.*, 11.

It should be noted that Grenville and Young have several refreshing and stimulating articles interlocking political and strategic aspects and frequently discount previously assigned roles to several prominent individuals, including Mahan and Roosevelt. The traditional view of the key role of Mahan in Tracy's 1889 report, advanced by the Sprouts and accepted by LaFeber, Herrick, Millis, West, myself, and others, is but one example. In their endeavor to place Mahan in perspective—a healthy antidote, as I have stated—they may at times overdo the case. For example: "In view of the defenseless position of the United States in the Pacific during the following decades [after acquisitions, 1890–1900], the military policy of the United States might have been better served if the millions of dollars spent on the canal had instead been used to build a large Pacific fleet and the necessary harbor facilities to serve it. But Mahan never conceived of such a solution, believing as he did that the first principle of naval strategy must be to keep the fleet undivided, able to pass from one ocean to the other as conditions demanded." (295). As I consider these sentences, the following questions come to mind: Why single out Mahan? Is not more influence being given Mahan relative to building the Canal than accorded him elsewhere? Does anyone really think that had Mahan been as strongly opposed to canal construction as he was in favor, he could have stopped the half-century urge to pierce the Isthmus? Was Mahan the only advocate of fleet concentration? Didn't President Theodore Roosevelt vehemently state that division would be "an act of utter folly"? And finally, granted the validity of the suggested choice of a Pacific fleet over the Canal, can it be convincingly argued that the money saved would have been appropriated for a Pacific fleet?

Another revisionist note is pertinent. These authors minimize the role played by Theodore Roosevelt, as Assistant Secretary of the Navy, in the plans for possible war with Spain and especially discount any special insight in the famous telegram to Dewey on the ground that action against the Phillipines were in the war plans drawn up as early as 1896 (269–78). See *supra*, 133–34.

15 Richard D. Challener, *Admirals, Generals and American Foreign Policy, 1898–1914*, 14, 12.

and monolithic character" following the publication of Mahan's initial sea power study.[16]

Recent research also supports the view that Mahan played an important role in American expansion at the close of the century. One well-recognized scholar writes: "The policy makers and others who embraced Mahan's teaching made them a central part of the expansionist ideology of the 1890's."[17] An unpublished doctoral dissertation on Mahan and American foreign policy analyzes Mahan's views within the broad setting of the period and concludes that he was "the leading polemicist of the American school of thought favoring expansion." This author is particularly impressed with Mahan's knowledge of the Far East and seeks to show him "the student of the Orient." He reaffirms the view that Mahan, aside from writing at an opportune moment, brought personal talents of merit. In his own words: "One of Mahan's most outstanding virtues as a propagandist was his ability to get to the heart of an issue and bring together the different elements of a particular problem into a clear, organized and comprehensive presentation."[18] Two books ably correlating diplomatic and military events in the Pacific give appropriate recognition to Mahan.[19]

Recent scholars agree with Mahan's evaluation and my own that he was but one of several who had participated in the national awakening. While fully supporting Mahan's

[16] Kenneth J. Hagan, *American Gunboat Diplomacy and the Old Navy,* *1877–1889,* 13.

[17] Walter LaFeber, *The New Empire: An Interpretation of American Expansion, 1860–1898,* 93.

[18] Morris Levy, "Alfred Thayer Mahan and the United States Foreign Policy" (Ph.D. diss., New York University, 1965), 9, 307, and 213.

[19] William R. Braisted, *The United States Navy in the Pacific, 1897–1909,* and *The United States Navy in the Pacific, 1909–1922.*

view that he had "to some extent helped turn thought," they also recognize others. One author chooses Frederick Jackson Turner, Josiah Strong, and Brooks Adams along with Mahan as individuals whose writings "typified and in some specific instances directly influenced the thought of American foreign policy makers who created the new empire."[20] Another author, in a study of the Naval War College from its founding in 1885 to 1915, recognizes Mahan's peculiarly important role but contends that the College as a whole was the "nursery of imperialism" and "evolved a philosophy of overseas expansion that paralleled and in many cases anticipated the ideas of the imperialists of the 1898 era."[21]

Much research has been done on the driving forces operative in the United States following the Civil War to the close of the century. And the query logically arises as to how Mahan was affected by them. What were the motivating forces for him and what was his order of priority? For the country as a whole, scholars find many forces but are not in agreement as to their importance. Most frequently mentioned are Manifest Destiny, Social Darwinism, missionary zeal, psychological malaise, security needs, awareness of ideas and events abroad, and a wide range of economic considerations, including increasing industrial production and limited home markets, the closing of the frontier, new investment opportunities, and the depression of 1893.[22]

20 LaFeber, *op. cit.*, 62–63.
21 Spector, *op. cit.*, 162–63. See also William H. Berge, "The Impulse for Expansion: John W. Burgess, Alfred Thayer Mahan, Theodore Roosevelt, Josiah Strong and the Development of a Rationale" (Ph.D. diss., Vanderbilt University, 1969); John P. Rasmussen, "The American Imperialist Elite: A Study in the Concept of National Efficiency" (Ph.D. diss., Stanford University, 1962). The latter study considers Alfred Thayer Mahan, Brooks Adam, and Theodore Roosevelt.
22 Julius W. Pratt, *Expansionists of 1898*, and LaFeber, *op. cit.*, offer contrasting views on the significance of economic forces. Paul S. Holbo believes that LaFeber's economic interpretation is overstressed and oversimplified and offers a more balanced multi-causal explanation in his "Eco-

Mahan would have been knowledgeable of these several forces and appreciative of their role, and selections from his writings could be found to support, at least limitedly, nearly all of them. His view of destiny, his belief in the superiority of the Anglo-Saxon race, his sense of moral mission, and his ideas on the preventive and remedial virtues of struggle have already been examined. These were important to him; they were no cloak for ulterior designs, at least in most instances, but in my opinion they were not central. One historian has recently proposed that Mahan's primary concern was for the future of American industrial growth.[23] Still more recently another historian, strongly disagreeing, insists that Mahan was first and foremost a navalist.[24] A case can be made for each view. Mahan was definitely aware of the extraordinary economic changes taking place and he wrote much about the need for larger horizons, wider trade, and

nomics, Emotion and Expansion: An Emerging Foreign Policy," in *The Gilded Age: Revised and Enlarged*, edited by H. Wayne Morgan, 199–221. For other viewpoints, see Robert E. Osgood, *Ideals of Self Interest in American Foreign Relations*; Merle E. Curti, *Growth of American Thought*; Richard Hofstader, *Social Darwinism in American Thought*; and Frederick Merk, *Manifest Destiny and Mission in American History: A Reinterpretation*. Ernest May in *American Imperialism: A Speculative Essay* attempts an explanation of the motivating forces behind this phenomenon. He associates Fred Merk with Manifest Destiny, Julius Pratt with Social Darwinism, Richard Hofstader with psychological malaise, Walter LaFeber with economic forces, and adds awareness of ideas and events abroad as his own. He raises an interesting question about the economic emphasis given by LaFeber. Speaking of the early years atfer 1900, he writes, "La Feber's businessmen had the same standing as before and regarded overproduction with only a little, if any less, concern. No economic factor would account for their different feeling about colonies" (16).

Two recent extended discussions of the background and culmination of expansion are Robert L. Beisner's *From the Old Diplomacy to the New, 1865–1900*, and Charles S. Campbell's *The Transformation of American Foreign Relations, 1865–1900*. The latter gives an excellent summary in his chapter, "Currents of the 1890s and Territorial Expansion" (Chapter VIII, 146–60); the former attempts an interesting restructuring in approach to this complex problem.

23 LaFeber, *op. cit.*, 87–88.
24 Karsten, *op. cit.*, 338–42.

greater markets. It will be recalled that on one occasion he explicitly stated, "The growing production of the country demands that we look outward." If one views the interests of the nation as a whole and its priorities, I would agree that economic needs would rate higher than naval needs; but I do not think this was the case with Mahan. As I see it, for him the navy was central and the advancement of his service was primary. Both personal and national welfare were involved. He contended that every national interest, whether of a commercial, financial, or political nature, demanded a navy and that "every danger of a military character" could be best met by naval preparedness.

Welfare of country, however, was not the sole motivating force with Mahan or his fellow officers in the desire for an improved navy. The state of the navy at this time with its decrepit ships, antique equipment, and promotion difficulties, arising from overcrowded lower grades with consequent low pay for several years, caused many younger officers to leave the service. Mahan made at least token efforts toward finding more satisfactory employment in civilian life. The "Young Turks" and the "Old Salts" were united in their desire for more and better ships with more jobs available and quicker promotion. After carefully surveying this lack of opportunity for advancement, one scholar concludes that the "career anxieties (of the "Young Turks") may properly be cited as one of the primary forces behind the growth of the 'new Navy' and the emergence of modern American navalism."[25]

Mahan believed that he was the best exponent, at least within the navy, of the needs and values of the navy. In 1892 he wrote to the editor of *The Atlantic Monthly*:

> The Navy—and I may even say the country—needs a voice

[25] *Ibid.*, 317.

to speak constantly of . . . matters touching the Navy . . . Except myself, I know of no one in the Navy better disposed to identify himself with such a career—and in lack of a better, I should greatly like to do it.[26]

As I previously stated, Mahan was aware that the final arbiter was public opinion. He knew all too well that an appeal restricted to the needs of the navy would find a limited audience, but if extended to include the interests of businessmen, merchants, shippers, and financiers he might hope for a favorable action. This is not to suggest hypocrisy; Mahan was sincere in his utterances here—the lessons of history spoke for him and through him but, as I analyze his motives, the economic needs of the country were not primary. Walter Millis states that he finds it "difficult to resist the impression that Mahan's major impulse was simply to produce an argument for more naval building."[27]

A word of caution is in order. This evaluation of priorities should not be pushed too far. The interrelatedness of industry, markets, marine, navy and bases as advanced by Mahan must be kept in mind and with obviously multiple forces operative in the country at large, it is unwise to emphasize one to the neglect of another. As one writer well states: "Although individuals might stress one or another facet of the movement, all were mutually reenforcing and can be completely understood only in terms of their mutual relationship."[28]

No one finds Mahan a systematic writer, yet scholars generally agree as to what he thought constituted sea power

26 Mahan to Horace Scudder, November 22, 1892: Mahan Papers.

27 Walter Millis, *Arms and Men: A Study of American Military History*, 144. In light of the comments earlier made on the subject, Millis makes this interesting quip that "if Mahan discovered nothing in particular he discovered it very well." *Ibid.*, 145.

28 David Healy, *U.S. Expansionism: The Imperialist Urge of the 1890s*, 5.

and as to how he evaluated its role in history. Sea power for Mahan involved three major factors: first, the active sea tools of combatant ships, service force, and merchant marine; second, those elements of national wealth, such as natural and financial resources, character of the government, number and character of the people which combine to make up a nation's military and industrial potential; third, geographic foundations of size, position, climate, sea lanes, and colonies or bases. As to the importance of sea power, he expressed this succinctly by stating that the due use and control of the sea was the central link in assisting a nation to achieve strength and wealth.

Although there is general agreement as to the meaning and import of sea power, there has been an encouraging number of scholars who are supporting the view I expressed thirty years ago that there are shortcomings as well as merits to Mahan's analysis of the period of history he covered, to the applicability of his conclusions for his own time, and to their vitality for subsequent years. Mahan's call to lecture at the Naval War College presented a twofold challenge. In the first place, once having grasped the idea "that the use and control of the sea is and has been a great factor in the history of the world," he recognized that the idea could not remain "vague and unsubstantiated," but must be supported by the collection and examination of specific instances in which the precise effect was clear. The second challenge was how to make the story of the past useful, or as he was to put it, how he might draw "lessons" from the past pertinent for the future. When one adds the pressure of time and the distraction of other assignments to this desire for lessons and this concern for demonstrating more than investigating, it is not surprising that his sea-power series is not completely satisfactory history.

It becomes increasingly evident that the particular

345

period of history Mahan surveyed was peculiarly important in the development of his ideas, and that an appreciation of this must be kept in mind by anyone who wishes to understand him. The period covered by his sea-power series marked the gradual growth of the British Empire and the rise of Britain to world pre-eminence and was replete with great naval wars. It was easy to affirm that a great state needed a colonial empire, and a colonial empire needed a great fleet, and a commercial or industrial state needed its own carrying ships. Production, shipping, and colonies—these were Mahan's three keys to greatness. These centuries also represented a period essentially dominated by mercantilist thought, although the latter years did witness the beginning of the shift from the closed mercantile economy to the more open *laissez-faire* economy as propounded by Adam Smith in *The Wealth of Nations,* as well as the ushering in of the early stages of the industrial revolution for Britain.

Most historians including myself have termed Mahan a mercantilistic imperialist. This is understandable when one recalls that Mahan's story covered the heyday of mercantilism and that he drew many of his examples from the period. Furthermore, there are many similarities between mercantilism and nineteenth-century expansion as expounded by Mahan. Both desired expansion, both sought a favorable balance of trade, both emphasized the need of a merchant marine, and both talked of colonies. A recent study on American expansion takes issue with this traditional view of Mahan as a mercantilistic imperialist. The author acknowledges that the "study of the seventeenth and eighteenth centuries heavily influenced Mahan's thinking" and that "some of his tenets mesh perfectly with mercantilist philosophy," yet as he examines Mahan's three keys of production, shipping, and colonies, he finds the driving forces between the two periods were quite different.[29] In most respects his point is well taken, but the case is not quite as simple as it might first appear. The confusion arises in part from the use of a word that has two meanings, in part because Mahan reversed positions on one of the three key elements, and in part as a matter of emphasis. For example, as regards production, the mercantilist solicitude was prompted more by desire for bullion than by fear of overproduction or underemployment, as was the case in the late nineteenth century, yet both sought favorable trade balances. Nevertheless, Mahan and the mercantilists were diametrically opposed on the issue of protection and free trade.[30]

As I earlier noted, Mahan originally maintained that any prosperous nation must have its own carrying trade, but that as time progressed he de-emphasized this feature.[31] Before the Merchant Marine Commission in 1904, he said it would be desirable for the United States to have its own merchant fleet, but he specifically stated he did not favor its receiving financial assistance that might otherwise go to the navy because the navy was primary.[32] After the Russo-Japanese War he disavowed the impression that he once held, and might possibly have helped diffuse, that "navies depend upon maritime commerce as the cause and justification of their existence."[33]

29 LaFeber, *op. cit.*, 85–91, or LaFeber, "A Note on the 'Mercantilist Imperialism' of Alfred Thayer Mahan," *Mississippi Valley Historical Review*, XLVIII (March, 1962), 674–85.

30 This is a striking difference, but it is interesting to observe that most of the business interests that Mahan, according to LaFeber, was supposed to "represent" did not generally share Mahan's view on this subject.

31 *Supra*, 265–66.

32 58 Cong., 3 sess., *Hearings before the Merchant Marine Commission*, 1745–48.

33 Mahan, *Naval Strategy Compared and Contrasted with the Principles of Military Operations on Land*, 445.

Finally, the fact that "colonies" can have two connotations helps create further confusion. Colonies may be seen as sources of raw materials and outlets for manufactured goods and also as military outposts and naval bases, or as both. Mahan generally emphasized the strategic aspects, but not exclusively, and therein lies some of the trouble. Certainly in his account of seventeenth- and eighteenth-century expansion, the commercial frequently loomed as important as the strategic and it is not strange that both aspects appear as part of the "lessons" to be gained. In the sentence that immediately preceded the much quoted statement setting forth the significance of production, shipping, and colonies, both views are found. He wrote: "Colonies and colonial posts were sometimes commercial, sometimes military in their character" and that "it was exceptional that the same position was equally important in both points of view."[34]

Despite this confusion in lesson-learning or lesson-giving and despite the fact that some of the late nineteenth-century expansion had clear colonial overtones in the commercial sense, Mahan did place the emphasis on the strategic aspects of all territorial acquisitions he advocated for the United States. All in all, the contention that Mahan does not fit the mercantilist pattern, though a trifle strained at times, is sufficiently well supported that I agree this characterization of his imperialism should be dropped.[35]

A British author thinks Mahan failed to appreciate the significance of the fact that the industrial revolution came much earlier to Britain than to other European powers. He thinks this headstart was an important factor in Britain's rise to greatness and believes that the crucial turning point in her history came shortly after the middle of the nine-

[34] Mahan, *Influence of Sea Power Upon History, 1660–1783,* 28.

[35] Several scholars either failed to catch this new interpretation or are not convinced, for they still portray the mercantilist emphasis. See Herrick, *op. cit.,* 50; Cooling, *op. cit.,* 74; and V. Davis, *The Admirals Lobby,* 107–108.

teenth century when other European powers, becoming aware of the resultant tremendous industrial and military opportunities, initiated their own revolutions. It is now known in light of recent research, he states, that certain features of Mahan's analysis were eroding even as the period under survey was drawing to a close; in the case of Britain, by 1792 or thereabouts, her colonial trade had ceased to be the main item in overseas trade and hence by 1830 only two of Mahan's links remained.[36]

Time has added to the dimensions of sea power as well as having eroded some of Mahan's views of it. Mahan saw the contiguity of the seas and recognized that over two-thirds of the globe's surface is sea. Consequently, he emphasized the maritime values of commercial transportation, stressing the great importance of sea lanes in peace as well as in war. He said little about the oldest extractive activity at sea, fishing. This traditional wealth is undergoing much change, in especially popular areas the once seemingly inexhaustible supply is now endangered, and certain species are even threatened with extinction. The most recent and most fascinating aspect of the exploitation of the seas is the prospect of extracting oil and other minerals from the ocean floors.[37] These resources are of great political and strategic importance, especially since the question of control and ownership is involved. Fishing has long been the subject of international disputes but these disputes have greatly intensified in recent years; the exploration and extraction of minerals have more recently given rise to intensive diplomatic discussion.

Mahan firmly believed that sea power was a prerequisite to national greatness, yet as I observed in the previous chap-

36 Gerald S. Graham, *The Politics of Naval Supremacy: Studies in British Maritime Ascendancy*, 120–21, 113–15.
37 L. W. Martin, *The Sea in Modern Strategy*, 15–26.

ter, the Soviet Union at mid-century was a world power even though the Red Navy was insignificant. He also thought that no nation with strong neighbors across its land frontiers could become a global sea power. The Soviet Union again presents the troublesome exception. It now has one of the two greatest navies, exhibiting world-wide deployment, possesses a superior merchant marine, is seeking and securing important bases, operates a highly organized fishing fleet, and supports the best oceanographic research fleet in the world.

It is beyond the scope of this study and the competence of this writer to analyze or assess the precise nature and purpose of these developments, but it is appropriate to indicate certain aspects that are pertinent. Several observers see a connection between this rise in Russian sea power and Mahan. Writes an American naval officer:

> The Kremlin's thorough understanding of the philosophy of that great naval strategist [Mahan] is demonstrated by this orchestrated employment of all aspects of their sea power, including their merchant, fishing, and survey fleets as well as their modern and powerful navy.[38]

A Danish officer observes:

> The strategists in the Kremlin . . . apparently understand Mahan better than most continental leaders have in the past. The Russians have also clearly digested Mahan's idea of quantity, and they are willing to pay the price for continued naval power and military preparedness.[39]

[38] Admiral R. G. Colbert in a speech, "Change and Challenge; The Shifting Balance of Power at Sea," at Istanbul, Turkey, as reported in *Vital Speeches*, XXXIX (December 15, 1972), 150–53.

[39] Commander Hans Garde, Royal Danish Navy, "Where is the Western Navy? The World Wonders," United States Naval Institute *Proceedings*, CI (April, 1975), 20. Bary M. Blackman has an informative chapter on "The Evolution of the Soviet Navy" in *Sea Power in the 1970s*, edited by George H. Quester.

The architect of this new Red Navy is Admiral S. G. Gorshkov, a flag officer for more than thirty years and commander-in-chief of the navy for over twenty years. It is significant that in a series of articles on the Russian Navy from the time of Peter the Great to the present, Admiral Gorshkov writes at times much like Mahan and also cites Mahan. He sees the ocean as playing a significant role in communications, commerce, and warfare, and extends Mahan to include the sea as a great potential source of food and minerals. Due appreciation and use of the ocean "directly affects the growth of the political prestige of the country and its economic and military power." He adds, "history shows that those states which do not have naval forces at their disposal have not been able to hold the status of a great power for long." He asserts Russian history is replete with failures on the part of the government to develop and maintain naval forces at adequate levels to win wars or achieve designated peacetime objectives. Finally, on one occasion in commenting on the resolution of naval warfare, Admiral Gorshkov declares: "Its ideologue was the creater [sic] of the 'theory of sea power,' one of the greatest apologists for American imperialism, A. T. Mahan. His theory of the decisive influence of seapower in history is reflected to this day in the U.S.A."[40]

These articles so impressed a leading American admiral that he wrote: "In the publication of this series Admiral Gorshkov emerges as a 20th century Russian Mahan, an

---

[40] These articles appeared serially in eleven issues in *Morskoy Sbornik*, the *Soviet Naval Digest*, during 1972–73 and were published in the United States Naval Institute *Proceedings* from January through November of 1974 under the title "Navies in War and Peace." Each article was followed by a commentary by an American naval officer, and it was the consensus of those dealing with this aspect that Gorshkov was writing essentially for home consumption, "an attempt to justify his policy which has shaped the current Russian navy." All quotations are from Volume C of the *Proceedings*—the first two from the January issue, 23, and the next from the March issue, 62 and 56.

articulate advocate of sea power as a vital—indeed indispensable—attribute of great power status." He further
thinks that both Gorshkov and Mahan "were able to appreciate new technology and to discern its relevance to the
changing art of warfare." Another American naval officer,
in a lengthy analysis of the Gorshkov articles, states that they
"provide a powerful rationale for expanded Soviet seapower
that is often Mahanian in the force of its appeal and in its
urgency."[41]

In light of my belief that there is a tendency to exaggerate Mahan's role as the determining influence during his
own lifetime, either at home or abroad, it is perhaps unnecessary to add a word of caution relative to Mahan and
recent Russian sea power. Similarity could imply indebtedness, but not necessarily. And in light of world events, indebtedness, if any, would surely be in the nature of cor-
roborative substantiation rather than creative impetus.

Sea power has never been a constant. Just as the navigators and explorers of the fifteenth and sixteenth centuries,
by their twofold discovery of a new world and a new route
to the Spice Islands, globalized sea power, so have the pure
and applied scientists in the nineteenth and twentieth centuries ushered in a new world. The extent and magnitude
of the technological developments greatly affecting civil or
military sea power, occurring in the century spanning Mahan's mature years and since, are almost unbelievable.
Among the more conspicuous are the changes from sail to
steam, from wind to coal to oil to uranium, from shot to
shell, from chemical explosion to nuclear fission and ocean-
spanning missiles with computerized warheads, from
muzzle-loading smooth bore to breech-loading rifle, from

41 Admiral Elmo R. Zumwalt, Jr., "Twentieth Century Mahan?", United
States Naval Institute *Proceedings*, C (November, 1974), 70; Commander
Clyde A. Smith, "The Meaning and Significance of the Gorshkov Articles,
"*Naval War College Review*, XXVI (March-April, 1974), 20.

Rear Admiral Alfred Thayer Mahan. The painting from which
this photograph was taken hangs over the mantel in "Mahan's
Corner" in the Naval War College Library. *Official U.S. Navy
photograph of the painting by Alexander James*

Admiral S. G. Gorshkov, architect of the new Red Navy; an American naval officer has termed him "a twentieth-century Russian Mahan." *"Novosti" photograph, approved by Soviet Embassy*

semaphore to wireless, from human eye and ear to electronics and oceanic observation via satellites, from surface vessels and actions to include sub- and super-marine crafts and modes of warfare. Furthermore, the ever-enlarging scope of markets and the ever-increasing demand for raw materials, often imported, the development of synthetics and the utilization on land of mobile steam and combustion engines have had very definite repercussions on sea power.[42]

Simply stated, the effects of these changes or developments on sea power are twofold. First, they affect military sea power in action, involving both the objective of sea power as well as the tools or instruments employed to gain that objective. Second, by influencing national civil and military potential, they affect the comparative ratio both among sea powers and between sea power and land power. Scholars venturing to discuss these features naturally differ. Their differences are in part dependent upon the stage of technological development at the time, in part from the changing political power structure, not necessarily related to the impacts of modern military science, and in part a question of personal perspective and value judgment.

Critics find less to quarrel with about Mahan's *objective* of sea power from the viewpoint of military action than they do about the *means* utilized. Mahan's objective was the coveted command of the sea which if gained would deny the enemy the use of the seas while securing one's own use. Even he recognized that this was a relative concept—a goal to be sought rather than an achievement gained, but a goal calling for the exertion of every effort. Other ideas such as concentration, communications, and strategic positions were corollaries, as it were, to this fundamental concept. Mahan saw the sea as indivisible and perhaps therein lies part of

---

[42] William E. Livezey, "Sea Power in a Changing World," *The Marine Corps Gazette*, XXXIII (April, 1949), 18–27 and (May, 1949), 16–19.

his trouble. In his own day, new powers arose to challenge the erstwhile British pre-eminence and Britain was forced by treaty, entente, or understanding to withdraw her fleets from the Far East, the Mediterranean, and the Western Atlantic in order to concentrate on threats closer home. Again, and more tied with technological developments, the triphibian war restricts command as to extent and duration. It is virtually impossible to deny enemy submarines access to the seas, and, similarly, enemy air power in certain areas makes attempts at command prohibitively costly. In light of these restrictions, naval strategists today frequently use the term "sea control" rather than "command of the sea." They now restrict the goal to *"denying* an enemy the right to use some seas at some times; and, *asserting* our own right to use some seas at some times."[43] Another writer, from a different point of view, states that superior naval forces have less freedom of action than formerly, "for a number of reasons, including the always present threat of nuclear war, the growing influence of international law and international organization, the development of rapid worldwide communications and a consequent increase in the impact of both domestic and international public opinion. . . ."[44]

Mahan repeatedly stressed the necessity of concentration. This elemental strategic principle of avoiding undue dispersion of strength to maximize the chances for superiority he adopted, as previously stated, from the great Swiss military strategist, Jomini. Involved were interior lines, mobility, and coordination of effort and command. The one aspect of this doctrine of concentration most often mentioned was his concern not to divide the fleet. His admonition to President Theodore Roosevelt on this subject has

43 Vice Admiral Stansfield Turner, "Missions of the U.S. Navy," United States Naval Institute *Proceedings*, C (December, 1974) , 18–20.

44 James A. Barber, "Mahan and Naval Strategy in the Nuclear Age," *Naval War College Review*, XXIV (March, 1972) , 81–82.

been discussed. Another interesting instance comes to light in the recent multi-volume biography of Franklin Roosevelt. After a trip to the west, Roosevelt, then Assistant Secretary of the Navy, grew fearful that with the completion of the Panama Canal there would be well-nigh irresistible demand for the fleet to be divided. He wrote Mahan and former President Roosevelt to seek their influence against any division of the fleet and their support for building a cruiser fleet to satisfy western demand and for a yearly transfer through the canal of the battle and cruise fleets. Both men responded; Mahan liked all the ideas and wrote an article on "The Panama Canal and the Distribution of the Fleet." He warned, "Halve the fleet and it is inferior in both oceans."[45]

Prior to the creation of the two-ocean navy, Mahan's "Don't Divide the Fleet" was a sound principle, but it lost its validity in the days of a navy second to none with multi-ocean fleets. Some authors are convinced that this axiom of Mahan's became a "strategic shibboleth" for several naval leaders. One critic, in commenting on this axiom, writes:

> For Mahan, historian and strategist, this belonged to the conceptual framework of his views on world strategy. But in the hands of later commanders it had been transferred in a most schematic way to the realm of tactics, with the result that in World War II the tactical commanders in many a

[45] Frank Freidel, *Franklin D. Roosevelt: The Apprenticeship*, 234–35. Letters dated May 28, June 2, June 16, and June 26 (1912). Freidel also cites three letters from Mahan to Roosevelt in August of 1914 on strategic subjects, among others, urging in light of the European situation that the fleet be brought together and put in state of readiness (245–46). Freidel calls F.D.R. Mahan's "greatest disciple." It is instructive to learn that Roosevelt had long been acquainted with Mahan's writings; relatives gave him *The Influence of Sea Power on History, 1660–1783* (12th ed.) for Christmas, 1897, and for his sixteenth birthday the following month sent him *The Interest of America in Sea Power, Present and Future* (47). It is rather surprising that these Mahan to Roosevelt letters are not in the new three-volume collection of Mahan's *Letters and Papers*.

case did not dare to detach parts of the fleet in order to deal with weak enemy forces.[46]

This is surely more a reflection on the commanders than on Mahan!

Students of strategy find cause for more drastic qualification and limitations as they consider Mahan's views on the means, the tools and instruments, by which sea power seeks to perform this historic function of securing command. For Mahan, history spoke clearly: the winning navy should consist of ships of the line, battleships, not overly large but numerous, with several calibers of guns. But, as we have earlier seen, on size and armament of the battleship Mahan lost in the very heyday of his reputation. At home and in Britain he "was almost the Bible for the anti-dreadnought forces," declares one historian.[47] Admiral Lord Fisher, the key figure in the reorganization of the British Navy and a strong proponent of the new vessel, was most displeased at Mahan's stance in light of the influence he carried in Britain. He took great delight in repeating to a friend that a Yankee officer had told him Mahan was "passé."[48]

It was in large part Mahan's conviction that the battleship was the primary vessel for fighting that caused him to downgrade the submarine and the airplane. It should be kept in mind, however, that both these instruments were in their infancy—mere toys in comparison to what comes to mind currently when we think of these crafts. The U.S.S. *Holland* was not commissioned until 1900 and used gas engines for surface propulsion. It was not until 1912, two years before Mahan's death, that the diesel engine was used,

[46] Urs Schwartz, *American Strategy: A New Perspective; The Growth of Politico-Military Thinking in the United States*, 29, 53–54. Cf. Bernard Brodie, *Strategy in the Missile Age*, 24–27.

[47] Marder, *op. cit.*, I, 60, n. 20.

[48] John Arbathrot Fisher, *Fear God and Dread Nought*, II, 96.

Saigon. A dramatic 98% of all war cargo brought to Vietnam
was carried on the navy's MSTS (Military Sea Transportation
Service) ships or MSTS-controlled ships. *Official U.S. Navy
photograph*

Aircraft carrier U.S.S. *Oriskany* refuels one escorting destroyer
while second destroyer waits her turn. *Official U.S. Navy photograph*

Shore bombardment by battleship and light cruiser. *Official U.S. Navy photograph*

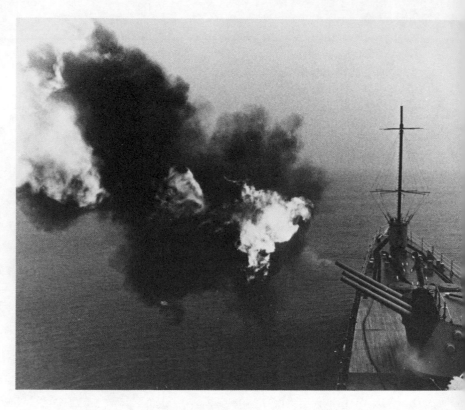

Light cruiser, U.S.S. *Oklahoma City*, provides naval gunfire support during Vietnam War. *Official U.S. Navy photograph*

and, as one authority rightly says, "It was the adoption of the Diesel engine for surfaced submarine propulsion that transformed the submarine from an accident-prone, short range, coastal defense auxiliary into an economic high seas raider."[49] Most naval experts, including Mahan, saw the submarine as a defensive weapon, and Mahan predicted it would make an attempted blockade more difficult. That some commentators thought Mahan more conservative on the submarine than he actually was appears certain in the light of his correspondence. In one letter he wrote, "I have not ventured so positive an adverse opinion as sometimes I see ascribed to me."[50]

There were a few individuals, however, who saw great potential for underseas craft. Some junior officers in both the United States and Great Britain urged greater support for it.[51] Admiral Lord Fisher saw the submarine as "the battleship of the future," with "vast dormant possibilities," and predicted an impending revolution as the craft became an offensive weapon. In commenting to a friend on Mahan's views on the subject, he said, "Mahan is an extinct volcano."[52] In this instance, in contrast to the "all-big-gun ship," the admiralities of Great Britain and Germany and those in authority in the United States agreed with Mahan.

Mahan's capital-ship theory dominated naval thinking at the start of World War I and, in certain respects, prevailed throughout. It was not until January 1915, that Admiral Tirpitz conceived the idea of using surface raiders and submarines to strangle British war effort. The havoc played, the enormous difficulties encountered, the counter-

49 Raymond O'Connor, *Force and Diplomacy*, 14, quoting Phillip Lundeberg.
50 Mahan, *Letters and Papers*, III, 550, 700.
51 Marder, *op. cit.*, 332–34; Spector, *op. cit.*, 251; and Karsten, *op. cit.*, 345–56.
52 Fisher, *op cit.*, II, 430.

measures employed, and the near success in this war of attrition need not be recounted. Parenthetically, it is instructive to learn that Mahan, after having studied the British-French struggle during the French Revolution and Empire, had written that the convoy was the best answer against commerce raiding.[53]

Perhaps because of the final victory against the *guerre de course*, coupled with the reluctance to accept new ideas, strategic thought changed surprisingly little in the years after the war. A vice admiral in the United States Navy states:

> Despite the difference between this kind of warfare [countermeasures employed] and the classic concept that battle fleet engagements would determine control of the seas, few strategists understood how radically the concept "control of the seas" had been altered by the advent of the submarine. British, German, Japanese, and American preparations for World War II all concentrated on potential battle fleet actions.[54]

The airplane attracted less attention among naval authorities prior to World War I than the submarine. It was seen primarily as a scouting craft and not as an offensive weapon. Some individuals thought it might increase the difficulty of the close blockade and others predicted it might help to neutralize the impact of the submarine. Its useful-

---

[53] Marder, *op. cit.*, IV, 116, and Mahan, *The Influence of Sea Power on the French Revolution and Empire, 1793–1812*, II, 217. Cf. Theodore Ropp, "German Sea Power: A Study in Failure" in *Dreadnought to Polaris: Maritime Strategy Since Mahan*, edited by A. M. J. Hyatt, 12–18.

[54] Turner, *loc. cit.*, 19. Vincent Davis elaborates on this idea when he writes: "A general indifference to the military implications of technological advances was a pervasive characteristic of the Navy's officer corps during most of years between 1890 and 1941," and he attributes this indifference in large part to Mahan, "who had taught the officers that these warships [the new battleships] comprised an all-purpose omnipotent naval weapons system if used according to his prescriptions." *The Admirals Lobby, op. cit.*, 170. An able presentation of Mahan in theory and in practice is given on pp. 106–37.

ness in the war, however, proved less than expected and required the enthusiastic post-war campaigns of Giulio Douhet and "Billy" Mitchell to bring it to the forefront of military thought. Yet, as the thirties progressed, "few strategists forecast the dominant role that control of the air over surface fleet would have."[55] Inklings of the value of the aircraft carrier were seen off Cape Matapan in Greece in March 1941, but it was at Midway and Coral Sea in 1942 that it was fully "demonstrated that the aircraft had replaced battleship gunfire as the primary punch of the fleet at sea, contrary to a half century of U.S. Navy strategic expectations."[56] Hindsight and perspective may enter into this conclusion, for the picture was not quite so clear at the time. Certainly the big guns did speak ably at the battle of the Philippines and frequently in amphibious operations; yet time supports the view that in World War II, "the aircraft carrier rather than the battleship was the key to defeating the enemy's surface fleet."[57]

Once again, at least for a period of time and in certain quarters, strategic thinking failed to perceive the significance of events in the fighting theaters. It was midway through the war, August 1943, that the Navy Department initiated its post-war planning. Several senior officers participated and, granted over-simplification in certain aspects and the need for qualification in others, it is safe to say that pre-war thinking dominated Plan Number One. Although the aircraft carrier was placed on a par with the battleship by one officer, and the desirability of emphasizing amphibious forces by another, still Mahan's capital-ship theory remained primary. After the return of junior staff officers from the

55 Turner, *loc. cit.*, 19–20.
56 Vincent Davis, *Post War Defense Policy and the U.S. Navy, 1943–46*, 8.
57 Arnold M. Kuzmack, "Where Does the Navy Go From Here?" in Quester, *op. cit.*, 47.

Pacific, significant modifications, even clear reversals in many respects, were made in subsequent plans.[58]

Some comments in the previous chapter show that lay writers, including myself, were a little slow, as were the naval planners, in immediately grasping the full impact of certain naval developments. The passage of time brings additional information as well as perspective. It can now be recognized that the major breakthrough in World War I was the development and extension of undersurface warfare, and that World War II brought refinements and improvements as well as countermeasures. Similarly, one sees that the major changes in World War II were the coming of age of the aircraft carrier and the development of amphibious operations.[59]

The most recent significant discovery of the pure and applied scientists affecting military sea power in action, beyond the pale of theoretical consideration in Mahan's day, is nuclear fission, applicable both for propulsion and for weaponry. The use of nuclear energy for propulsion is important in many areas but nowhere so conspicuous as in the

[58] Davis, *Post War Defense Planning and the U.S. Navy, 1943–46*, 3–38. The later plans which incorporated the "carrier-fleet" concept are developed in succeeding chapters.

[59] Valuable insights on these points may be found in Stephen F. Ambrose, "Sea Power in World War I and II," *Naval War College Review*, XXII (March, 1970), 26–40; Arthur C. Herrington, "U.S. Naval Policy," *Naval War College Review*, XXII (September, 1969), 4–13; the introductory chapter on "Naval Strategy Before 1939," in John Creswell, *Sea Warfare, 1939–45*; Sir Arthur R. Hezlet, *Aircraft and Sea Power, 139–352*. See also Captain S. W. W. Roskill, *The Strategy of Sea Power*, for a valuable, concise appraisal of the development and application of sea power, particularly as seen from the point of view of Great Britain, from 1914 through World War II, 101–265.

An interesting development in the Korean and Vietnamese wars was the movement of such a large number of troops by plane. This may be a portent for the future but it was most certainly influenced by the peculiar circumstances surrounding these conflicts. As Vice Admiral Sir Arthur Hezlet states, Western sea power which made intervention possible, "has, however, never been challenged except in a very minor way." Hezlet, *op. cit.*, 345.

William Mitchell (1879–1936), brigadier general in the U.S. Army and passionate advocate for a large and independent air force. *Library of Congress*

RA-5C Vigilante is launched from catapult of aircraft carrier
U.S.S. *Saratoga*. *Official U.S. Navy photograph*

submarine. Here we have a technological evolution so drastic that in a very real sense a new vessel has been created. The erstwhile submersible has become a true submarine capable of almost unlimited underwater endurance and at speeds greater than on the surface. Endurance, maneuverability, and mobility have always been features sought in sea vessels. Sir Julian Corbett, the great British naval historian and contemporary of Mahan, wrote that at the "root of all naval history [is] the problem of reconciling sea endurance with free movement."[60] The nuclear-powered submarine combines well both of these features, and one writer goes so far as to state that it "marks a new era in sea power" and that in light of its potential the submarine "is destined to be the capital ship of the modern navy." He enthusiastically asserts that "no other ship, nor indeed any other realistic vehicle of war, can attain the invulnerability, the performance, the mobility, the flexibility of choice or the command of force which the undersea ship can have."[61]

Although significant in propulsion, nuclear energy has at present had even more far-reaching effects in the field of thermonuclear weaponry with its vast array of launching and delivery systems. This is a much too complicated story to present here but let it suffice to say that the leading military nations have reacted by developing a wide range of weaponry and strategies. The potential destructiveness of thermonuclear weapons causes nations to seek to avoid total war. While preparing the most sophisticated weapons modern science can produce and in an almost unbelievable range and depth, military planners do this basically with the hope that they will not be used; for ironically, "if the forces

[60] Julian S. Corbett, *Drake and the Tudor Navy*, I, 3, as cited by Robert E. Walters, *Sea Power and the Nuclear Fallacy: A Reevaluation of Global Strategy.*

[61] Walters, *op. cit.*, 125 and 130. Cf. Ian Smart, "From Polaris to the Future," in Hyatt, *op. cit.*, 101–10; Martin, *op. cit.*, 91–108.

allocated for the purpose have to be used they will have failed." This deterrence strategy for avoidance of a general war leads to the preparation and strategy for wars along conventional lines, permitting conflicts of intervention to occur, restricted, it can be hoped, in area and weaponry. And finally, in this sophisticated age, local wars and diplomatic presence suggest still different preparations and strategies.[62]

In the midst of all these developments, the naval forces have regained in the 1960's and 1970's a position of favor somewhat lost in the heyday of the airplane in the decade and a half following World War II. One author states: "Investigation suggests that naval forces will continue to be the best and frequently the only way to serve many military purposes. But now and in the future the case must be argued against a wider range of alternatives than ever before."[63] After surveying the American situation and carefully weighing the strengths and weaknesses of air, sea, and land power, Hanson Baldwin concludes that the United States should concentrate on what he calls a modernized and modified oceanic strategy. He explains: "A modernized oceanic strategy means air power and missile power as well as a nuclear-powered navy and a large and more modern merchant marine and secure bases for all forms of military power."[64]

And where does Mahan fit into the picture of sea power in a changing world? In light of the technological developments affecting military sea power in action, it is obvious

62 Hezlet, op. cit., 345. Martin, op. cit., 27–90, has a good discussion of the role of the navy in these several "levels" of war. Cf. André Beaufre, "Future of Naval Strategies," in his Strategy for Tomorrow, 59–65.

63 Martin, op. cit., 12.

64 Hanson Baldwin, Strategy for Tomorrow, 300. Despite increasing logistical independence seen in the ability to refuel and make limited repairs at sea and the benefits of nuclear propulsion, Baldwin argues that land bases are more and more important (300). Walters, op. cit., 200–201, argues just the opposite.

that we are in a new world. Mahan's battleship has been replaced, first, it was thought, by the aircraft carrier, and now by the nuclear-powered submarine. His mastery of the sea falling to the nation whose battle fleet could defeat its opposite number, or, failing that, could gain command of the sea through blockade, has largely gone; like no longer meets like, and the command of the sea, usually tenuous even for Mahan, has now become control of some of the seas some of the time. Surely the strategic framework today is different than in Mahan's day, or at the end of World War I, or at the opening, or even at the close, of World War II. Modern warfare is vastly more complex, and some writers contend that Mahan's strategic concepts are too simplistic and monistic to be of value presently. Others do not want to reject him so quickly, arguing that one can neither ignore him nor accept him without reservations. One author believes that, "His lessons on command of the sea, concentration, mobility, and strategic position are, when correctly applied, as useful as ever." In my judgment, it seems safe to conclude that the impact of technology, especially in the three areas discussed—submarines, airplanes, and nuclear energy—has so altered naval warfare from the days of Mahan that the erstwhile dean of naval strategy, though generally appreciated for his wide-ranging historical background and his insightful analyses, and though not infrequently serving as the starting point for discussion and debate in the field, is no longer the leading authority in current naval strategic thinking.[65]

[65] Davis, *Post War Defense Policy and the U.S. Navy, 1943–1946*, in a chapter entitled "The New Order and the Future" (259–70), discusses key elements in the new thinking and points out (264) the ways Mahan has been outmoded. Barber, *loc. cit.*, 88, finds Mahan still valid if proper limitations are accepted.

Captain Carl H. Amme, while admitting that "Hardly anyone reads Mahan today; too much about sea power has changed," asserts: "His influence has been lasting. His principles form a large part of the core of beliefs

Turning now to the second broad area in which technological developments are important, it can be seen that they affect national civil and military potential in two ways: the comparative standing among sea powers and the comparative relationship between sea power and land power. Perhaps not enough was written previously about the first of these. The absence or presence of strategic resources greatly affects the ability of nations to exploit new developments, and this is nowhere better seen than in Great Britain in the late nineteenth and early twentieth centuries when significant changes in ordnance, armor, and propulsion followed one after the other. As steam replaced sail, the possession of coal was most important and Great Britain, the great coal country of the world, producing more coal until 1880 than the rest of the world combined, profited greatly. The change from coal to petroleum did not equally benefit her; when this change came on the eve of World War I (the *Queen Elizabeth*, completed in 1915, was the first battleship to use petroleum exclusively), Britain found herself controlling only two per cent of the world's petroleum production. Other major powers, except the United States, were similarly deficient in their home territories in naval oil supplies, and obviously there were civilian demands for petroleum as well. The world struggle for oil was on and has greatly intensified in recent years. The same sort of struggle for fissionable minerals now exists, though it is less acute and understandably is less publicized.

The shift from timber to iron for ship construction was likewise significant. Great Britain, long dependent on timber imports, especially for naval needs, now found herself with splendid resources in iron ore, the necessary reduction

around which the Navy sees its role. They provide a framework within which naval strategy is made. But it would be a mistake to accept these principles uncritically." "Seapower and the Superpowers," United States Naval Institute *Proceedings*, XCIV (October, 1968), 27.

Vice Admiral Hyman G. Rickover, prickly pioneer of nuclear-reactor development, visits the U.S.S. *Nautilus*, first nuclear-powered submarine (1954). *Official U.S. Navy photograph*

A Poseidon missile launched from the nuclear-powered ballistic missile submarine, U.S.S. *James Madison*, October 23, 1970. *Official U.S. Navy photograph*

materials, and an advanced metallurgical plant. Similarly, the introduction of heavy armor and powerful ordnance favored Britain, the world's greatest producer of iron, pig iron, and finished steel products until 1890. However, one point often overlooked in evaluating these changes is that the rapidity with which they took place caused quick obsolescence in materiel and this constant supersession struck the mistress of the seas most disadvantageously. Germany, the United States, and Japan, able largely to write off through obsolescence the headstart of the British, became significant, even competitive naval powers by comparatively moderate efforts.[66]

Mahan identified British monopoly of the seas in the nineteenth century with world power, and rightly so. And as we have seen, he was aware of some of the peculiarly favorable circumstances partially responsible for British pre-eminence—insularity, centrality, and strategically located bases to mention three—but Mahan did not apprehend sufficiently the points just cited or certain other aspects of the industrial revolution noted earlier in accounting for British primacy; and he did not anticipate adequately the disintegration of the highly favorable British position as this revolution reached other parts of the world.[67]

As technological developments alter the power equation among sea powers, so also do they alter it between land power and sea power. Mahan was aware of this and scholars have given attention to it. As might be expected, Mahan gave most thought to how these changes in weapons and propulsion might affect strategy, modify tactics, and limit the earlier fruits of command and thereby weaken the sea power component of total power. The relation of sea power to land power, however, was more drastically altered by the

66 Livezey, loc. cit., May issue, 16–17.
67 Graham, op. cit., 120 ff.

greatly increased mobility of land power resulting from the use of the railroad, automobile, tank, and airplane. Others in his day sensed this development more fully than did Mahan, most notably Sir Halford Mackinder.

This subject has interested scholars, intrigued strategists, and influenced military planners. A brief background with some development was sketched in one of my earlier chapters thirty years ago. Further insights are now available. One of the best analyses of Mahan and Mackinder is given by Harold and Margaret Sprout in their *Foundations of International Politics*. They provide a careful comparison and contrast of these two geopoliticians, discuss both their initial and later views, and summarize the strengths and shortcomings of each. They are impressed with "the imagination and insight" of Mahan, and state that "some of his most striking concepts and perspectives are still current today," and they assert that "Mackinder especially has left a deep imprint."

Their conclusion is "that geographical configuration— the global layout of land and sea—has become very much less politically significant today than formerly," and that "the patterns of international political potential are increasingly affected by social changes and by paramilitary and nonmilitary forms of political interaction." The lessened import once accorded geographical configuration is interestingly expressed:

> When ballistic rockets armed with thermonuclear warheads can be fired from nearly any point upon the earth's surface, either from land or from ships at sea, with a range and accuracy that enable them to devastate whole cities at nearly every other point upon the earth's surface, we shall have reached the end of the line for geopolitical concepts and theories which purport to explain and to forecast the over-

all design of international politics by reference to the configuration of lands and seas.[68]

More recently, in a provocative re-evaluation of global strategy, the author examines at length Mackinder's Heartland thesis and finds the premises unsound. He and the Sprouts agree that Mackinder's views came to the United States in the 1940's and have greatly affected our military planning. This critic argues that the West has been overly impressed with the strategic superiority of the Heartland, its impregnability in fact, and as a result has been misled into the adoption of the nuclear deterrent. This has become such an obsession, he thinks, that it has kept the United States from seeing the true future of the nuclear-powered submarine.[69] Another commentator on Mahan and Mackinder also thinks that the ideas of both are in need of revision, especially in light of recent technological developments. He believes that the views of the two men are not necessarily contradictory or mutually exclusive, and the Sprouts would subscribe to this viewpoint. The thrust of his article is that the Soviets may well be attempting a sophisticated synthesis of both Mahan and Mackinder.[70]

A discussion of the pros and cons of the Heartland thesis must not divert us from the larger problem from which it arises, i.e., the impact of technological developments on the comparative relationship of land and sea power. There is general agreement that sea power suffered in relation to land power as the railroad, automobile, tank, and aircraft brought increased mobility in land transportation. There are some scholars, however, who believe the trend has been

68 Harold and Margaret Sprout, Foundations of International Politics, 325, 332, 337, 338.

69 Walters, op. cit., 8–9. Actually, much of the book deals with an exposition and criticism of Mackinder and of American reaction.

70 Benton V. Davis, "Soviet Naval Strategy: Mahan and Mackinder Revisited," Naval War College Review, XXI (October, 1968), 1–13.

halted, if not indeed reversed. With the new frontier of under-sea riches and the application of nuclear propulsion for the submarine, giving both endurance and difficulty of detection, the world is entering a new maritime era, thinks one scholar. In his words: "Rather than seeing the end of sea power, we are moving into a period which will bring a vast expansion of sea power."[71] Another author writes:

> . . . [I]t is difficult to avoid concluding that the strategic significance of sea power has increased, most notably in its impact on land warfare. It is now capable of operating inland, with an even greater potential for what is called "blackmail" and for affecting the outcome of wars, either unconventional, limited or general. In fact, it is likely that sea power is destined to become a more potent force on the international scene as the two major powers compete in various dimensions of activity for what they deem to be their essential interests.[72]

There is little reason to question Mahan's view that the sea, covering over two-thirds of the earth's surface, was a great highway, a wide common, upon which man might travel in all directions. Modern industry, demanding an ever-increasing quantity and variety of strategic raw materials, makes no nation self-sufficient. The import of certain crucial items has become essential to the very life of all industrial nations and in many instances, if not most, this involves transport by sea. There is abundant evidence that the due use, if not the control of the sea still remains not merely one link but the central link, as Mahan would say, in the life of a nation.

Technological developments have greatly increased the problem of logistics in modern war. Five times the equipment per soldier was transported in World War II as in

71 Walters, *op. cit.*, 125, 133, 157.
72 O'Conner, *op. cit.*, 21.

World War I. In fact, in the last war twelve tons of supplies and equipment were shipped for each soldier overseas and each month another ton was sent in food, clothing, and ammunition. Eight major fronts and a near dozen additional combat zones were involved; some across a 3,000-mile ocean and others across a 7,000-mile ocean. Also, the Service Fleet gave logistical support at distances and for periods of time without parallel in history. Not infrequently it maintained the fleet as far as 5,000 miles from a permanent base; the First Carrier Task Force that left the Marshall Islands in February 1944 had not returned to a permanent base at war's end seventeen months later. More than 98 per cent of the over 100,000 crafts of all types in the United States Navy on V-E Day were non-combatant vessels, such as supply ships, tenders, oilers, repair ships, ammunition ships, hospital ships, and transports. In light of these facts, it seems safe to state that the role of the sea has not lessened but rather grown greater and more complicated with the many developments of technology.

The views previously expressed relative to Mahan as historian have been supported by recent scholarship. An American historian, in a bibliographical essay on naval history for the half-century following Mahan's death, confirms the view expressed by his American Historical Association colleagues in the resolution adopted at their 1914 meeting, that Mahan had revolutionized the writing of naval history. In the introductory paragraph this author writes:

> Alfred Thayer Mahan left an imprint on the writing of American naval history that remained clearly visible in 1960. After his death in 1914, Mahan's successors tended to overlook the wider implications of his concepts and to follow closely his dictum that naval history should emphasize "lessons learned." Naval authors devoted most of their re-

379

search to the operational aspect of the field. Only gradually did non-operational approaches—dealing with such subjects as diplomacy, policy and internal organization of the navy—begin to provide the broader contexts and thorough treatment that the field requires.[73]

A British historian comments on the absence of resources and refined techniques of Mahan, Corbett, and other contemporary British naval historians as compared with more recent historians. As regards Mahan:

On the evidence of a far flung miscellany of sources, he developed the doctrine of the "command of the seas" and the strategic consequences that followed from it—the effect of the "command" upon land warfare, on the history of west European expansion and on the acquisition and retention of empires.

And continues:

As a great historical synthesis *The Influence of Sea Power* was a masterpiece and it remains a classic, but in terms of scholarship it was premature. Because Mahan tended to concentrate on strategy divorced from policy and diplomacy, he unwittingly encouraged the quarantining of naval history from the main stream of knowledge.

He reflectively adds that had Mahan delved into all these aspects he would never have written more than one book and that it would have lacked scope or breadth and "might have lost the authority and perspective which his peculiar genius for generalization brought to bear on broad strategic problems."[74] This evaluation would be rather close to

[73] James M. Merrill, "Successors to Mahan: A Survey of American Naval History, 1914–1960," *Mississippi Valley Historical Review*, L (June, 1963), 79.

[74] Graham, *op. cit.*, 4–6.

Mahan's own when he recognized that he was not a historian "after the high modern pattern."[75]

Mahan's doctrine of force was previously rather carefully analyzed with frequent quotations to avoid, it was hoped, the danger of reading him out of context. This aspect of his thought has been less extensively and less often discussed by writers in the past thirty years than his views on the purpose and use of navies and his interest in expansion. One scholar, after surveying the history of the Naval War College, concluded that it had been "the nursery of imperialism," and further states that the evidence he finds "would seem to support Joseph Schumpeter's contention [in his *Imperialism*, 23–66] that a self-conscious military class will always find reasons for war and expansion whatever the objective situation. . . . It would appear that the more 'professionalized' and self-conscious the American officers became the more imperialistic they were likely to be." Of the several "professors of war," he mentions Luce, Mahan, and Captain Henry C. Taylor, all presidents of the College, as among the most influential in this respect. With few commitments abroad and two great oceans separating the United States from other major powers, it was necessary, "in order to convince the people that a navy was needed," to play up the importance of the defense of the Monroe Doctrine, the building of an Isthmian Canal, the extension of commerce, and the virtues of struggle. War was depicted as not only possible or probable, but by some as inevitable, and by men like Luce, Mahan, and Taylor as even desirable.[76]

In an evaluation of Mahan and his messmates at Annapolis, another author finds this professionalized group as force oriented as were their colleagues at the Naval War

[75] *Supra*, 38.
[76] Spector, *op. cit.*, 176, n. 25 and 169–70.

College. He concludes that, "From whatever perspective the naval officers might view human behavior, war and warships were always in the foreground." Or in the words of one rear admiral whom he quotes: "If you wish to preserve the peace of the world, give us more battleships and fewer statesmen."[77] In a short article, "Mahan: Historian With a Purpose," a different writer suggests that Mahan's doctrine of power came not only from his military training as a naval officer but also from his sincere Christianity. He believes that Mahan saw God as the motivating power in history, with force His servant and competition a divine manifestation working in wondrous ways.[78]

The validity of a philosophy of empire and power comparable to that held by Mahan, has come under increased scrutiny by many thoughtful citizens in the past thirty years. Without necessarily calling into question whether unrestrained nationalism and unrestricted militarism, frequently leading to large-scale wars, have been effective or salutary in the past, there is a growing awareness that new approaches are demanded in the nuclear age. There is a deepening apprehension that even if we can avoid a general nuclear war, pyrrhic stalemates, like Vietnam, and ever-mounting expenditures for essentially non-productive ends will so deplete our resources, disrupt our economy, and disenchant our society that the American dream we prize, already threatened by forces often not directly related to the

[77] Karsten, *op. cit.*, 218–20.

[78] Francis Duncan, "Mahan: Historian With a Purpose," United States Naval Institute *Proceedings*, LXXXIII (May, 1957) , 499–500. Calvin D. Davis carefully appraises Mahan's role at the First Hague Peace Conference in his *United States and the First Hague Peace Conference*. In "The World of Captain Mahan," (Ph.D. diss., Princeton University, 1961) , Bates M. Gilliam describes the geopolitical worlds of 1890, 1900, and 1910 and Mahan's reactions to each and at one point asserts: "He [Mahan] contributed to the development of thinking in international politics as few other writers have done." (3)

military, will at best remain a dream, or at worst, as a result of our failure, will haunt us as a nightmare.

Many statesmen and scholars, including a widely renowned economist, have termed arms control and nuclear proliferation by far the most urgent issue of the age. Some world leaders have sensed this urgency and have spoken out with courage. Five-star General Dwight D. Eisenhower, in his farewell presidential address of January 17, 1961, warned his fellow countrymen to beware of the growing power of the "military-industrial complex." Sixteen years later, President Carter proposed that the two super powers reduce their arsenals by twenty per cent. Whether our nation and other nations of the world are ready to heed these calls and warnings is far from sure, yet it is more than certain that to drift invites disaster.

Timeliness, as has been emphasized both in this appraisal and my earlier one, is an important factor as one evaluates Mahan and his influence. This alone, however, is not a sufficient explanation for his place in history; one cannot dismiss Mahan so readily. We all live in time and place, and contingency is a fact for everyone. One may thoroughly disagree with Mahan in his judgment that he would have done better in civilian life than in the military; one may well believe he would have continued as an inconspicuous naval officer drifting along on the line of simple respectability had the call not come to lecture at the Naval War College; one may even speculate that had Mahan not developed the sea-power doctrine and elucidated his concepts of naval strategy so ably, someone else might have done so; one may cogently argue that most, if not all, of the events with which his name is closely associated would have occurred had he not become a public figure—yet these are not the alternatives with which we work. History records that

383

Mahan did join the navy, did receive the call to lecture on naval history and strategy, did develop intriguing and revelatory ideas on sea power and strategy, and finally as publicist and propagandist did find a receptive audience both at home and abroad.

Recent scholarship essentially supports the generally moderate conclusions I earlier advanced regarding Mahan's role during his own lifetime as navalist, expositor of sea power, philosopher of force, historian, expansionist, and publicist-propagandist, and perhaps to a slightly less extent my evaluation for the quarter of a century following. Myopia and prejudice as well as insight and strength are present in Mahan's many writings and account for the fact that in his own day he had detractors as well as admirers. With the passage of years, it is only natural to find a lessening of the validity of certain of his ideas. This is most conspicuous in the field of naval strategy and my appraisal in the previous chapter of the continued applicability of Mahan's views in this respect needs modification. New information, increased perspective, and technological developments have all contributed to this revision, but even here there remains a clear residual core of validity. When one adds to the technological advances the drastic modifications in the power structure and the tremendous changes in social, economic, and political thought and practice, this is assuredly a vastly different world from that which Mahan knew. However, as one recognizes that under these circumstances Mahan does not have continued vitality in certain respects, equally, in my judgment, one cannot wisely assert that his significance in all areas has ceased. Nations still value the due use and control of the sea, still strive for power and vie for position, still find merit in his sea-power thesis and his doctrine of power.

Mahan's influence today is obviously less specific, more general, and clearly more difficult to pinpoint than it was

384

half a century ago. And most certainly, if one should be on guard against unduly emphasizing Mahan's influence during his lifetime, one must exercise care to avoid overstating the case in subsequent years when his immediacy has receded. However, I do believe that in the midst of change there is a continuity in human affairs. As a friend of mine whose insight and judgment I greatly respect recently observed: "One cannot escape the thought that any example of landmark writing retains a certain validity, if not in actual application, then in its often immense power to suggest, to extend, to produce, almost in reverie, the new intellectualizations which have stricter applications to our times. And present reality is always transformed by those who look beyond it." When my friend made this statement did he have the writings of some specific author in mind? Yes, those of Alfred Thayer Mahan.

As I revisit Mahan, I find that he continues to interest scholars of several disciplines and of varying persuasions and that most consider him an individual whose influence, though exaggerated by some and belittled by others, is still judged impressive. I also discover that others are intrigued, as I am, by the fact that his story has its full share of inconsistency and paradox. For example, Mahan spent forty years of active service in the navy, yet he was clearly less a sailor than a scholar, more at home in the library than in command of a ship; his ideas on strategy and sea power were forward looking and progressive, yet in virtually all other naval affairs as well as in general lifestyle and social, economic, and political views he was clearly conservative. His doctrine of sea power and his prescription as to how nations should shape their policies and actions if they wished to become great were adjudged revelatory, almost novel by some, yet they embodied relatively simple and almost commonplace facts that had been discussed for years, if not for centuries. His naval histories, the sea-power series, were recognized by his historical colleagues as revolutionizing the views on that subject held not only in this country but in the world, yet entering the navy at sixteen Mahan had no university education. His devotion to the church and its mission, the intensity of his religious beliefs and his life of rectitude evoked warm praise from his pastor and fellow parishioners and were considered qualities of an exemplary Christian, yet his philosophy of power—glorifying expansion, rationalizing imperialism, exalting force, contending that under no circumstances could a state pre-engage to arbitrate concerning its interests, defending war on moral and beneficial grounds, holding war as productive of great good and peace as not adequate for progress, viewing war as noble and peace as an alluring but somewhat ignoble ideal—is difficult for some to reconcile with the principles of the Prince of Peace.

Some of these statements may not seem paradoxical to everyone or perhaps not fairly stated, and with consistency in thought and practice so rare, it may be questioned whether Mahan should be held to higher standards than others. But whether these paradoxes are seen as fair and valid, whether Mahan should be expected to be more than a child of his age, whether his views elicit agreement or disagreement, whether his impact is deemed beneficial or harmful or both, in my opinion, one can assert with confidence that Mahan's influence during his own lifetime, and to a lesser extent in the years following, is impressive. And while no justifiable claim can be made that he is a central figure in history, Mahan assuredly occupies a place of importance and significance.

BOOKS AND ARTICLES BY MAHAN
IN ORDER OF PUBLICATION

1879. "Naval Education for Officers and Men," United States Naval Institute *Proceedings*, Vol. V (December, 1879), 345–76.

1883. *The Gulf and Inland Waters*. New York, Charles Scribner's Sons, 1883.

1888. "The Necessity and Objects of a Naval War College," United States Naval Institute *Proceedings*, Vol. XIV (December, 1888), 621–39. Reprinted in *Naval Administration and Warfare* (1908).

1890. *The Influence of Sea Power upon History, 1660–1783*. Boston, Little, Brown and Company, 1890.
    "The United States Looking Outward," *Atlantic Monthly*, Vol. LXVI (December, 1890), 816–24. Reprinted in *The Interest of America in Sea Power, Present and Future* (1897).

1892. "Pitt's War Policy," *Quarterly Review*, Vol. 175 (July, 1892), 70–101. Reprinted in *The Influence of Sea Power upon the French Revolution and Empire, 1793–1812* (1892).
    The Influence of Sea Power upon the French Revolution and Empire, 1793–1812. 2 vols. Boston, Little, Brown and Company, 1892.
    Admiral Farragut. New York, D. Appleton and Company, 1892.

1893. "Hawaii and Our Future Sea Power," *The Forum*, Vol. XV (March, 1893), 1–11. Reprinted in *The Interest of America in Sea Power, Present and Future* (1897).
    "Admiral the Earl of St. Vincent [Jervis]," *Atlantic Monthly*, Vol. LXXI (March, 1893), 303–15. Reprinted in *Types of Naval Officers* (1901).

"Admiral Saumarez," *Atlantic Monthly*, Vol. LXXI (May, 1893), 605–19. Reprinted in *ibid.*

"The Practical Character of a Naval War College," United States Naval Institute *Proceedings*, Vol. XIX (June, 1893), 153–66. Reprinted in *Naval Administration and Warfare* (1908).

"Admiral Lord Exmouth [Pellew]," *Atlantic Monthly*, Vol. LXXII (July, 1893), 27–41. Reprinted in *Types of Naval Officers* (1901).

"The Isthmus and Sea Power," *Atlantic Monthly*, Vol. LXXII (October, 1893), 459–72. Reprinted in *The Interest of America in Sea Power, Present and Future* (1897).

"Two Maritime Expeditions," *United Service Magazine*, Vol. CXXIX (October, 1893), 1–13. Reprinted in *Naval Strategy* (1911).

1894. "Admiral Earl Howe," *Atlantic Monthly*, Vol. LXXIII (January, 1894), 20–37. Reprinted in *Types of Naval Officers* (1901).

"Possibilities of an Anglo-American Reunion," *North American Review*, Vol. CLIX (November, 1894), 551–63. Reprinted in *The Interest of America in Sea Power, Present and Future* (1897).

1895. "Lessons from the Yalu Fight," *Century Magazine*, Vol. L (August, 1895), 629–32.

"The Future in Relation to American Naval Power," *Harper's Monthly*, Vol. XCI (October, 1895), 767–75. Reprinted in *The Interest of America in Sea Power, Present and Future* (1897).

"The Navy as a Career," *The Forum*, Vol. XX (November, 1895), 277–83.

"Blockade in Relation to Naval Strategy," *Journal of the Royal United Service Institution*, Vol. XXXIX (November, 1895), 1057–69. Also in United States Institute *Proceedings*, Vol. XXI (December, 1895), 851–66.

1896. "Nelson at Cape St. Vincent," *Century Magazine*, Vol. LI (February, 1896), 604–15.

"The Engineer in Naval Warfare," *North American Review*, Vol. CLXIII (December, 1896), 648–54.

1897. "Nelson at the Battle of the Nile," *Century Magazine,* Vol. LIII (January, 1897), 435–47.

"The Battle of Copenhagen," *Century Magazine,* Vol. LIII (February, 1897), 525–41.

"Nelson at Trafalgar," *Century Magazine,* Vol. LIII (March, 1897), 741–59.

The Life of Nelson: The Embodiment of the Sea Power of Great Britain. 2 vols. Boston, Little, Brown and Company, 1897.

"Preparedness for a Naval War," *Harper's Monthly,* Vol. XCIV (March, 1897), 579–88. Reprinted in *The Interest of America in Sea Power, Present and Future* (1897).

"A Twentieth-Century Outlook," *Harper's Monthly,* Vol. XCV (September, 1897), 521–33. Reprinted in *ibid.*

"Strategic Features of the Caribbean Sea and the Gulf of Mexico," *Harper's Monthly,* Vol. XCV (October, 1897), 680–91. Reprinted in *ibid.*

The Interest of America in Sea Power, Present and Future. Boston, Little, Brown and Company, 1897.

1898. "The Battle of Trafalgar," a paper read before the Military Historical Society of Massachusetts, February 1, 1898. Printed in Vol. XI of *Naval Actions and Operations Against Cuba and Porto Rico, 1593–1815.* Boston, published for the Historical Society of Massachusetts by E. B. Stillings and Company, 1901.

"Major Operations of the Royal Navy, 1762–1783," in Sir William Laird Clowes, *A History of the Royal Navy,* III, 353–565. London, Sampson, Low, Marston and Company, 1898. Published separately in 1913 by Mahan as noted below.

"John Paul Jones in the Revolution," *Scribner's Magazine,* Vol. XXIV (July, 1898), 22–36.

"John Paul Jones in the Revolution," *Scribner's Magazine,* Vol. XXIV (August, 1898), 204–19.

"Current Fallacies upon Naval Subjects," *Harper's Monthly,* Vol. XCVII (June, 1898), 42–53. Reprinted in *Lessons of the War with Spain and Other Articles* (1899).

"Distinguishing Qualities of Ships of War," *Scripps-McRae Newspaper League,* November, 1898. Reprinted in *ibid.*

"The War on the Sea and Its Lessons. Part I. How the Motive of the War Gave Direction to Its Earliest Movements," *Mc-*

Clure's Magazine, Vol. XII (December, 1898), 110–18. Reprinted in *ibid.*

1899. "The War on the Sea and Its Lessons. Part II. The Effect of Deficient Coast Defense on the Movement of the Navy," *McClure's Magazine,* Vol. XII (January, 1899), 231–40. Reprinted in *ibid.*

"The Relation of the United States to Their New Dependencies," *Engineering Magazine,* Vol. XVI (January, 1899), 521 ff. Reprinted in *ibid.*

"The War on the Sea and Its Lessons. Part III. Reasons for Blockading Cuba," *McClure's Magazine,* Vol. XII (February, 1899), 353–62. Reprinted in *ibid.*

"The War on the Sea and Its Lessons. Part IV. Problems Presented by Cervera's Appearance in West Indies Waters," *McClure's Magazine,* Vol. XII (March, 1899), 470–80. Reprinted in *ibid.*

"The War on the Sea and Its Lessons. Part V. The Guard Set over Cervera and the Watch Kept on Camara," *McClure's Magazine,* Vol. XII (April, 1899), 527–34. Reprinted in *ibid.*

"The Peace Conference and the Moral Aspect of War," *North American Review,* Vol. CLXIX (October, 1899), 433–47. Reprinted in *ibid.* Also reprinted in *Some Neglected Aspects of War* (1907).

"The Neapolitan Republicans and Nelson's Accusers," *English Historical Review,* Vol. XIV (July, 1899), 471–501. Data utilized in revised edition of *Life of Nelson* (1899).

Lessons of the War with Spain and Other Articles. Boston, Little, Brown and Company, 1899.

The Life of Nelson: The Embodiment of the Sea Power of Great Britain. 2 vols. Boston, Little, Brown and Company, 1899. Revised edition. Enlarged upon Nelson's activities at Naples.

1900. "The Transvaal and the Philippine Islands," *The Independent,* Vol. LII (February, 1900), 289–91.

"Merits of the Transvaal Dispute," *North American Review,* Vol. CLXX (March, 1900), 312–26. Reprinted in *The Problem of Asia* (1900).

"The Philippines and the Future," *The Independent,* Vol. LII (March 22, 1900), 697–98.

"The Problem of Asia," *Harper's Monthly,* Vol. C (March, 1900), 536–47. Reprinted in *The Problem of Asia* (1900).

"The Problem of Asia," *Harper's Monthly*, Vol. C (April, 1900), 747–59. Reprinted in *ibid.*
"The Problem of Asia," *Harper's Monthly*, Vol. C (May, 1900), 929–41. Reprinted in *ibid.*
"The Boer Republic and the Monroe Doctrine," *The Independent*, Vol. LII (May 10, 1900), 1101–1103.
"Nelson at Naples," *English Historical Review*, Vol. XV (October, 1900), 699–727.
"Effect of Asiatic Conditions upon World Policies," *North American Review*, Vol. CLXXI (November, 1900), 609–26. Reprinted in *The Problem of Asia* (1900).
"War from the Christian Standpoint," a paper read before the Church Congress, Providence, Rhode Island, November 15, 1900. Printed in *Some Neglected Aspects of War* (1907).
The Story of War in South Africa, 1899–1900. London, Sampson, Low, Marston and Company, 1900.
The War in South Africa. New York, P. F. Collier and Son, 1900. Profusely illustrated.
The Problem of Asia and Its Effects upon International Policies. Boston, Little, Brown and Company, 1900.

1901. "The Influence of the South African War upon the Prestige of the British Empire," *National Review*, Vol. XXXVIII (December, 1901), 501–12. Also in *Living Age*, Vol. CCXXXII (January 18, 1902), 129–37. Reprinted in *Retrospect and Prospect* (1902).
Types of Naval Officers Drawn from the History of the British Navy. Boston, Little, Brown and Company, 1901. Includes, in addition to the sketches of Jervis, Saumarez, Pellew, and Howe which had appeared in the *Atlantic Monthly* in 1893–94, accounts of Hawke and Rodney.

1902. "The Growth of Our National Feeling" (renamed "Retrospect and Prospect"), *World's Work*, Vol. III (February, 1902), 1763–68. Reprinted in *Retrospect and Prospect* (1902).
"The Military Rule of Obedience," *National Review*, Vol. XXXIX (March, 1902), 26–38. Also in *International Monthly*, Vol. V (March, 1902), 247–61. Reprinted in *ibid.*
"Motives to Imperial Federation," *National Review*, Vol. XXXIX (May, 1902), 390–408. Reprinted in *ibid.*
"Conditions Governing the Dispositions of Navies," *Na-*

MAHAN ON SEA POWER

tional Review, Vol. XXXIX (July, 1902), 701–19. Reprinted in *ibid.*

"Sampson's Naval Career," *McClure's Magazine,* Vol. XIX (July, 1902), 217–21. Published also as "Rear Admiral Wm. R. Sampson," *Fortnightly Review,* Vol. LXXII (August, 1902), 227–39. Reprinted in *ibid.*

"The Persian Gulf and International Relations," *National Review,* Vol. XL (September, 1902), 27–45. Reprinted in *ibid.*

"Why We Must Have a Greater Navy" (renamed "Conditions Determining the Naval Expansion of the United States"), *Leslie's Weekly,* Vol. XCV (October 2, 1902), 318 ff. Reprinted in *ibid.*

Retrospect and Prospect: Studies in International Relations, Naval and Political. Boston, Little, Brown and Company, 1902.

1903. "The Monroe Doctrine," *National Review,* Vol. XL (February, 1903), 871–89. Reprinted in *Naval Administration and Warfare* (1908).

"Subordination in Historical Treatment" (renamed "Writing of History"), *Atlantic Monthly,* Vol. XCI (March, 1903), 289–98. Reprinted in *ibid.* This was the President's Address at the annual meeting of the American Historical Association in 1902 and was printed in the *Annual Report* for that year.

"The Apparent Decadence of the Church's Influence" (read before the Church Club), *The Churchman,* Vol. LXXXVII (April 25, 1903), 537–38.

"The United States Navy Department," *Scribner's Magazine,* Vol. XXXIII, (May, 1903), 567–77. Reprinted in *Naval Administration and Warfare* (1908).

"Principles of Naval Administration," *National Review,* Vol. XLI (June, 1903), 546–65. Reprinted in *ibid.*

1904. "The War of 1812. Part I. Antecedents and Causes," *Scribner's Magazine,* Vol. XXXV (January, 1904), 19–33. Rapid résumé of the first 282 pages of *Sea Power in Its Relations to the War of 1812* (1905).

"The War of 1812. Part II. The Approach of War," *Scribner's Magazine,* Vol. XXXV (February, 1904), 190–203. Reprinted in *ibid.*

"Appreciation of Conditions in the Russo-Japanese Conflict. Part I," *Collier's Weekly*, Vol. XXXII (February 20, 1904), 7–8.

"The War of 1812. Part III. Early Cruises and Engagements, *Constitution* and *Guerriere, Scribner's Magazine*, Vol. XXXV (March, 1904), 333–51. Reprinted in *Sea Power in Its Relations to the War of 1812* (1905).

"The War of 1812. Part IV. Operations on the Northern Frontier after Hull's Surrender," *Scribner's Magazine*, Vol. XXXV (April, 1904), 459–75. Reprinted in *ibid*.

"Appreciation of Conditions in the Russo-Japanese Conflict. Part II," *Collier's Weekly*, Vol. XXXIII (April 30, 1904), 10–13.

"The War of 1812. Part V. Naval Actions *Wasp* and *Frolic, United States* and *Macedonian, Scribner's Magazine*, Vol. XXXV (May, 1904), 591–608. Reprinted in *Sea Power in Its Relations to the War of 1812* (1905).

"Torpedo Craft vs. Battleships," *Collier's Weekly*, Vol. XXXIII (May 21, 1904), 16–17.

"The War of 1812. Part VI. The Winter of 1812–1813. Action between *Constitution* and *Java, Scribner's Magazine*, Vol. XXXV (June, 1904), 713–28. Reprinted in *Sea Power in Its Relations to the War of 1812* (1905).

"The War of 1812. Part VII. Lake Frontier Campaign of 1813," *Scribner's Magazine*, Vol. XXXVI (July, 1904), 98–112. Reprinted in *ibid*.

"The War of 1812. Part VIII. The Battle of Lake Erie and Perry's Victory," *Scribner's Magazine*, Vol. XXXVI (September, 1904), 363–79. Reprinted in *ibid*.

"Some Considerations of the Principles Involved in the Present War" (renamed "Principles Involved in the War between Japan and Russia"), *National Review*, Vol. XLIV (September, 1904), 27–46. Reprinted in *Naval Administration and Warfare* (1908).

"The War of 1812. Part IX. British Offensive Operations on the Coast, 1813–1814," *Scribner's Magazine*, Vol. XXXVI (October, 1904), 485–97. Reprinted in *Sea Power in Its Relations to the War of 1812* (1905).

"The War of 1812. Part X. Maritime Operations External to United States Waters," *Scribner's Magazine*, Vol. XXXVI (November, 1904), 601–14. Reprinted in *ibid*.

1905. "The War of 1812. Part XI. The Campaign of 1814," *Scribner's Magazine,* Vol. XXXVII (January, 1905), 101–116. Reprinted in *ibid.*

"The Problems That Rojestvensky And Togo Must Solve," *Collier's Weekly,* Vol. XXXV (May 13, 1905), 12–14.

"The Battle of the Sea of Japan," *Collier's Weekly,* Vol. XXXV (June 17, 1905), 12–13.

"Negotiations at Ghent in 1814," *American Historical Review,* Vol. XI (October, 1905), 68–87. Reprinted in *Sea Power in Its Relations to the War of 1812* (1905).

"The Personality of Nelson," *United Service Magazine,* Vol. CLIII (Old Series) (October, 1905), 7–8.

"The Strength of Nelson," *National Review,* Vol. XLVI (November, 1905), 411–27.

Sea Power in Its Relations to the War of 1812. 2 vols. Boston, Little, Brown and Company, 1905.

1906. "Peace Terms of the War of 1812," *The Dial,* Vol. XL (April 16, 1906), 253.

"Some Reflections upon the Far-Eastern War" (renamed "Retrospect upon the War between Japan and Russia"), *National Review,* Vol. XLVII (May, 1906), 383–405. Also in *Living Age,* Vol. XXXII (July 14, 1906), 67-81. Reprinted in *Naval Administration and Warfare* (1908).

"Reflections, Historic and Others, Suggested by the Battle of the Sea of Japan," United States Naval Institute *Proceedings,* Vol. XXXII (June, 1906), 447–71. Also in *Journal of the Royal United Service Institution,* Vol. L (November, 1906), 1327–46.

1907. "Our Navy Fifty Years Ago," *Harper's Monthly,* Vol. CXIV (February, 1907), 375–80. Reprinted in *From Sail to Steam* (1907).

"The Submarine and Its Enemies," *Collier's Weekly,* Vol. XXXIX (April 6, 1907), 17–21.

"Our Navy before the War of Secession," *Harper's Monthly,* Vol. CXIV (May, 1907), 869–74. Reprinted in *From Sail to Steam* (1907).

"The Hague Conference; the Question of Immunity of Belligerent Merchant Shipping," *National Review,* Vol. XLIX (June, 1907), 521–37. Also in *Living Age,* Vol. XXXVI (July 6,

1907), 3–15. Reprinted in *Some Neglected Aspects of War* (1907).

"The Hague Conference and the Practical Aspect of War," *National Review*, Vol. XLIX (July, 1907), 688–704. Also in *Living Age*, Vol. XXXVI (July 27, 1907), 195–207. Reprinted in *ibid.*

"Old Times at the Naval Academy," *Harper's Monthly*, Vol. CXV (August, 1907), 372–78. Reprinted in *From Sail to Steam* (1907).

"Night Watches at Sea," *Harper's Weekly*, Vol. LI (September 21, 1907), 1374 and 1391. Reprinted in *ibid.*

"Eleven Knots," *Harper's Weekly*, Vol. LI (September 28, 1907), 1420 and 1430. Reprinted in *ibid.*

"Old Time Naval Officials," *Harper's Monthly*, Vol. CXV (October, 1907), 771–76. Reprinted in *ibid.*

"Sailing Home to War," *Harper's Weekly*, Vol. LI (October 5, 1907), 1453. Reprinted in *ibid.*

"Clearing for Action," *Harper's Weekly*, Vol. LI (October 19, 1907), 1518 and 1538. Reprinted in *ibid.*

"The Minor Trials of Blockade Duty," *Harper's Weekly*, Vol. LI (October 26, 1907), 1556. Reprinted in *ibid.*

"When Newport Was Annapolis," *Harper's Weekly*, Vol. LI (November 16, 1907), 1687: Reprinted in *ibid.*

"Off to Japan in '67," *Harper's Weekly*, Vol. LI (November 23, 1907), 1732. Reprinted in *ibid.*

"When United States Warships Held Japan's Waters," *Harper's Weekly*, Vol. LI (December 7, 1907), 1793. Reprinted in *ibid.*

"The Value of the Pacific Cruise of the United States Fleet, Prospect," *Scientific American*, Vol. XCVII (December 7, 1907), 407 and 412–13. Reprinted in *Naval Administration and Warfare* (1908).

Some Neglected Aspects of War. Boston, Little, Brown and Company, 1907.

From Sail to Steam: Recollections of Naval Life. New York and London, Harper and Brothers, 1907.

1908. "The Value of the Pacific Cruise of the United States Fleet, Retrospect," *Collier's Weekly*, Vol. XLI (August 28, 1908), 8–9. Reprinted in *Naval Administration and Warfare* (1908).

Naval Administration and Warfare, Some General Principles With Other Essays. Boston, Little, Brown and Company, 1908.

1909. "Germany's Naval Ambition," *Collier's Weekly*, Vol. XLIII (April 24, 1909), 12–13.
The Harvest Within: Thoughts on the Life of a Christian. Boston, Little, Brown and Company, 1909.
"Address," U. S. Naval Institute *Proceedings*, Vol. XXXV (1909), 271–82. Address on the occasion of the unveiling of the Sampson Memorial Window in the Naval Academy chapel.
1910. *The Interest of America in International Conditions.* Boston, Little, Brown and Company, 1910.

1911. "The Battleship of All Big Guns," *World's Work*, Vol. XXI (January, 1911), 13888–902.
"Why Fortify the Panama Canal?," *North American Review*, Vol. CXCIII (March, 1911), 331–39. Reprinted in *Armaments and Arbitration* (1912).
"Armaments and Arbitration," *North American Review*, Vol. CXCIII (May, 1911), 641–52. Reprinted in *ibid.*
"The Panama Canal and Sea Power in the Pacific," *Century Magazine*, Vol. LXXXII (June, 1911), 240–48. Reprinted in *ibid.*
"Diplomacy and Arbitration," *North American Review*, Vol. CXCIV (July, 1911), 124–35. Reprinted in *ibid.*
"Navies as International Factors," *North American Review*, Vol. CXCIV (September, 1911), 344–55. Reprinted in *ibid.*
"The Deficiencies of Law as an Instrument of International Adjustments," *North American Review*, Vol. CXCIV (November, 1911), 674–84. Reprinted in *ibid.*
Naval Strategy, Compared and Contrasted with the Principles of Military Operations on Land. Boston, Little, Brown and Company, 1911.
"Importance of Command of the Sea," *Scientific American*, Vol. CV (December 9, 1911), 512.

1912. "The Place of Force in International Relations," *North American Review*, Vol. CXCV (January, 1912), 28–39. Reprinted in *Armaments and Arbitration* (1912).

"The Great Illusion," *North American Review*, Vol. CXCV (March, 1912), 319–32. Reprinted in *ibid.*
"The Naval War College," *North American Review*, Vol. CXCVI, 72–84. Reprinted in *ibid.*
"Was Panama 'A Chapter of National Dishonor,' " *North American Review*, Vol. CXCVI (October, 1912), 549–68. Reprinted in *ibid.*
Armaments and Arbitration, or the Place of Force in the International Relations of States. New York and London, Harper and Brothers, 1912.

1913. "The Panama Canal from a Military Point of View," *Revue Économique Internationale*, Brussels, Vol. I (January, 1913), 57–75.
"Japan Among the Nations," *Living Age,* Vol. CCLXXVIII (August 2, 1913), 312–15. Copy of letter in New York *Times* of June 23, 1913.
"Freedom in the Use of the Prayer Book," *The Churchman*, Vol. CVIII (November, 1913), 623–24.
The Major Operations of the Navies in the War of American Independence. Boston, Little, Brown and Company, 1913.

1914. "Twentieth Century Christianity," *North American Review*, Vol. CXCIX (April, 1914), 589–98.
"Sea Power in the Present European War," *Leslie's Weekly,* Vol. CXIX (August 20, 1914), 174 and 185.
"Commodore Macdonough at Plattsburg," *North American Review*, Vol. CC (August, 1914), 203–21.
"The Panama Canal and the Distribution of the Fleet," *North American Review*, Vol. CC (September, 1914), 406–17.
"Prayer Book Revision," *The Churchman*, Vol. CX (October 10, 1914), 465–66.
"Prayer Book Revision," *The Churchman*, Vol. CX (October 17, 1914), 497–98.

1918. *Mahan on Naval Warfare—Selections from the Writings of Rear Admiral Alfred Thayer Mahan.* Edited by Allan Westcott. Boston, Little, Brown and Company, 1918.

1931. *Letters of Alfred Thayer Mahan to Samuel A'Court Ashe, 1858–59.* Edited by R. P. Chiles. Durham, N. C., Duke University Press, 1931.

397

SELECTED BIBLIOGRAPHY

(With few exceptions, the following bibliography has been confined to material to which reference is made in the text.)

MANUSCRIPT SOURCES

The Flowers Collection—Mahan to Ashe Letters, Duke University, Durham, North Carolina.

The Hay Papers—Library of Congress.

The Lodge Papers—Massachusetts Historical Society, Boston, Massachusetts.

The Long Papers—Massachusetts Historical Society, Boston, Massachusetts.

The Luce Papers—Navy Department Archives.

The McKinley Papers—Library of Congress.

The Mahan Papers—Library of Congress.

The Navy Department—Bureau of Naval Personnel.

The Roosevelt Papers (to March, 1909)—Library of Congress.

The State Department—Domestic Letters and Miscellaneous Letters.

Albert Shaw to writer, March 24, 1937.

OFFICIAL PUBLICATIONS

Bemis, S. F., and Griffin, G. G. *Guide to the Diplomatic History of the United States, 1775–1921.* Washington, Government Printing Office, 1935.

Congressional Record, 1874– . Washington, Government Printing Office, 1874– .

Gooch, G. P. and Temperley, H. *British Documents on the Origins of the War, 1898–1914.* 11 vols. London, H. M.'s Stationery Office, 1926–38.

Die Grosse Politik der Europäischen Kabinette, 1871–1914. 40 vols. Berlin, Deutsche Verlagsgesellschaft für Politik und Geschichte M. B. H., 1922–27.

Hearings before Merchant Marine Commission, 58 Cong., 3 sess.

Hearings before Committee on Naval Affairs, House of Representatives.
58 Cong., 2 sess.
58 Cong., 3 sess.
60 Cong., 1 sess.
61 Cong., 3 sess.
62 Cong., 2 sess.
63 Cong., 2 sess.
House Document No. 485, 57 Cong., 1 sess. 2 vols. Schley Court of Inquiry.
House Executive Document No. 1, Part III, 51 Cong., 1 sess. Secretary Tracy's report of 1889.
House Executive Document No. 1, Part III, 53 Cong. 2 sess. Secretary Herbert's report of 1893.
House Report No. 1355, 55 Cong., 2 sess. Report of Committee on Foreign Affairs on joint resolution for annexation of Hawaii, May 17, 1898.
House Report No. 1132, 60 Cong., 1 sess. Report of Committee on Naval Affairs *re* establishment of a naval base at Pearl Harbor, March 2, 1908.
House Report No. 2078, 61 Cong., 3 sess. Report of Committee on Naval Affairs relative to the council of National Defense.
House Report No. 584, 62 Cong., 2 sess. Report on the same topic as the immediately preceding item.
Journal of the Executive Proceedings of the Senate of the United States of America, 55 Cong. Washington, 1909.
Malloy, W. M., *Treaties, Conventions, International Protocols, and Agreements, between the United States of America and Other Powers, 1776–1909.* 2 vols. Washington, Government Printing Office, 1910.
Moore, John B. *Digest of International Law.* 8 vols. Washington, Government Printing Office, 1906.
Navy Department, *Annual Report, 1915.* Washington, 1915.
Papers Relating to the Foreign Relations of the United States, 1862– . Washington, Government Printing Office, 1864– .
Register of the Commissioned and Warrant Officers of the United States, and of the Marine Corps. Washington, Government Printing Office, 1893.
Report of the Merchant Marine Commission No. 2755, 58 Cong., 3 sess.

Richardson, James D. *A Compilation of the Messages and Papers of the Presidents.* 10 vols. Washington, Bureau of National Literature and Art, 1910.

Scott, James Brown. *The Proceedings of the Hague Peace Conferences.* New York, Oxford University Press, 1920.

—— (ed.). *The Reports to the Hague Conferences of 1899 and 1907.* Oxford, Eng., Clarendon Press, 1917.

Senate Document No. 188, 55 Cong., 2 sess. Statement on the Pacific interests of the United States by G. W. Melville.

Senate Document No. 62, 55 Cong., 3 sess. Material relevant to the treaty of peace with Spain, including consular reports anent the Philippines.

Senate Document No. 148, 56 Cong., 2 sess. Telegraphic correspondence between the Department of State and the peace commissioners in Paris.

Senate Document No. 85, 57 Cong., 1 sess. Interoceanic canal negotiations.

Senate Document No. 284, 57 Cong., 2 sess. Data relative to the cession of the Danish West Indies.

Senate Document No. 213, 59 Cong., 2 sess. The views of Mahan and Sims on the size of battleships.

Senate Document No. 466, 61 Cong., 2 sess. Reprint of T. G. Roberts' article, "The Merchant Marine and the Navy."

Senate Document No. 471, 63 Cong., 2 sess. A diplomatic history of the Panama Canal.

Senate Executive Report No. 1, 57 Cong., 1 sess. Report by Committee on Foreign Relations relative to the 1902 treaty for the purchase of the Danish Islands.

Senate Report No. 1944, 51 Cong., 2 sess. Report of Committee on Foreign Relations about Maritime Canal Company of Nicaragua and United States interests in the Isthmus.

Senate Report No. 227, 53 Cong., 2 sess. Report of Committee on Foreign Relations concerning Hawaiian matters.

Senate Report No. 681, 55 Cong., 2 sess. Report of Committee on Foreign Relations on joint resolution for Hawaiian annexation, March 16, 1898.

Senate Report No. 885, 55 Cong., 2 sess. Report of Committee on Foreign Relations relative to affairs in Cuba.

The Statutes at Large of the United States, 1873– . Volume 18 ff. Washington, Government Printing Office, 1875–

PERIODICAL LITERATURE

Abel, Anna Heloise. "Sea Power and the War of 1812," *The Dial*, Vol. XL (January 16, 1906), 45–47.

Angell, Norman. "The Great Illusion," *North American Review*, Vol. CLXCV (July, 1912), 754–72.

Ashe, Samuel. "Memories of Annapolis," *South Atlantic Quarterly*, Vol. XVIII (July, 1919), 197–210.

Bailey, T. A. "Japan's Protest against the Annexation of Hawaii," *Journal of Modern History*, Vol. III (April, 1931), 46–61.

———. "The United States and Hawaii during the Spanish-American War," *American Historical Review*, Vol. XXXVI (April, 1931), 552–60.

Barrett, John. "Our Interests in China—a Question of the Hour," *The Review of Reviews*, Vol. XXI (January, 1900), 42–49.

———. "The Cuba of the Far East," *North American Review*, Vol. CLXIV (February, 1897), 173–80.

Bradford, R. B. "Coaling Stations for the Navy," *Forum*, Vol. XXVI (February, 1899), 732–47.

Brodie, Bernard. "War at Sea: Changing Techniques and Unchanging Fundamentals," *The Virginia Quarterly Review*, Vol. XIX (Winter, 1943), 1–19.

———. "New Tactics in Naval Warfare," *Foreign Affairs*, Vol. XXIV (January, 1946), 210–23.

Bryce, James. "The Policy of Annexation for America," *Forum*, Vol. XXIV (December, 1897), 385–95.

Chamberlain, Dr. Leander. "A Chapter in National Dishonor," *North American Review*, Vol. CXCV (February, 1912), 145–74.

Clarke, George Sydenham. "Captain Mahan's Counsels to the United States," *Nineteenth Century*, Vol. XLIII (February, 1898), 292–300.

Colomb, P. H. "The United States Navy under the New Conditions of National Life," *North American Review*, Vol. CLXVII (October, 1898), 434–44.

Corbett, Julian. "A Revival of Naval History," *Contemporary Review*, Vol. CX (December, 1916), 734–40.

Craven, Wesley Frank. "Historical Study of the British Empire," *Journal of Modern History*, Vol. VI (March, 1934), 40–69.

De Kay, Charles. "Authors at Home," *Critic*, Vol. XXXII (May 28, 1898), 353–55.
Dennett, Tyler. "The Future in Retrospect: Mahan's 'The Problem of Asia,'" *Foreign Affairs*, Vol. XIII (April, 1935), 464–72.
Eddy, Ulysses D. "Our Chance for Commercial Supremacy," *Forum*, Vol. XI (June, 1891), 419–28.
"Excubitor" [pen name]. "Admiral Mahan's Warning," *Fortnightly Review*, Vol. LXXXVIII (August, 1910), 224–34.
Eyre, James K., Jr. "Russia and the American Acquisition of the Philippines," *Mississippi Valley Historical Review*, Vol. XXVIII (March, 1942), 539–62.
Fiske, Bradley A. "Naval Power," U. S. Naval Institute *Proceedings*, Vol. XXXVII (1911), 1684 ff.
Giddings, F. H. "Imperialism?," *Political Science Quarterly*, Vol. XIII (December, 1898), 585–605.
Godkin, E. L. "The Sea Power," *The Nation*, Vol. LXVII (September, 1898), 198–99.
H. H. "Naval History: Mahan and His Successors," *The Military Historian and Economist*, Vol. III (January, 1918), 7–19.
Hacker, L. M. "The Holy War of 1898," *American Mercury*, Vol. XXI (November, 1930), 316–26.
———. "The Incendiary Mahan: A Biography," *Scribner's*, Vol. XCV (April, 1934), 263–68, 311–20.
Halstead, Murat. "American Annexation and Armaments," *Forum*, Vol. XXIV (September, 1897), 56–66.
Harrington, Fred H. "The Anti-Imperialist Movement in the United States, 1898–1900," *Mississippi Valley Historical Review*, Vol. XXII (September, 1935), 211–30.
Hunt, Gaillard. "Sea Power in Its Relations to the War of 1812," *American Historical Review*, Vol. XI (July, 1906), 924–26.
Jane, Fred T. "Naval Warfare: Present and Future," *Forum*, Vol. XXIV (October, 1897), 234–45.
Johnson, A. H. "Mahan on Sea Power," *English Historical Review*, Vol. VIII (October, 1893), 784–88.
Jordan, Thomas. "Why We Need Cuba," *Forum*, Vol. XI (June, 1891), 559–67.
Judson, W. V. "Strategic Value of Her West Indian Possession to the United States," *Annals* of the American Academy of Political and Social Science, Vol. XIX (1902), 383–91.

Laughton, J. K. "Captain Mahan on Maritime Power," *Edinburgh Review*, Vol. CLXXII (October, 1890), 420–53.

———. "Captain Mahan on Maritime Power," *Edinburgh Review*, Vol. CLXXVII (April, 1893), 484–518.

Lodge, Henry Cabot. "Our Blundering Foreign Policy," *Forum*, Vol. XIX (March, 1895), 8–17.

———. "Our Duty to Cuba," *Forum*, Vol. XXI (May, 1896), 278–87.

Luce, Stephen B. "Naval Strategy," U. S. Naval Institute *Proceedings*, Vol. XXXV (1909), 93–112.

Lüttwitz, Baron von. "German Naval Policy and Strategy," *Journal of the Royal United Service Institution*, Vol. XLI (February, 1897), 315–30.

Mackinder, H. J. "The Geographical Pivot of History," *The Geographical Journal*, Vol. XXIII (April, 1904), 421–44.

Maude, Captain F. N. "The Influence of Sea Power," *National Review*, Vol. XXIII (March, 1894), 110–17.

Mead, Lucia Ames. "Some Fallacies of Captain Mahan," *Arena*, Vol. XL (September, 1908), 163–70.

Melville, Commodore G. W. "Our Future in the Pacific—What We Have There to Hold and Win," *North American Review*, Vol. CLXVI (March, 1898), 281–96.

Moireau, Auguste. "La Maîtresse de la Mer," *Revue des deux Mondes*, Vol. XI (October, 1902), 618–708.

Money, H. D. "Our Duty to Cuba," *Forum*, Vol. XXV (March, 1898), 17–24.

"Nauticus" [Laird Clowes]. "Sea Power: Its Past and Its Future," *Fortnightly Review*, Vol. LIV (December, 1893), 849–68.

Olney, Richard. "Growth of Our Foreign Policy," *Atlantic Monthly*, Vol. LXXXV (March, 1900), 289–301.

Paullin, C. O. "The Major Operations of the Navies in the War of American Independence," *American Historical Review*, Vol. XIX (April, 1914), 689.

———. "A. T. Mahan," *Mississippi Valley Historical Review*, Vol. I (March, 1915), 613–14.

Pratt, Julius W. "The 'Large Policy' of 1898," *Mississippi Valley Historical Review*, Vol. XIX (September, 1932), 219–42.

———. "The Collapse of American Imperialism," *American Mercury*, Vol. XXXI (March, 1934), 269–78.

Proctor, John R. "Hawaii and the Changing Front of the World," *Forum*, Vol. XXIV (September, 1897), 34–45.

Puleston, Captain W. D. "Mahan: Naval Philosopher," *Scribner's*, Vol. XCVI (November, 1934), 294–98.

Rice, Wallace. "Some Current Fallacies of Captain Mahan," *The Dial*, Vol. XXVIII (March 16, 1900), 198–200.

Roberts, T. G. "The Merchant Marine and the Navy," U. S. Naval Institute *Proceedings*, Vol. XXXVI (1910), 1–39.

Roosevelt, Theodore. "The Influence of Sea Power upon History," *Atlantic Monthly*, Vol. LXVI (October, 1890), 563–67.

———. "The Influence of Sea Power upon the French Revolution," *Atlantic Monthly*, Vol. LXXI (April, 1893), 556–59.

———. "The Influence of Sea Power upon History, 1660–1783," and "The Influence of Sea Power upon the French Revolution and Empire," *Political Science Quarterly*, Vol. IX (March, 1894), 171–73.

———. "Captain Mahan's Life of Nelson," *Bookman*, Vol. V (June, 1897), 331–34.

———. "A Great Public Servant," *Outlook*, Vol. CIX (January 13, 1915), 85–86.

Schammell, J. M. "Thucydides and Sea Power," U. S. Naval Institute *Proceedings*, Vol. XLVII (1921), 701–704.

Schofield, J. M., and Alexander, B. S. "Report on Pearl Harbor, 1873," *American Historical Review*, Vol. XXX (April, 1925), 561–65.

Schurz, Carl. "Manifest Destiny," *Harper's Monthly*, Vol. LXXXVII (November, 1893), 737–46.

Sherman, John. "The Nicaragua Canal," *Forum*, Vol. XI (March, 1891), 1–9.

Sloane, William Milligan. "Two Historians," *Columbia University Quarterly*, Vol. XVIII (March, 1916), 106–12.

Smith, T. C. "Expansion after the Civil War, 1865–1871," *Political Science Quarterly*, Vol. XVI (September, 1901), 412–36.

Stephens, H. Morse. "Some Living American Historians," *World's Work*, Vol. IV (July, 1902), 2316–27.

Stevens, John L. "A Plea for Annexation," *North American Review*, Vol. CLVII (December, 1893), 736–45.

Stevens, William Oliver. "Scrapping Mahan," *Yale Review*, Vol. XII (April, 1923), 528–42.

Winn, F. L. "Nicaragua Canal," *Overland Monthly*, Vol. XXIII (May, 1894), 489–97.

REVIEWS AND EDITORIALS NOT OTHERWISE LISTED

American Historical Review, Vol. IV (July, 1899), 719–21.
Ibid., Vol. XX (January, 1915), 445–46.
Blackwood's Edinburgh Magazine, Vol. CXLVII (October, 1890), 576–84.
Ibid., Vol. CLXIII (April, 1898), 563–65.
Current Opinion, Vol. LVIII (February, 1915), 103–104.
Harper's Monthly, Vol. LXXXVII (November, 1893), 962–63.
Literary World, Vol. XXI (July 5, 1890), 217–18.
The Nation, Vol. LXXXII (January 11, 1906), 39–41.
The Review of Reviews, Vol. IV (September, 1891), 125–36.
Ibid., Vol. VII (April, 1893), 324–27.
Ibid., Vol. IX (June, 1894), 644.
Ibid., Vol. X (July, 1894), 2.
Ibid., Vol. X (November, 1894), 481.
Ibid., Vol. XV (March, 1897), 331–32.
Ibid., Vol. XVII (January, 1898), 68.
Ibid., Vol. XVII (January, 1898), 71–72.
Ibid., Vol. XVII (June, 1898), 719–21.
Ibid., Vol. XIX (May, 1899), 553–54.
Ibid., Vol. XXI (February, 1900), 134–35.
Ibid., Vol. XXVI (November, 1902), 613–14.
Ibid., Vol. XXX (October, 1904), 470–72.
Sea Power, Vol. VII (September, 1919), 125.

NEWSPAPERS

Portland *Oregonian*.
New York *Times*
Boston Evening *Transcript*
New York *Tribune*

BIOGRAPHIES, LETTERS, AND MEMOIRS

Acheson, Sam Hanna. *Joe Bailey, the Last Democrat.* New York, The Macmillan Company, 1932.
Alden, C. S. and Earle R. *Makers of Naval Tradition.* New York, Ginn and Company, 1926.
Ashton, Sir George. *Memoirs of a Marine.* London, John Murray, 1919.
Bacon, Reginald. *A Naval Scrap-Book.* London, Hutchinson and Company, 1925.

Bemis, S. F. (ed.). *The American Secretaries of State and Their Diplomacy*. 10 vols. New York, A. Knopf, 1927–29.

Bishop, Joseph B. *Notes and Anecdotes of Many Years*. New York, Charles Scribner's Sons, 1925.

———. *Theodore Roosevelt and His Time*. 2 vols. New York, Charles Scribner's Sons, 1920.

Busbey, L. White. *Uncle Joe Cannon*. New York, Henry Holt and Company, 1927.

Castle, William R. "John W. Foster," in Bemis (ed.), *The American Secretaries of State and Their Diplomacy*, IX.

Cortissoz, Royal. *The Life of Whitelaw Reid*. 2 vols. New York, Charles Scribner's Sons, 1921.

Cowles, Anna Roosevelt. *Letters from Theodore Roosevelt to Anna Roosevelt Cowles, 1870–1918*. New York, Charles Scribner's Sons, 1924.

Croly, Herbert. *Marcus Alonzo Hanna*. New York, The Macmillan Company, 1912.

Curti, Merle E. *Bryan and World Peace*. Northampton, Mass., Smith College, 1931.

Dennett, Tyler. *John Hay: from Poetry to Politics*. New York, Dodd, Mead and Company, 1933.

Dewey, George. *The Autobiography of George Dewey, Admiral of the Navy*. New York, Charles Scribner's Sons, 1913.

Falk, E. A. *Togo and the Rise of Japanese Sea Power*. New York and Toronto, G. P. Putnam's Sons, 1936.

Fisher, John Arbuthnot. *Records* by Admiral of the fleet, Lord Fisher. London, Hodder and Stoughton, 1919.

Fuess, Claude Moore. *Carl Schurz, Reformer*. New York, Dodd, Mead and Company, 1932.

Gillett, F. H. *George Frisbie Hoar*. Boston and New York, Houghton Mifflin Company, 1934.

Hibben, Paxton. *The Peerless Leader: William Jennings Bryan*. New York, Farrar and Rinehart, 1929.

Hoar, George F. *Autobiography of Seventy Years*. 2 vols. New York, Charles Scribner's Sons, 1903.

Hunt, Thomas. *Life of William H. Hunt*. Brattleboro, Vermont, E. L. Hildreth and Company, 1922.

Lodge, Henry Cabot. *Selections from the Correspondence of Theodore Roosevelt and Henry Cabot Lodge*. 2 vols. New York and London, Charles Scribner's Sons, 1925.

Maurice, Sir F., and Arthur, Sir G. *Life of Lord Wolseley*. London, W. Heinemann, 1924.

Mayo, Lawrence Shaw. *America of Yesterday as Reflected in the Diary of John D. Long*. Boston, Atlantic Monthly Press, 1923.

Morison, E. E. *Admiral Sims and the Modern American Navy*. New York, Houghton Mifflin Company, 1942.

Nevins, Allan. *Henry White, Thirty Years of Diplomacy*. New York, Harper and Brothers, 1930.

————. *Grover Cleveland: A Study in Courage*. New York, Dodd, Mead and Company, 1933.

————. *Letters of Grover Cleveland*. Boston and New York, Houghton Mifflin Company, 1933.

Ogasawara, Admiral Viscount Nagayo. *Life of Admiral Togo*. Tokyo, Seitoshorin Press, 1934.

Olcott, C. S. *The Life of William McKinley*. 2 vols. Boston and New York, Houghton Mifflin Company, 1916.

Pratt, Julius W. "Alfred Thayer Mahan," in William T. Hutchinson (ed.), *The Marcus W. Jernegan Essays in American Historiography*. Chicago, University of Chicago Press, 1937.

Pringle, H. F. *Theodore Roosevelt, a Biography*. New York, Harcourt, Brace and Company, 1931.

Puleston, W. D. *The Life and Work of Captain Alfred Thayer Mahan*. New Haven, Yale University Press, 1939.

Repington, Charles A'Court. *Vestigia*. Boston and New York, Houghton Mifflin Company, 1919.

Robinson, William A. *Thomas B. Reed, Parliamentarian*. New York, Dodd, Mead and Company, 1930.

Roosevelt, Theodore. *An Autobiography*. New York, The Macmillan Company, 1913.

Schuyler, Montgomery. "Walter Q. Gresham," in Bemis (ed.), *The American Secretaries and Their Diplomacy*, IX.

Sprout, Margaret T. "Mahan: Evangelist of Sea Power," in Edward M. Earle (ed.), *Makers of Modern Strategy*. Princeton, N. J., Princeton University Press, 1943.

Sydenham of Combe [George Sydenham Clarke]. *My Working Life*. London, John Murray, 1927.

Taylor, Charles Carlisle. *The Life of Admiral Mahan*. New York, George H. Doran Company, 1920. Printed in Great Britain, with copyright held by John Murray, London.

Thayer, William R. *The Life and Letters of John Hay.* 2 vols. (American Statesmen Series, XXVI–XXVII). Boston and New York, Houghton Mifflin Company, 1908.

Tirpitz, Alfred von. *My Memoirs.* New York, Dodd, Mead and Company, 1919.

White, Andrew D. *Autobiography.* 2 vols. New York, The Century Company, 1905.

OTHER SPECIAL AND GENERAL WORKS

Adams, C. F. *Lee at Appomattox and Other Papers.* Boston and New York, Houghton Mifflin Company, 1903.

Adams, E. D. *The Power of Ideals in American History.* New Haven, Yale University Press, 1913.

Angell, Norman. *The Great Illusion.* London, W. Heinemann, 1910.

———. *The World's Highway.* New York, George H. Doran Company, 1915.

Bailey, T. A. *Theodore Roosevelt and the Japanese-American Crisis.* Los Angeles, Stanford University Press, 1934. London, Oxford University Press, 1934.

Beard, Charles A. *The Navy: Defense or Portent?* New York and London, Harper and Brothers, 1932.

———. *The Idea of National Interest.* New York, The Macmillan Company, 1934.

Bemis, S. F. *A Diplomatic History of the United States.* New York, Henry Holt and Company, 1936.

Brodie, Bernard. *Sea Power in the Machine Age.* Princeton, N. J., Princeton University Press, 1941.

———. *A Guide to Naval Strategy.* Princeton, N. J., Princeton University Press, 1944. Third edition.

Burgess, John W. *Political Science and Comparative Constitutional Law.* 2 vols. Boston and London, Ginn and Company, 1890.

Cant, Gilbert. *The War at Sea.* New York, John Day Company, 1940.

Carter, John. *Conquest: America's Painless Imperialism.* New York, Harcourt, Brace and Company, 1928.

Castex, Raoul. *Les Théories Stratégiques.* 5 vols. Paris, Société de Éditions géographiques, maritimes et coloniales, 1929.

Colomb, D. H. *Naval Warfare: Its Ruling Principles and Practices Historically Treated.* London, W. A. Allen and Company, 1891.

Corbett, Julian S. *Some Principles of Maritime Strategy.* London, Longmans, Green and Company, 1919. Second edition.

Davis, Forrest. *The Atlantic System: The Story of Anglo-American Control of the Sea.* New York, Reynal and Hitchcock, 1941.

Davis, George T. *A Navy Second to None: the Development of Modern American Naval Policy.* New York, Harcourt, Brace and Company, 1940.

Dennett, Tyler. *Americans in Eastern Asia.* New York, The Macmillan Company, 1922.

―――. *Roosevelt and the Russo-Japanese War.* Garden City, Doubleday, Page and Company, 1925.

Dennis, A. L. P. *Adventures in American Diplomacy, 1896–1906.* New York, E. P. Dutton and Company, 1928.

Dillon, E. J. *The Eclipse of Russia.* New York, George H. Doran Company, 1918.

Dulles, Foster Rhea. *America in the Pacific.* Boston and New York, Houghton Mifflin Company, 1932.

Dunn, A. W. *From Harrison to Harding.* 2 vols. New York and London, G. P. Putnam's Sons, 1922.

Earle, Edward Mead (ed.), *Makers of Modern Strategy.* Princeton, N. J., Princeton University Press, 1943.

Fiennes, Gerard. *Sea Power and Freedom.* New York and London, G. P. Putnam's Sons, 1918.

Foster, John W. *The Annexation of Hawaii.* Washington, Gibson Brothers, 1897.

Griswold, A. Whitney. *The Far Eastern Policy of the United States.* New York, Harcourt, Brace, and Company, 1938.

Gooch, G. P. *History and Historians in the Nineteenth Century.* London, Longmans, Green and Company, 1928.

Halle, von E. *Die Seemacht in der Deutschen Geschichte.* Leipzig, G. J. Goscherische, 1907.

Hallgren, Mauritz. *The Tragic Fallacy, a Study of America's War Policies.* New York and London, A. Knopf, 1937.

Hallmann, Hans. *Der Weg zum Deutschen Schlachtflottenbau.* Stuttgart, W. Kohlhammer, 1933.

―――. *Krügerdepesche und Flottenfrage.* Stuttgart, W. Kohlhammer, 1927.

Heindel, R. H. *The American Impact on Great Britain*. Philadelphia, University of Pennsylvania Press, 1940.

Hill, H. C. *Roosevelt and the Caribbean*. Chicago, University of Chicago Press, 1927.

Holls, Frederick W. *The Peace Conference at The Hague*. New York, The Macmillan Company, 1900.

Holt, W. S. *Treaties Defeated by the Senate*. Baltimore, Johns Hopkins Press, 1933.

Hurd, Archibald, and Castle, Henry. *German Sea Power, Its Rise, Progress and Economic Basis*. London, John Murray, 1914.

Inman, Samuel G. "The Significance of the Caribbean," in Wilgus (ed.), *The Caribbean Area*. Washington, George Washington University Press, 1934.

Jane, Fred T. *Heresies of Sea Power*. London and New York, Longmans, Green and Company, 1906.

Kehr, Eckart. *Schlachtflottenbau und Parteipolitik, 1894–1901*. Berlin, E. Ebering, 1930.

Kenworthy, J. M. "Navy," in *The Encyclopedia of the Social Sciences*, XI. New York, The Macmillan Company, 1933.

————. "Alfred Thayer Mahan (1840–1914)," in *The Encyclopedia of the Social Sciences*, X. New York, The Macmillan Company, 1933.

Kirkham, George K. *The Books and Articles of Rear-Admiral A. T. Mahan, U. S. N.* New York, Ballou Press, 1929.

Knowles, L. C. A. *The Industrial and Commercial Revolution*. New York, E. P. Dutton and Company, 1921.

Knox, Dudley W. *A History of the United States Navy*. New York, G. P. Putnam's Sons, 1936.

Kohlsaat, H. H. *From McKinley to Harding*. New York, Charles Scribner's Sons, 1923.

Langer, W. L. *The Diplomacy of Imperialism*. 2 vols. New York and London, A. Knopf, 1935.

Latané, J. H. *A History of American Foreign Policy*. New York, Doubleday, Page and Company, 1927.

Leyland, John. "Recent Naval Literature," in *Brassey's Naval Annual, 1897*. Portsmouth, Eng., J. Griffin and Company, 1897.

Long, John D. *The New American Navy*. 2 vols. New York, The Outlook Company, 1903.

Mackinder, Halford. *Britain and British Seas.* Oxford, Eng., Clarendon Press, 1922.

———. *Democratic Ideals and Reality: A Study in the Politics of Reconstruction.* London, Constable and Company, 1919.

Marder, Arthur J. *The Anatomy of British Sea Power.* New York, A. Knopf, 1940.

Millis, Walter. *The Martial Spirit.* Boston, The Literary Guild, 1931.

———. *The Future of Sea Power in the Pacific.* New York and Boston, Foreign Policy Association and World Peace Foundation, 1935.

Munro, D. G. *The United States and the Caribbean Area.* Boston, World Peace Foundation, 1934.

Nasmyth, George W. *Organized Insanity.* Washington, American Peace Society, 1914.

Nearing, Scott, and Freeman, Joseph. *Dollar Diplomacy, a Study in American Imperialism.* New York, Viking Press, 1926.

Pratt, Fletcher. *Sea Power and Today's War.* New York, Harrison-Hilton, 1939.

Pratt, Julius W. *Expansionists of 1898.* Baltimore, Johns Hopkins Press, 1936.

Richmond, Admiral Sir Herbert. *Sea Power in the Modern World.* New York, Reynal and Hitchcock, 1934.

Ropp, Theodore. "Continental Doctrines of Sea Power," in Edward M. Earle (ed.), *Makers of Modern Strategy.* Princeton, N. J., Princeton University Press, 1943.

Rosinski, Herbert. "Command of the Sea," in H. G. Thursfield (ed.), *Brassey's Naval Annual, 1939.* London, Clowes, 1939.

———. "German Theories of Sea Warfare," in H. G. Thursfield (ed.), *Brassey's Naval Annual, 1940.* London, Clowes, 1940.

———. "Mahan and the Present War," in H. G. Thursfield (ed.), *Brassey's Naval Annual, 1941.* London, Clowes, 1941.

Scott, James Brown. *The Hague Peace Conferences of 1899 and 1907.* 2 vols. Baltimore, Johns Hopkins Press, 1909.

Silburn, P. A. *The Evolution of Sea Power.* London, Longmans, Green and Company, 1912.

Sprout, Harold, and Sprout, Margaret. *The Rise of American Naval Power.* Princeton, N. J., Princeton University Press, 1939.

————. *Toward A New Order of Sea Power*. Princeton, N. J., Princeton University Press, 1940.

Stanwood, E. *A History of the Presidency from 1788 to 1897*. Boston and New York, Houghton Mifflin Company, 1898.

Strausz-Hupé, R. *Geo-Politics: The Struggle for Space and Power*. New York, G. P. Putnam's Sons, 1942.

Strong, Josiah. *Our Country: Its Possible Future and Its Present Crisis*. New York, Baker and Taylor Company, 1891.

Sullivan, Mark. *Our Times*. 6 vols. New York and London, Charles Scribner's Sons, 1926–35.

Tansill, C. C. *The Purchase of the Danish West Indies*. Baltimore, Johns Hopkins Press, 1932.

Tyler, Alice F. *The Foreign Policy of James G. Blaine*. Minneapolis, University of Minnesota Press, 1927.

Vagts, Alfred. *Deutchland und die Vereinigten Staaten in der Weltpolitik*. 2 vols. New York, The Macmillan Company, 1935.

Weigert, Hans. *Generals and Geographers*. New York, Oxford University Press, 1942.

Weinberg, Albert K. *Manifest Destiny*. Baltimore, Johns Hopkins Press, 1935.

Welles, Sumner. *Naboth's Vineyard*. 2 vols. New York, Payson and Clarke, 1928.

Wilgus, A. Curtis (ed.), *The Caribbean Area*. Washington, George Washington University Press, 1934.

Wilkerson, M. M. *Public Opinion and the Spanish-American War*. Baton Rouge, Louisiana State University Press, 1932.

Williams, Mary Wilhemine. *Anglo-American Isthmian Diplomacy, 1815–1915*. Washington, American Historical Association, 1916.

Wisan, Josephe E. *The Cuban Crisis as Reflected in the New York Press, 1895–1898*. New York, Columbia University Press, 1934.'

Woodward, E. L. *Great Britain and the German Navy*. Oxford, Eng., Clarendon Press, 1935.

ADDENDA FOR THE REVISED EDITION
BIBLIOGRAPHY

(Only cited items listed)

A. BOOKS

Baldwin, Hanson W. *Strategy for Tomorrow.* New York, Harper and Row, 1970.

Beaufre, André. *Strategy for Tomorrow.* New York, Crane Russok, 1974.

Beisner, Robert L. *From the Old Diplomacy to the New, 1865–1900.* New York, Crowell, 1975.

Braisted, William R. *The United States Navy in the Pacific, 1909–1922.* Austin, University of Texas Press, 1971.

———. *The United States Navy in the Pacific, 1897–1909.* Austin, University of Texas Press, 1958.

Brodie, Bernard. *Strategy in the Missile Age.* Princeton, Princeton University Press, 1959.

Campbell, Charles S. *The Transformation of American Foreign Relations, 1865–1900.* New York, Harper and Row, 1976.

Challener, Richard D. *Admirals, Generals and American Foreign Policy, 1898–1914.* Princeton, Princeton University Press, 1973.

Cooling, Benjamin Franklin. *Benjamin Franklin Tracy: Father of the Modern American Fighting Navy.* Hamden, Connecticut, Shoe String Press, 1973.

Creswell, John. *Sea Warfare, 1939–1945.* Rev. ed., Berkeley and Los Angeles, University of California Press, 1967.

Curti, Merle. *Growth of American Thought.* 3d ed. New York and London, Harper and Row, 1964.

Davis, Calvin D. *United States and the First Hague Peace Conference.* Ithaca, Cornell University Press, 1962.

Davis, Vincent. *Post War Defense Policy and the U.S. Navy, 1943–1946.* Chapel Hill, University of North Carolina Press, 1966.

————. *The Admirals Lobby.* Chapel Hill, University of North Carolina Press, 1967.

Fisher, John Arbathrot. *Fear God and Dread Nought.* Edited by Arthur J. Marder, 3 vols., London, Cape, 1952–59.

Freidel, Frank. *Franklin D. Roosevelt: The Apprenticeship.* Boston, Little Brown and Company, 1952.

Graham, Gerald S. *The Politics of Naval Supremacy: Studies in British Maritime Ascendancy.* Cambridge, Cambridge University Press, 1965.

Grenville, John A. S., and Young, George Berkley. *Politics, Strategy, and American Diplomacy.* New Haven and London, Yale University Press, 1966.

Hagan, Kenneth J. *American Gunboat Diplomacy and the Old Navy, 1877–1889.* Westport, Connecticut, Greenwood Press, 1973.

Healy, David. *U.S. Expansionism: The Imperialist Urge in the 1890s.* Madison, University of Wisconsin Press, 1970.

Herrick, Walter R., Jr. *The American Naval Revolution.* Baton Rouge, Louisiana State University Press, 1966.

Hezlet, Sir Arthur Richard. *Aircraft and Sea Power.* New York, Stein and Day, 1970.

Hofstader, Richard. *Social Darwinism in American Thought.* Boston, Beacon Press, 1955.

Hyatt, A. M. J. (ed.). *Dreadnought to Polaris: Maritime Strategy Since Mahan.* Toronto, Montreal and Vancouver, Copp Clark Publishing Company, 1973.

Karsten, Peter. *The Naval Aristocracy: The Golden Age of Annapolis and the Emergence of Modern American Navalism.* New York, Free Press, 1972.

Kuehl, Warren F. *Dissertations in History*, 2 vols. Lexington, University of Kentucky Press, 1965 and 1972.

LaFeber, Walter. *The New Empire: An Interpretation of American Expansion, 1860–1898*. Ithaca and London, Cornell University Press, 1963.

Mahan, Alfred Thayer. *Letters and Papers*. Edited by Robert Seager II and Doris D. Maguire. 3 vols. Annapolis, Naval Institute Press, 1975.

Marder, Arthur J. *From the Dreadnought to Scapa Flow: The Royal Navy in the Fisher Era, 1904–1919*. 5 vols. London, Oxford University Press, 1961–1969.

Martin, L. W. *The Sea in Modern Strategy*. New York, Frederick A. Praeger, 1967.

May, Ernest. *American Imperialism: A Speculative Theory*. New York, Atheneum, 1968.

Merk, Frederick. *Manifest Destiny and Mission in American History; A Reinterpretation*. New York, Alfred A. Knopf, 1963.

Millis, Walter. *Arms and Men: A Study of American Military History*. New York, Mentor Book, 1958.

Morgan, H. Wayne, (ed.). *The Gilded Age: Revised and Enlarged Edition*. Syracuse, Syracuse University Press, 1970.

O'Connor, Raymond G. *Force and Diplomacy: Essays, Military and Diplomatic*. Coral Gables, University of Miami Press, 1972.

Osgood, Robert Endicott. *Ideals and Self Interest in American Foreign Relations*. Chicago, University of Chicago Press, 1953.

Quester, George H. (ed.). *Sea Power in the 1970s*. New York and London, Dunellen, 1975.

Roskill, Captain S. W. *The Strategy of Sea Power: Its Development and Application*. London, Collins, 1962.

Schwarz, Urs. *American Strategy: A New Perspective; The Growth of Politico-Military Thinking in the United States*. Garden City, Doubleday and Company, 1966.

Sprout, Harold and Margaret. *Foundations of International Politics.* New York, Nostrand, 1962.

Walters, Robert E. *Sea Power and the Nuclear Fallacy: A Reevaluation of Global Strategy.* New York, Holmes and Meir, 1975.

B. MAGAZINE ARTICLES

Ambrose, Stephen E. "Seapower in World Wars I and II," *Naval War College Review,* Vol. XXII (March, 1970), 26–40.

Amme, Captain Carl H. "Seapower and the Superpowers," United States Naval Institute *Proceedings,* Vol. XCIV (October, 1968), 27–35.

Barber, Commander James A. "Mahan and Naval Strategy in the Nuclear Age," *Naval War College Review,* Vol. XXIV (March, 1972), 78–88.

Colbert, Admiral R. G. "Change and Challenges: The Shifting Balance of Power at Sea," *Vital Speeches,* Vol. XXXIX (December 15, 1972), 150–53.

Davis, Benton V. "Soviet Naval Strategy: Mahan and Mackinder Revisited," *Naval War College Review,* Vol. XXI (October, 1968), 1-13.

Duncan, Francis. "Mahan: Historian With a Purpose," United States Naval Institute *Proceedings,* Vol. LXXXIII (May, 1957), 498–503.

Garde, Commander Hans Garde (Danish Navy). "Where is the Western Navy Today? The World Wonders," United States Naval Institute *Proceedings,* Vol. CI (April, 1975), 18–23.

Gorshkov, Admiral S. G. "Navies in Peace and War," United States Naval Institute *Proceedings,* Vol. C, (January through November, 1974).

Herrington, Arthur C. "U.S. Naval Policy," *Naval War College Review,* Vol. XXII (September, 1969), 4–13.

LaFeber, Walter. "A Note on the 'Mercantilist Imperialism' of Alfred Thayer Mahan," *Mississippi Valley Historical Review,* Vol. XLVIII (March, 1962), 674–85.

Langer, Walter L. "Farewell to Empire," *Foreign Affairs*, Vol. XLI (October, 1962), 113–30.

Livezey, William E. "Sea Power in a Changing World," *The Marine Corps Gazette*, Vol. XXXIII, Part I (April, 1949), 18–27 and Part II (May, 1949), 16–19.

Merrill, James M. "Successors to Mahan: A Survey of Writings of American Naval History, 1914–1960," *Mississippi Valley Historical Review*, Vol. L (June, 1963), 79–99.

St. John, Captain Ronald B. "European Naval Expansion and Mahan, 1889–1906," *Naval War College Review*, Vol. XXIII (March, 1971), 74–83.

Seager, Robert II. "Ten Years Before Mahan: The Unofficial Case for the New Navy, 1880–1890," *Mississippi Valley Historical Review*, Vol. XL (December, 1953), 491–512.

Smith, Commander Clyde A. "The Meaning and Significance of the Gorshkov Articles," *Naval War College Review*, Vol. XXVI (March-April, 1974), 18–37.

Turner, Vice Admiral Stansfield. "Missions of the U.S. Navy," United States Naval Institute *Proceedings*, Vol. C (December, 1974), 18–25.

Zumwalt, Admiral Elmo R. "Twentieth Century Mahan?" United States Naval Institute *Proceedings*, Vol. C (November, 1974) 70–73.

C. UNPUBLISHED MATERIAL

Berge, William H. "The Impulse for Expansion: John W. Burgess, Alfred Thayer Mahan, Theodore Roosevelt, Josiah Strong and the Development of a Rationale." Ph.D. dissertation, Vanderbilt University, 1969.

*Davis, Calvin D. "The United States and the First Hague Conference," Ph.D. dissertation, University of Indiana, 1961.

Gilliam, Bates M. "The World of Captain Mahan." Ph.D. dissertation, Princeton University, 1961.

* These dissertations have not been examined since books based on them have been utilized.

*Herrick, Walter R., Jr. "General Tracy's Navy: A Study of the Development of American Sea Power, 1889–1893," Ph.D. dissertation, University of Virginia, 1962.

*Karsten, Peter D. "The Naval Aristocracy: U.S. Naval Officers from 1840's to the 1920's: Mahan's Messmates," Ph.D. dissertation, University of Wisconsin, 1968.

Levy, Morris. "Alfred Thayer Mahan and the United States Foreign Policy." Ph.D. dissertation, New York University, 1965.

Rasmussen, John P. "The American Imperialist Elite: A Study in the Concept of National Efficiency." Ph.D. dissertation, Stanford University, 1962.

Spector, Ronald. "Professors of War: The U.S. Naval War College and the Modern American Navy, 1865–1915." Ph.D. dissertation. Yale University, 1967.

INDEX